MINI THESAURUS

The Editors of Webster's
New World™ Dictionaries

MICHAEL AGNES
EDITOR IN CHIEF

MACMILLAN • USA

Webster's New World™ Mini Thesaurus

Macmillan General Reference
A Simon & Schuster Macmillan Company
1633 Broadway
New York, NY 10019-6785

A Webster's New World™ Book

Dictionary Editorial Offices:
New World Dictionaries
850 Euclid Avenue
Cleveland, OH 44114-3354

ISBN 0-02-862062-3

Manufactured in the United States of America

1 2 3 4 5 6   97 98 99 00 01 02

GUIDE TO THE USE OF THIS BOOK

Webster's New World™ Mini Thesaurus has been prepared as a handy source of synonyms for terms encountered in everyday written and spoken English. It provides readers with essential information about the meanings of these synonyms and how to understand the subtle differences between them. If a writer or speaker is uncertain, for example, whether to "predict," "prophesy," or "prognosticate" a course of events, the entry at **foretell** will explain how these differ from each other and will give a clear indication of which would be the right choice.

Kinds of Entries. There are two kinds of entries in this thesaurus, main entries and brief entries. All entries are listed alphabetically by their headword, or first boldface term.

Main Entries - A main entry is a paragraph in which related synonyms are differentiated. After the headword and also in boldface is a list of the closest synonyms for that term. Following the list are brief definitions for the headword and synonyms. The definitions begin with "refers to," "implies," "denotes," "is used with reference to," or similar expressions. Often, an example that illustrates the proper use of the synonym is given in square brackets. The synonym under discussion appears in italics in the bracketed sentence or phrase.

Main entries may conclude by providing one or more common antonyms for the headword. They may also end with a cross-reference to another, related, main entry. Such cross-references are introduced by "*See also synonyms at...*" or "*For other antonyms see...*".

Brief Entries - A brief entry consists simply of a headword and a cross-reference to a main entry where the term and its synonyms are discussed and their differences are clarified. For example:

speechless for synonyms see **voiceless**.

Brief entries may also direct the reader to a list of antonyms:

wordy for antonyms see **concise**.

For more extensive information on the meanings of synonyms and antonyms, the reader is encouraged to consult *Webster's New World™ Thesaurus, Third Edition,* and *Webster's New World™ College Dictionary, Third Edition.*

A

abandon, desert, forsake, quit —**Abandon** implies leaving a person or thing, either as a final necessary measure [to *abandon* a drought area] or as a complete rejection of one's responsibilities, claims, etc. [She *abandoned* her child.] (*See also synonyms at* **relinquish**.) **Desert** emphasizes leaving in willful violation of one's obligation, oath, etc. [The soldier *deserted* his post.] **Forsake** stresses renouncing a person or thing formerly dear to one [to *forsake* one's friends, ideals, etc.] **Quit**, basically implying to leave or give up, is now commonly used to mean stop [She *quit* her job.] —*Antonym:* **reclaim**.

abase for synonyms see **degrade**.

abash for synonyms see **embarrass**.

abate for synonyms see **wane**.

abbey for synonyms see **cloister**.

abbreviate for synonyms see **shorten**.

abdicate, renounce, resign —**Abdicate** most commonly refers to the formal giving up by a sovereign of his or her throne, but sometimes describes a surrender of any prerogative. **Renounce**, often interchangeable with **abdicate**, is the more frequent usage when the voluntary surrender of any right, claim, title, practice, etc. is meant, and often suggests sacrifice [She *renounced* the pleasures of society.] **Resign** is applied to the deliberate giving up of a position, unexpired term, etc. by formal notice. —*Antonym:* **assume**.

abhor for synonyms see **hate**.

abhorrence for synonyms see **aversion**.

abhorrent for synonyms see **hateful**.
abide for synonyms see **continue, stay**.
abject for synonyms see **base**[1].
able, capable, competent, qualified —**Able** implies
power or ability to do something [*able* to make pay-
ments] but sometimes suggests superior power or skill
[an *able* orator]. **Capable** usually implies the mere meeting of ordinary requirements [a *capable* machinist].
Competent and **qualified** both imply the possession of
the requisite qualifications for the specified work, situation, etc., but **qualified** stresses compliance with specified requirements [a *competent* critic of modern art; a
qualified voter]. —*Antonym:* **inept**.
abnormal for synonyms see **irregular**.
abnormal for antonyms see **normal**.
abolish, annul, abrogate, rescind, revoke, repeal
—**Abolish** denotes a complete doing away with something, as an institution, custom, practice, condition, etc.
[to *abolish* slavery, ignorance, etc.] **Annul** and **abrogate**
stress a canceling by authority or formal action [The
marriage was *annulled*. The law *abrogated* certain
privileges.] **Rescind, revoke,** and **repeal** all agree in describing the setting aside of laws, orders, permits, etc. [to
rescind an order; *revoke* a charter; *repeal* an Amend-
ment]. —*Antonym:* **establish**.
abominable for synonyms see **hateful**.
aboriginal for synonyms see **native**.
abortive for synonyms see **futile**.
abridge for synonyms see **shorten**.
**abridgment, abstract, brief, summary, synopsis, di-
gest, epitome** —**Abridgment** describes a work condensed from a larger work by omitting the less important
parts, but keeping the main contents more or less unal-

tered. An **abstract** is a short statement of the essential contents of a book, court record, etc. often used as an index to the original material. **Brief** and **summary** both imply a statement of the main points of the matter under consideration [the *brief* of a legal argument], **summary**, especially, connoting a recapitulating statement. A **synopsis** is a condensed, orderly treatment, as of the plot of a novel, that permits a quick general view of the whole. A **digest** is a concise, systematic treatment, generally more comprehensive in scope than a synopsis, and, in the case of technical material, often arranged under titles for quick reference. An **epitome** is a statement of the essence of a subject in the shortest possible form. —*Antonym:* **expansion**.

abrogate for synonyms see **abolish**.

abrupt for synonyms see **steep** and **sudden**.

absent-minded, abstracted, preoccupied, distrait, distraught, inattentive —**Absent-minded** suggests an aimless wandering of the mind away from the immediate situation, often implying a habitual tendency of this kind [the *absent-minded* professor]. **Abstracted** suggests a withdrawal of the mind from the immediate present and a serious concern with some other subject. **Preoccupied** implies that the attention cannot be readily turned to something new because of its concern with a present matter. **Distrait** suggests inability to concentrate, often emphasizing such a condition as a mood. **Distraught** implies a similar inability to concentrate, specifically because of worry, grief, etc. **Inattentive** implies a failure to pay attention, emphasizing such behavior as a lack of discipline.

absolve, acquit, exonerate, pardon, forgive, vindicate —**Absolve** implies a setting free from responsibilities or obligation [*absolved* from her promise] or from the penalties for their violation. **Acquit** means to release from a specific charge by a judicial decision, usually for lack of evidence. To **exonerate** is to relieve of the blame for a wrongdoing. To **pardon** is to release from punishment for an offense [The prisoner was *pardoned* by the governor.] **Forgive** implies giving up all claim to punishment as well as any resentment or vengeful feelings. To **vindicate** is to clear (a person or thing under attack) through evidence of the unfairness of the charge, criticism, etc. —*Antonym:* **blame.**

abstain for synonyms see **refrain.**

abstract for synonyms see **abridgment.**

abstracted for synonyms see **absent-minded.**

absurd, ludicrous, preposterous, foolish, silly, ridiculous —**Absurd** means laughably inconsistent with what is judged as true or reasonable [an *absurd* hypothesis]. **Ludicrous** is applied to what is laughable from incongruity or exaggeration [a *ludicrous* facial expression]. **Preposterous** is used to describe anything flagrantly absurd or ludicrous. **Foolish** describes that which shows lack of good judgment or of common sense [Don't take *foolish* chances.] **Silly** and **ridiculous** apply to whatever excites amusement or contempt by reason of its extreme foolishness, **silly** often indicating an utterly nonsensical quality. —*Antonyms:* **sensible, logical, rational.**

abundant for synonyms see **plentiful.**

abundant for antonyms see **meager, rare.**

abuse for synonyms see **wrong.**

accede for synonyms see **consent.**

accept for synonyms see **receive.**

accept for antonyms see **decline.**

accidental, fortuitous, casual, incidental, adventi-

tious —**Accidental** describes that which occurs by chance [an *accidental* encounter]. **Fortuitous,** which frequently suggests a complete absence of cause, now usually refers to chance events of a fortunate nature. **Casual** describes the unpremeditated, random, informal, or irregular quality of something [a *casual* visit, remark, dress, etc.] **Incidental** emphasizes the nonessential or secondary nature of something [an *incidental* consideration]. **Adventitious** refers to that which is added extrinsically and connotes a lack of essential connection.

acclaim for synonyms see **praise.**

accommodate for synonyms see **adapt** and **contain.**

accompany, attend, escort, convoy, chaperon —**Accompany** means to go or be together with as a companion, associate, attribute, etc., and usually connotes equality of relationship [He *accompanied* her to the theater.] **Attend** implies presence either in a subordinate position or to render services, etc. [Dr. Jones *attended* the patient.] **Escort** and **convoy** are both applied to the accompanying, as by an armed guard, of persons or things needing protection (**convoy,** especially in the case of sea travel and **escort,** in the case of land travel). **Escort** also implies an accompanying as a mark of honor or an act of courtesy. **Chaperon** implies accompaniment, for reasons of propriety, of young unmarried people by an older or married person.

accomplice for synonyms see **comrade.**

accomplish for synonyms see **perform, reach.**

accord for synonyms see **agree.**

accord for antonyms see **conflict.**

accountable for synonyms see **responsible.**

accredit for synonyms see **authorize.**

accurate for synonyms see **correct.**

accuse, charge, indict, arraign, impeach —Accuse is used with reference to finding fault for offenses of varying gravity [to *accuse* one of murder, to *accuse* one of carelessness]. **Charge** usually implies an accusation of a legal or formal nature. **Indict** describes the action of a grand jury, etc. in finding a case against a person and ordering him or her brought to trial. **Arraign** refers to the actual process of calling the person before the court and informing that person of the charges against him or her. **Impeach** is applied to charging a public official with misconduct of office, but in nonlegal usage denotes a challenging of a person's motives, etc.

accustomed for synonyms see **usual**.

achieve for synonyms see **perform, reach**.

acid for synonyms see **sour**.

acidulous for synonyms see **sour**.

acknowledge, admit, own, avow, confess —Acknowledge implies the reluctant disclosure of something one might have kept secret [He *acknowledged* the child as his.] **Admit** describes assent that has been elicited by persuasion and implies a conceding of a fact, etc. [I'll *admit* you're right.] **Own** denotes an informal acknowledgment of something in connection with oneself [to *own* to a liking for turnips]. **Avow** implies an open, emphatic declaration, often as an act of affirmation. **Confess** is applied to a formal acknowledgment of a sin, crime, etc., but in a weakened sense is used interchangeably with **admit** in making simple declarations [I'll *confess* I don't like him.]

acknowledge for antonyms see **deny**.

acme for synonyms see **summit**.

acquaint for synonyms see **notify**.

acquiesce for synonyms see **consent**.

acquiesce for antonyms see **object.**

acquire for synonyms see **get.**

acquisitive for synonyms see **greedy.**

acquit for synonyms see **absolve** and **behave.**

acting for synonyms see **temporary.**

action for synonyms see **battle.**

active, energetic, vigorous, strenuous, brisk —**Active** implies a state of motion, operation, etc. ranging from cases of normal functioning to instances of quickened activity [He's still *active* at eighty. There is an *active* market in commodities.] **Energetic** suggests a concentrated exertion of energy or effort [an *energetic* workout]. **Vigorous** implies forcefulness, robustness, and strength as inherent qualities [a *vigorous* plant]. **Strenuous** is applied to things that make trying demands on one's strength, energy, etc. [a *strenuous* trip]. **Brisk** implies liveliness and vigor of motion [a *brisk* walk]. *See also synonyms at* **agile.**

active for antonyms see **inactive, latent.**

actual for synonyms see **true.**

actual for antonyms see **imaginary, latent, plausible.**

acute, crucial, critical —**Acute** suggests severe intensification of an event, condition, etc. that is sharply approaching a climax [an *acute* shortage]. **Critical** is applied to a turning point which will decisively determine an outcome [the *critical* battle of a war]. **Crucial** comes into contrast with **critical** where a trial determining a line of action rather than a decisive turning point is involved [a *crucial* debate on foreign policy]. *See also synonyms at* **sharp.**

adage for synonyms see **saying.**

adamant for synonyms see **inflexible.**

adapt, adjust, accommodate, conform —**Adapt** implies

a modifying so as to suit new conditions and suggests flexibility [to *adapt* oneself to a new environment]. **Adjust** describes the bringing of things into proper relation through the use of skill or judgment [to *adjust* brakes, to *adjust* differences]. **Accommodate** implies a subordinating of one thing to the needs of another and suggests concession or compromise [He *accommodated* his walk to the halting steps of his friend.] **Conform** means to bring or act in harmony with some standard pattern, principle, etc. [to *conform* to specifications].

address for synonyms see **speech**.

adequate for synonyms see **sufficient**.

adhere for synonyms see **stick**.

adherent for synonyms see **follower**.

ad interim for synonyms see **temporary**.

adjacent, adjoining, contiguous, tangent, neighboring —**Adjacent** things may or may not be in actual contact with each other but they are not separated by things of the same kind [*adjacent* angles, our *adjacent* farmhouses]. That which is **adjoining** something else touches it at some point or along a line [*adjoining* rooms]. Things are **contiguous** when they touch along the whole or most of one side [*contiguous* farms]. **Tangent** implies contact at a single, nonintersecting point with a curved line or surface [a line *tangent* to a circle]. **Neighboring** things lie near to each other [*neighboring* villages].

adjoining for synonyms see **adjacent**.

adjourn, prorogue, dissolve, postpone, suspend —**Adjourn** is applied to the action of a deliberative body etc. in bringing a session to a close, with the intention of resuming at a later date. **Prorogue** applies to the formal dismissal of a parliament by the crown, subject to reassembly. To **dissolve** an assembly is to terminate it as constituted, so that an election must be held to reconstitute it. **Postpone** implies the intentional delaying of an action until a later time. **Suspend** denotes the breaking off of proceedings, privileges, etc. for a time, sometimes for such an indefinite time as to suggest cancellation [to *suspend* a sentence].

adjust for synonyms see **adapt**.

administer for synonyms see **govern**.

admire for synonyms see **regard**.

admit for synonyms see **acknowledge, receive**.

admit for antonyms see **exclude**.

admonish for synonyms see **advise**.

adolescent for synonyms see **young**.

adore for synonyms see **venerate**.

adorn, decorate, ornament, embellish, beautify, bedeck —**Adorn** is used of that which adds to the beauty of something by gracing it with beauty [Roses *adorned* her hair.] **Decorate** implies the addition of something to render attractive what would otherwise be plain or bare [to *decorate* a wall with pictures]. **Ornament** is used with reference to accessories which enhance the appearance [a crown *ornamented* with jewels]. **Embellish** suggests the addition of something highly ornamental or ostentatious for effect. To **beautify** is to lend beauty to, or heighten the beauty of. **Bedeck** emphasizes the addition of showy things [*bedecked* with jewelry].

adroit for synonyms see **dexterous**.

adult for synonyms see **ripe**.

advance, promote, forward, further —**Advance** is used to describe assistance in hastening the course of anything or in moving toward an objective. To **promote** is to help in the establishment, development, or success of something [to *promote* good will]. **Forward** emphasizes the idea of action as an impetus [Concessions were made to *forward* the pact.] **Further** emphasizes assistance in bringing a desired goal closer [to *further* a cause]. —*Antonyms:* retard, check. *For other antonyms see* **hinder**.

advanced for synonyms see **liberal**.

adventitious for synonyms see **accidental**.

adversary for synonyms see **opponent**.

advise, counsel, admonish, caution, warn —**Advise** implies the making of recommendations as to a course of action by someone with actual or supposed knowledge, experience, etc. **Counsel** implies the giving of advice after careful deliberation and suggests that weighty matters are involved. **Admonish** suggests earnest, gently reproving advice concerning a fault, error, etc., given by someone fitted to do so by age or position. To **caution** is to give advice that puts one on guard against possible danger, failure, etc. **Warn**, often interchangeable with **caution**, is used when a serious danger or penalty is involved.

✓**advocate** for synonyms see **support**.

aesthete, dilettante, connoisseur, virtuoso —**Aesthete**, although applied to one highly sensitive to art and beauty, is often used derogatorily to connote effeteness, decadence, etc. **Dilettante** refers to one who appreciates art as distinguished from one who creates it, but is used disparagingly of one who dabbles superficially in the arts. A **connoisseur** is one who has expert knowledge or a keen discrimination in matters of art and, by extension, in any matters of taste [a *connoisseur* of fine foods]. **Virtuoso**, in this comparison, denotes a collector or connoisseur of art objects, and is sometimes used derogatorily to suggest faddishness.

✓**affable** for synonyms see **amiable**.

affect, influence, impress, touch, move, sway —**Affect** implies the producing of an effect strong enough to evoke a reaction. (*See also synonyms at* **assume**.) To **influence** is to affect in such a way as to produce a change in action, thought, nature, or behavior [to *influence* legislation]. **Impress** is used of that which produces a deep or lasting effect on the mind. **Touch** and the stronger **move**, as considered here, are both applied to the arousing of emotion, sympathy, etc., but **move** also denotes an influencing so as to effect a change. **Sway** emphasizes the influencing of a person so as to turn him or her from a given course [Threats will not *sway* us.]

affectation for synonyms see **pose**.

affecting for synonyms see **moving**.

affection for synonyms see **disease** and **love**.

affiliate for synonyms see **related**.

affirm for synonyms see **assert**.

affliction, trial, tribulation, misfortune —**Affliction** implies pain, suffering, or distress imposed by illness, loss, misfortune, etc. **Trial** suggests suffering that tries one's endurance, but in a weaker sense refers to annoyance that tries one's patience. **Tribulation** describes severe affliction continuing over a long and trying period. **Misfortune** is applied to a circumstance or event involving adverse fortune and to the suffering or distress occasioned by it.

affluence for antonyms see **poverty**.

affluent for synonyms see **rich**.

affront for synonyms see **offend**.

afraid, frightened, scared, timid, timorous, fearful, terrified —**Afraid** is applied to a general feeling of fear or disquiet and is the broadest in application of all the words considered here [to be *afraid* of the dark, to be *afraid* to die]. **Frightened** and **scared** imply a sudden, usually temporary seizure of fear [The child was *frightened* by the dog. He ran like a *scared* rabbit.] **Timid** implies a lack of courage or self-confidence and suggests overcautiousness, shyness, etc. [He is *timid* about investing money.] **Timorous** and **fearful** suggest a feeling of disquiet and a tendency to worry rather than an alarming fear [*fearful* of making an error.] **Terrified** suggests a feeling of intense, overwhelming fear [He stood *terrified* as the tiger charged.] —*Antonym:* **self-controlled**. *For other antonyms see* **brave**.

age for synonyms see **period**.

aggravate for synonyms see **intensify**.

aggregate for synonyms see **sum**.

aggressive, militant, assertive, pushy —**Aggressive** implies a bold and energetic pursuit of one's ends, connoting, in derogatory usage, a ruthless desire to dominate and, in a favorable sense, enterprise, initiative, etc. **Militant** implies a vigorous, unrelenting espousal of a cause, movement, etc. and rarely suggests the furthering of one's own ends. **Assertive** emphasizes self-confidence and a persistent determination to express oneself or one's opinions. **Pushy** is applied derogatorily to a forwardness of personality that manifests itself in officiousness, rudeness, etc.

aggrieve for synonyms see **wrong**.

agile, nimble, quick, spry, sprightly —**Agile** and **nimble** both imply rapidity and lightness of movement, **agile** emphasizing dexterity in the use of the limbs and **nimble**, deftness in the performance of some act. **Quick** implies rapidity and promptness, seldom indicating, out of context, the degree of skillfulness. **Spry** suggests nimbleness or alacrity, especially as displayed by vigorous elderly people. **Sprightly** implies animation or vivacity and suggests gaiety, lightness, etc. —*Antonyms:* **torpid, sluggish, lethargic.**

agitate for synonyms see **disturb.**

agitated for antonyms see **calm, cool.**

agnostic for synonyms see **atheist.**

agony for synonyms see **distress.**

agree, conform, accord, harmonize, correspond, coincide, tally —**Agree** implies a being or going together without conflict and is the general term used in expressing an absence of inconsistencies, inequalities, unfavorable effects, etc. **Conform** emphasizes agreement in form or essential character. **Accord** emphasizes fitness for each other of the things that are being considered together. **Harmonize** implies a combination or association of different things in a proportionate, orderly, or pleasing arrangement [*harmonizing* colors]. **Correspond** is applied to that which matches, complements, or is analogous to something else [Their Foreign Office *corresponds* to our State Department.] **Coincide** stresses the identical character of the things considered [Their interests *coincide.*] **Tally** is applied to a thing that corresponds to another thing as a counterpart or duplicate. *See also synonyms at* **consent.** —*Antonym:* **differ.** *For other antonyms see* **object.**

agreeable for synonyms see **pleasant.**

aid for synonyms see **help.**

ailing for synonyms see **sick.**

ailment for synonyms see **disease.**

aim for synonyms see **intention.**

air for synonyms see **melody.**

airs for synonyms see **pose.**

alarm for synonyms see **fear, frighten.**

alert for synonyms see **intelligent, watchful.**

alias for synonyms see **pseudonym.**

alien, foreigner, stranger, immigrant, émigré —**Alien** is applied to a resident who bears political allegiance to some other country. (*See also synonyms at* **extrinsic.**) **Foreigner** is applied to a visitor or resident from another country, especially one with a different language, cultural pattern, etc. **Stranger** is used of a person from another region who is unacquainted with local people, customs, etc. **Immigrant** is applied to a person who comes to another country to settle. **Émigré** is a word for one who has left his or her country to take political refuge elsewhere.

alien for antonyms see **citizen, native.**

alive for synonyms see **living.**

alive for antonyms see **dead.**

allay for synonyms see **relieve.**

allegiance, fidelity, loyalty, fealty, homage —**Allegiance** refers to the duty of a citizen to his or her government or a similarly felt obligation to support a cause or leader. **Fidelity** implies strict adherence to an obligation, trust, etc. **Loyalty** suggests a steadfast devotion of an unquestioning kind that one may feel for one's family, friends, or country. **Fealty**, now chiefly a literary word, suggests faithfulness that one has sworn to uphold. **Homage** implies respect, reverence, or honor rendered to a person because of his or her rank, achievement, etc. —*Antonyms:* **faithlessness, disaffection.**

alleviate for synonyms see **relieve.**

alliance, league, coalition, confederacy, confederation, federation, union —**Alliance** refers to any association entered into for mutual benefit. **League**, often interchangeable with **alliance,** stresses formality of organization and definiteness of purpose. **Coalition** implies a temporary alliance of opposing parties, etc., as in times of emergency. **Confederacy** and **confederation** in political usage refer to a combination of independent states for the joint exercise of certain governmental functions, as defense or customs. A **federation** is a league of states or organizations that give up part of their independence to a central authority. **Union** implies a close, permanent alliance and suggests complete unity of purpose and interest.

allied for synonyms see **related**.

allocate for synonyms see **allot**.

allot, assign, apportion, allocate —**Allot** and **assign** both imply the giving of a share or portion with no indication of uniform distribution, **assign** having the extra connotation of authoritativeness [I was *assigned* the task of *allotting* the seats.] **Apportion** connotes the just, proportionate, often uniform distribution of a fixed number of portions. **Allocate** usually implies the allowance of a fixed amount for a specific purpose [to *allocate* $50 for books].

allow for synonyms see **let**.

allude for synonym see **refer**.

allure for synonyms see **attract**.

alluvium for synonyms see **wash**.

ally for synonyms see **comrade**.

ally for antonyms see **opponent**.

alone, solitary, lonely, lone, lonesome —**Alone,** unqualified, denotes the simple fact of being by oneself or itself. **Solitary** conveys the same sense but suggests more strongly the lack of companionship or association [a *solitary* tree in the meadow]. **Lonely,** and the more poetic **lone,** convey a heightened sense of solitude and gloom [The *lonely* sentinel walks his post]. **Lonesome** suggests a longing or yearning for companionship, often for a particular person [The child is *lonesome* for his mother]. —*Antonym:* **accompanied.**

alter for synonyms see **change.**

altercation for synonyms see **quarrel.**

alternate for synonyms see **intermittent.**

alternative for synonyms see **choice.**

altitude for synonyms see **height.**

altruistic for synonyms see **philanthropic.**

amateur, dilettante, novice, neophyte, tyro —**Amateur** refers to one who does something for the pleasure of it rather than for pay and often implies a relative lack of skill. A **dilettante** is an amateur in the arts, but the word is also applied disparagingly to a superficial dabbler in the arts. **Novice** and **neophyte** refer to one who is a beginner, hence inexperienced, in some activity, **neophyte** carrying additional connotations of youthful enthusiasm. **Tyro** refers to an inexperienced but self-assertive beginner and generally connotes incompetence.

amateur for antonyms see **professional.**

amaze for synonyms see **surprise.**

ambiguous for synonyms see **obscure.**

ambitious, aspiring, enterprising, emulous —**Ambitious** implies a striving for advancement, wealth, fame, etc., and is used with both favorable and unfavorable connotation. **Aspiring** suggests a striving to reach some lofty end regarded as somewhat beyond one's normal expectations [an *aspiring* young poet]. **Enterprising** implies an energetic readiness to take risks or undertake new projects in order to succeed. **Emulous** suggests ambition characterized by a competitive desire to equal or surpass another.

ambulatory for synonyms see **itinerant**.

ameliorate for synonyms see **improve**.

amenable for synonyms see **obedient**.

amiable, affable, good-natured, obliging, genial, cordial —**Amiable** and **affable** suggest qualities of friendliness, easy temper, etc. that make one likable, **affable** also implying a readiness to be approached, to converse, etc. A **good-natured** person is one who is disposed to like as well as be liked and is sometimes easily imposed on. **Obliging** implies a ready, often cheerful, desire to be helpful [The *obliging* clerk took my order.] **Genial** suggests good cheer and sociability [our *genial* host]. **Cordial** suggests graciousness and warmth [a *cordial* greeting]. —*Antonym:* **ill-natured.** *For other antonyms see* **sullen.**

amount for synonyms see **sum**.

ample for synonyms see **plentiful**.

ample for antonyms see **meager**.

amuse, divert, entertain, beguile —**Amuse** suggests the agreeable occupation of the mind, especially by something that appeals to the sense of humor [The monkey's antics *amused* him.] To **divert** is to take the attention from serious thought or worry to something gay or light. **Entertain** implies planned amusement or diversion, often with some intellectual appeal [Another guest *entertained* us with folk songs.] **Beguile** suggests the occupation of time with an agreeable activity, largely to dispel boredom or tedium. —*Antonym:* **bore.**

amusing for synonyms see **funny**.

analogy for synonyms see **likeness**.

anathematize for synonyms see **curse**.

ancient for synonyms see **old**.

anecdote for synonyms see **story**.

angel for synonyms see **sponsor**.

anger, indignation, rage, fury, ire, wrath —**Anger** is broadly applicable to feelings of resentful or revengeful displeasure. **Indignation** implies righteous anger aroused by what seems unjust, mean, or insulting. **Rage** suggests a violent outburst of anger in which self-control is lost. **Fury** implies a frenzied rage that borders on madness. **Ire**, chiefly a literary word, suggests a show of great anger in acts, words, looks, etc. **Wrath** implies deep indignation expressing itself in a desire to punish or get revenge. —*Antonyms:* **pleasure, forbearance.**

angle for synonyms see **phase**.

anguish for synonyms see **distress**.

animal for synonyms see **carnal**.

animate, quicken, exhilarate, stimulate, invigorate, vitalize —**Animate** implies a making alive or lively [an *animated* conversation] or an imparting of motion or activity [an *animated* doll]. *(See also synonyms at **living**.)* To **quicken** is to rouse to action that which is lifeless or inert [The insulting rebuff *quickened* his resolution.] **Exhilarate** implies an enlivening or elevation of the spirits. **Stimulate** implies a rousing from inertia, inactivity, or lethargy, as if by goading. **Invigorate** means to fill with vigor or energy in a physical sense [an *invigorating* tonic]. **Vitalize** implies the imparting of vigor or animation in a nonphysical sense [to *vitalize* a dull story]. —*Antonyms:* **deaden, depress, enervate.**

animated for synonyms see **lively, living**.

animosity for synonyms see **enmity**.

annihilate for synonyms see **destroy**.

announce for synonyms see **declare**.

annoy, vex, irk, bother, tease, plague —**Annoy** implies temporary disturbance of mind caused by something that displeases one or tries one's patience. **Vex** implies a more serious source of irritation and greater disturbance, often intense worry. **Irk** stresses a wearing down of one's patience by persistent annoyance. **Bother** implies minor disturbance of one's peace of mind and may suggest mild perplexity or anxiety. To **tease** is to annoy by persistent, irritating actions, remarks, etc. **Plague** suggests mental torment comparable to the physical suffering caused by an affliction.

annoy for antonyms see **comfort.**

annul for synonyms see **abolish.**

annular for synonyms see **round.**

anomalous for synonyms see **irregular.**

answer, respond, reply, retort, rejoin —**Answer** implies a saying, writing, or acting in return, as required by the situation or by courtesy [to *answer* a letter, the phone, etc.] **Respond** implies an appropriate reaction made voluntarily or spontaneously to that which serves as a stimulus [to *respond* to an appeal]. **Reply** in its strictest application refers to an answer that satisfies in detail the question asked. **Retort** suggests a reply, especially one that is sharp or witty, provoked by a charge, criticism, etc. **Rejoin** implies an answer, originally to a reply, now often to an objection.

answer for antonyms see **ask.**

answerable for synonyms see **responsible.**

antagonism for synonyms see **enmity.**

antagonist for synonyms see **opponent.**

antecedent for synonyms see **cause** and **previous.**

anticipate for synonyms see **expect.**

antipathy for synonyms see **aversion.**

antiquated, antique for synonyms see **old.**

antisocial for synonyms see **unsocial.**

antithetical for synonyms see **opposite.**

antonymous for synonyms see **opposite.**

anxiety for synonyms see **care.**

anxious for synonyms see **eager.**

apathetic for synonyms see **impassive.**

ape for synonyms see **imitate.**

aperient for synonyms see **physic.**

apex for synonyms see **summit.**

aphorism for synonyms see **saying.**

aplomb for synonyms see **confidence.**

apocryphal for synonyms see **fictitious.**

appall for synonyms see **dismay.**

apparent for synonyms see **evident.**

appeal, plead, sue, petition, pray, supplicate —**Appeal** implies an earnest, sometimes urgent request and in legal usage connotes resort to a higher court or authority.   **Plead,** applied to formal statements in court answering to allegations or charges, carries into general usage the implication of entreaty by argument [He *pleaded* for tolerance.]   **Sue** implies respectful or formal solicitation for relief, a favor, etc.   **Petition** implies a formal request, usually in writing and in accordance with established rights.   **Pray** and **supplicate** suggest humility in entreaty and imply that the request is addressed to God or to a superior authority, **supplicate** in addition suggesting a kneeling or other abjectly prayerful attitude.

✓**appearance, look, aspect, semblance, guise** —**Appearance** and **look** refer generally to the outward impression of a thing, but the former often implies mere show or pretense [an *appearance* of honesty] and the latter (often in the plural) refers specifically to physical details [the drab *look* of an abandoned house, good *looks*].   **Aspect** also refers to physical details, especially to facial features or expression [a man of handsome *aspect*] or to the distinguishing features at a given time or place [In spring the yard had a refreshing *aspect*.] **Semblance**, which also refers to the outward impression as contrasted with the inner reality, usually does not imply deception [a *semblance* of order]. **Guise** is usually used of a deliberately misleading appearance [under the *guise* of patriotism].

appease for synonyms see **pacify.**
appliance for synonyms see **implement.**
applicable for synonyms see **relevant.**
appoint for synonyms see **furnish.**
apportion for synonyms see **allot.**
apposite for synonyms see **relevant.**
appraise for synonyms see **estimate.**
appreciable for synonyms see **perceptible.**
appreciate, value, prize, treasure, esteem, cherish
—**Appreciate**, in this comparison, implies sufficient critical judgment to see the value or to enjoy [She *appreciates* good music.] *(See also synonyms at* **understand.**) To **value** is to rate highly because of worth [I *value* your friendship.] To **prize** is to value highly or take great satisfaction in [He *prizes* his Picasso collection.] To **treasure** is to regard as precious and implies special care to protect from loss. To **esteem** is to hold in high regard and implies warm attachment or respect [an *esteemed* statesman]. To **cherish** is to prize or treasure, but connotes greater affection for or attachment to the thing cherished [She *cherished* her friends.]

appreciate for antonyms see **despise.**
apprise for synonyms see **notify.**
appropriate for synonyms see **fit.**
approve, endorse, sanction, certify, ratify —**Approve,**

the most general of the following terms, means simply to regard as good or satisfactory. **Endorse** adds the further implication of active support or advocacy [to *endorse* a candidate for office]. **Sanction** implies authoritative approval [a practice *sanctioned* by the charter]. **Certify** implies official approval because of compliance with the requirements or standards [She is a *certified* public accountant.] **Ratify** implies official approval of that which has been done by one's representative [to *ratify* a peace treaty]. —*Antonyms:* **disapprove, reject.**

apropos for synonyms see **relevant.**
apt for synonyms see **fit, likely, quick.**
aptitude for synonyms see **talent.**
arbiter for synonyms see **judge.**
arbitrary for synonyms see **dictatorial.**
archaic for synonyms see **old.**
archetype for synonyms see **model.**
ardent for synonyms see **passionate.**
ardor for synonyms see **passion.**
arduous for synonyms see **hard.**
argot for synonyms see **dialect.**
argue for synonyms see **discuss.**
argument, dispute, controversy —**Argument** refers to a discussion in which there is disagreement and suggests the use of logic and the bringing forth of facts to support or refute a point. **Dispute** basically refers to a contradiction of an assertion and implies vehemence or anger in debate. **Controversy** connotes a disagreement of lengthy duration over a matter of some weight or importance [the Darwinian *controversy*].
arid for synonym see **dry.**
arise for synonyms see **rise.**
arm for synonyms see **furnish.**

aroma for synonyms see **smell**.

arouse for synonyms see **incite, stir**.

arraign for synonyms see **accuse**.

arrogant for synonyms see **proud**.

art, skill, artifice, craft —**Art**, the word of widest application in this group, denotes in its broadest sense merely the ability to make something or to execute a plan. **Skill** implies expertness or great proficiency in doing something. **Artifice** implies skill used as a means of trickery or deception. **Craft** implies ingenuity in execution, sometimes even suggesting trickery or deception. In another sense, **craft** is distinguished from **art** in its application to a lesser skill involving little or no creative thought.

artifice for synonyms see **art** and **trick**.

artificial, synthetic, ersatz, counterfeit, spurious —**Artificial** is applied to anything made by human work, especially if it is in imitation of something natural [*artificial* hair]. **Synthetic** is applied to a substance that is produced by chemical synthesis and is used as a substitute for a natural substance which it resembles [*synthetic* dyes]. **Ersatz**, which refers to an artificial substitute, always implies an inferior substance [*Ersatz* coffee made of acorns.] **Counterfeit** and **spurious** are applied to a careful imitation deliberately intended to deceive [*counterfeit* money, a *spurious* signature]. —*Antonym:* **natural**.

artless for synonyms see **naive**.

ascertain for synonyms see **learn**.

ascetic for synonyms see **severe**.

ascribe, attribute, impute, assign, credit, attach —**Ascribe**, in this comparison, implies assignment to someone of something that may reasonably be deduced [to *ascribe* a motive to someone]. **Attribute** implies assignment of a quality, factor, or responsibility that may reasonably be regarded as applying [to *attribute* an error to carelessness]. **Impute** usually implies the assignment of something unfavorable or accusatory [to *impute* evil to someone]. **Assign** implies the placement of something in a particular category because of some quality, etc. attributed to it [He *assigned* the poem to the 17th century.] **Credit** implies belief in the possession by someone of some quality, etc. [to *credit* one with intelligence]. **Attach** implies the connection of something with something else as being appropriate to it [Different people *attach* different meanings to words.]

ashamed, humiliated, mortified, chagrined —**Ashamed** implies embarrassment, and sometimes guilt, felt because of one's own or another's wrong or foolish behavior [*ashamed* of his tears]. **Humiliated** implies a sense of being humbled or disgraced [*humiliated* by my failure]. **Mortified** suggests humiliation so great as to seem almost fatal to one's pride or self-esteem [She was *mortified* by his obscenities.] **Chagrined** suggests embarrassment coupled with irritation or regret over what might have been prevented [*chagrined* at his error]. —*Antonym:* proud.

ashen for synonyms see **pale**.

asinine for synonyms see **silly**.

ask, inquire, query, question, interrogate, catechize, quiz —**Ask** and the more formal **inquire** and **query** usually denote no more than the seeking of an answer or information, but **query** also often implies doubt as to the correctness of something [The printer *queried* the spelling of several words.] **Question** and **interrogate** imply the asking of a series of questions [to *question* a witness], **interrogate** adding the further implication of systematic examination [to *interrogate* a prisoner of war]. **Cate-chize** is equivalent to **interrogate** but implies the expectation of certain fixed answers, especially with reference to religious doctrine. **Quiz**, used especially in schools, implies a short, selective questioning to test factual knowledge of some subject.

ask for antonyms see **answer, tell**.

aspect for synonyms see **appearance, phase**.

aspiring for synonyms see **ambitious**.

assail for synonyms see **attack**.

assassinate for synonyms see **kill**.

assault for synonyms see **attack**.

assemble for synonyms see **gather**.

assemble for antonyms see **scatter**.

assent for synonyms see **consent**.

assert, declare, affirm, aver, avouch, warrant —To **assert** is to state positively with great confidence but with no objective proof [He *asserted* that the nature of human beings would never change.] To **declare** is to assert openly or formally, often in the face of opposition [They *declared* their independence.] **Affirm** implies deep conviction in one's statement and the unlikelihood of denial by another [I cannot *affirm* that she was there.] **Aver** connotes implicit confidence in the truth of one's statement from one's own knowledge of the matter. **Avouch** implies firsthand knowledge or authority on the part of the speaker. **Warrant**, in this comparison, is colloquial, and implies positiveness by the speaker [I *warrant* he'll be late again.] —*Antonym:* **controvert**. *For other antonyms see* **deny**.

assertive for synonyms see **aggressive**.

assiduous for synonyms see **busy**.

assign for synonyms see **allot, ascribe**.

assignment for synonyms see **task**.

assist for synonyms see **help**.

associate for synonyms see **comrade**.

assuage for synonyms see **relieve**.

assume, pretend, feign, affect, simulate —Assume implies the putting on of a false appearance but suggests a harmless or excusable motive [an *assumed* air of bravado]. (See also synonyms at **presume**.) **Pretend** and **feign** both imply a profession or display of what is false, the more literary **feign** sometimes suggesting an elaborately contrived situation [to *pretend* not to hear, to *feign* deafness]. To **affect** is to make a show of being, having, using, wearing, etc., usually for effect [to *affect* a British accent]. **Simulate** emphasizes the imitation of typical signs involved in assuming an appearance or characteristic not one's own [to *simulate* interest].

assurance for synonyms see **conviction, confidence**.

assurance for antonyms see **uncertainty**.

astonish for synonyms see **surprise**.

astound for synonyms see **surprise**.

astute for synonyms see **shrewd**.

asylum for synonyms see **shelter**.

atheist, agnostic, deist, freethinker, unbeliever, infidel —An **atheist** rejects all religious belief and denies the existence of God. An **agnostic** questions the existence of God, heaven, etc. in the absence of material proof and in unwillingness to accept supernatural revelation. **Deist**, a historical term, was applied to 18th century rationalists who believed in God as a creative, moving force but who otherwise rejected formal religion and its doctrines of revelation, divine authority, etc. **Freethinker**, the current parallel term, similarly implies rejection of the tenets and traditions of formal religion as incompatible with reason. **Unbeliever** is a more negative term, simply designating, without further qualification, one who does not accept any religious belief. **Infidel** is applied to a person not believing in a certain religion or the prevailing religion. —*Antonym:* **theist.**

atrocious for synonyms see **outrageous.**

attach for synonyms see **ascribe** and **bind.**

attachment for synonyms see **love.**

attack, assail, assault, beset, storm, bombard —**Attack** implies vigorous, aggressive action, whether in actual combat or in an undertaking [to *attack* a city, a problem, etc.] **Assail** means to attack by repeated blows, thrusts, etc. [*assailed* by reproaches]. **Assault** implies a sudden, violent attack or onslaught and suggests direct contact and the use of force. **Beset** implies an attack or onset from all sides [*beset* with fears]. **Storm** suggests a rushing, powerful assault that is stormlike in its action and effect. **Bombard** means to attack with artillery or bombs, and in figurative use suggests persistent, repetitious action [to *bombard* a public speaker with questions]. —*Antonym:* **resist.** *For other antonyms see* **defend.**

attain for synonyms see **reach.**

attempt for synonyms see **try.**

attend for synonyms see **accompany.**

attentive for synonyms see **thoughtful.**

attitude for synonyms see **posture.**

attorney for synonyms see **lawyer.**

attract, allure, charm, fascinate, enchant, captivate —**Attract** implies the exertion of a force such as magnetism to draw a person or thing into a susceptibility in the thing drawn. **Allure** implies attraction by that which seductively offers pleasure, delight, reward, etc. **Charm** suggests the literal or figurative casting of a spell and implies very pleasing qualities in the agent. **Fascinate** and **enchant** both also suggest a magical power, **fascinate** stressing irresistibility and **enchant** the evoking of great admiration. **Captivate** implies a capturing of the attention or affection, but suggests a light, passing influence. —*Antonym:* **repel.**

attraction for antonyms see **aversion.**

attribute for synonyms see **ascribe** and **quality.**

auction for synonyms see **sell.**

audacious for synonyms see **brave.**

audacity for synonyms see **temerity.**

augment for synonyms see **increase.**

august for synonyms see **grand.**

auspicious for synonyms see **favorable.**

austere for synonyms see **severe.**

authentic, genuine, bona fide, veritable —**Authentic** implies reliability and trustworthiness, stressing that the thing considered is in agreement with fact or actuality [an *authentic* report]. **Genuine** is applied to that which really is what it is represented to be, emphasizing freedom from admixture, adulteration, sham, etc. [*genuine* silk, *genuine* grief]. **Bona fide** is properly used when a question of good faith is involved. **Veritable** implies correspondence with the truth and connotes absolute affirmation [a *veritable* fool]. —*Antonyms:* **spurious, counterfeit, sham.**

authenticate for synonyms see **confirm.**

authority for synonyms see **influence, power.**

authorize, commission, accredit, license —**Authorize** implies the giving of power or right to act, ranging in application from a specific legal power to discretionary powers in dealings of any kind. To **commission** a person is to authorize as well as instruct him or her to perform a certain duty, as the execution of an artistic work, or to appoint that person to a certain rank or office. **Accredit** implies the sending of a person, duly authorized and with the proper credentials, as an ambassador, delegate, etc. **License** implies the giving of formal legal permission to do some specified thing and often emphasizes regulation [to *license* hunters].

automatic for synonyms see **spontaneous**.

avaricious for synonyms see **greedy**.

avenge, revenge —**Avenge** implies the infliction of deserved or just punishment for wrongs or oppressions. **Revenge** implies the infliction of punishment as an act of retaliation, usually for an injury against oneself, and connotes personal malice, bitter resentment, etc. as the moving force.

aver for synonyms see **assert**.

average, mean, median, norm —**Average** refers to the result obtained by dividing a sum by the number of quantities added [The *average* of 7, 9, 17 is 33 divided by 3, or 11.] and in extended use is applied to the usual or ordinary kind, instance, etc. (*See also synonyms at* **normal**.) **Mean** commonly designates a figure intermediate between two extremes [The *mean* temperature for a day with a high of 56° and a low of 34° is 45°.] and figuratively implies moderation [the golden *mean*]. The **median** is the middle number or point in a series arranged in order of size [The *median* grade in the group 50, 55, 85, 88, 92 is 85; the average is 74.] **Norm** implies a standard of average performance for a given group [a child below the *norm* for his age in reading comprehension].

averse for synonyms see **reluctant**.

aversion, antipathy, repugnance, loathing, revulsion,

abhorrence —**Aversion** and **antipathy** both imply an ingrained feeling against that which is disagreeable or offensive, **aversion** stressing avoidance or rejection, and **antipathy**, active hostility. **Repugnance** emphasizes the emotional resistance or opposition one offers to that which is incompatible with one's ideas, tastes, etc. **Loathing** suggests a feeling of extreme disgust or intolerance. **Revulsion** suggests a drawing back or away from in disgust, horror, etc. **Abhorrence** implies a feeling of extreme aversion or repugnance.

avert for synonyms see **prevent**.

avid for synonyms see **eager**.

avoid for synonyms see **escape**.

avouch for synonyms see **assert**.

avow for synonyms see **acknowledge**.

await for synonyms see **expect**.

awaken for synonyms see **stir**.

award for synonyms see **reward**.

aware, conscious, cognizant, sensible —**Aware** implies having knowledge of something through alertness in observing or in interpreting what one sees, hears, feels, etc. [to be *aware* of a fact]. **Conscious** implies awareness of a sensation, feeling, fact, condition, etc. and may suggest mere recognition or a focusing of attention [*conscious* of a draft in the room, *conscious* humor]. One is **cognizant** of something when one has certain or special knowledge of it through observation or information [*cognizant* of the terms of the will]. **Sensible** implies awareness of something that is not expressed directly or explicitly [*sensible* of their solemn grief].

awe, reverence, veneration, dread —**Awe** refers to a feeling of fearful or profound respect or wonder inspired by the greatness, superiority, grandeur, etc. of a person or thing and suggests an immobilizing effect. **Reverence** is applied to a feeling of deep respect mingled with love for something one holds sacred or inviolable and suggests a display of homage, deference, etc. **Veneration** implies worshipful reverence for a person or thing regarded as hallowed or sacred and specifically suggests acts of religious devotion. **Dread,** as it comes into comparison here, suggests extreme fear mixed with awe or reverence [a *dread* of divine retribution].

awkward, clumsy, maladroit, inept —**Awkward** implies unfitness for smooth, easy functioning, has the broadest application of the terms here, suggesting ungracefulness, unmanageableness, inconvenience, tactlessness, embarrassment, etc. [an *awkward* implement, step, position, remark, etc.] **Clumsy,** emphasizing stiffness or bulkiness, suggests a lack of flexibility or dexterity, unwieldiness, etc. [a *clumsy* build, *clumsy* old galoshes]. **Maladroit** and **inept** both imply tactlessness in social relations, **maladroit** often emphasizing this as a tendency and **inept** stressing inappropriateness of a particular act or remark. —*Antonym:* **graceful.** *For other antonyms see* **dexterous.**

B

baby for synonyms see **indulge.**
back, back up for synonyms see **support.**
backbone for synonyms see **fortitude.**
backer for synonyms see **sponsor.**
bad, evil, wicked, ill, naughty —**Bad,** in this comparison, is the broadest term, ranging in implication from merely unsatisfactory to utterly depraved. **Evil** and

wicked connote willful violation of a moral code, but **evil** often has ominous or malevolent implications [an *evil* hour] and **wicked** is sometimes weakened in a playful way to mean merely mischievous [*wicked* wit]. **Ill**, which is slightly weaker than **evil** in its implications of immorality, is now used chiefly in certain idiomatic phrases [*ill*-gotten gains]. **Naughty** today implies mere mischievousness or disobedience [He is a *naughty* child.] —*Antonym: good. For more antonyms see* **moral.**

badger for synonyms see **bait.**

badlands for synonyms see **waste.**

baffle for synonyms see **frustrate.**

bait, badger, hound, heckle, hector, torment, ride —To **bait** is to torment or goad and implies malicious delight in the persecution [Jew-*baiting*]. To **badger** is to pester so persistently as to bring to a state of frantic confusion. To **hound** is to pursue or attack relentlessly until the victim succumbs [He was *hounded* out of office.] **Heckle** denotes the persistent questioning and taunting of a public speaker so as to annoy or confuse him or her. **Hector** implies a continual bullying or nagging in order to intimidate or break down resistance. **Torment,** in this comparison, suggests continued harassment so as to cause acute suffering [*tormented* by her memories]. **Ride** is colloquial and implies harassment or teasing by ridiculing, criticizing, etc. [They were *riding* the rookie unmercifully from the dugout.]

balance for synonyms see **remainder** and **symmetry.**

bald for synonyms see **bare.**

bale for synonyms see **bundle.**

baleful for synonyms see **sinister.**

balk for synonyms see **frustrate.**

balky for synonyms see **contrary.**

ban for synonyms see **forbid**.

banal for synonyms see **insipid**.

band for synonyms see **troop**.

baneful for synonyms see **pernicious**.

banish, exile, expatriate, deport, transport, ostracize
—**Banish** implies removal from a country (not necessarily one's own) as a formal punishment. **Exile** implies
compulsion to leave one's own country, either because of
a formal decree or through force of circumstance. **Expatriate** suggests more strongly voluntary exile and often
implies the acquiring of citizenship in another country.
To **deport** is to send (an alien) out of the country, either
because of unlawful entry or because his or her presence
is regarded as undesirable. To **transport** is to banish (a
convict) to a penal colony. **Ostracize** today implies
forced exclusion from society, or a certain group, as because of disgrace [He was *ostracized* for his part in the
scandal.]

bank¹ for synonyms see **rely**.

bank² for synonyms see **shoal, shore**.

bar¹ for synonyms see **hinder**.

bar² for synonyms see **shoal**.

barbarian, barbaric, barbarous, savage —**Barbarian**
basically refers to a civilization regarded as primitive,
usually without further connotation [The Anglo-Saxons
were a *barbarian* people.] **Barbaric** suggests the crudeness and lack of restraint regarded as characteristic of
primitive peoples [*barbaric* splendor]. **Barbarous** connotes the cruelty and brutality regarded as characteristic
of primitive peoples [*barbarous* warfare]. **Savage** implies
a more primitive civilization than **barbarian** and connotes even greater fierceness and cruelty [a *savage* in-
quisition]. —*Antonym:* **civilized**.

barbaric for synonyms see **barbarian**.

barbarous for synonyms see **barbarian**.

bare, naked, nude, bald, barren —Bare, in this comparison, implies the absence of the conventional or appropriate covering [*bare* legs, *bare*headed]. (*See also synonyms at* **strip**.) **Naked** implies the absence of clothing, either entirely or from some part, and connotes a revealing of the body [a *naked* bosom]. **Nude**, which is somewhat euphemistic for **naked**, is commonly applied to the undraped human figure in art. **Bald** suggests a lack of natural covering, especially of hair on the head. **Barren** implies a lack of natural covering, especially vegetation, and connotes destitution and fruitlessness [*barren* lands]. —*Antonyms:* **covered, clothed.**

barren for synonyms see **bare, sterile**.

barren for antonyms see **fertile**.

barrier for synonyms see **obstacle**.

barrister for synonyms see **lawyer**.

barter for synonyms see **sell**.

base¹, mean, ignoble, abject, sordid, vile, low, degrading —Base implies a putting of one's own interests ahead of one's obligations, as because of greed or cowardice [*base* motives]. **Mean** suggests a contemptible pettiness of character or conduct [his *mean* attempts to slander her]. **Ignoble** suggests a lack of high moral or intellectual qualities [to work for an *ignoble* end]. **Abject** implies debasement and a contemptible lack of self-respect [an *abject* servant]. **Sordid** connotes the depressing drabness of that which is mean or base [the *sordid* details of their affair]. **Vile** suggests disgusting foulness or depravity [*vile* epithets]. **Low** suggests rather generally coarseness, vulgarity, depravity, etc., specifically in reference to taking grossly unfair advantage [so *low* as to kick a cripple's crutch]. **Degrading** suggests a lowering or corruption of moral standards [the *degrading* aspects of army life]. —*Antonym:* **noble.** *For other antonyms see* **moral.**

base², basis, foundation, groundwork —**Base,** as compared here, refers to a part or thing at the bottom acting as a support or underlying structure [the *base* of a lamp]. **Basis,** conveying the same idea, is the term preferred for nonphysical things [the *basis* of a theory]. **Foundation** stresses solidity in the underlying or supporting thing and often suggests permanence and stability in that which is built on it [the *foundation* of a house]. **Groundwork,** closely synonymous with **foundation,** is principally applied to nonphysical things [the *groundwork* of a good education].

bashful for synonyms see **shy.**

basis for synonyms see **base².**

bathos for synonyms see **pathos.**

battle, engagement, campaign, encounter, skirmish, action, combat —**Battle** denotes a conflict between armed forces in a war and implies a large-scale, prolonged contest over a particular area. **Engagement,** the more formal term, stresses the actual meeting of opposing forces, with no restrictive connotation as to duration. A **campaign** is a series of military operations with a particular objective and may involve a number of battles. **Encounter** usually suggests a chance meeting of hostile forces. **Skirmish** refers to a brief, light encounter between small detachments. **Action** stresses the detailed operations of active fighting [killed in *action*]. **Combat,** the most general of these terms, simply implies armed fighting, without further qualification.

beach for synonyms see **shore.**

bear, suffer, endure, tolerate, stand, brook —Bear implies a putting up with something that distresses, annoys, pains, etc., without suggesting the way in which one sustains such an imposition. (*See also synonyms at* carry.) **Suffer** suggests passive acceptance of or resignation to that which is painful or unpleasant. **Endure** implies a holding up against prolonged pain, distress, etc. and stresses stamina or patience. **Tolerate** and the more informal **stand** both imply self-imposed restraint of one's opposition to something that is offensive or repugnant. **Brook**, a literary word, is usually used in the negative, suggesting determined refusal to put up with what is distasteful.

bearing, carriage, demeanor, mien, deportment, manner —Bearing, in this comparison denoting manner of carrying or conducting oneself, refers to characteristic physical and mental posture. **Carriage**, also applied to posture, specifically stresses the physical aspects of a person's bearing [an erect *carriage*]. **Demeanor** refers to behavior as expressing one's attitude or a specified personality trait [a demure *demeanor*]. **Mien**, a literary word, refers to one's bearing and manner [a man of melancholy *mien*]. **Deportment** refers to one's behavior with reference to standards of conduct or social conventions. **Manner** is applied to customary or distinctive attitude, actions, speech, etc. and, in the plural, refers to behavior conforming with polite conventions.

beat, pound, pummel, thrash, flog, whip, maul —Beat, the most general word in this comparison, conveys the basic idea of hitting or striking repeatedly, whether with the hands, feet, an implement, etc. **Pound** suggests heavier, more effective blows than **beat** [to *pound* with a hammer]. **Pummel** implies the beating of a person with the fists and suggests a continuous, indiscriminate rain of damaging blows. **Thrash**, originally referring to the beating of grain with flail, suggests similar broad, swinging strokes, as in striking a person repeatedly with a stick or other object. **Flog** implies a punishing by the infliction of repeated blows with a stick, strap, whip, etc. **Whip**, often used as an equivalent of **flog**, specifically suggests lashing strokes or motions. **Maul** implies the infliction of repeated heavy blows such as to bruise or lacerate. Most of these terms are used loosely, especially by journalists, in describing a decisive victory in a contest.

beautiful, lovely, handsome, pretty, comely, fair, good-looking, beauteous —**Beautiful** is applied to that which gives the highest degree of pleasure to the senses or to the mind and suggests that the object of delight approximates one's conception of an ideal. **Lovely** refers to that which delights by inspiring affection or warm admiration. **Handsome** implies attractiveness by reason of pleasing proportions, symmetry, elegance, etc. and carries connotations of masculinity, dignity, or impressiveness. **Pretty** implies a dainty, delicate, or graceful quality in that which pleases and carries connotations of femininity or diminutiveness. **Comely** applies to persons only and suggests a wholesome attractiveness of form and features rather than a high degree of beauty. **Fair** suggests beauty that is fresh, bright, or flawless and, when applied to persons, is used especially of complexion and features. **Good-looking** is closely equivalent to **handsome** or **pretty**, suggesting a pleasing appearance but not expressing the fine distinctions of either word. **Beauteous**, equivalent to **beautiful** in poetry and lofty prose, is now often used in humorously disparaging references to beauty. —*Antonym:* **ugly.**

beautify for synonyms see **adorn.**

bedeck for synonyms see **adorn.**

beg, solicit, entreat, beseech, implore, importune —**Beg** implies humbleness or earnestness in asking for something and is now often used in polite formulas [I *beg* to differ, I *beg* to report]. **Solicit** stresses courtesy and formality in requesting something [We *solicit* your aid. He *solicits* our trade.] **Entreat** implies the use of all the persuasive power at one's command. **Beseech** suggests fervor or passion in the asking and connotes anxiety over the outcome. **Implore** is stronger still, suggesting desperation or great distress. **Importune** suggests persistence in entreating, often to the point of becoming offensive.

begin, commence, start, initiate, inaugurate —**Begin,** the most general of these terms, indicates merely a setting into motion of some action, process, or course [to *begin* eating]. **Commence,** the more formal term, is used with reference to a ceremony or an elaborate course of action [to *commence* a court action]. **Start** carries the particular implication of leaving a point of departure in any kind of progression [They wanted to *start* a journey on Tuesday. The boulder *started* a landslide.] **Initiate,** in this connection, refers to the carrying out of the first steps in some course or process, with no indication of what is to follow [to *initiate* peace talks]. **Inaugurate** suggests a formal or ceremonial beginning or opening [to *inaugurate* a new library].

begin for antonyms see **close², stop.**

beginning for synonyms see **origin.**

begrudge for synonyms see **envy.**

beguile for synonyms see **amuse** and **deceive, lure.**

behave, conduct, demean, deport, comport, acquit
—**Behave,** used reflexively (as also the other words in
this comparison), implies action in conformity with the
required standards of decorum [Did the children *behave*
themselves?] **Conduct** implies the direction or guidance
of one's actions in a specified way [He *conducted* himself
well at the trial.] **Demean** suggests behavior or appearance that is indicative of the specified character trait
[She *demeaned* herself like a gracious hostess.] **Deport**
and **comport** suggest behavior in accordance with the
fixed rules of society [They always *deport* themselves like
ladies.] **Acquit** suggests behavior in accordance with the
duties of one's position or with one's obligations [The
rookie *acquitted* himself like a major leaguer.]

behold for synonyms see **see.**

belief, faith, trust, confidence, credence —**Belief,** the
term of broadest application in this comparison, implies
mental acceptance of something as true, even though absolute certainty may be absent. (*See also synonyms at*
opinion.) **Faith** implies complete, unquestioning acceptance of something even in the absence of proof and,
especially, of something not supported by reason. **Trust**
implies assurance, often apparently intuitive, in the reliability of someone or something. **Confidence** also suggests such assurance, especially when based on reason or
evidence. **Credence** suggests mere mental acceptance of
something that may have no solid basis in fact. —*Antonym:* **doubt.** *For other antonyms see* **unbelief.**

belittle for synonyms see **disparage.**

**belligerent, bellicose, pugnacious, quarrelsome, con-
tentious** —**Belligerent** implies a taking part in war or
fighting or in actions that are likely to provoke fighting
[*belligerent* nations]. **Bellicose** implies a warlike or hos-

tile nature, suggesting a readiness to fight [a *bellicose* mood]. **Pugnacious** and **quarrelsome** both connote aggressiveness and a willingness to initiate a fight, but **quarrelsome** more often suggests pettiness and eagerness to fight for little or no reason. **Contentious** suggests an inclination to argue or quarrel, usually with annoying persistence. —*Antonyms:* **peaceful, friendly.**

bend for synonyms see **curve.**
benevolent for synonyms see **kind.**
benign for synonyms see **kind.**
bent for synonyms see **inclination.**
berate for synonyms see **scold.**
beseech for synonyms see **beg.**
beset for synonyms see **attack.**
bestow for synonyms see **give.**
betray for synonyms see **deceive, reveal.**
better for synonyms see **improve.**
bevy for synonyms see **group.**
bewilder, puzzle, perplex, confuse, confound, nonplus, dumbfound —**Bewilder** implies such utter confusion that the mind is staggered beyond the ability to think clearly. **Puzzle** implies such a baffling quality or such intricacy, as of a problem, situation, etc., that one has great difficulty in understanding or solving it. (*See also synonyms at* **mystery.**) **Perplex**, in addition, implies uncertainty or even worry as to what to think, say, or do. **Confuse** implies a mixing up mentally to a greater or lesser degree. **Confound** implies such confusion as completely frustrates or greatly astonishes one. To **nonplus** is to cause such perplexity or confusion that one is utterly incapable of speaking, acting, or thinking further. **Dumbfound** specifically implies as its effect a nonplussed or confounded state in which one is momentarily

struck speechless.

bias for synonyms see **prejudice**.

big for synonyms see **large**.

big for antonyms see **small**.

bigot for synonyms see **zealot**.

billow for synonyms see **wave**.

bind, tie, fasten, attach —Bind and **tie** are often interchangeable, but in discriminative use, **tie** specifically implies the connection of one thing with another by means of a rope, string, etc. which can be knotted [to *tie* a horse to a hitching post], and **bind** suggests the use of an encircling band which holds two or more things firmly together [to *bind* someone's legs]. **Fasten**, a somewhat more general word, implies a joining of one thing to another, as by tying, binding, gluing, nailing, pinning, etc. **Attach** emphasizes the joining of two or more things in order to keep them together as a unit [to *attach* one's references to an application].

birthright for synonyms see **heritage**.

biting for synonyms see **incisive**.

bizarre for synonyms see **fantastic**.

blame for synonyms see **criticize**.

blame for antonyms see **absolve**.

bland for synonyms see **soft** and **suave**.

bland for antonyms see **pungent**.

blasphemy, profanity, swearing, cursing —Blasphemy, the strongest of the following terms, is used especially of any remark deliberately mocking or contemptuous of God. **Profanity** extends the concept to irreverent remarks referring to any person or thing regarded as sacred. **Swearing** and **cursing**, in this connection, both refer to the utterance of profane oaths and imprecations, the latter, especially, to the calling down of evil upon someone or something.

blast for synonyms see **wind**.

blatant for synonyms see **vociferous**.

blaze, flame, flicker, flare, glow, glare —**Blaze** suggests a hot, intensely bright, relatively large and steady fire [the *blaze* of a burning house]. **Flame** generally refers to a single, shimmering, tonguelike emanation of burning gas [the *flame* of a candle]. **Flicker** suggests an unsteady, fluttering flame, especially one that is dying out [the last *flicker* of his oil lamp]. **Flare** implies a sudden, bright, unsteady light shooting up into darkness [the *flare* of a torch]. **Glow** suggests a steady, warm, subdued light without flame or blaze [the *glow* of burning embers]. **Glare** implies a steady, unpleasantly bright light [the *glare* of a bare light bulb].

blemish for synonyms see **defect**.

blend for synonyms see **mix**.

blink for synonym see **wink**.

bliss for synonyms see **ecstasy**.

block for synonyms see **hinder**.

blubber for synonyms see **cry**.

bluff for synonyms see **blunt**.

blunder for synonyms see **error**.

blunt, bluff, brusque, curt, gruff —**Blunt** implies a candor and tactlessness that show little regard for another's feelings ["You're a fool," was his *blunt* reply.] (See also synonyms at **dull**.) **Bluff** suggests a coarse heartiness of manner and a good nature that causes the candor to seem inoffensive [a *bluff* old gardener]. **Brusque** implies apparent rudeness, as evidenced by abruptness of speech or behavior [a *brusque* rejection]. **Curt** suggests a terseness of expression that implies a lack of tact or courtesy [a *curt* dismissal]. **Gruff** suggests bad temper and roughness of speech and manner, connoting, in addition, a harshness or throatiness in utterance [He was a *gruff* sergeant]. —*Antonym:* **tactful**. *For other antonyms see* **suave**.

boast, brag, vaunt, swagger, crow —**Boast,** the basic term in this list, merely suggests pride or satisfaction, as in one's deeds or abilities [You may well *boast* of your efficiency.] **Brag** suggests greater ostentation and overstatement [He *bragged* of what he would do in the race.] **Vaunt,** a formal, literary term, implies greater vainglory but either of the preceding [*Vaunt* not in your triumph.] **Swagger** suggests a proclaiming of one's superiority in an insolent or overbearing way. **Crow** suggests loud boasting in exultation or triumph [Stop *crowing* over your victory.]

bodily, physical, corporeal, corporal, somatic —**Bodily** refers to the human body as distinct from the mind or spirit [*bodily* ills]. **Physical,** while often interchangeable with **bodily,** suggests somewhat less directly the anatomy and physiology of the body [*physical* exercise]. **Corporeal** refers to the material substance of the body and is opposed to *spiritual* [his *corporeal* remains]. **Corporal** refers to the effect of something upon the body [*corporal* punishment]. **Somatic** is the scientific word and refers to the body as distinct from the psyche, with no philosophical or poetic overtones [the *somatic* differences between individuals]. —*Antonyms:* **mental, psychic, spiritual.**

body, corpse, remains, carcass, cadaver —**Body** refers to the whole physical substance of a person or animal, whether dead or alive. **Corpse** and the euphemistic **remains** refer to a dead human body. **Carcass** is used of the dead body of an animal or, contemptuously, of a human being. **Cadaver** refers primarily to a dead human body used for medical dissection.

bogus for synonyms see **false.**

boil, seethe, simmer, stew —**Boil,** the basic word, refers to the vaporization of a liquid over direct heat or, metaphorically, to great agitation, as with rage [Her stubbornness made my blood *boil.*] **Seethe** suggests violent boiling with much bubbling and foaming or, in an extended sense, violent excitement [The country *seethed* with rebellion.] **Simmer** implies a gentle, continuous cooking at or just below the boiling point or, metaphorically, imminence of eruption, as in anger or revolt. **Stew** refers to slow, prolonged boiling or, in an extended colloquial sense, unrest caused by worry or anxiety.

boisterous for synonyms see **vociferous.**

bold for synonyms see **brave.**

bold for antonyms see **afraid, shy.**

bombard for synonyms see **attack.**

bombastic, grandiloquent, flowery, euphuistic, turgid —**Bombastic** refers to speech or writing that is pompous and inflated and suggests extravagant verbal padding and little substance. **Grandiloquent** suggests an overreaching eloquence and implies the use of grandiose, high-flown language and an oratorical tone. **Flowery** language is full of figurative and ornate expressions and high-sounding words. **Euphuistic** is applied to an extremely artificial style of writing in which there is a straining for effect at the expense of thought. **Turgid** implies such inflation of style as to obscure meaning.

bona fide for synonyms see **authentic.**

bondage for synonyms see **servitude.**

boner for synonyms see **error.**

bonus, bounty, premium, dividend —**Bonus** refers to

anything given over and above the regular wages, salary, remuneration, etc. [a Christmas *bonus*, a soldier's *bonus*]. A **bounty** is a reward given by a government for a specific undertaking considered in the public interest, as the production of certain crops, the destruction of vermin, etc. **Premium**, as compared here, implies a reward or prize offered as an inducement to buy, sell, compete, etc. [A toy is given as a *premium* with each package.] **Dividend** refers to a prorated share in an amount distributed among stockholders, policyholders, etc. from profits or surplus.

booboo for synonyms see **error**.

boorish for synonyms see **rude**.

boost for synonyms see **lift**.

booty for synonyms see **spoil**.

border, margin, edge, rim, brim, brink —**Border** refers to the boundary of a surface and may imply the limiting line itself or the part of the surface immediately adjacent to it. **Margin** implies a bordering strip more or less clearly defined by some distinguishing feature [the *margin* of a printed page]. **Edge** refers to the limiting line itself or the terminating line at the sharp convergence of two surfaces [the *edge* of a box]. **Rim** is applied to the edge of a circular or curved surface. **Brim** refers to the inner rim at the top of a cup or other container. **Brink** refers to the edge at the top of a steep slope. All of these terms have figurative application [the *border* of good taste, a *margin* of error, an *edge* on one's appetite, the *rim* of consciousness, a mind filled to the *brim*, the *brink* of disaster].

bosom for synonyms see **breast**.

bother for synonyms see **annoy**.

bound[1] for synonyms see **limit**.

bound² for synonyms see **skip**.

bountiful for synonyms see **generous, profuse**.

bounty for synonyms see **bonus**.

bouquet for synonyms see **scent**.

brace for synonyms see **couple**.

brag for synonyms see **boast**.

brass for synonyms see **temerity**.

brave, courageous, bold, audacious, valiant, intrepid, plucky —**Brave** implies fearlessness in meeting danger or difficulty and has the broadest application of the words considered here. **Courageous** suggests constant readiness to deal with things fearlessly by reason of a stout-hearted temperament or a resolute spirit. **Bold** stresses a daring temperament, whether displayed courageously, presumptuously, or defiantly. **Audacious** suggests an imprudent or reckless boldness. **Valiant** emphasizes a heroic quality in the courage or fortitude shown. **Intrepid** implies absolute fearlessness and especially suggests dauntlessness in facing the new or unknown. **Plucky** emphasizes gameness in fighting against something when one is at a decided disadvantage.

brave for antonyms see **afraid, cowardly**.

break, smash, crash, crush, shatter, crack, split, fracture, splinter —**Break**, the most general of these terms, expresses their basic idea of separating into pieces as a result of impact, stress, etc. **Smash** and **crash** add connotations of suddenness, violence, and noise. **Crush** suggests a crumpling or pulverizing pressure. **Shatter** means sudden fragmentation and a scattering of pieces. **Crack** implies incomplete separation of parts or a sharp, snapping noise in breaking. **Split** means separation lengthwise, as along the direction of grain or layers. **Fracture** means the breaking of a hard or rigid substance, as bone or rock. **Splinter** refers to the splitting of wood, etc. into long thin, sharp pieces. All of these terms are used figuratively to imply great force or damage [to *break* one's heart, *smash* one's hopes, *crush* the opposition, *shatter* one's nerves, etc.]

breaker for synonyms see **wave**.

breast, bosom, bust —Breast refers to the front part of the human torso from the shoulders to the abdomen, or it designates either of the female mammary glands. **Bosom** refers to the entire human breast but, except in euphemistic applications (a big-*bosomed* matron), is now more common in figurative usage where it implies the human breast as a source of feeling, a protective, loving enclosure, etc. [the *bosom* of his family]. **Bust**, as considered here, almost always implies the female breasts and is the conventional term in referring to silhouette, form, etc., as in garment fitting, beauty contests, etc.

breeze for synonyms see **wind**.

bridle for synonyms see **restrain**.

brief, short —Brief and short are opposites of *long* in their application to duration [a *brief* or *short* interval], although **brief** often emphasizes compactness, conciseness, etc. [a *brief* review] and **short** often implies incompleteness or curtailment [a *short* measure, to make *short* work of it]. **Short** is usually used where linear extent is referred to [a *short* man]. *See also synonyms at* **abridgment.** —Antonyms: **long, prolonged.**

bright, radiant, shining, brilliant, luminous, lustrous —Bright, the most general term here, implies the giving forth or reflecting of light, or a being filled with light [a *bright* day, star, shield, etc.] (*See also synonyms at* **intelligent.**) **Radiant** emphasizes the actual or apparent emission of rays of light. **Shining** implies a steady, continuous brightness [the *shining* sun]. **Brilliant** implies intense or flashing brightness [*brilliant* sunlight, diamonds, etc.] **Luminous** is applied to objects that are full of light or give off reflected or phosphorescent light. **Lustrous** is applied to objects whose surfaces gleam by reflected light and emphasizes gloss or sheen [*lustrous* silk].

bright for antonyms see **dark**.

brilliant for synonyms see **bright**.

brim for synonyms see **border**.

bring, take, fetch —Bring (in strict usage) implies a carrying or conducting to, and **take**, similar action away from, a specified or implied place [*Bring* the book to me. I will *take* it back to the library.] **Fetch** implies a going after something, getting it, and bringing it back [He threw the stick and the dog *fetched* it back to him.]

brink for synonyms see **border**.

brisk for synonyms see **active**.

brittle for synonyms see **fragile**.

brittle for antonyms see **pliable**.

broach for synonyms see **utter**.

broad, wide, deep —Broad and **wide** both are applied to extent from side to side of surfaces having height or length, **wide** being preferred when the distance between limits is stressed [two feet *wide*, a *wide* aperture]. **Broad** is used when the full extent of surface is considered [*broad* hips, *broad* plains]. **Deep**, in this connection, refers to extent backward, as from the front, an opening, etc. [a *deep* lot, a *deep* cave]. —Antonym: **narrow**.

bromide for synonyms see **platitude**.

brook for synonyms see **bear**.

brusque for synonyms see **blunt**.

brutal for synonyms see **cruel**.

bucolic for synonyms see **rural**.

buff for synonyms see **polish.**

building, edifice, structure, pile —Building is the general term applied to a fixed structure in which people dwell, work, etc. **Edifice** implies a large or stately building and is sometimes used figuratively [the *edifice* of democracy]. **Structure** also suggests an imposing building, but has special application when the material of construction is being stressed [a steel *structure*]. **Pile** is applied in poetry and lofty prose to a very large building or mass of buildings.

bulge for synonyms see **projection.**

bulk, mass, volume —These words all refer to a quantity of matter or collection of units forming a body or whole. **Bulk** implies a body of great size, weight, or numbers [the lumbering *bulk* of a hippopotamus, the *bulk* of humanity]. **Mass** refers to an aggregate, multitude, or expanse forming a cohesive, unified, or solid body [an eggshaped *mass*, a *mass* of color, the *mass* of workers]. **Volume** means a moving or flowing mass, often of a fluctuating nature [*volumes* of smoke, the *volume* of production].

bum for synonyms see **vagrant.**

bundle, bale, parcel, package, pack —Bundle refers to a number of things bound together for convenience in carrying, storing, etc. and does not in itself carry connotations as to size, compactness, etc. [a *bundle* of discarded clothing]. **Bale** implies a standardized or uniform quantity of goods, as raw cotton, hay, etc., compressed into a rectangular mass and tightly bound. **Parcel** and **package** are applied to something wrapped or boxed for transportation, sale, etc. and imply moderateness of size and a compact or orderly arrangement. **Pack** is applied to a package of a standard amount [a *pack* of cigarettes] or to a compact bundle carried on the back of a person or animal.

burdensome for synonyms see **onerous**.

burglary for synonyms see **theft**.

burlesque for synonyms see **caricature**.

burn, scorch, singe, sear, char —Burn is the broadest term in this comparison, denoting injury to any extent by fire, intense heat, friction, acid, etc. [a *burnt* log, *sun-burned, windburned*]. **Scorch** and **singe** both imply superficial burning, **scorch** emphasizing discoloration or damaging of texture [to *scorch* a shirt in ironing], and **singe,** the burning off, often intentional, of bristles, feathers, the ends of hair, etc. **Sear** implies the burning of animal tissue and is applied specifically to the quick browning of the outside of roasts, etc. in cooking to seal in the juices. **Char** implies a reduction by burning to charcoal or carbon. All of these terms have figurative applications [a *burning* desire, a *scorching* tirade, a *singed* reputation, a soul-*searing* experience, *charred* hopes].

burnish for synonyms see **polish**.

bury for synonyms see **hide**.

business, commerce, trade, industry —Business, in this comparison, refers generally to the buying and selling of commodities and services and connotes a profit motive. **Commerce** and **trade** are both used in referring to the distribution or exchange of commodities, especially as this involves their transportation, but **commerce** generally implies such activity on a large scale between cities, countries, etc. **Industry** refers chiefly to the large-scale manufacture of commodities.

bust for synonyms see **breast**.

busy, industrious, diligent, assiduous, sedulous —Busy suggests active employment in some task or activity, either temporarily or habitually [I'm *busy* just now.] **Industrious** suggests habitual devotion to one's work or activity [an *industrious* salesclerk]. **Diligent** implies unremitting attention, usually to a particular task, and connotes enjoyment in the task itself [a *diligent* student of music]. **Assiduous** suggests painstaking, persevering preoccupation with some task [*assiduous* study]. **Sedulous** implies unremitting devotion to a task until the goal is reached [a *sedulous* investigation of the crime]. —*Antonym:* idle. *For other antonyms see* **lazy**.

butchery for synonyms see **slaughter**.

butt in (or **into**) for synonyms see **intrude**.

C

cabal for synonyms see **conspiracy**.

cache for synonyms see **hide**.

cadaver for synonyms see **body**.

cajole for synonyms see **coax**.

calamity for synonyms see **disaster**.

calculate for synonyms see **compute**.

call, summon, convoke, convene, invite —Call, in this comparison, is the basic word signifying to request the presence of someone at some place [He *called* the waiter over to our table.] **Summon**, the more formal term, implies authority or peremptoriness in the request [to *summon* a witness]. **Convoke** and **convene** refer to the summoning of a group to assemble as for deliberation or legislation, but **convoke** implies greater authority or formality [to *convene* a class, to *convoke* a congress]. **Invite** suggests a courteous request for someone's presence, especially as a guest or participant, and usually suggests that the decision to come rests with the invited.

caller for synonyms see **visitor**.

calm, tranquil, serene, placid, peaceful —**Calm,** basically applied to the weather, suggests a total absence of agitation or disturbance [a *calm* sea, a *calm* mind, a *calm* answer]. **Tranquil** implies a more intrinsic or permanent peace and quiet than **calm** [They lead a *tranquil* life]. **Serene** suggests an exalted tranquillity [He died with a *serene* smile on his lips.] **Placid** implies an undisturbed or unruffled calm and is sometimes used in jocular disparagement to suggest dull equanimity [She's as *placid* as a cow.] **Peaceful** suggests a lack of turbulence or disorder [a *peaceful* gathering]. —*Antonyms:* **stormy, agitated, excited.**

campaign for synonyms see **battle**.

can, may —**Can,** in formal usage, denotes ability, either physical or mental [He *can* walk. I *can* understand you.] **May** denotes possibility [I *may* go tomorrow.] or, in formal usage, permission [You *may* have another cooky.] In informal and colloquial usage, **can** is most frequently used to express permission, especially in interrogative and negative statements [*Can't* I go? You *cannot!*]

candid for synonyms see **frank**.

canon for synonyms see **law**.

cant for synonyms see **dialect**.

capable for synonyms see **able**.

capacity for synonyms see **function**.

capital for synonyms see **chief**.

capitulate for synonyms see **yield**.

caprice, whim, whimsy, vagary, crotchet —**Caprice** refers to a sudden, impulsive, apparently unmotivated turn of mind or emotion [discharged at the *caprice* of a foreman]. **Whim** and **whimsy** both refer to an idle, quaint, or curious notion, but **whim** more often suggests willfulness and **whimsy** fancifulness [Pursuing a *whim* he wrote a poem full of *whimsy*.] **Vagary** suggests a highly unusual or extravagant notion [the *vagaries* in fashion in women's clothes]. **Crotchet** implies great eccentricity and connotes stubbornness in opposition to prevailing thought, usually on some insignificant point [his *crotchets* concerning diet].

capricious for synonyms see **inconstant**.

capsize for synonyms see **upset**.

captious for synonyms see **critical**.

captivate for synonyms see **attract**.

capture for synonyms see **catch**.

carcass for synonyms see **body**.

care, concern, solicitude, worry, anxiety —**Care** suggests a weighing down of the mind, as by dread, apprehension, or great responsibility [worn out by the *cares* of the day]. **Concern** suggests mental uneasiness over someone or something in which one has an affectionate interest [I feel *concern* for their welfare.] **Solicitude** implies thoughtfulness, often excessive apprehension, for the welfare, safety, or comfort of another [She stroked his head with great *solicitude*.] **Worry** suggests mental distress or agitation over some problem [His chief *worry* was that he might fail.] **Anxiety** suggests an apprehensive or uneasy feeling with less mental activity than **worry**, often over some indefinite but anticipated evil [He viewed the current world situation with *anxiety*.] —*Antonyms:* **unconcern, indifference.**

careful, meticulous, scrupulous, circumspect, cautious, prudent, discreet, wary —**Careful** implies close attention to or great concern for whatever is one's work or responsibility, and usually connotes thoroughness, a guarding against error or injury, etc. **Meticulous** implies extreme, sometimes finicky, carefulness about details. **Scrupulous** implies a conscientious adherence to what is considered right, true, accurate, etc. **Circumspect** implies a careful consideration of all circumstances to avoid error or unfavorable consequences. **Cautious** implies a careful guarding against possible dangers or risks. **Prudent** implies the exercise of both caution and circumspection, suggesting careful management in economic and practical matters. **Discreet** implies the exercise of discernment and judgment in the guidance of one's speech and action and suggests careful restraint. **Wary** implies a cautiousness that is prompted by suspicion. —*Antonyms:* **careless, negligent, lax.**

caress, fondle, pet, cuddle, dandle —**Caress** refers to a display of affection by gentle stroking or patting. **Fondle** implies a more demonstrative show of love or affection, as by hugging, kissing, etc. **Pet,** as applied generally, implies treatment with special affection and indulgence, including patting, fondling, etc., but informally it refers to indulgence, especially by young couples, in hugging, kissing, and amorous caresses. **Cuddle** implies affectionate handling, as of a small child by its mother, by pressing or drawing close within the arms. **Dandle** implies a playful affection displayed toward a child by moving him or her up and down lightly on the knee.

caricature, burlesque, parody, travesty, satire, lampoon —**Caricature** refers to an imitation or representation of a person or thing, in drawing, writing, or performance, that ludicrously exaggerates its distinguishing features. **Burlesque** implies the handling of a serious subject lightly or flippantly, or of a trifling subject with mock seriousness. A **parody** ridicules a written work or

writer by imitating the style closely, especially so as to
point up its peculiarities or affectations, and by distorting the content nonsensically or changing it to something
absurdly incongruous. **Travesty**, in contrast, implies
that the subject matter is retained, but that the style and
language are changed so as to give a grotesquely absurd
effect. **Satire** refers to a literary composition in which
follies, vices, stupidities, and abuses in life are held up to
ridicule and contempt. **Lampoon** refers to a piece of
strongly satirical writing that uses broad humor in attacking and ridiculing the faults and weaknesses of an
individual.

carnage for synonyms see **slaughter**.

carnal, fleshly, sensual, animal —**Carnal** implies relation to the body or flesh as the seat of basic physical
appetites, now especially sexual appetites, and usually
stresses absence of intellectual or moral influence [*carnal*
lust]. **Fleshly**, expressing less censure, stresses these
appetites and their gratification as natural to the flesh
[*fleshly* frailty]. **Sensual** stresses relation to or preoccupation with gratifying the bodily senses and usually implies grossness or lewdness [*sensual* lips]. **Animal** is applied to the physical nature of people as distinguished
from their intellectual and spiritual nature, and now
rarely carries a derogatory implication [*animal* spirits].

carping for synonyms see **critical**.

carriage for synonyms see **bearing**.

carry, bear, convey, transport, transmit —**Carry** means
to take something from one place to another and implies
a person as the agent or the use of a vehicle or other
medium. **Bear** emphasizes the support of the weight or
the importance of that which is carried [*borne* on a sedan
chair, to *bear* good tidings]. **Convey**, often simply a for-

mal equivalent of *carry*, is preferred where continuous movement is involved [boxes *conveyed* on a moving belt] or where passage by means of an agent or medium is implied [Words *convey* ideas.] **Transport** is applied to the movement of goods or people from one place to another, especially over long distances. **Transmit** stresses causal agency in connection with the sending or conducting of things [The telegrapher *transmitted* the message.]

cartel for synonyms see **monopoly**.

case for synonyms see **instance**.

cast for synonyms see **throw**.

castigate for synonyms see **punish**.

casual for synonyms see **accidental** and **random**.

cataclysm for synonyms see **disaster**.

catalog for synonyms see **list**.

catastrophe for synonyms see **disaster**.

catch, capture, nab, trap, snare —**Catch**, the most general term here, refers to a seizing or taking of a person or thing, whether by skill or cunning, and usually implies pursuit. **Capture** implies a greater measure of resistance or elusiveness than **catch** and therefore stresses seizure by force or stratagem [to *capture* an outlaw]. **Nab**, an informal word, specifically implies a sudden or quick taking into custody [The police *nabbed* the thief.] **Trap** and **snare** both imply the literal or figurative use of a device for catching a person or animal and suggest a situation from which escape is difficult or impossible [to *trap* a bear, *snared* by her womanly wiles].

catechize for synonyms see **ask**.

cathartic for synonyms see **physic**.

cause, reason, motive, antecedent, determinant, occasion —**Cause**, in its distinctive sense, refers to a situation, event, or agent that produces an effect or result

[Carelessness is often a *cause* of accident.] **Reason** implies the mental activity of a rational being in explaining or justifying some act or thought [She had a *reason* for laughing.] A **motive** is an impulse, emotion, or desire that leads to action [the *motive* for a crime]. An **antecedent** is an event or thing that is the predecessor of, and is responsible for, a later event or thing [War always has its *antecedent*.] A **determinant** is a cause that helps to determine the character of an effect or result [Ambition was a *determinant* in his success.] An **occasion** is a situation or event that allows a cause to have an effect [The court case was an *occasion* for stating a new legal principle.]

cause for antonyms see **effect**.

caustic for synonyms see **sarcastic**.

caution for synonyms see **advise**.

cautious for synonyms see **careful**.

caviling for synonyms see **critical**.

cavity for synonyms see **hole**.

cease for synonyms see **stop**.

cease for antonyms see **continue**.

celebrate, commemorate, solemnize, observe, keep —**Celebrate** implies the marking of an occasion or event, especially a joyous one, with ceremony or festivity [Let's *celebrate* his promotion.] To **commemorate** is to honor the memory of some person or event by a ceremony [to *commemorate* Lincoln's birthday]. **Solemnize** suggests the use of formal, grave ritual in signalizing an event, especially a religious ceremony [to *solemnize* a marriage]. **Observe** and the less formal **keep** suggest the respectful marking of a day or occasion in the prescribed or appropriate manner [to *observe*, or *keep*, a religious holiday].

celebrated for synonyms see **famous.**

censure for synonyms see **criticize.**

center for synonyms see **middle.**

ceremony, rite, ritual, formality —**Ceremony** refers to a formal, usually solemn, act established as proper to some religious or state occasion [the *ceremony* of launching a ship]. **Rite** refers to the prescribed form for a religious practice [burial *rites*]. **Ritual** refers to rites or ceremonies collectively, especially to the rites of a particular religion [the *ritual* of voodooism]. **Formality** suggests a conventional, often meaningless, act or custom, usually one associated with social activity [the *formalities* of polite conversation].

certain for synonyms see **sure.**

certain for antonyms see **doubtful.**

certainty for synonyms see **conviction.**

certify for synonyms see **approve.**

certitude for synonyms see **conviction.**

certitude for antonyms see **uncertainty.**

chagrined for synonyms see **ashamed.**

chain for synonyms see **series.**

chance for synonyms see **happen** and **random.**

change, alter, vary, modify, transform, convert —**Change** denotes a making or becoming distinctly different and implies either a radical transmutation of character or replacement with something else [I'll *change* my shoes.] **Alter** implies a partial change, as in appearance, so that the identity is preserved [to *alter* a garment]. **Vary** suggests irregular or intermittent change [to *vary* one's reading]. **Modify** implies minor change, often so as to limit or moderate [to *modify* the language of a report]. **Transform** implies a change in form and now, usually, in nature or function [to *transform* matter into energy]. **Convert** suggests more strongly change to suit a new function [They decided to *convert* the dining room into a bedroom.]

chaos for synonyms see **confusion**.

chaperon for synonyms see **accompany**.

char for synonyms see **burn**.

character for synonyms see **disposition** and **quality**.

characteristic, individual, distinctive —**Characteristic** suggests the indication of a quality that is peculiar to, and helps identify, something or someone [the *characteristic* taste of honey]. **Individual** and **distinctive** refer to, or suggest the possession of, a quality or qualities that distinguish something from others of its class or kind, **distinctive** often implying a meritorious difference [an *individual*, or *distinctive*, literary style].

charge for synonyms see **accuse** and **command**.

charity for synonyms see **mercy**.

charlatan for synonyms see **quack**.

charm for synonyms see **attract**.

charter for synonyms see **hire**.

chaste, virtuous, pure, modest, decent —**Chaste** and **virtuous**, in this connection, imply moral excellence manifested by forbearance from acts or thoughts that do not accord with virginity or strict marital fidelity. **Pure** impies chastity through innocence and an absence of seductive influences rather than through self-restraint. **Modest** and **decent** are both applied to propriety in behavior, dress, bearing, or speech as exhibiting morality or purity.

chaste for antonyms see **immoral**.

chasten, chastise for synonyms see **punish**.

cheap, inexpensive —**Cheap** and **inexpensive** both mean low in cost or price, but **inexpensive** simply suggests value comparable to the price and **cheap**, in this sense, stresses a bargain. **Cheap** may also imply inferior quality or value, tawdriness, contemptibleness, etc. [*cheap* jewelry, to feel *cheap*].

cheap for antonyms see **costly**.

cheat, defraud, swindle, trick, dupe, hoax —**Cheat**, the most general term in this comparison, implies dishonesty or deception in dealing with someone, to obtain some advantage or gain. **Defraud**, chiefly a legal term, stresses the use of deliberate deception in criminally depriving a person of his or her rights, property, etc. **Swindle** stresses the winning of a person's confidence in order to cheat or defraud him or her of money, etc. **Trick** implies a deluding by means of a ruse or stratagem, but does not always suggest fraudulence or a harmful motive. **Dupe** stresses credulity in the person who is tricked or fooled. **Hoax** implies a trick skillfully carried off simply to demonstrate the gullibility of the victim.

check for synonyms see **restrain**.

check for antonyms see **advance**.

cheek for synonyms see **temerity**.

cheerful for synonyms see **happy**.

cheerful for antonyms see **sad**.

cherish for synonyms see **appreciate**.

chicanery for synonyms see **deception**.

chief, principal, main, leading, foremost, capital —**Chief** is applied to the person or thing first in rank, authority, importance, etc., and usually connotes subordination of all others [His *chief* problem was getting a job.] **Principal** is applied to the person who directs or controls others [a *principal* clerk] or to the thing or person having precedence over all others by reason of size, position, importance, etc. [the *principal* products of Africa]. **Main**, in strict usage, is applied to the thing, often part of a system or an extensive whole, that is preeminent in size, power, importance, etc. [the *main* line of a railroad]. **Leading** stresses capacity for guiding, conducting, or drawing others [a *leading* light, question, etc.] **Foremost** suggests a being first by having moved ahead to that position [the *foremost* statesman of our time]. **Capital** is applied to that which is ranked at the head of its kind or class because of its importance or its special significance [the *capital* city]. —*Antonyms:* **subordinate, subservient.**

childlike, childish —Both of these words are applied to persons of any age in referring to characteristics or qualities considered typical of a child. **Childlike** suggests the favorable qualities such as innocence, guilelessness, trustfulness, etc., and **childish** suggests the unfavorable qualities, such as immaturity, foolishness, petulance, etc.

chivalrous for synonyms see **civil.**

choice, option, alternative, preference, selection —**Choice** implies the chance, right, or power to choose, usually by the free exercise of one's judgment [a bachelor by *choice*]. **Option** suggests the privilege of choosing as granted by a person or group in authority that normally exercises the power [local *option* on liquor sales]. **Alternative**, in strict usage, limits a choice to one of two possibilities [the *alternative* of paying a fine or serving 30 days]. **Preference** suggests the determining of choice by predisposition or partiality [a *preference* for striped ties]. **Selection** implies a wide choice and the exercise of careful discrimination [*selections* from the modern French poets].

choleric for synonyms see **irritable.**

choose, select, pick, elect, prefer —Choose implies the exercise of judgment in settling upon a thing or course from among those offered. **Select**, and the more informal **pick**, imply a choosing by careful discrimination from a large number available, **pick** sometimes connoting random selection [*Pick* a number from 1 to 10.] **Elect** implies formal action in officially choosing a person or thing. **Prefer** implies preconceived partiality for one thing over another but does not always connote the actual getting of what one chooses. —*Antonym:* **reject.**

chop for synonyms see **grind.**

chore for synonyms see **task.**

chronic, inveterate, confirmed, hardened —Chronic suggests long duration or frequent recurrence and is used especially of diseases or habits that resist all efforts to eradicate them [*chronic* sinusitis]. **Inveterate** implies firm establishment as a result of continued indulgence over a long period of time [an *inveterate* liar]. **Confirmed** suggests fixedness in some condition or practice, often from a deep-seated aversion to change [a *confirmed* bachelor]. **Hardened** implies fixed tendencies and a callous indifference to emotional or moral considerations [a *hardened* criminal].

chuckle for synonyms see **laugh.**

circle for synonyms see **coterie.**

circuit for synonyms see **circumference.**

circular for synonyms see **round.**

circumference, perimeter, periphery, circuit, compass —Circumference refers to the line bounding a circle or any approximately circular or elliptical area. **Perimeter** extends the meaning to a line bounding any area, as a triangle, square, or polygon. **Periphery**, in its literal sense identical with **perimeter**, is more frequently

used of the edge of a concrete object or in an extended
metaphorical sense [the *periphery* of understanding]. **Circuit** now usually refers to a traveling around a periphery
[the moon's *circuit* of the earth]. **Compass** refers literally to an area within specific limits but is often used
figuratively [the *compass* of the city, the *compass* of freedom].

circumscribe for synonyms see **limit**.

circumspect for synonyms see **careful**.

circumstance for synonyms see **occurrence**.

citizen, subject, national, native —**Citizen** refers to a
member of a state or nation, especially one with a republican government, who owes it allegiance and is entitled
to full civil rights either by birth or naturalization. **Subject** is the term used when the government is headed by
a monarch or other sovereign. **National** is applied to a
person residing away from the country of which he or
she is, or once was, a citizen or subject, and is especially
used of one another by fellow countrymen living abroad.
Native refers to one who was born in the country under
question and is applied specifically to an original or indigenous inhabitant of the region.

citizen for antonyms see **alien**.

civil, polite, courteous, chivalrous, gallant —**Civil** implies merely a refraining from rudeness [Keep a *civil*
tongue in your head.] **Polite** suggests a more positive
observance of etiquette in social behavior [It is not *polite*
to interrupt.] **Courteous** suggests a still more positive
and sincere consideration of others that springs from an
inherent thoughtfulness [always *courteous* to strangers].
Chivalrous implies disinterested devotion to the cause of
the weak, especially to helping women [quite *chivalrous*
in her defense]. **Gallant** suggests a dashing display of

courtesy, especially to women [her *gallant* lover].

civil for antonyms see **rude**.

claim for synonyms see **demand**.

clamor for synonyms see **noise**.

clamorous for synonyms see **vociferous**.

clandestine for synonyms see **secret**.

clean, cleanse —In this comparison **clean** is the broader term and denotes generally the removal of dirt or impurities, as by washing, brushing, etc. **Cleanse** suggests more specifically the use of chemicals, purgatives, etc. and is often used metaphorically to imply purification [to *cleanse* one's mind of evil thoughts]. —*Antonyms:* **soil, dirty.**

clear, transparent, translucent, pellucid —**Clear** suggests freedom from cloudiness, haziness, muddiness, etc., either literally or figuratively [a *clear* liquid, *clear* logic]. *(See also synonyms at* **evident.***)* **Transparent** suggests such clearness that objects on the other side (or by extension, meanings, etc.) may be seen distinctly [Plate glass is *transparent*.] **Translucent** implies the admission of light, but so diffused that objects on the other side cannot be clearly distinguished [Stained glass is *translucent*.] **Pellucid** suggests the sparkling clearness of crystal [a slab of *pellucid* ice, *pellucid* writing]. —*Antonyms:* **opaque, cloudy, turbid.**

cleave for synonyms see **stick**.

clemency for synonyms see **mercy**.

clever, cunning, ingenious, shrewd —**Clever**, in this comparison, implies quick-wittedness or adroitness, as in contriving the solution to a problem [a *clever* reply]. **Cunning** suggests great skill or ingenuity, but often implies deception or craftiness [*cunning* as a fox]. **Ingenious** stresses inventive skill, as in origination or fabrication [an *ingenious* explanation]. **Shrewd** suggests cleverness accompanied by practicality [a *shrewd* understanding of the situation], sometimes verging on craftiness [a *shrewd* politician]. *See also synonyms at* **intelligent**.

cliché for synonyms see **platitude**.

climax for synonyms see **summit**.

cling for synonyms see **stick**.

clique for synonyms see **coterie**.

cloister, convent, nunnery, monastery, abbey, priory —**Cloister** is the general term for a place of religious seclusion, for either men or women, and emphasizes in connotation retirement from the world. **Convent**, once a general term synonymous with **cloister**, is now usually restricted to such a place for women (nuns), formerly called a **nunnery**. **Monastery** usually refers to a cloister for men (monks). An **abbey** is a cloister ruled by an abbot or abbess. A **priory** is a cloister ruled by a prior or prioress and is sometimes a subordinate branch of an abbey.

close¹, dense, compact, thick —**Close** suggests something whose parts or elements are near together with little space between [*close*-order drill]. *(See also synonyms at* **familiar** *and* **stingy**.) **Dense** suggests such a crowding together of elements or parts as to form an almost impervious mass [a *dense* fog]. **Compact** suggests close and firm packing, especially within a small space, and usually implies neatness and order in the arrangement of parts [a *compact* bundle]. **Thick**, in this connection, suggests a great number of parts massed tightly together [*thick* fur]. —*Antonyms:* **open, dispersed**.

close², end, conclude, finish, complete, terminate —**Close** suggests a coming or bringing to a stop, as if by shutting something regarded as previously open [nomi-

nations are now *closed*]. **End** suggests the stopping of
some process, whether or not it has been satisfactorily
completed [Let's *end* this argument.] To **conclude** is to
bring or come to a formal termination, often by arriving
at some decision [to *conclude* negotiations]. **Finish** emphasizes the bringing to a desired end of that which one
has set out to do, especially by adding perfecting touches
[to *finish* a painting]. **Complete**, in its distinctive sense,
suggests a finishing by filling in the missing or defective
parts [The award will *complete* his happiness.] To **terminate** is to bring or come to an end regarded as a limit or
boundary [to *terminate* a privilege].

close² for antonyms see **begin**.
cloudy for synonyms see **opaque**.
cloudy for antonyms see **clear**.
cloy for synonyms see **satiate**.
clumsy for synonyms see **awkward**.
clumsy for antonyms see **dexterous**.
clutch for synonyms see **take**.
coalesce for synonyms see **mix**.
coalition for synonyms see **alliance**.

coarse, gross, indelicate, vulgar, obscene, ribald
—**Coarse**, in this comparison, implies such a lack of refinement in manners or speech as to be offensive to one's
esthetic or moral sense [*coarse* laughter]. **Gross** suggests
a brutish crudeness or roughness [*gross* table manners].
Indelicate suggests a verging on impropriety or im-
modesty [an *indelicate* remark]. **Vulgar**, in this connection, emphasizes a lack of proper training, culture, or
good taste [the *vulgar* ostentation of her home]. **Obscene** is used of that which is offensive to decency or
modesty and implies lewdness [*obscene* gestures]. **Ribald**
suggests such mild indecency or lewdness as might bring

laughter from those who are not too squeamish [*ribald* jokes]. —*Antonym:* **refined**.

coast for synonyms see **shore**.

coax, cajole, wheedle —**Coax** suggests repeated attempts to persuade someone to do something and implies the use of soothing words, an insinuating manner, etc. **Cajole** suggests the use of flattery or other blandishments. **Wheedle** implies even more strongly the use of subtle flattery or seduction in gaining one's ends.

coerce for synonyms see **force**.

coeval for synonyms see **contemporary**.

cogent for synonyms see **valid**.

cogitate for synonyms see **think**.

cognate for synonyms see **related**.

cognizant for synonyms see **aware**.

cohere for synonyms see **stick**.

coincide for synonyms see **agree**.

collate for synonyms see **compare**.

colleague for synonyms see **comrade**.

collect for synonyms see **gather**.

collect for antonyms see **scatter**.

collected for synonyms see **cool**.

color, shade, hue, tint, tinge —**Color** is the general term for the property of reflecting light of a particular wavelength: the distinct colors of the spectrum are red, orange, yellow, green, blue, indigo, and violet. **Shade** refers to any of the gradations of a color with reference to its degree of darkness [a light *shade* of green]. **Hue**, often equivalent to **color**, is used specifically to indicate a modification of a basic color [orange of a reddish *hue*]. **Tint** refers to a gradation of a color with reference to its degree of whiteness and suggests a paleness or delicacy of color [pastel *tints*]. **Tinge** suggests the presence of a small amount of color, usually diffused throughout [white with a *tinge* of blue].

colossal for synonyms see **huge**.

combat for synonyms see **battle**.

combine for synonyms see **join**.

combine for antonyms see **separate**.

comely for synonyms see **beautiful**.

comfort, console, solace, relieve, soothe —Comfort suggests the lessening of misery or grief by cheering, calming, or inspiring with hope. **Console** suggests less positive relief but implies a moderation of the sense of loss or disappointment [to *console* someone on the death of a parent]. **Solace** suggests the relieving of melancholy, boredom, loneliness, etc. [He *solaced* himself by playing the flute.] **Relieve** suggests the mitigation, often temporary, of misery or discomfort so as to make it bearable [to *relieve* the poor]. **Soothe** implies the calming or allaying of pain or distress [She *soothed* the child with a lullaby.] —*Antonym:* **afflict**. *For other antonyms see* **annoy, distress, torment**.

comfortable, cozy, snug, restful —Comfortable implies the absence of disturbing, painful, or distressing features and, in a positive sense, stresses ease, contentment, freedom from care, etc. [a *comfortable* climate]. **Cozy** suggests such comfort as might be derived from shelter against storm, cold, hardship, etc. [a *cozy* nook by the fire]. **Snug** is used of something that is small and compact, but just large enough to provide ease and comfort, and often carries additional connotations of coziness [a *snug* apartment]. **Restful** is applied to that which promotes relaxation, freedom from care, etc. [*restful* music]. —*Antonym:* **miserable**.

comic, comical for synonyms see **funny**.

command, order, direct, instruct, enjoin, charge
—**Command**, when it refers to a giving of orders, implies the formal exercise of absolute authority, as by a sovereign, military leader, etc. *(See also synonyms at* **power**.) **Order** often stresses peremptoriness, sometimes suggesting an arbitrary exercise of authority [I *ordered* him out of the house.] **Direct** and **instruct** are both used in connection with supervision, as in business relations, **instruct** perhaps more often stressing explicitness of details in the directions given. **Enjoin** suggests a directing with urgent admonition [He *enjoined* them to secrecy.] and sometimes implies the legal prohibiting of an action. **Charge** implies the imposition of a task as a duty, trust, or responsibility.

commemorate for synonyms see **celebrate**.
commence for synonyms see **begin**.
commence for antonyms see **close²**, **stop**.
commensurable for synonyms see **proportionate**.
commensurate for synonyms see **proportionate**.
comment, commentary for synonyms see **remark**.
commerce for synonyms see **business**.
commiseration for synonyms see **pity**.
commission for synonyms see **authorize**.
commit, entrust, confide, consign, relegate —**Commit**, the basic term here, implies the delivery of a person or thing into the charge or keeping of another. **Entrust** implies committal based on trust and confidence. **Confide** stresses the private nature of information entrusted to another and usually connotes intimacy of relationship. **Consign** suggests formal action in transferring something to another's possession or control. **Relegate** implies a consigning to a specific class, sphere, place, etc., especially one of inferiority, and usually suggests the

literal or figurative removal of something undesirable.
common, general, ordinary, familiar, popular, vulgar
—**Common** refers to that which is met with most frequently or is shared by all or most individuals in a group, body, etc., and may imply prevalence, usualness, or, in a depreciatory sense, inferiority [a *common* belief, a *common* hussy]. *(See also synonyms at* **mutual.**) **General** implies connection with all or nearly all of a kind, class, or group and stresses extensiveness [*general* unrest among the people]. **Ordinary** implies accordance with the regular or customary pattern, stressing commonplaceness and lack of special distinction [an *ordinary* workday]. **Familiar** applies to that which is widely known and readily recognized [a *familiar* feeling]. **Popular** and, in this connection, **vulgar** imply widespread currency, acceptance, or favor among the general public or the common people [a *popular* song, *Vulgar* Latin]. —Antonym: **exceptional.** *For other antonyms see* **rare.**
commonplace for synonyms see **platitude** and **trite.**
compact for synonyms see **close**[1].
companion for synonyms see **comrade.**
company for synonyms see **troop.**
compare, contrast, collate —**Compare** refers to a literal or figurative putting together in order to note points of resemblance and difference, and implies the weighing of parallel features for relative values [to *compare* Shakespeare with Schiller]. **Contrast** implies a comparing for the purpose of emphasizing differences [to *contrast* farm life with city life]. **Collate** implies detailed, critical comparison, specifically of different versions of the same text.
compass for synonyms see **circumference, range.**
compassion for synonyms see **pity.**

compassionate for synonyms see **tender**.

compel for synonyms see **force**.

compensate for synonyms see **pay**.

competent for synonyms see **able**.

competition, rivalry, emulation —**Competition** denotes a striving for the same object, position, prize, etc., usually in accordance with certain fixed rules. **Rivalry** implies keen competition between opponents more or less evenly matched, and, unqualified, it often suggests unfriendliness or even hostility. **Emulation** implies endeavor to equal or surpass in achievement, character, etc. another, usually one greatly admired. —*Antonym:* **cooperation**.

complete, full, total, whole, entire, intact —**Complete** implies inclusion of all that is needed for the integrity, perfection, or fulfillment of something [a *complete* set, *complete* control]. (*See also synonyms at* **close**[2].) **Full** implies the inclusion of all that is needed [a *full* dozen] or all that can be held, achieved, etc. [in *full* bloom]. **Total** implies an adding together of everything without exception [*total* number] and is, in general applications, equivalent to **complete** [*total* abstinence]. **Whole** and **entire** imply unbroken unity, stressing that not a single part, individual, instance, etc. has been omitted or diminished [the *whole* student body, one's *entire* attention]. **Intact** is applied to that which remains whole after passing through an experience that might have impaired it [The tornado left the barn *intact*.] —*Antonyms:* **partial, defective**.

complex, complicated, intricate, involved —**Complex** refers to that which is made up of many elaborately interrelated or interconnected parts, so that much study or knowledge is needed to understand or operate it [a *com-*

plex mechanism]. **Complicated** is applied to that which is highly complex and hence very difficult to analyze, solve, or understand [a *complicated* problem]. **Intricate** specifically suggests a perplexingly elaborate interweaving of parts that is difficult to follow [an *intricate* maze]. **Involved**, in this connection, is applied to situations, ideas, etc. whose parts are thought of as intertwining in complicated, often disordered, fashion [an *involved* argument]. —*Antonym:* simple.

compliant for synonyms see **obedient**.

compliant for antonyms see **inflexible, stubborn**.

complicated for synonyms see **complex**.

component for synonyms see **element**.

comport for synonyms see **behave**.

composed for synonyms see **cool**.

composure for synonyms see **equanimity**.

comprehend for synonyms see **include** and **understand**.

compress for synonyms see **contract**.

comprise for synonyms see **include**.

compunction for synonyms see **penitence, qualm**.

compute, calculate, estimate, reckon —**Compute** suggests the use of simple mathematics to determine a quantity, amount, etc. and implies a determinable, hence precise, result [to *compute* the volume of a cylinder]. **Calculate** implies the use of higher mathematics [to *calculate* distances in astronomy]. **Estimate** means the judging, usually in advance, of a quantity, cost, etc. and connotes an approximate result [to *estimate* the cost of building a house]. **Reckon**, an informal substitute for **compute**, suggests the use of simple arithmetic such as can be performed mentally [to *reckon* the days before election].

comrade, associate, colleague, companion, ally, con-

federate, accomplice —**Comrade** refers to a person with whom one is closely associated and implies a sharing in activities and fortunes [my *comrades* in arms]. **Associate** refers to a person who is frequently in one's company, usually because of some work or project shared in common [business *associates*]. *(See also synonyms at* **join**.*)* **Colleague** denotes a fellow worker, especially in one of the professions, and may or may not imply a close personal relationship [his *colleagues* at the university]. **Companion** always refers to a person who actually accompanies one and usually implies a close personal relationship [a dinner *companion*, the *companions* of one's youth]. **Ally** now usually refers to a government joined with another or others in a common pursuit, especially war. A **confederate** is one who joins with another or others for some common purpose, specifically in some unlawful act. An **accomplice** is one who unites with others, either as a principal or a subordinate, with criminal intent to commit an offense.

conceal for synonyms see **hide**.
conceal for antonyms see **reveal**.
conceit for synonyms see **pride**.
concept, conception for synonyms see **idea**.
concern for synonyms see **care**.
conciliate for synonyms see **pacify**.

concise, terse, laconic, succinct, pithy —**Concise** implies the stating of much in few words, by removing all superfluous or expanded details [a *concise* summary]. **Terse** adds to this the connotation of polished smoothness [a *terse* style]. **Laconic**, on the other hand, suggests brevity to the point of curtness or ambiguity ["You'll see," was his *laconic* reply]. **Succinct** implies clarity but compactness in the briefest possible number of words

[He spoke in *succinct* phrases.] **Pithy** suggests forcefulness and wit resulting from compactness [*pithy* axioms].
—*Antonym:* **prolix**. *For other antonyms see* **wordy**.

conclude for synonyms see **close²** and **decide**, **infer**.
conclude for antonyms see **begin**.
concur for synonyms see **consent**.
condemn for synonyms see **criticize**.
condense for synonyms see **contract**.
condescend for synonyms see **stoop**.
condition for synonyms see **state**.
condolence for synonyms see **pity**.
conduct, direct, manage, control —Conduct, in this comparison, implies a supervising by using one's executive skill, knowledge, wisdom, etc. [to *conduct* a sales campaign]. *(See also synonyms at* **behave**.) **Direct** implies less supervision of actual details, but stresses the issuance of general orders or instructions [to *direct* the construction of a dam]. **Manage** implies supervision that involves the personal handling of all details [to *manage* a department]. **Control** implies firm direction by regulation or restraint and often connotes complete domination [The school board *controls* the system.]
confederacy for synonyms see **alliance**.
confederate for synonyms see **comrade**.
confederate for antonyms see **opponent**.
confederation for synonyms see **alliance**.
confer for synonyms see **give**.
confess for synonyms see **acknowledge**.
confide for synonyms see **commit**.
confidence, self-confidence, assurance, self-possession, aplomb —Confidence, in this comparison, implies belief in one's own abilities, or especially in the form **self-confidence**, reliance on one's own powers [He

has *confidence* he will win.] **Assurance,** in this connection, suggests an even stronger belief in one's ability, but in an unfavorable sense, it may connote (as may **confidence**) conceited or arrogant self-sufficiency. **Self-possession** suggests that presence of mind which results from the ability to control one's feelings and behavior. **Aplomb** refers, usually in a favorable sense, to an evident assurance of manner manifesting self-possession [He stood his ground with admirable *aplomb.*] *See also synonyms at* **belief, certainty.** —*Antonyms:* **diffidence, shyness.**

confident for synonyms see **sure.**

confident for antonyms see **shy.**

confidential for synonyms see **familiar.**

configuration for synonyms see **form.**

confine for synonyms see **limit.**

confine for antonyms see **free.**

confirm, substantiate, corroborate, verify, authenticate, validate —To **confirm** is to establish as true that which was doubtful or uncertain [to *confirm* a rumor]. **Substantiate** suggests the producing of evidence that proves or tends to prove the validity of a previous assertion or claim [The census figures *substantiate* his charge.] **Corroborate** suggests the strengthening of one statement or testimony by another [The witnesses *corroborated* her version of the event.] To **verify** is to prove to be true or correct by investigation, comparison with a standard, or reference to ascertainable facts [to *verify* an account]. **Authenticate** implies proof of genuineness by an authority or expert [to *authenticate* a painting]. **Validate** implies official confirmation of the validity of something [to *validate* a will]. —*Antonym:* **contradict.** *For other antonyms see* **disprove.**

confirmed for synonyms see **chronic.**

conflict, fight, struggle, contention, contest —**Conflict** refers to a sharp disagreement or collision in interests, ideas, etc. and emphasizes the process rather than the end [the *conflict* over slavery]. **Fight,** a rather general word for any contest, struggle, or quarrel, stresses physical or hand-to-hand combat. **Struggle** implies great effort or violent exertion, physical or otherwise [the *struggle* for existence]. **Contention** most frequently applies to heated verbal strife, or dispute [religious *contention* broke out]. **Contest** refers to a struggle, either friendly or hostile, for supremacy in some matter [athletic *contests,* a *contest* of wits]. —*Antonyms:* **accord, harmony.**

conform for synonyms see **adapt, agree.**

confound for synonyms see **bewilder.**

confuse for synonyms see **bewilder.**

confusion, disorder, disarray, chaos, jumble, muddle —**Confusion** suggests an indiscriminate mixing or putting together of things so that it is difficult to distinguish the individual elements or parts [The hall was a *confusion* of language.] **Disorder** and **disarray** imply a disturbance of the proper order or arrangement of parts [The room was in *disorder.* Her clothes were in *disarray.*] **Chaos** implies total and apparently irremediable lack of organization [The troops are in a state of *chaos.*] **Jumble** suggests a confused mixture of dissimilar things [His drawer was a *jumble* of clothing, books, etc.] **Muddle** implies a snarled confusion resulting from mismanagement or incompetency [They've made quite a *muddle* of the negotiations.] —*Antonyms:* **order, system.**

confute for synonyms see **disprove.**

congenital for synonyms see **innate.**

conjecture for synonyms see **guess**.

connect for synonyms see **join**.

connoisseur for synonyms see **aesthete**.

conquer, vanquish, defeat, overcome, subdue, subjugate, overthrow, rout —**Conquer** implies gaining mastery over someone or something by physical, mental, or moral force [to *conquer* bad habits]. **Vanquish** implies a thorough overpowering or frustrating, often in a single conflict or battle [a *vanquished* army]. To **defeat** is to get the better of, often only for the time being [The *defeated* troops rallied and counterattacked.] **Overcome** implies the overpowering of an antagonist or the surmounting of difficulties. To **subdue** is to defeat so as to break the spirit of resistance. To **subjugate** is to bring under complete subjection. **Overthrow** implies a victory in which a prevailing power is dislodged by force. To **rout** is to defeat so overwhelmingly that the enemy is put to disorderly flight.

conquest for synonyms see **victory**.

conscious for synonyms see **aware**.

consecrate for synonyms see **devote**.

consecrated for synonyms see **holy**.

consent, assent, agree, concur, accede, acquiesce —**Consent** implies compliance with something proposed or requested, stressing this as an act of the will. To **assent** is to express acceptance of or adherence to an opinion or proposition. **Agree** implies accord reached by settling differences of opinion or overcoming resistance. **Concur** implies agreement arrived at formally on a specific matter, often with regard to a line of action. To **accede** is to yield one's assent to a proposal. **Acquiesce** implies tacit agreement or restraint of opposition in accepting something about which one has reservations.

—*Antonyms*: **dissent, refuse.**   *For other antonyms see* **deny, object.**

consequence for synonyms see **effect** and **importance.**

consider, study, contemplate, weigh, reflect —**Consider** basically denotes a directing of the mind to something in order to understand it or to make a decision about it.   **Study** implies more intense concentration of the mind and methodical attention to details.   **Contemplate** implies a deep, continued mental viewing of a thing, sometimes suggesting the use of intuitive powers in envisioning something or dwelling upon it.   **Weigh** suggests a balancing of contradictory information, conflicting opinions, or possible eventualities, in reaching a decision.   **Reflect**, suggesting a turning of one's thoughts back to something, implies quiet, earnest consideration.

considerate for synonyms see **thoughtful.**

consign for synonyms see **commit.**

console for synonyms see **comfort.**

consolidate for synonyms see **join.**

conspicuous for synonyms see **noticeable.**

conspiracy, plot, intrigue, machination, cabal —**Conspiracy** is used of a project or scheme in which a number of people plan and act together secretly for an unlawful or harmful purpose [a *conspiracy* to seize the throne].   **Plot** is used of a secret, usually evil, plan the details of which have been carefully worked out [The *plot* to deprive him of his inheritance failed.]   **Intrigue**, implying more intricate scheming, suggests furtive, underhanded maneuvering often of an illicit nature [the *intrigues* at the royal court].   **Machination** stresses deceit and cunning in devising plots or schemes intended to harm someone [the *machinations* of the villain].   **Cabal** suggests a small group of persons involved in a political intrigue.

constant for synonyms see **continual, faithful.**
constant for antonyms see **inconstant.**
constituent for synonyms see **element.**
constrain for synonyms see **force.**
construct for synonyms see **make.**
construe for synonyms see **explain.**
contain, hold, accommodate —Contain, in strict usage, signifies an enclosing within or including as a component, part, or fraction, and **hold**, the capacity for containing [The bottle *contains* two ounces of liquid, but it *holds* a pint.] To **accommodate** is to hold comfortably without crowding [an elevator built to *accommodate* twelve people].
contaminate, taint, pollute, defile —Contaminate refers to that which on coming into contact with something will make it impure, unclean, or unfit for use [Fumes were *contaminating* the air.] **Taint** emphasizes effect over cause and implies that some measure of decay or corruption has taken place [*tainted* food]. **Pollute** implies complete befoulment, decay, or corruption through contamination. **Defile** implies pollution or desecration of that which should be held sacred.
contemn for synonyms see **despise.**
contemplate for synonyms see **consider.**
contemplative for synonyms see **pensive.**
contemporaneous for synonyms see **contemporary.**
contemporary, contemporaneous, coeval, synchronous, simultaneous —Contemporary and contemporaneous both mean existing or happening in the same period of time, **contemporary** (often applied to the present) referring more often to persons or their works, and **contemporaneous**, to events. **Coeval** implies extension over the same period of time when a remote time or very

long duration is involved. **Synchronous** implies exact correspondence in time of occurrence or rate of movement. **Simultaneous** implies occurrence at the same point or brief interval of time.

content for synonym see **satisfy.**
contention for synonyms see **conflict, discord.**
contentious for synonyms see **belligerent.**
contest for synonyms see **conflict.**
contiguous for synonyms see **adjacent.**
contingency for synonyms see **emergency.**
continual, continuous, constant, incessant, perpetual, eternal —**Continual** applies to that which recurs repeatedly or goes on unceasingly over a long period of time [*continual* arguments]. **Continuous** applies to that which extends without interruption in either space or time [a *continuous* expanse]. **Constant** stresses uniformity, steadiness, or regularity in occurrence or recurrence [the *constant* beat of the heart]. **Incessant** implies unceasing or uninterrupted activity [*incessant* chatter]. **Perpetual** applies to that which lasts or persists for an indefinitely long time [a *perpetual* nuisance]. **Eternal** stresses endlessness or timelessness [the *eternal* verities]. —*Antonym:* **interrupted.** For other antonyms see **intermittent.**
continue, last, endure, abide, persist —**Continue** implies a going on in a specified course or condition and stresses uninterrupted existence rather than duration. **Last** stresses duration, either for the specified time, or if unqualified, for a time beyond that which is usual. **Endure** implies continued resistance to destructive influences or forces. **Abide** is applied to that which remains stable and steadfast, especially in contrast to that which is changing and transitory. **Persist** implies con-

tinued existence beyond the expected or normal time.
continue for antonyms see **stop.**

continuous for synonyms see **continual.**

continuous for antonyms see **intermittent.**

contort for synonyms see **deform.**

contour for synonyms see **outline.**

contract, shrink, condense, compress, deflate —Contract implies a drawing together of surfaces or parts and
a resultant decrease in size, bulk, or extent. To **shrink** is
to contract so as to be short of the normal or required
length, amount, extent, etc. [Those shirts have *shrunk*.]
Condense suggests reduction of something into a more
compact or more dense form without loss of essential
content [*condensed* milk]. To **compress** is to press or
squeeze into a more compact, orderly form [a lifetime's
work *compressed* into one volume]. **Deflate** implies a reduction in size or bulk by the removal of air, gas, or in
extended use, anything insubstantial [to *deflate* a balloon, one's ego, etc.]

contract for antonyms see **expand.**

contradict for synonyms see **deny.**

contradict for antonyms see **confirm.**

contrary, perverse, restive, balky —Contrary, in this
comparison, implies a disinclination to accept
orders, advice, etc. (*See also synonyms at* **opposite.**)
Perverse implies an unreasonable obstinacy in deviating
from what is considered right or acceptable. **Restive** is
applied to persons who are impatient under restraint or
discipline and hence are hard to control or keep in order.
Balky implies a stopping short and stubbornly refusing
to go on.

contrast for synonyms see **compare.**

contrition for synonyms see **penitence.**

control for synonyms see **conduct** and **power**.

controversy for synonyms see **argument**.

controvert for synonyms see **disprove**.

controvert for antonyms see **assert**.

conundrum for synonyms see **mystery**.

convene for synonyms see **call**.

convent for synonyms see **cloister**.

converse for synonyms see **speak**.

convert for synonyms see **change**, **transform**.

convey for synonyms see **carry**.

conviction, certainty, certitude, assurance —Conviction suggests a being convinced because of satisfactory reasons or proof and sometimes implies earlier doubt. *(See also synonyms at* **opinion.**) **Certainty** suggests a firm, settled belief or positiveness in the truth of something. **Certitude** is sometimes distinguished from the preceding as implying an absence of objective proof, hence suggesting unassailable blind faith. **Assurance** suggests confidence, but not necessarily positiveness, usually in something that is yet to happen [I have *assurance* of his continuing support.] —*Antonyms:* **doubt, skepticism.**

conviction for antonyms see **uncertainty**.

convincing for synonyms see **valid**.

convoke for synonyms see **call**.

convoy for synonyms see **accompany**.

cool, composed, collected, unruffled, nonchalant —Cool, in this comparison, implies freedom from the heat of emotion or excitement, suggesting a calm, dispassionate attitude or a controlled alertness in difficult circumstances. **Composed** suggests readiness to meet a trying situation through self-possession or the disciplining of one's emotions. **Collected** stresses a being in full command of one's faculties or emotions in a distracting situation. **Unruffled** suggests the maintenance of poise or composure in the face of something that might agitate or embarrass one. **Nonchalant** stresses a cool lack of concern or casual indifference. —*Antonyms:* **excited, agitated**.

copious for synonyms see **plentiful**.

copy, reproduction, facsimile, duplicate, replica —**Copy**, the broadest of these terms, refers to any imitation, often only approximate, of an original [a carbon *copy*]. (*See also synonyms at* **imitate**.) **Reproduction** implies a close imitation of the original, often, however, with differences, as of material, size, or quality [a *reproduction* of a painting]. A **facsimile** is an exact reproduction in appearance, sometimes, however, differing in scale [a photostated *facsimile* of a document]. A **duplicate** is a double, or counterpart, of something, serving all the purposes of the original [all the books of a single printing are *duplicates*]. A **replica** is an exact reproduction of a work of art, in strict usage, one made by the original artist.

coquet for synonyms see **trifle**.

cordial for synonyms see **amiable**.

corner for synonyms see **monopoly**.

corporal for synonyms see **bodily**.

corporeal for synonyms see **bodily, material**.

corpse for synonyms see **body**.

correct, accurate, exact, precise —**Correct** connotes little more than absence of error [a *correct* answer] or adherence to conventionality [*correct* behavior]. (*See also synonyms at* **punish**.) **Accurate** implies a positive exercise of care to obtain conformity with fact or truth [an *accurate* account of the events]. **Exact** stresses perfect conformity to fact, truth, or some standard [the *exact* time, an *exact* quotation]. **Precise** suggests minute accuracy of detail and often connotes a finicky or overly fastidious attitude [*precise* in all his habits].

correct for antonyms see **false, wrong**.

correspond for synonyms see **agree**.

corroborate for synonyms see **confirm**.

corrupt for synonyms see **debase**.

costly, expensive, dear, valuable, invaluable —Costly refers to something that costs much and usually implies richness, magnificence, rareness, etc. [*costly* gems]: it is often applied to that which it would cost much in money or effort to correct or replace [a *costly* error]. **Expensive** implies a price in excess of the article's worth or of the purchaser's ability to pay [an *expensive* hat]. **Dear** implies an exorbitant price or one considerably beyond the normal or fair price [Meat is *dear* these days]. **Valuable**, in this connection, implies such great value as to bring a high price [a *valuable* collection]. **Invaluable** suggests value so great that it cannot be appraised in monetary terms [*invaluable* aid].

costly for antonyms see **cheap**.

coterie, circle, set, clique —A coterie is a small, intimate, somewhat select group of people associated for social or other reasons [a literary *coterie*]. **Circle** suggests any group of people having in common some particular interest or pursuit [in music *circles*]. **Set** refers to a group, usually larger and, hence, less exclusive than a **coterie**, having a common background, interests, etc. [the sporting *set*]. **Clique** refers to a small, highly exclusive group, often within a larger one, and implies snobbery, selfishness, or, sometimes, intrigue [a *clique* of obscurantist poets].

counsel for synonyms see **advise** and **lawyer**.

counselor for synonyms see **lawyer**.

count for synonyms see **rely**.

countenance for synonyms see **face**.

counterfeit for synonyms see **artificial, false**.

counterfeit for antonyms see **authentic**.

couple, pair, brace, yoke, span —**Couple** applies to any two persons or things of the same sort that are somehow associated [a *couple* of plates] or it is used colloquially to mean several or a few [I must buy a *couple* of things.] **Pair** is used of two similar things that are associated together or are necessary in twos for proper use [a *pair* of socks] or of a single thing made up of two corresponding parts [a *pair* of scissors]. A **brace** is a couple, especially of certain birds or animals [a *brace* of pheasants, hounds, etc.] **Yoke** applies to a pair of animals harnessed together for pulling [a *yoke* of oxen]. **Span** is used especially of a pair of horses harnessed together.

courageous for synonyms see **brave**.

courteous for synonyms see **civil**.

covert for synonyms see **secret**.

covet for synonyms see **envy**.

covetous for synonyms see **greedy**.

covey for synonyms see **group**.

cowardly, craven, pusillanimous, dastardly —**Cowardly**, the general term, suggests a reprehensible lack of courage in the face of danger or pain [a *cowardly* deserter]. **Craven** implies abject or fainthearted fear [a *craven* fear for one's life]. **Pusillanimous** implies an ignoble, contemptible lack of courage or endurance [*pusillanimous* submission]. **Dastardly** connotes a sneaking, malicious cowardice that is manifested in a despicable act [a *dastardly* informer].

cowardly for antonyms see **brave**.

cozy for synonyms see **comfortable**.

crack for synonyms see **break**.

craft for synonyms see **art**.

crafty for synonyms see **sly**.

cranky for synonyms see **irritable**.

crash for synonyms see **break**.

crave for synonyms see **desire**.

craven for synonyms see **cowardly**.

craven for antonyms see **brave**.

crawl, creep —**Crawl**, in its strict usage, suggests movement by dragging the prone body along the ground [a snake *crawls*], and, figuratively, connotes abjectness or servility [She came *crawling* to apologize.] **Creep** suggests movement, often furtive, on all fours [a baby *creeps*], and, figuratively, connotes slow, stealthy, or insinuating progress [The bleak winter days *crept* by.]

craze for synonyms see **fashion**.

credence for synonyms see **belief**.

credible for synonyms see **plausible**.

credit for synonyms see **ascribe**.

creep for synonym see **crawl**.

cripple for synonyms see **maim**.

crisis for synonyms see **emergency**.

crisp for synonyms see **fragile**.

criterion for synonyms see **standard**.

critical, hypercritical, faultfinding, captious, caviling, carping —**Critical**, in its strictest use, implies an attempt at objective judging so as to determine both merits and faults [a *critical* review], but it often (and **hypercritical**, always) connotes emphasis on the faults or shortcomings. (See also synonyms at **acute**.) **Faultfinding** implies a habitual or unreasonable emphasis on faults or defects.

Captious suggests a characteristic tendency to find fault
with, or argue about, even the pettiest details [a *captious*
critic]. **Caviling** stresses the raising of quibbling objections on the most trivial points [a *caviling* grammarian].
Carping suggests peevishness, perversity, or censorious-
ness in seeking out faults.

**criticize, reprehend, blame, censure, condemn, de-
nounce** —Criticize, in this comparison, is the general
term for finding fault with or disapproving of a person
or thing. **Reprehend** suggests sharp or severe disapproval, generally of faults, errors, etc. rather than of persons. **Blame** stresses the fixing of responsibility for an
error, fault, etc. **Censure** implies the expression of
severe criticism or disapproval by a person in authority
or in a position to pass judgment. **Condemn** and **denounce** both imply an emphatic pronouncement of
blame or guilt, **condemn** suggesting the rendering of a
judicial decision, and **denounce**, public accusation
against persons or their acts.

criticize for antonyms see **praise**.

cross for synonyms see **irritable**.

crotchet for synonyms see **caprice**.

crow for synonyms see **boast**.

crowd, throng, multitude, swarm, mob, host, horde
—Crowd is applied to an assembly of persons or things
in close proximity or densely packed together and may
suggest lack of order, loss of personal identity, etc.
[*Crowds* lined the street.] **Throng** specifically suggests a
moving crowd of people pushing one another [*throngs* of
celebrators at Times Square]. **Multitude** stresses greatness of number in referring to persons or things assembled or considered together [a *multitude* arrayed against
him]. **Swarm** suggests a large, continuously moving

group [a *swarm* of sightseers]. **Mob**, properly applied to a disorderly or lawless crowd, is an abusive term when used to describe the masses or any specific group of people. **Host** specifically suggests a large organized body marshaled together but may be used generally of any sizable group considered collectively [He has a *host* of friends.] **Horde** specifically refers to any large predatory band [a *horde* of office seekers].

crucial for synonyms see **acute.**

cruel, brutal, inhuman, pitiless, ruthless —**Cruel** implies indifference to the suffering of others or a disposition to inflict it on others [*cruel* fate]. **Brutal** implies an animallike or savage cruelty that is altogether unfeeling [a *brutal* prison guard]. **Inhuman** stresses the complete absence of those qualities expected of a civilized human being, such as compassion, mercy, or benevolence. **Pitiless** implies a callous refusal to be moved or influenced by the suffering of those one has wronged. **Ruthless** implies a cruel and relentless disregard for the rights or welfare of others, while in pursuit of a goal. —*Antonym:* **humane.** *For other antonyms see* **kind.**

crush for synonyms see **break.**

cry, weep, sob, wail, keen, whimper, moan, blubber —**Cry** implies the expression of grief, sorrow, pain, or distress by making mournful, convulsive sounds and shedding tears. **Weep** more specifically stresses the shedding of tears. To **sob** is to weep aloud with a catch in the voice and short, gasping breaths. **Wail** implies the uttering of loud, prolonged, mournful cries in unsuppressed lamentation. **Keen**, specifically an Irish term, signifies a wailing in lamentation for the dead. To **whimper** is to cry with subdued, whining, broken sounds, as a fretful or frightened child does. **Moan** suggests the expression of sorrow or pain in a low, prolonged, mournful sound or sounds. **Blubber,** a derisive term used chiefly of children, implies a contorting or swelling of the face with weeping, and broken, inarticulate speech.

cryptic for synonyms see **obscure.**

cuddle for synonyms see **caress.**

cumbersome for synonyms see **heavy.**

cunning for synonyms see **clever, sly.**

curb for synonyms see **restrain.**

cure, heal, remedy —Cure and **heal** both imply a restoring to health or soundness, **cure** specifically suggesting the elimination of disease, distress, evil, etc., and **heal,** the making or becoming whole of a wound, sore, lesion, cut, etc. or, figuratively, the mending of a breach. **Remedy** stresses the use of medication or a specific corrective treatment in relieving disease, injury, distress, etc.

curious, inquisitive, meddlesome, prying —Curious, in this comparison, implies eagerness or anxiousness to find out about things and may suggest a wholesome desire to be informed. **Inquisitive** implies a habitual tendency to be curious, especially about matters that do not concern one, and an attempt to gain information by persistent questioning. **Meddlesome** suggests unwelcome intrusion into the affairs of others. **Prying** suggests an officious inquisitiveness and meddlesomeness that persist against resistance. —*Antonym:* **uninterested.** *For other antonyms see* **indifferent.**

current for synonyms see **prevailing** and **tendency.**

curse, damn, execrate, imprecate, anathematize —Curse is the general word for calling down evil or injury on someone or something. **Damn** carries the same general meaning but, in strict usage, implies the use of

the word "damn" in the curse [He *damned* his enemies —
he said, "*Damn* my enemies!"] **Execrate** suggests cursing prompted by great anger or abhorrence. **Imprecate**
suggests the calling down of calamity on someone, especially from a desire for revenge. **Anathematize** strictly
refers to the formal utterance of solemn condemnation
by ecclesiastical authority, but in general use it is
equivalent to **imprecate**. —*Antonym:* **bless**.

cursing for synonyms see **blasphemy**.

cursory for synonyms see **superficial**.

curt for synonyms see **blunt**.

curtail for synonyms see **shorten**.

curve, bend, twist, turn, bend —Curve suggests a
swerving or deflection in a line that follows or approximates the arc of a circle [He *curved* the next pitch.]
Bend refers to the curving of something that is normally
straight but that yields to pressure or tension [to *bend* a
wire]. **Twist**, in this connection, implies greater resistance in the object to be bent and often connotes a
wrenching out of the normal line [to *twist* one's arm].
Turn, in this comparison often interchangeable with
bend, is used specifically where the object is curved
back upon itself [*Turn* back the sheet before you get into
bed.]

custom for synonyms see **habit**.

customary for synonyms see **usual**.

cutting for synonyms see **incisive**.

cynical, misanthropic, pessimistic —Cynical implies a
contemptuous disbelief in human goodness and sincerity
[He is *cynical* about recovering his missing watch.] **Misanthropic** suggests a deep-seated hatred or distrust of
people in general [a *misanthropic* hermit]. **Pessimistic**
implies an attitude, often habitual, of expecting the worst

to happen [*pessimistic* about one's chances to *win*]. —*Antonym:* **optimistic**.

D

dainty, nice, particular, fastidious, squeamish
—**Dainty**, in this comparison, suggests delicate taste and
implies a tendency to reject that which does not fully accord with one's refined sensibilities [a *dainty* appetite].
*(See also synonyms at **delicate**.)* **Nice** suggests fine or
subtle discriminative powers, especially in intellectual
matters [a *nice* distinction in definition]. **Particular** implies dissatisfaction with anything that fails to conform
in detail with one's standards [*particular* in one's choice
of friends]. **Fastidious** implies adherence to such high
standards as to be disdainfully critical of even minor
nonconformities [her *fastidious* taste in literature].
Squeamish suggests such extreme sensitiveness to what
is unpleasant, or such prudishness, as to result in disgust
or nausea [not too *squeamish* in his business dealings].
dally for synonyms see **loiter, trifle.**
damage for synonyms see **injure.**
damn for synonyms see **curse.**
damp for synonyms see **wet.**
dandle for synonyms see **caress.**
danger, peril, jeopardy, hazard, risk —**Danger** is the
general term for liability to injury or evil, of whatever
degree or likelihood of occurrence [the *danger* of falling
on icy walks]. **Peril** suggests great and imminent danger
[The burning house put them in *peril* of death.] **Jeopardy** emphasizes exposure to extreme danger [Liberty is
in *jeopardy* under tyrants.] **Hazard** implies a foreseeable

but uncontrollable possibility of danger, but stresses the element of chance [the *hazards* of hunting big game]. **Risk** implies the voluntary taking of a dangerous chance [He jumped at the *risk* of his life.] —*Antonyms:* **safety, security.**

dank for synonyms see **wet.**

dark, dim, dusky, murky, gloomy —Dark, the general word in this comparison, denotes an absence of light, entirely or partly [a *dark* night]. **Dim** implies so little light that objects can be seen only indistinctly. **Dusky** suggests the grayish, shadowy light of twilight [a *dusky* winter evening]. **Murky** now usually suggests the thick, heavy darkness of fog or smoke-filled air [the *murky* ruins of a temple]. **Gloomy** suggests a cloudy, cheerless darkness [a *gloomy* forest]. —*Antonym:* **light.** For other antonyms see **bright.**

darn for synonyms see **mend.**

dastardly for synonyms see **cowardly.**

daunt for synonyms see **dismay.**

dawdle for synonyms see **loiter.**

dead, deceased, departed, late, defunct, extinct, inanimate, lifeless —Dead is the general word for someone or something that was alive but is no longer so. **Deceased** and **departed** are both euphemistic, especially for one who has recently died, but the former is largely a legal, and the latter a religious, usage. **Late** always precedes the name or title of one who has recently died [the *late* Mr. Green] or of one who preceded the incumbent in some office or function [his *late* employer]. **Defunct,** applied to a person, is now somewhat rhetorical or jocular, but it is also commonly used of something that because of failure no longer exists or functions [a *defunct* government]. **Extinct** is applied to a species, race, etc. that has no living member. **Inanimate** refers to that which has never had life [*inanimate* rocks]. **Lifeless** is equivalent to either **dead** or **inanimate** [her *lifeless* body, *lifeless* blocks].

dead for antonyms see **living**.

deadly for synonyms see **fatal**.

dear for synonyms see **costly**.

dear for antonyms see **cheap**.

debar for synonyms see **exclude**.

debase, deprave, corrupt, debauch, pervert —**Debase** implies generally a lowering in quality, value, dignity, etc. [Greed had *debased* his character.] *(See also synonyms at* **degrade**.) **Deprave** suggests gross degeneration, especially with reference to morals [a mind *depraved* by crime]. **Corrupt** implies a deterioration or loss of soundness by some destructive or contaminating influence [a government *corrupted* by bribery]. **Debauch** implies a loss of moral purity or integrity as through dissipation or intemperate indulgence [*debauched* young profligates]. **Pervert** suggests a distorting of or departure from what is considered right, natural, or true [a *perverted* sense of humor]. —*Antonym:* **elevate**. *For other antonyms see* **improve**.

debate for synonyms see **discuss**.

debauch for synonyms see **debase**.

debilitate for synonyms see **weaken**.

decay, rot, putrefy, spoil, molder, disintegrate, decompose —**Decay** implies gradual, often natural, deterioration from a normal or sound condition [His teeth have begun to *decay*.] **Rot** refers to the decay of organic, especially vegetable, matter, caused by bacteria, fungi, etc. [*rotting* apples]. **Putrefy** suggests the offensive, foul-smelling rotting of animal matter [bodies *putre-*

fying in the fields]. **Spoil** is the common informal word for the decay of foods [Fish *spoils* quickly in summer.] **Molder** suggests a slow, progressive, crumbling decay [Old buildings *molder* away.] **Disintegrate** implies the breaking up of something into parts or fragments so that the wholeness of the original is destroyed [the *disintegration* of rocks]. **Decompose** suggests the breaking up or separation of something into its component elements [a *decomposing* chemical compound]: it is also a somewhat euphemistic substitute for **rot** and **putrefy**.

decease for synonyms see **die**.

deceased for synonyms see **dead**.

deceitful for synonyms see **dishonest**.

deceive, mislead, beguile, delude, betray —**Deceive** implies deliberate misrepresentation of facts by words, actions, etc., generally to further one's ends [*deceived* into buying fraudulent stocks]. To **mislead** is to cause to follow the wrong course or to err in conduct or action, although not always by deliberate deception [*misled* by the sign into going to the wrong floor]. **Beguile** implies the use of wiles and enticing prospects in deceiving or misleading [*beguiled* by promises of a fortune]. To **delude** is to fool people so completely that they accept what is false as true. **Betray** implies a breaking of faith while appearing to be loyal.

decency for synonyms see **decorum**.

decent for synonyms see **chaste**.

deception, fraud, subterfuge, trickery, chicanery —**Deception** is applied to anything that deceives, whether by design or illusion. **Fraud** suggests deliberate deception in dishonestly depriving a person of property, rights, etc. **Subterfuge** suggests an artifice or stratagem used to deceive others in evading something or gaining some end. **Trickery** implies the use of tricks or ruses in fraudulently deceiving others. **Chicanery** implies the use of petty trickery and subterfuge, especially in legal actions.

decide, determine, settle, conclude, resolve —**Decide** implies the bringing to an end of vacillation, doubt, or dispute by making up one's mind as to an action, course, or judgment. **Determine** in addition suggests that the form, character, functions, and scope of something are precisely fixed [The club *decided* on a lecture series and appointed a committee to *determine* the speakers and the dates.] **Settle** stresses finality in a decision, often one arrived at by arbitration, and implies the termination after all doubt or controversy. To **conclude** is to decide after careful investigation or reasoning. **Resolve** implies firmness of intention to carry through a decision [He *resolved* to go to bed early every night.]

declare, announce, publish, proclaim —**Declare** implies a making known openly by an explicit or clear statement, often one expressed formally [He *declared* his intention to run for office.] *(See also synonyms at assert.)* To **announce** is to make something of interest known publicly or officially, especially something of the nature of news [to *announce* a sale]. To **publish** is to make known through a medium that reaches the general public, now especially the medium of printing. **Proclaim** implies official, formal announcement, made with the greatest possible publicity, of something of great moment or significance ["*Proclaim* liberty throughout all the land. . . ."]

decline, refuse, reject, repudiate, spurn —**Decline** implies courtesy in expressing one's nonacceptance of an invitation, proposal, etc. [He *declined* the nomination.]

Refuse is a more direct, sometimes even blunt term, implying an emphatic denial of a request or demand [to *refuse* a person money]. **Reject** stresses a negative or antagonistic attitude and implies positive refusal to accept, use, believe, etc. [They *rejected* the damaged goods.] **Repudiate** implies the disowning, disavowal, or casting off with condemnation of a person or thing as having no authority, worth, validity, or truth [to *repudiate* the claims of faith healers]. To **spurn** is to refuse or reject with contempt or disdain [She haughtily *spurned* his attentions.] —*Antonym:* **accept**.

decompose for synonyms see **decay**.

decorate for synonyms see **adorn**.

decorum, decency, propriety, dignity, etiquette —**Decorum** implies stiffness or formality in rules of conduct or behavior established as suitable to the circumstances [levity not in keeping with *decorum*]. **Decency** implies observance of the requirements of modesty, good taste, etc. [Have the *decency* to thank her.] **Propriety** suggests conformity with conventional standards of proper or correct behavior, manners, etc. [His offensive language oversteps the bounds of *propriety*.] **Dignity**, in this connection, implies conduct in keeping with one's position or one's self-respect. **Etiquette** refers to the forms established by convention or prescribed by social arbiters for behavior in polite society.

decoy for synonyms see **lure**.

decrease, dwindle, lessen, diminish, reduce —**Decrease** and **dwindle** suggest a growing gradually smaller in bulk, size, volume, or number, but **dwindle** emphasizes a wasting away to the point of disappearance [His hopes *decreased* as his fortune *dwindled* away to nothing.] **Lessen** is equivalent to **decrease**, except that it does not imply any particular rate of decline [His influence *lessened* overnight.] **Diminish** emphasizes subtraction from the whole by some external agent [Disease had *diminished* their ranks.] **Reduce** implies a lowering, or bringing down [to *reduce* prices].

decrease for antonyms see **increase**.

decrepit for synonyms see **weak**.

decry for synonyms see **disparage**.

dedicate for synonyms see **devote**.

deduce for synonyms see **infer**.

deep for synonyms see **broad**.

deep for antonyms see **superficial**.

defeat for synonyms see **conquer**.

defeat for antonyms see **victory**.

defect, imperfection, blemish, flaw —**Defect** implies a lack of something essential to completeness or perfection [a *defect* in vision]. An **imperfection** is any faulty detail that detracts from perfection [minor *imperfections* of style]. A **blemish** is a superficial or surface imperfection that mars the appearance [skin *blemishes*]. A **flaw** is an imperfection in structure or substance, such as a crack or gap, that mars the wholeness or continuity [a *flaw* in a metal bar].

defend, guard, protect, shield, preserve —**Defend** implies an active effort to repel an actual attack or invasion [to *defend* oneself in court]. **Guard** suggests a watching over to keep safe from any potential attack or harm [to *guard* a coastline]. **Protect** and **shield** imply a keeping safe from harm or injury by interposing a barrier [He built a fence to *protect* his garden.], but **shield** also connotes a present or imminent attack or harmful agency [to *shield* one's eyes against a glare]. **Preserve** implies a keeping safe from encroaching deterioration or decay [to *preserve* civil liberties].

defend for antonyms see **attack**.

defer for synonyms see **yield**.

deference for synonyms see **honor**.

defile for synonyms see **contaminate**.

deflate for synonyms see **contract**.

deform, distort, contort, warp —**Deform** implies a marring of form, appearance, or character, as if by pressure or stress [a body *deformed* by disease]. **Distort** implies a twisting or wrenching out of the normal or proper shape or form [a mind *distorted* by fear]. **Contort** suggests an even more violent wrenching out of shape so as to produce a grotesque or unpleasant result [a face *contorted* by pain]. **Warp** implies a bending out of shape, as of wood in drying, and hence, suggests a turning aside from the true or right course [judgment *warped* by prejudice].

defraud for synonyms see **cheat**.

deft for synonyms see **dexterous**.

deft for antonyms see **awkward**.

defunct for synonyms see **dead**.

degrade, abase, debase, humble, humiliate —**Degrade** literally means to lower in grade or rank, but it commonly implies a lowering or corrupting of moral character, self-respect, etc. **Abase** suggests a loss, often merely temporary and self-imposed, of dignity, respect, etc. [He *abased* himself before his employer.] **Debase** implies a decline in value, quality, or character [a *debased* mind]. To **humble** is to lower the pride or increase the humility, especially of another, and, unqualified, suggests that such lowering is deserved [*humbled* by the frightening experience]. To **humiliate** is to humble or shame (another) painfully and in public [*humiliated* by their laughter]. —*Antonyms:* **exalt, dignify.**

degrading for synonyms see **base**².

deign for synonyms see **stoop.**

deist for synonyms see **atheist.**

dejected for synonyms see **sad.**

delay, retard, slacken, impede, hinder —Delay implies the interference of something that causes a detainment or postponement [I was *delayed* by the storm.] **Retard** implies the action of something in causing a slowing down of movement or progress [The advancing army had been *retarded.*] **Slacken** suggests a slowing down by relaxation of activity or intensity [Trade had *slackened* somewhat.] **Impede** implies interference with movement or progress by some obstruction [The muddy roads *impeded* our journey.] **Hinder** suggests a holding back or restraining of movement or action, often of that which has not yet begun [The search was *hindered* by his arrival.] —*Antonyms:* **hasten, expedite.**

deleterious for synonyms see **pernicious.**

deliberate for synonyms see **think** and **voluntary.**

deliberate for antonyms see **random** and **spontaneous, sudden.**

delicate, dainty, exquisite —Delicate and dainty are both used to describe things that are pleasing to highly refined tastes or sensibilities, **delicate** implying fragility, subtlety, or fineness, and **dainty,** smallness, fastidiousness, or gracefulness. **Exquisite** is applied to something so delicately wrought or subtly refined as to be appreciated by only the most keenly discriminating or fastidious. —*Antonyms:* **gross, crude, coarse.**

delight for synonyms see **pleasure.**

delirium for synonyms see **mania.**

deliver for synonyms see **rescue.**

delude for synonyms see **deceive**.

delusion, illusion, hallucination, mirage —**Delusion** implies belief in something that is contrary to fact or reality, resulting from deception, a misconception, or a mental disorder [to have *delusions* of grandeur]. **Illusion** suggests the false perception or interpretation of something that has objective existence [Perspective in drawing gives the *illusion* of depth.] **Hallucination** implies the apparent perception, in a nervous or mental disorder, of something that is actually not present. **Mirage** refers to an optical illusion caused by atmospheric conditions, and, in figurative use, implies an unrealizable hope or aspiration.

demand, claim, require, exact —**Demand** implies a calling for as owing or necessary, connoting a peremptory exercise of authority or an imperative need [to *demand* obedience]. **Claim** implies a demanding of something as allegedly belonging to one [to *claim* a throne]. **Require** suggests a pressing need, often one inherent in the nature of a thing, or the binding power of rules or laws [Aliens are *required* to register.] **Exact** implies a demanding and the enforcing of the demand at the same time [an *exacting* foreman].

demean for synonyms see **behave**.

demeanor for synonyms see **bearing**.

dementia for synonyms see **insanity**.

demolish for synonyms see **destroy**.

demur for synonyms see **object**.

demure for synonyms see **shy**.

denounce for synonyms see **criticize**.

dense for synonyms see **close**[1] and **stupid**.

denude for synonyms see **strip**.

deny, gainsay, contradict, impugn —**Deny** implies a

refusal to accept as true, real, valid, existent, or tenable [He *denied* the charge.] To **gainsay** is to dispute what a person says or to challenge the person saying it [facts that cannot be *gainsaid*]. **Contradict** not only implies emphatic denial, but, in addition, often suggests belief or evidence that the opposite or contrary is true. **Impugn** implies a direct, forceful attack against that which one calls into question [She *impugned* his motives.]

deny for antonyms see **acknowledge, assert, consent.**

depart for synonyms see **go.**

depart for antonyms see **stay.**

departed for synonyms see **dead.**

depend for synonyms see **rely.**

dependable, reliable, trustworthy, trusty —**Dependable** refers to a person or thing that can be depended on as in an emergency and often connotes levelheadedness or steadiness [She is a *dependable* friend.] **Reliable** is applied to a person or thing that can be counted upon to do what is expected or required [his *reliable* assistant]. **Trustworthy** applies to a person, or sometimes a thing, whose truthfulness, integrity, discretion, etc. can be relied on [a *trustworthy* source of information]. **Trusty** applies to a person or thing which continued experience has shown to be completely trustworthy or dependable [his *trusty* steed].

deport for synonyms see **banish** and **behave.**

deportment for synonyms see **bearing.**

deprave for synonyms see **debase.**

depreciate for synonyms see **disparage.**

depressed for synonyms see **sad.**

derelict for synonyms see **remiss.**

deride for synonyms see **ridicule.**

derive for synonyms see **rise.**

descry for synonyms see **see**.

desecration for synonyms see **sacrilege**.

desert for synonyms see **abandon**, **waste**.

design for synonyms see **intend**, **plan**.

desire, wish, want, crave —Desire, generally interchangeable with the other words here in the sense of "to long for," stresses intensity or ardor [to *desire* success]. **Wish** is not so strong a term as **desire** and has special application when an unrealizable longing is meant [He *wished* summer were here.] **Want**, specifically suggesting a longing for something lacking or needed, generally is a more informal equivalent of **wish** [She *wants*, or *wishes*, to go with us.] **Crave** suggests desire to gratify a physical appetite or an urgent need [to *crave* affection].

desist for synonyms see **stop**.

despairing for synonyms see **hopeless**.

desperate for synonyms see **hopeless**.

despise, scorn, disdain, contemn —Despise implies a strong emotional response toward that which one looks down upon with contempt or aversion [to *despise* a hypocrite]. (See also synonyms at **hate**.) To **scorn** is to feel indignation toward or deep contempt for [to *scorn* the offer of a bribe]. **Disdain** implies a haughty or arrogant contempt for what is considered to be beneath one's dignity [to *disdain* flattery]. **Contemn**, chiefly a literary word, implies a vehement disapproval of a person or thing as base, vile, or despicable.

despise for antonyms see **appreciate**.

despoil for synonyms see **ravage**.

despondent for synonyms see **hopeless**.

destiny for synonyms see **fate**.

destitute for synonyms see **poor**.

destitution for synonyms see **poverty**.

destroy, demolish, raze, annihilate —**Destroy** implies a tearing down or bringing to an end by wrecking, ruining, killing, eradicating, etc. and is the term of broadest application here [to *destroy* a city, to *destroy* one's influence]. **Demolish** implies such destructive force as to completely smash to pieces [The bombs *demolished* the factories.] **Raze** means to level to the ground, either destructively or by systematic wrecking with a salvaging of useful parts. To **annihilate** is to destroy so completely as to blot out of existence [rights that cannot be *annihilated*].

destruction for synonyms see **ruin**.

desultory for synonyms see **random**.

detached for synonyms see **indifferent**.

determinant for synonyms see **cause**.

determine for synonyms see **decide, learn**.

detest for synonyms see **hate**.

detestable for synonyms see **hateful**.

detrimental for synonyms see **pernicious**.

devastate for synonyms see **ravage**.

deviate, swerve, veer, diverge, digress —**Deviate** suggests a turning aside, often to only a slight degree, from the correct or prescribed course, standard, doctrine, etc. [to *deviate* from the truth]. **Swerve** implies a sudden or sharp turning from a path or course [The car *swerved* to avoid hitting us.] **Veer**, originally used of ships and wind, suggests a turning or series of turnings so as to change direction. **Diverge** suggests the branching off of a single path or course into two courses constantly leading away from each other [The sides of an angle *diverge* from a single point.] **Digress** suggests a wandering, often deliberate and temporary, from the main topic in speaking or writing.

devote, dedicate, consecrate, hallow —Devote suggests the giving up or applying of oneself or something with the seriousness or earnestness evoked by a formal vow [to *devote* one's life to a cause]. To **dedicate** is to set apart or assign (something), as in a formal rite, to some serious, often sacred, purpose [to *dedicate* a temple]. To **consecrate** is to set apart for some religious or holy use [to *consecrate* ground for a church]. **Hallow**, a stronger word, suggests an intrinsic holiness in the thing set apart [to *hallow* the Sabbath].

devout for synonyms see **pious.**

dexterous, adroit, deft, handy —Dexterous implies an expertness, natural or acquired, demonstrated in the ability to do things with skill and precision [a *dexterous* mechanic]. **Adroit** adds to this a connotation of cleverness and resourcefulness and is now generally used of mental facility [an *adroit* evasion]. **Deft** suggests a nimbleness and sureness of touch [a *deft* seamstress]. **Handy** suggests skill, usually without training, at a variety of small tasks [a *handy* man around the house].

dexterous for antonyms see **awkward.**

dialect, vernacular, cant, jargon, argot, lingo —Dialect, in this comparison, refers to a form of a language peculiar to a locality or group and differing from the standard language in matters of pronunciation, syntax, etc. **Vernacular** today commonly refers to the informal or colloquial variety of a language as distinguished from the formal or literary variety. **Cant**, in this connection, refers to the distinctive stock words and phrases used by a particular sect, class, etc. [clergymen's *cant*]. **Jargon** is used of the special vocabulary and idioms of a particular class, occupational group, etc., especially by one who is unfamiliar with these. **Argot** refers especially to the secret jargon of thieves and tramps. **Lingo** is a humorous or mildly contemptuous term applied to any language, dialect, or jargon by one to whom it is unintelligible.

dictatorial, arbitrary, dogmatic, doctrinaire —**Dictatorial** implies the domineering, autocratic methods or manner of a dictator [the *dictatorial* enunciation of his opinions]. **Arbitrary** suggests the unreasoned, unpredictable use of one's power or authority in accord only with one's own will or desire [an *arbitrary* decision]. **Dogmatic** suggests the attitude of a religious teacher in asserting certain doctrines as absolute truths not open to dispute [The scientific method is not *dogmatic*.] **Doctrinaire** implies a rigid adherence to abstract doctrines or theories, without regard to their practical application.

die, decease, expire, pass away, pass on, perish —**Die** is the basic, simple, direct word meaning to stop living or to become dead. **Decease, expire,** and **pass away** (or **pass on**) are all euphemisms, **decease** being also the legal term. **Expire** means literally to breathe one's last breath. **Pass away** and **pass on** are used informally to suggest a coming to an end. **Perish** implies death by a violent means or under difficult circumstances.

different, diverse, divergent, distinct, dissimilar, disparate, various —**Different,** applied to things that are not alike, implies individuality [three *different* doctors] or contrast [The twins wore *different* hats.] **Diverse** more emphatically sets apart the things referred to, suggesting a conspicuous difference [*diverse* interests]. **Divergent** suggests a branching off in different directions with an ever-widening distance between, and stresses irreconcilability [*divergent* schools of thought]. **Distinct,** as applied to two or more things, stresses that each has a different identity and is unmistakably separate from the others, whether or not they are similar in kind, class, etc. [charged with two *distinct* offenses]. **Dissimilar** stresses absence of similarity in appearance, properties, or nature [*dissimilar* techniques]. **Disparate** implies essential or thoroughgoing difference, often stressing an absence of any relationship between things [*disparate* concepts]. **Various** emphasizes the number and diversity of kinds, types, etc. [*various* gifts]. —*Antonyms:* alike, similar. *For other antonyms see* **same.**

differentiate for synonyms see **distinguish.**

difficult for synonyms see **hard.**

difficult for antonyms see **easy.**

difficulty, hardship, rigor, vicissitude —**Difficulty** is applied to anything hard to contend with, without restriction as to nature, intensity, etc. [a slight *difficulty*, great *difficulty*]. **Hardship,** stronger in connotation, suggests suffering, privation, or trouble that is extremely hard to bear [the *hardships* of poverty]. **Rigor** suggests severe hardship but further connotes that it is imposed by external, impersonal circumstances beyond one's control [the *rigors* of winter]. **Vicissitude,** a bookish word, suggests a difficulty that is likely to occur in the course of something, often one inherent in a situation [the *vicissitudes* of political life].

diffident for synonyms see **shy.**

diffuse for synonyms see **wordy.**

digest for synonyms see **abridgment.**

dignity for synonyms see **decorum.**

digress for synonyms see **deviate.**

dilapidation for synonyms see **ruin.**

dilate for synonyms see **expand.**

dilemma for synonyms see **predicament.**

dilettante for synonyms see **aesthete, amateur.**

diligent for synonyms see **busy.**

dim for synonyms see **dark.**

dim for antonyms see **bright.**

diminish for synonyms see **decrease.**

diminish for antonyms see **increase, intensify.**

diminutive for synonyms see **small.**

din for synonyms see **noise.**

diplomacy for synonyms see **tact.**

diplomatic for synonyms see **suave.**

direct for synonyms see **command, conduct.**

dirty, soiled, grimy, filthy, foul —Dirty is applied to that which is covered or filled with any kind of dirt and is the broadest of these terms [a *dirty* face, a *dirty* room]. **Soiled** generally suggests the presence of superficial dirt in an amount sufficient to impair cleanness or freshness [a *soiled* shirt]. **Grimy** suggests soot or granular dirt deposited on or ingrained in a surface [a miner with a *grimy* face]. **Filthy** is applied to that which is disgustingly dirty [*filthy* as a pigpen]. **Foul** implies extreme filth that is grossly offensive or loathsome because of its stench, putridity, or corruption [*foul* air]. —*Antonym:* **clean.**

disable for synonyms see **maim.**

disappear for synonyms see **vanish.**

disarray for synonyms see **confusion.**

disaster, calamity, catastrophe, cataclysm —Disaster implies great or sudden misfortune that results in loss of life, property, etc. or that is ruinous to an undertaking. **Calamity** suggests a grave misfortune that brings deep distress or sorrow to an individual or to the people at large. **Catastrophe** is specifically applied to a disastrous end or outcome. **Cataclysm** suggests a great upheaval, especially a political or social one, that causes sudden and violent change with attending distress and suffering.

disastrous for antonyms see **lucky**.

disbar for synonyms see **exclude**.

disbelief for synonyms see **unbelief**.

discern, perceive, distinguish, observe, notice —**Discern** implies a making out or recognizing of something visually or mentally [to *discern* a person's motives]. **Perceive** implies recognition by means of any of the senses, and, with reference to mental apprehension, often implies keen understanding or insight [to *perceive* a change in attitude]. **Distinguish**, in this connection, implies a perceiving clearly or distinctly by sight, hearing, etc. [He *distinguished* the voices of men down the hall.] **Observe** and **notice** both connote some measure of attentiveness, and usually suggest use of the sense of sight [to *observe* an eclipse, to *notice* a sign].

discharge for synonyms see **free**.

disciple for synonyms see **follower**.

discipline for synonyms see **punish**.

discipline for antonyms see **indulge**.

disclose for synonyms see **reveal**.

discomfit for synonyms see **embarrass**.

discompose for synonyms see **disturb**.

disconcert for synonyms see **embarrass**.

discontinue for synonyms see **stop**.

discord, strife, contention, dissension —**Discord** denotes disagreement or lack of concord and may imply quarreling between persons, clashing qualities in things, dissonance in sound, etc. **Strife** stresses the struggle to win out where there is a conflict or disagreement. **Contention** suggests verbal strife as expressed in argument, controversy, or dispute. **Dissension** implies difference of opinion, usually suggesting contention between opposing groups in a body. —*Antonyms:* **harmony, agreement**.

discourse for synonyms see **speak**.

discourteous for synonyms see **rude**.

discover for synonyms see **learn**.

discreet for synonyms see **careful**.

discriminate for synonyms see **distinguish**.

discuss, argue, debate, dispute —**Discuss** implies a talking about something in a deliberative fashion, with varying opinions offered constructively and, usually amicably, so as to settle an issue, decide on a course of action, etc. **Argue** implies the citing of reasons or evidence to support or refute an assertion, belief, proposition, etc. **Debate** implies a formal argument, usually on public questions, in contests between opposing groups. **Dispute** implies argument in which there is a clash of opposing opinions, often presented in an angry or heated manner.

disdain for synonyms see **despise**.

disdain for antonyms see **appreciate**.

disdainful for synonyms see **proud**.

disease, affection, malady, ailment —**Disease** may apply generally to any deviation of the body from its normal or healthy state or it may refer to a particular disorder with a specific cause and characteristic symptoms. **Affection** is an older term referring to a disorder of a specific organ or part [an *affection* of the spleen]. **Malady** usually refers to a deep-seated chronic disease, frequently one that is ultimately fatal. **Ailment** refers to a chronic, annoying disorder of whatever degree of seriousness [the minor *ailments* of the aged].

diseased for antonyms see **healthy**.

disgrace, dishonor, shame, infamy, ignominy, odium, scandal —**Disgrace** refers to a loss of favor or respect and a sense of humiliation brought on by one's own or another's actions [I felt *disgrace* at his expulsion.] **Dishonor** implies a loss of honor or self-respect brought on by one's own actions. **Shame** emphasizes the humiliation felt at a loss of esteem [His guilt brought him great *shame*.] **Infamy** stresses the notoriety occasioned by a great disgrace. **Ignominy** stresses the contemptible nature of that which causes disgrace. **Odium** refers to the disgrace or infamy brought on by hateful action. **Scandal**, in this connection, stresses the severe criticism, gossip, etc. brought on by a shameful or infamous act. —*Antonyms:* **respect, esteem.** *For other antonyms see* **honor.**

dishonest, deceitful, lying, untruthful —**Dishonest** implies the act or practice of telling a lie, or of cheating, deceiving, stealing, etc. [a *dishonest* official]. **Deceitful** implies an intent to make someone believe what is not true, as by giving a false appearance, using fraud, etc. [a *deceitful* advertisement]. **Lying** suggests only the act of telling a falsehood [Curb your *lying* tongue.] **Untruthful** is used as a somewhat softened substitute for lying, especially with reference to statements and reports [an *untruthful* account].

dishonest for antonyms see **upright.**

dishonor for synonyms see **disgrace.**

disinclined for synonyms see **reluctant.**

disintegrate for synonyms see **decay.**

disinterested for synonyms see **indifferent.**

disloyal for synonyms see **faithless.**

dismantle for synonyms see **strip.**

dismay, appall, horrify, daunt —**Dismay** suggests fear or, especially in modern usage, discouragement at the prospect of some difficulty or problem which one does not quite know how to resolve [*dismayed* at his lack of understanding]. **Appall** suggests terror or (now more commonly) dismay at a shocking but apparently unalterable situation [an *appalling* death rate]. **Horrify** suggests horror or loathing (or, in a weakened sense, irritation) at that which shocks or offends one [*horrified* at the suggestion]. **Daunt** implies a becoming disheartened in the performance of an act that requires some courage [never *daunted* by adversity].

dismiss for synonyms see **eject**.

disorder for synonyms see **confusion**.

disparage, depreciate, decry, belittle, minimize —**Disparage** is to attempt to lower in esteem, as by insinuation, invidious comparison, faint praise, etc. To **depreciate** is to lessen (something) in value as by implying that it has less worth than is usually attributed to it [He *depreciated* her generosity.] **Decry** implies vigorous public denunciation, often from the best of motives [to *decry* corruption in government]. **Belittle** is equivalent to **depreciate**, but stresses a contemptuous attitude toward the subject. **Minimize** suggests an ascription of the least possible value or importance [Don't *minimize* your own efforts.] —*Antonym:* **magnify**. *For other antonyms see* **praise**.

disparate for synonyms see **different**.

dispassionate for synonyms see **fair**.

dispatch for synonyms see **haste** and **kill**.

dispel for synonyms see **scatter**.

dispense, distribute, divide, dole —**Dispense** suggests the careful measuring out of that which has been ordered or is otherwise given out [to *dispense* drugs]. **Distribute**

implies a dealing out of portions or a spreading about of units among a number of recipients [to *distribute* leaflets]. **Divide** suggests separation of a whole into parts to be shared [an inheritance *divided* among five children]. **Dole** implies a distributing of money, food, or other necessities as an act of charity or in a sparing or niggardly manner.

disperse for synonyms see **scatter**.

displace for synonyms see **replace**.

display for synonyms see **show**.

displeasure for synonyms see **offense**.

disposition, temperament, temper, character, personality —Disposition refers to the normal or prevailing aspect of one's nature [a genial *disposition*]. **Temperament** refers to the balance of traits that are manifested in one's behavior or thinking [an artistic *temperament*]. **Temper** refers to one's basic emotional nature, especially as regards relative quickness to anger [a hot *temper*, an even *temper*]. **Character** is applied to the sum of moral qualities associated with a distinctive individual [a weak *character*] and, unqualified, suggests moral strength, self-discipline, etc. [a man of *character*]. **Personality** is applied to the sum of physical, mental, and emotional qualities that distinguish one as a person [a negative *personality*] and, unqualified, suggests attractiveness or charm [a girl with *personality*].

disprove, refute, confute, controvert, rebut —Disprove implies the presenting of evidence or reasoned arguments that demonstrate an assertion or other statement to be false or erroneous. **Refute** implies a more thorough assembly of evidence and a more careful development of argument and hence suggests conclusiveness of proof against. **Confute** suggests the overwhelming or

silencing of a person by argument or proof. **Controvert**
implies a disputing or denying of statements, arguments,
etc. in an endeavor to refute them. **Rebut** stresses formality in refuting an argument, such as is observed in
debate or court procedure.

disprove for antonyms see **confirm.**

dispute for synonyms see **argument** and **discuss.**

disregard for synonyms see **neglect.**

dissension for synonyms see **discord.**

dissent for antonyms see **consent.**

dissimilar for synonyms see **different.**

dissipate for synonyms see **scatter.**

dissolve for synonyms see **adjourn** and **melt.**

distant for synonyms see **far.**

distend for synonyms see **expand.**

distinct for synonyms see **different.**

distinct for antonyms see **obscure.**

distinctive for synonyms see **characteristic.**

distinguish, discriminate, differentiate —Distinguish
implies a recognizing or marking apart from others by
special features or characteristic qualities [to *distinguish*
good from evil]. (*See also synonyms at* **discern.**) **Discriminate,** in this connection, suggests a distinguishing
of minute or subtle differences between similar things [to
discriminate scents]. **Differentiate** suggests the noting or
ascertaining of specific differences between things by
comparing in detail their distinguishing qualities or features.

distinguished for synonyms see **famous.**

distort for synonyms see **deform.**

distrait for synonyms see **absent-minded.**

distraught for synonyms see **absent-minded.**

distress, suffering, agony, anguish —Distress implies

mental or physical strain imposed by pain, trouble, worry, or the like and usually suggests a state or situation that can be relieved [*distress* caused by famine]. **Suffering** stresses the actual enduring of pain, distress, or tribulation [the *suffering* of the wounded]. **Agony** suggests mental or physical torment so excruciating that the body or mind is convulsed with the force of it [in mortal *agony*]. **Anguish** has equal force but is more often applied to acute mental suffering [the *anguish* of despair].

distress for antonyms see **comfort**.

distribute for synonyms see **dispense**.

disturb, discompose, perturb, agitate —**Disturb** implies the unsettling of normal mental calm or powers of concentration by worry, interruption, etc. [to *disturb* one's train of thought]. **Discompose** implies the upsetting of one's self-possession [Her sudden outburst *discomposed* him.] To **perturb** is to cause to have a troubled or alarmed feeling [The bad news *perturbed* him.] **Agitate** suggests an arousing of intense mental or emotional excitement [He was so *agitated*, he could not answer.]

diverge for synonyms see **deviate**.

divergent for synonyms see **different**.

diverse for synonyms see **different**.

divert for synonyms see **amuse**.

divest for synonyms see **strip**.

divide for synonyms see **dispense, separate**.

dividend for synonyms see **bonus**.

divine for synonyms see **holy**.

division for synonyms see **part**.

divulge for synonyms see **reveal**.

do for synonyms see **perform**.

docile for synonyms see **obedient**.

doctrinaire for synonyms see **dictatorial**.

doctrine, dogma, tenet, precept —**Doctrine** refers to a theory based on carefully worked out principles and taught or advocated by its adherents [scientific or social *doctrines*]. **Dogma** refers to a belief or doctrine that is handed down by authority as true and indisputable, and often connotes arbitrariness, arrogance, etc. [religious *dogma*]. **Tenet** emphasizes the maintenance or defense, rather than the teaching, of a theory or principle [the *tenets* of a political party]. **Precept** refers to an injunction or dogma intended as a rule of action or conduct [to teach by example rather than by *precept*].

dogged for synonyms see **stubborn**.

dogma for synonyms see **doctrine**.

dogmatic for synonyms see **dictatorial**.

dole for synonyms see **dispense**.

doleful for synonyms see **sad**.

dominant, predominant, paramount, preeminent, preponderant —**Dominant** refers to that which dominates or controls, or has the greatest effect [*dominant* characteristics in genetics]. **Predominant** refers to that which is at the moment uppermost in importance or influence [the *predominant* reason for his refusal]. **Paramount** is applied to that which ranks first in importance, authority, etc. [of *paramount* interest to me]. **Preeminent** implies prominence because of surpassing excellence [the *preeminent* writer of his time]. **Preponderant** implies superiority in amount, weight, power, importance, etc. [the *preponderant* religion of a country].

domineering for synonyms see **masterful**.

domineering for antonyms see **servile**.

dominion for synonyms see **power**.

donate for synonyms see **give**.

donation for synonyms see **present**.

doom for synonyms see **fate**.

dormant for synonyms see **latent**.

doubt for synonyms see **uncertainty**.

doubt for antonyms see **belief, conviction**.

doubtful, dubious, questionable, problematical —**Doubtful** implies strong uncertainty as to the probability, value, honesty, validity, etc. of something [a *doubtful* remedy]. **Dubious** is less strong, suggesting merely vague suspicion or hesitancy [*dubious* about the future]. **Questionable** strictly suggests only that there is some reason for doubt, but it is often used as a euphemism to imply strong suspicion, almost amounting to certainty, of immorality, dishonesty, etc. [a *questionable* reputation]. **Problematical** implies only uncertainty with no suggestion of a moral question [a *problematical* success].

doubtful for antonyms see **sure**.

drag for synonyms see **pull**.

draw for synonyms see **pull**.

draw for antonyms see **push**.

dread for synonyms see **awe, fear**.

drench for synonyms see **soak**.

drift for synonyms see **tendency** and **wash**.

droll for synonyms see **funny**.

drove for synonyms see **group**.

drowsy for synonyms see **sleepy**.

drunk, drunken, intoxicated, inebriated —**Drunk** is the simple, direct word, usually used in the predicate, for one who is overcome by alcoholic liquor [He is *drunk*.] **Drunken**, usually used attributively, is equivalent to **drunk** but sometimes implies habitual, intemperate drinking of liquor [a *drunken* bum]. **Intoxicated** and **inebriated** are euphemisms, the former often expressing slight drunkenness and the latter, a state of drunken exhilaration. There are many euphemistic and slang terms in English expressing varying degrees of drunkenness.

dry, arid —**Dry** suggests a lack or insufficiency of moisture, in either a favorable or unfavorable sense [a *dry* climate, a *dry* river bed]. **Arid** implies an abnormal, intense dryness, especially with reference to a region or climate, and connotes barrenness or lifelessness [an *arid* waste].

dry for antonyms see **wet**.

dubiety for synonyms see **uncertainty**.

dubiosity for synonyms see **uncertainty**.

dubious for synonyms see **doubtful**.

ductile for synonyms see **pliable**.

dull, blunt, obtuse —**Dull** is specifically applied to a point or edge that has lost its previous sharpness [a *dull* knife] and generally connotes a lack of keenness, zest, spirit, intensity, etc. [a *dull* book, a *dull* pain]. (*See also synonyms at* **stupid**.) **Blunt** is often equivalent to **dull**, but specifically refers to a point or edge that is intentionally not sharp [a *blunt* fencing saber]. **Obtuse** literally applies to a pointed end whose sides form an angle greater than 90° and figuratively connotes great dullness of understanding or lack of sensitivity [too *obtuse* to comprehend].

dull for antonyms see **bright**, **intelligent**, **lively**, **sharp**.

dumb for synonyms see **voiceless**.

dumbfound for synonyms see **bewilder**.

dupe for synonyms see **cheat**.

duplicate for synonyms see **copy**.

dusky, swarthy, tawny —**Dusky** suggests a darkness of color or an absence of light, verging on blackness [*dusky* twilight]. (*See also synonyms at* **dark**.) **Swarthy** and **tawny** both refer only to color, **swarthy** suggesting a dark brown verging on black [a *swarthy* complexion] and

tawny, a yellowish-brown, or tan [*tawny* hair].

duty, obligation, responsibility —Duty refers to the general conduct required by one's sense of justice, morality, etc. or by the dictates of one's conscience [*duty* to one's fellow human beings]. (*See also synonyms at* **function.**) **Obligation** refers to what one is bound to do to fulfill a particular contract, promise, social requirement, etc. [You are under *obligation* to care for her.] **Responsibility** refers to a particular task, trust, or the like for which one is accountable or answerable [The garden is her *responsibility.*]

dwarf, midget, Pygmy —Dwarf refers to any individual that is considerably smaller than the average for the species and sometimes implies malformation or disproportion of parts. **Midget** refers to a normally formed and proportioned, but diminutive, human being. **Pygmy** strictly refers to a member of any of several small-sized African or Asiatic peoples, but it is sometimes used (written **pygmy**) as a synonym for **dwarf** or **midget.**

dwindle for synonyms see **decrease.**

E

eager, avid, keen, anxious —**Eager** implies great enthusiasm, zeal, or sometimes impatience, in the desire for
or pursuit of something [*eager* to begin work]. **Avid** suggests an intense, sometimes greedy, desire to enjoy or
possess something [*avid* for power]. **Keen** implies deep
interest and a spirited readiness to achieve something
[The team was *keen* on winning.] **Anxious**, in this connection, suggests an eagerness that is accompanied with
some uneasiness over the outcome [*anxious* to do his
best].

eager for antonyms see **reluctant**.

earnest for synonyms see **pledge** and **serious**.

earth, universe, world —**Earth** is applied to the globe or
planet we live on, but in religious use is opposed to
heaven or hell. **Universe** refers to the whole system of
planets, stars, and space, and to everything that exists in
it. **World** is equivalent to **earth**, especially in its relation to human beings and their activities, but it is sometimes
a generalized synonym for **universe**.

earthly, terrestrial, worldly, mundane —**Earthly** is applied to that which belongs to the earth or to the present
life and is chiefly contrasted with *heavenly* [*earthly* pleas-
ures]. **Terrestrial**, having as its opposite *celestial* (both
Latin-derived parallels of the preceding terms), has special application in formal and scientific usage [*terrestrial*
magnetism]. **Worldly** implies reference to the material
concerns or pursuits of humankind and is chiefly contrasted with *spiritual* [*worldly* wisdom]. **Mundane**, although often used as a close synonym of **worldly**, now

especially stresses the commonplace or practical aspects of life [to return to *mundane* matters after a flight of fancy].

easy, facile, effortless, smooth, simple —Easy is the broadest term here in its application to that which demands little effort or presents little difficulty [*easy* work]. **Facile** means occurring, moving, working, etc. easily and quickly, sometimes unfavorably suggesting a lack of thoroughness or depth [a *facile* style]. **Effortless**, in contrast, favorably suggests expert skill or knowledge as responsible for performance that seems to require no effort [the *effortless* grace of the skater]. **Smooth** suggests freedom from or riddance of irregularities, obstacles, or difficulties as bringing ease of movement [a *smooth* path to success]. **Simple**, in this connection, suggests freedom from complication, elaboration, or involvement, as making something easy to understand [a *simple* explanation].

easy for antonyms see **hard**.

ebb for synonyms see **wane**.

eccentricity for synonym see **idiosyncrasy**.

economical for synonyms see **thrifty**.

ecstasy, bliss, rapture, transport —Ecstasy implies extreme emotional exaltation, now usually intense delight, that overpowers the senses and lifts one into a trancelike state. **Bliss** implies a state of great happiness and contentment, often literally or figuratively suggesting heavenly joy. **Rapture** now generally suggests the mental exaltation experienced when one's entire attention is captured by something that evokes great joy or pleasure. **Transport** implies a being carried away by any powerful emotion.

edge for synonyms see **border**.

edifice for synonyms see **building**.

educate for synonyms see **teach**.

educe for synonyms see **extract**.

eerie for synonyms see **weird**.

efface for synonyms see **erase**.

effect, consequence, result, issue, outcome —**Effect** is applied to that which is directly produced by an action, process, or agent and is the exact correlative of *cause*. (*See also synonyms at* **perform**.) **Consequence** suggests that which follows something else on which it is dependent in some way, but does not connote as direct a connection with *cause*. **Result** stresses that which is finally brought about by the effects or consequences of an action, process, etc. **Issue**, in this connection, suggests a result in which there is emergence from difficulties or conflict. **Outcome** refers to the result of something that was in doubt.

effect for antonyms see **cause**.

effective, efficacious, effectual, efficient —**Effective** is applied to that which produces a definite effect or result [an *effective* speaker]. **Efficacious** refers to that which is capable of producing the desired effect or result [an *efficacious* remedy]. **Effectual** specifically implies the production of the desired effect or result in a decisive manner [an *effectual* reply to his charge]. **Efficient** implies skill and economy of energy in producing the desired result and is often applied to persons [an *efficient* worker].

effective for antonyms see **futile**.

effectual for synonyms see **effective**.

effectual for antonyms see **futile**.

effeminate for synonyms see **female**.

efficacious for synonyms see **effective**.

efficient for synonyms see **effective**.

effort, exertion, endeavor, pains —**Effort** implies a conscious attempt to achieve a particular end [Make some *effort* to be friendly.] **Exertion** implies an energetic, even violent, use of power, strength, etc., often without reference to any particular end [She feels faint after any *exertion*.] **Endeavor** suggests an earnest, sustained attempt to accomplish a particular, usually meritorious, end [a life spent in the *endeavor* to do good]. **Pains** suggests a laborious, diligent attempt [to take *pains* with one's work]. —*Antonym:* **ease**.

effortless for synonyms see **easy**.

effrontery for synonyms see **temerity**.

eject, expel, evict, dismiss, oust —**Eject**, the term of broadest application here, implies generally a throwing or casting out from within [to *eject* saliva from the mouth]. **Expel** suggests a driving out, as by force, specifically, a forcing out of a country, organization, etc., often in disgrace [*expelled* from school]. **Evict** refers to the forcing out, as of a tenant, by legal procedure. **Dismiss**, in this connection, refers to the removal of an employee, etc. but does not in itself suggest the reason for the separation [*dismissed* for incompetence]. **Oust** implies the getting rid of something undesirable, as by force or the action of law [to *oust* corrupt officials].

elastic, resilient, flexible, supple —**Elastic** implies ability to return without permanent injury to the original size or shape after being stretched, expanded, etc. [an *elastic* garter]. **Resilient** implies ability to spring back quickly into shape after being deformed, especially by compression [a healthy, *resilient* skin]. **Flexible** refers to anything that can be bent without breaking, whether or not it returns to its original form [a *flexible* wire]. **Supple** is applied to that which is easily bent, twisted, or folded without breaking, cracking, etc. [kidskin is *supple*].

elastic for antonyms see **stiff**.

elect for synonyms see **choose**.

element, component, constituent, ingredient, factor
—**Element**, in its general use, is the broadest term for
any of the basic, irreducible parts or principles of anything, concrete or abstract [the *elements* of a science].
Component and **constituent** both refer to any of the
simple or compound parts of some complex thing or
concept, but **constituent** also implies that the part is essential to the complex [Hemoglobin is a *constituent* of
blood.]   **Ingredient** refers to any of the substances
(sometimes nonessential) that are mixed together in preparing a food, medicine, etc. [the *ingredients* of a cock-
tail].   **Factor** applies to any of the component parts that
are instrumental in determining the nature of the complex [Luck was a *factor* in his success.]

elevate for synonyms see **lift**.

elevate for antonyms see **debase**.

elevation for synonyms see **height**.

elicit for synonyms see **extract**.

eliminate for synonyms see **exclude**.

elongate for synonyms see **extend**.

elucidate for synonyms see **explain**.

elude for synonyms see **escape**.

emanate for synonyms see **rise**.

emancipate for synonyms see **free**.

embarrass, abash, discomfit, disconcert, rattle, faze
—To **embarrass** is to cause to feel ill at ease so as to result in a loss of composure [*embarrassed* by their compli-
ments].   **Abash** implies a sudden loss of self-confidence
and a growing feeling of shame or inadequacy [I stood
abashed at his rebukes.]   **Discomfit** implies a frustration

of plans or expectations and often connotes a resultant feeling of discomposure or humiliation. To **disconcert** is to cause to lose quickly one's self-possession so as to result in confusion or mental disorganization [His interruptions were *disconcerting.*] **Rattle** and **faze** are colloquial equivalents for **disconcert**, but the former emphasizes emotional agitation, and the latter is most commonly used in negative constructions [Danger does not *faze* him.] —*Antonyms:* **compose, assure.**

embellish for synonyms see **adorn.**

embrace for synonyms see **include** and **caress.**

emergency, exigency, contingency, crisis, strait (or **straits**) —**Emergency** refers to any sudden or unforeseen situation that requires immediate action [The flood had created an *emergency.*] **Exigency** may refer either to such a situation or to the need or urgency arising from it [The *exigencies* of the moment require drastic action.] **Contingency** is used of an emergency regarded as remotely possible in the future [Prepare for any *contingency.*] **Crisis** refers to an event regarded as a turning point which will decisively determine an outcome [an economic *crisis*]. **Strait** (or **straits**) refers to a trying situation from which it is difficult to extricate oneself [The loss left them in dire *straits.*]

emigrate for synonyms see **migrate.**

émigré for synonyms see **alien.**

eminent for synonyms see **famous.**

emolument for synonyms see **wage.**

emotion for synonyms see **feeling.**

employ for synonyms see **use.**

empty, vacant, void, vacuous —**Empty** means having nothing in it [an *empty* box, an *empty* street, an *empty* stomach]. (*See also synonyms at* **vain.**) **Vacant** means lacking that which appropriately or customarily occupies or fills it [a *vacant* apartment, a *vacant* position]. **Void**, as discriminated here, specifically stresses complete or vast emptiness [*void* of judgment]. **Vacuous**, now rare in its physical sense, suggests the emptiness of a vacuum. —*Antonym:* **full**.

emulation for synonyms see **competition**.

emulous for synonyms see **ambitious**.

enchant for synonyms see **attract**.

encomium for synonyms see **tribute**.

encounter for synonyms see **battle**.

encroach for synonyms see **trespass**.

end for synonyms see **close**², **stop** and **intention**.

end for antonyms see **begin**.

endeavor for synonyms see **effort**, **try**.

endemic for synonyms see **native**.

endorse for synonyms see **approve**.

endurance, **patience**, **fortitude**, **forbearance**, **stoicism** —**Endurance** stresses the capacity to bear suffering or hardship [Job's *endurance* of his afflictions]. **Patience** implies the bearing of suffering, provocation, delay, tediousness, etc. with calmness and self-control [her *patience* with children]. **Fortitude** suggests the resolute endurance that results from firm, sustained courage [the *fortitude* of the pioneers]. (*See also synonyms at* **fortitude**.) **Forbearance** implies restraint under provocation or a refraining from retaliation for a wrong [He acted with *forbearance* toward the hecklers.] **Stoicism** suggests such endurance of suffering without flinching as to indicate an almost austere indifference to either pain or pleasure. —*Antonym:* **impatience**.

endure for synonyms see **bear**, **continue**.

enemy for synonyms see **opponent**.

energetic for synonyms see **active**.

energy for synonyms see **strength**.

enervate for synonyms see **unnerve, weaken**.

engagement for synonyms see **battle**.

enhance for synonyms see **intensify**.

enigma for synonyms see **mystery**.

enigmatic for synonyms see **obscure**.

enjoin for synonyms see **command** and **forbid**.

enjoyable for synonyms see **pleasant**.

enjoyment for synonyms see **pleasure**.

enlarge for synonyms see **increase**.

enmity, hostility, animosity, antagonism —Enmity denotes a strong, settled feeling of hatred, whether concealed, displayed, or latent. **Hostility** usually suggests enmity expressed in active opposition, attacks, etc. **Animosity** suggests bitterness of feeling that tends to break out in open hostility. **Antagonism** stresses the mutual hostility or enmity of persons, forces, etc.

enormous for synonyms see **huge**.

enough for synonyms see **sufficient**.

ensue for synonyms see **follow**.

enterprising for synonyms see **ambitious**.

entertain for synonyms see **amuse**.

enthusiasm for synonyms see **passion**.

enthusiast for synonyms see **zealot**.

entice for synonyms see **lure**.

entire for synonyms see **complete**.

entreat for synonyms see **beg**.

entrust for synonyms see **commit**.

enunciate for synonyms see **utter**.

envy, begrudge, covet —To envy another is to feel ill will, jealousy, or discontent at that person's possession of something that one keenly desires to have or achieve

oneself. **Begrudge** implies an unwillingness that someone should possess or enjoy something that he or she
needs or deserves. To **covet** is to long ardently and
wrongfully for something that belongs to another.

eon for synonyms see **period**.

ephemeral for synonyms see **transient**.

epicure, gourmet, gourmand, gastronome, glutton
—An **epicure** is a person who has a highly refined taste
for fine foods and drinks and takes great pleasure in indulging it. A **gourmet** is a connoisseur in eating and
drinking who discriminatingly appreciates differences in
flavor or quality. **Gourmand**, occasionally equivalent to
gourmet, is more often applied to a person who has a
hearty liking for good food or one who is inclined to eat
to excess. A **gastronome** is an expert in all phases of
the art or science of good eating. A **glutton** is a greedy,
voracious eater and drinker.

epicurean for synonyms see **sensuous**.

epigram for synonyms see **saying**.

episode for synonyms see **occurrence**.

epitome for synonyms see **abridgment**.

epoch for synonyms see **period**.

equable for synonyms see **steady**.

equal for synonyms see **same**.

equanimity, composure, serenity, nonchalance, sangfroid —**Equanimity** implies an inherent evenness of
temper or disposition that is not easily disturbed. **Composure** implies the disciplining of one's emotions in a
trying situation or habitual self-possession in the face of
excitement. **Serenity** implies a lofty, clear peace of
mind that is not easily clouded by ordinary stresses or
excitement. **Nonchalance** implies a casual indifference
to or a cool detachment from situations that might be ex

pected to disturb one emotionally. **Sang-froid** implies great coolness and presence of mind in dangerous or trying circumstances.

equip for synonyms see **furnish**.

equivalent for synonyms see **same**.

equivocal for synonyms see **obscure**.

equivocate for synonyms see **lie**.

era for synonyms see **period**.

eradicate for synonyms see **exterminate, kill**.

erase, expunge, efface, obliterate, delete —Erase implies a scraping or rubbing out of something written or drawn, or figuratively, the removal of an impression. To **expunge** is to remove or wipe out completely. **Efface** implies a rubbing out from a surface, and, in extended use, suggests a destroying of the distinguishing marks, or even of the very existence, of something. **Obliterate** implies a thorough blotting out of something so that all visible traces of it are removed. **Delete** implies the marking of written or printed matter for removal, or the removal of the matter itself.

error, mistake, blunder, slip, faux pas, boner, booboo —Error implies deviation from truth, accuracy, correctness, right, etc. and is the broadest term in this comparison [an *error* in judgment, an *error* in arithmetic]. **Mistake** suggests an error resulting from carelessness, inattention, misunderstanding, etc. and does not in itself carry a strong implication of criticism [a *mistake* in reading a blueprint]. **Blunder** implies stupidity, clumsiness, inefficiency, etc. and carries a suggestion of more severe criticism [A tactical *blunder* cost them the war.] A **slip** is a mistake, usually slight, made inadvertently in speaking or writing. A **faux pas** is a social blunder or error in etiquette that causes embarrassment. **Boner** and **booboo**, slang terms, are applied to a silly or ridiculous blunder.

ersatz for synonyms see **artificial**.

erudite for synonyms see **profound**.

erudite for antonyms see **ignorant**.

erudition for synonyms see **information**.

escape, avoid, evade, elude —**Escape**, as compared here, implies a getting out of, a keeping away from, or simply a remaining unaffected by an impending or present danger, evil, confinement, etc. [to *escape* death, to *escape* criticism]. **Avoid** suggests the display of conscious effort in keeping clear of something undesirable or harmful [to *avoid* crowds during a flu epidemic]. To **evade** is to escape or avoid by artifice, cunning, adroitness, etc. [to *evade* pursuit, to *evade* one's duty]. To **elude** is to escape the grasp of someone or something by artful or slippery dodges or because of a baffling quality [The criminal *eluded* the police. The meaning *eluded* him.]

escort for synonyms see **accompany**.

especial for synonyms see **special**.

espy for synonyms see **see**.

essay for synonyms see **try**.

essential, indispensable, requisite, necessary —**Essential**, in strict usage, is applicable to that which constitutes the absolute essence or the fundamental nature of a thing and therefore must be present for the thing to exist, function, etc. [Food is *essential* to life.] An **indispensable** person or thing cannot be done without if the specified or implied purpose is to be achieved. **Requisite** is applied to that which is required by the circumstances or for the purpose and generally suggests a requirement that is imposed externally rather than an inherent need [the *requisite* experience for a position].

Necessary implies a pressing need but does not always connote absolute indispensability.

esteem for synonyms see **appreciate, regard**.

esteem for antonyms see **disgrace**.

estimate, appraise, evaluate, rate —Estimate, in this comparison, refers broadly to the forming of a personal opinion or judgment. (*See also synonyms at* **compute**.) **Appraise** implies the aim of giving an accurate or expert judgment, as of value or worth [to *appraise* a new house]. **Evaluate** also connotes an attempt at an exact judgment, but rarely with reference to value in terms of money [Let us *evaluate* the evidence.] **Rate** implies assignment of comparative value, quality, etc. [He is *rated* the best in his field.]

eternal for synonyms see **continual**.

ethical for synonyms see **moral**.

etiquette for synonyms see **decorum**.

eulogize for synonyms see **praise**.

eulogy for synonyms see **tribute**.

euphuistic for synonyms see **bombastic**.

evade for synonyms see **escape**.

evaluate for synonyms see **estimate**.

evanescent for synonyms see **transient**.

even for synonyms see **level, steady**.

event for synonyms see **occurrence**.

evict for synonyms see **eject**.

evidence for synonyms see **proof**.

evident, apparent, manifest, obvious, palpable, clear, plain —Evident and apparent apply to that which can be readily perceived or easily inferred, but **evident** implies the existence of external signs [his *evident* disappointment] and **apparent** suggests the use of deductive reasoning [It's *apparent* he'll win.] **Manifest** applies to that which is immediately, often intuitively, clear to the understanding. **Obvious** refers to that which is so noticeable or obtrusive that no one can fail to perceive it. **Palpable** applies especially to that which can be perceived through some sense other than that of sight [*palpable* signs of fever]. **Clear** implies that there is no confusion or obscurity to hinder understanding [*clear* proof]. **Plain** implies such simplicity or lack of complexity as to be easily perceptible [The *plain* facts are these.]

evident for antonyms see **obscure**.

evil for synonyms see **bad**.

evoke for synonyms see **extract**.

exact for synonyms see **correct** and **demand**.

exacting for synonyms see **onerous**.

examine for synonyms see **scrutinize**.

example for synonyms see **instance, model**.

exasperate for synonyms see **irritate**.

excavation for synonyms see **hole**.

excel, surpass, transcend, outdo —**Excel** implies superiority in some quality, skill, achievement, etc. over all or over the one (or ones) specified [to *excel* at chess]. **Surpass** implies a going beyond (someone or something specified) in degree, amount, or quality [No one *surpasses* him in generosity]. **Transcend** suggests a surpassing to an extreme degree [It *transcends* all understanding.] **Outdo** implies a going beyond someone else or a previous record in performance [He will not be *outdone* in bravery.]

excellent for synonyms see **good**.

exceptional, extraordinary —**Exceptional** means much above average in ability, quality, etc. [her *exceptional* talent as an actress]. **Extraordinary** implies a going beyond the ordinary limit or degree [an *extraordinary* increase in the cost of living].

exceptional for antonyms see **common**.

excessive, exorbitant, extravagant, immoderate, inordinate —**Excessive** applies to that which goes beyond what is proper, right, or usual [*excessive* demands]. **Exorbitant** is applied to that which is unreasonably excessive and often connotes a greedy desire for more than is just or due [*exorbitant* prices]. **Extravagant** and **immoderate** both imply excessiveness resulting from a lack of restraint or of prudence [*extravagant* praise, *immoderate* laughter]. **Inordinate** implies a going beyond the orderly limits of convention or the bounds of good taste [his *inordinate* pride].

excessive for antonyms see **moderate**.

excite for synonyms see **provoke**.

excited for antonyms see **calm, cool**.

exclude, debar, disbar, eliminate, suspend —**Exclude** implies a keeping out or prohibiting of that which is not yet in [to *exclude* someone from membership]. **Debar** connotes the existence of some barrier, as legal authority or force, which excludes someone from a privilege, right, etc. [to *debar* certain groups from voting]. **Disbar** refers only to the expulsion of a lawyer from the group of those who are permitted to practice law. **Eliminate** implies the removal of that which is already in, usually connoting its undesirability or its irrelevancy [to *eliminate* waste products]. **Suspend** refers to the removal, usually temporary, of someone from some organization, institution, etc., as for the infraction of some rule [to *suspend* a student from school]. —*Antonym:* **admit**. For other antonyms see **include**.

execrate for synonyms see **curse**.

execute for synonyms see **kill** and **perform**.

exemption, immunity, impunity —**Exemption** implies release from some obligation or legal requirement, especially where others are not so released [*exemption* from the military draft]. **Immunity** implies freedom from or protection against something disagreeable or menacing to which all or many are liable [*immunity* from a penalty, disease, taxes]. **Impunity** specifically implies escape or freedom from punishment [to commit a crime with *impunity*]. —*Antonym:* **liability.**

exertion for synonyms see **effort.**

exhausted for synonyms see **tired.**

exhibit for synonyms see **proof, show.**

exhilarate for synonyms see **animate.**

exhort for synonyms see **urge.**

exigency for synonyms see **emergency, need.**

exile for synonyms see **banish.**

exonerate for synonyms see **absolve.**

exorbitant for synonyms see **excessive.**

expand, swell, distend, inflate, dilate —**Expand** implies an increasing in size, bulk, or volume and is the broadest term here, being applicable when the enlarging force operates from either the inside or the outside or when the increase comes about by unfolding, puffing out, spreading, or opening. **Swell** implies expansion beyond the normal limits or size. **Distend** implies a swelling as a result of pressure from within that forces a bulging outward. **Inflate** suggests the use of air or gas, or of something insubstantial, to distend or swell a thing. **Dilate** suggests a widening or stretching of something circular.

expand for antonyms see **contract, limit.**

expatriate for synonyms see **banish.**

expect, anticipate, hope, await —**Expect** implies a

considerable degree of confidence that a particular event will happen [to *expect* guests for dinner]. **Anticipate** implies a looking forward to something with a foretaste of the pleasure or distress it promises, or a realizing of something in advance, and a taking of steps to meet it [to *anticipate* trouble]. **Hope** implies a desire for something, accompanied by some confidence in the belief that it can be realized [to *hope* for the best]. **Await** implies a waiting for, or a being ready for, a person or thing [A hearty welcome *awaits* you.]

expedient for synonyms see **resource**.

expedition for synonyms see **haste** and **trip**.

expel for synonyms see **eject**.

expensive for synonyms see **costly**.

expensive for antonyms see **cheap**.

experiment for synonyms see **trial**.

expert for synonym see **professional**.

expert for antonyms see **amateur**.

expire for synonyms see **die**.

explain, expound, explicate, elucidate, interpret, construe —**Explain** implies a making clear or intelligible of something that is not known or understood [to *explain* how a machine operates]. **Expound** implies a systematic and thorough explanation, often one made by a person having expert knowledge [to *expound* a theory]. **Explicate** implies a scholarly analysis or exposition that is developed in detail [the *explication* of a Biblical passage]. **Elucidate** implies a shedding light upon by clear and specific explanation, illustration, etc. [to *elucidate* the country's foreign policy]. **Interpret** is to bring out meanings not immediately apparent, as by translation, searching insight, or special knowledge [How do you *interpret* his silence?] **Construe** suggests a particular inter-

pretation of something whose meaning is ambiguous
[His statement is not to be lightly *construed*.]

explicate for synonyms see **explain**.

expose for synonyms see **show**.

expose for antonyms see **hide**.

expostulate for synonyms see **object**.

expound for synonyms see **explain**.

express for synonyms see **utter**.

expunge for synonyms see **erase**.

exquisite for synonyms see **delicate**.

extemporaneous, extemporary, extempore for synonyms see **impromptu**.

extend, lengthen, elongate, prolong, protract —**Extend** and **lengthen** both imply a making longer in space
or time, but **extend**, in addition, may signify an enlarging in area, scope, influence, meaning, etc. **Elongate** is a
synonym for **lengthen** in the spatial sense and is more
commonly used in technical applications. **Prolong** and
protract both primarily imply an extending in time,
prolong suggesting continuation beyond the usual or expected time, and **protract** a being drawn out needlessly
or wearingly.

extend for antonyms see **shorten**.

exterminate, extirpate, eradicate —**Exterminate** implies the complete, wholesale destruction of things or living beings whose existence is considered undesirable.
Extirpate and **eradicate** both suggest the extinction or
abolition of something, **extirpate** implying a deliberate
and violent destruction at the very source so that the
thing cannot be regenerated, and **eradicate** connoting
less violence and, often, the working of natural processes
or a methodical plan.

extinct for synonyms see **dead**.

extirpate for synonyms see **exterminate**.

extol for synonyms see **praise**.

extol for antonyms see **disparage**.

extort for synonyms see **extract**.

extract, educe, elicit, evoke, extort —**Extract** implies a drawing out of something, as if by pulling, sucking, etc. [to *extract* a promise]. **Educe** suggests a drawing out or evolving of something that is latent or undeveloped [Laws were *educed* from tribal customs.] **Elicit** connotes difficulty or skill in drawing out something hidden or buried [His jokes *elicited* no smiles.] **Evoke** implies a calling forth or summoning, as of a mental image, by stimulating the emotions [The odor *evoked* a memory of childhood.] **Extort** suggests a forcing or wresting of something, as by violence or threats [to *extort* a ransom].

extraneous for synonyms see **extrinsic**.

extraneous for antonyms see **relevant**.

extraordinary for synonym see **exceptional**.

extraordinary for antonyms see **usual**.

extravagant for synonyms see **excessive, profuse**.

extrinsic, extraneous, foreign, alien —**Extrinsic** refers to that which coming from outside a thing is not inherent in its real nature [the *extrinsic* advantages of wealth]. **Extraneous**, often synonymous with **extrinsic**, may connote the possibility of integration of the external object into the thing to which it is added [*extraneous* grace notes]. **Foreign** implies that the external object is organically so different that it cannot become assimilated [a *foreign* substance in the blood]. **Alien** emphasizes the incompatibility of the external object with the subject in question ["Nothing human is *alien* to me."] —Antonym: **intrinsic**.

F

fabricate for synonyms see **lie** and **make**.

fabulous for synonyms see **fictitious**.

face, countenance, visage, physiognomy —**Face** is the basic, direct word for the front of the head. **Countenance** refers to the face as it reflects the emotions or feelings and is, hence, often applied to the facial expression [his happy *countenance*]. **Visage** refers to the form, proportions, and expression of the face, especially as indicative of general temperament [a man of stern *visage*]. **Physiognomy** refers to the general cast of features, especially as characteristic of an ethnic group or as supposedly indicative of character [the *physiognomy* of an honest man].

facet for synonyms see **phase**.

facetious for synonyms see **witty**.

facile for synonyms see **easy**.

facsimile for synonyms see **copy**.

factor for synonyms see **element**.

faculty for synonyms see **talent**.

fad for synonyms see **fashion**.

fade for synonyms see **vanish**.

fagged for synonyms see **tired**.

failing for synonyms see **fault**.

fair, just, impartial, unbiased, dispassionate, objective —**Fair**, the general word, implies the treating of both or all sides alike, without reference to one's own feelings or interests [a *fair* exchange]. (*See also synonyms at* **beautiful**.) **Just** implies adherence to a standard of rightness or lawfulness without reference to one's own inclinations [a *just* decision]. **Impartial** and **unbiased**

both imply freedom from prejudice for or against any side [an *impartial* chairman, an *unbiased* account]. **Dispassionate** implies the absence of passion or strong emotion, hence connotes cool, disinterested judgment [a *dispassionate* critic]. **Objective** implies a viewing of persons or things without reference to oneself, one's feelings, interests, etc. [an *objective* newspaper]. —Antonyms: **prejudiced, biased.**

faith for synonyms see **belief.**

✓**faithful, loyal, constant, staunch** or **stanch, resolute** —**Faithful** implies continued, steadfast adherence to a person or thing to which one is bound by an oath, duty, obligation, etc. [a *faithful* wife]. **Loyal** implies undeviating allegiance to a person, cause, institution, etc. which one feels morally bound to support or defend [a *loyal* friend]. **Constant** suggests freedom from fickleness in affections or loyalties [a *constant* lover]. **Staunch** (or **stanch**) implies such strong allegiance to one's principles or purpose as not to be turned aside by any cause [a *staunch* defender of the truth]. **Resolute** stresses unwavering determination, often in adhering to one's personal ends or aims [She was *resolute* in her decision to stay.]

✓**faithless, false, disloyal, traitorous, treacherous, perfidious** —**Faithless** implies failure to adhere to an oath, duty, obligation, etc. [a *faithless* wife]. **False**, in this connection more or less synonymous with **faithless**, stresses failure in devotion to someone or something that has a moral claim to one's support [a *false* friend]. **Disloyal** implies a breach of allegiance to a person, cause, institution, etc. [*disloyal* to one's family]. **Traitorous** strictly implies the commission of an act of treason. **Treacherous** means a proclivity to commit treason or to betray a trust [His *treacherous* colleagues cheated him out of the honors due him.] **Perfidious** adds to the meaning of **treacherous** a connotation of sordidness or depravity [a *perfidious* informer].

fake for synonyms see **false**.

faker for synonyms see **quack**.

fallacious for antonyms see **valid**.

false, sham, counterfeit, bogus, fake —**False,** in this comparison, refers to anything that is not in essence that which it purports to be and may or may not connote deliberate deception [*false* hair]. (*See also synonyms at* **faithless.**) **Sham** refers to an imitation or simulation of something and usually connotes intent to deceive [*sham* piety]. **Counterfeit** and the colloquial **bogus** apply to a very careful imitation and always imply intent to deceive or defraud [*counterfeit,* or *bogus,* money]. **Fake** is a less formal term for any person or thing that is not genuine [a *fake* doctor, chimney, etc.] —*Antonyms:* **genuine, real.** *For other antonyms see* **correct.**

falter for synonyms see **hesitate**.

familiar, close, intimate, confidential —**Familiar** is applied to that which is known through constant association, and, with reference to persons, suggests informality, or even presumption, such as might prevail among members of a family. (*See also synonyms at* **common.**) **Close** is applied to persons or things very near to one in affection, attraction, interests, etc. **Intimate** implies very close association, acquaintance, relationship, etc. or suggests something of a very personal or private nature. **Confidential** implies a relationship in which there is mutual trust and a sharing of private thoughts, problems, etc.

familiar for antonyms see **strange**.

famished for synonyms see **hungry**.

famous, renowned, celebrated, noted, notorious, distinguished, eminent, illustrious —**Famous** is applied to persons or things that have received wide public attention and are generally known and talked about. **Renowned** suggests a being named publicly again and again for some outstanding quality, achievement, etc. **Celebrated** is applied to persons or things that have received much public honor or praise. **Noted** implies a being brought to the wide notice of the public for some particular quality. **Notorious**, in current usage, suggests a being widely but unfavorably known or talked about. **Distinguished** implies a being noted as superior in its class or of its kind. **Eminent** more strongly stresses the conspicuous superiority of persons or things. **Illustrious** suggests a reputation based on brilliance of achievement or splendidness of character. —*Antonyms:* **obscure, unknown.**

fanatic for synonyms see **zealot.**

fanciful for synonyms see **imaginary.**

fang for synonyms see **tooth.**

fantastic, bizarre, grotesque —**Fantastic** implies a lack of restraint in imagination, suggesting that which is extravagantly fanciful or unreal in design, conception, construction, etc. [*fantastic* notions]. (*See also synonyms at* **imaginary.**) **Bizarre** suggests that which is extraordinarily eccentric or strange because of startling incongruities, extreme contrasts, etc. [music with a *bizarre* atonality]. **Grotesque** suggests a ludicrously unnatural distortion of the normal or real, or a fantastic combination of elements [the *grotesque* grimaces of the comedian].

far, distant, remote, removed —**Far** generally suggests that which is an indefinitely long way off in space, time, relation, etc. [*far* lands]. **Distant**, although also suggesting a considerable interval of separation [a *distant* sound], is the term used when the measure of any interval is specified [desks four feet *distant* from one another]. **Remote** is applied to that which is far off in space, time, connection, etc. from a place, thing, or person understood as a point of reference [a *remote* village]. **Removed**, used predicatively, stresses separateness, distinctness, or lack of connection more strongly than **remote**. —*Antonyms:* **near, close.**

farcical for synonyms see **funny.**

fare for synonyms see **food.**

fascinate for synonyms see **attract.**

fashion, style, mode, vogue, fad, rage, craze —**Fashion** is the prevailing custom in dress, manners, speech, etc. of a particular place or time, especially as established by the dominant section of society or the leaders in the fields of art, literature, etc. (*See also synonyms at* **make** *and* **method.**) **Style,** often a close synonym for **fashion,** in discriminating use suggests a distinctive fashion, especially the way of dressing, living, etc. that distinguishes persons with money and taste. **Mode,** the French word expressing this idea, suggests the height of fashion in dress, behavior, etc. at any particular time. **Vogue** stresses the general acceptance or great popularity of a certain fashion. **Fad** stresses the impulsive enthusiasm with which a fashion is taken up for a short time. **Rage** and **craze** both stress an intense, sometimes irrational enthusiasm for a passing fashion.

fast, rapid, swift, fleet, quick, speedy, hasty —**Fast** and **rapid** are generally interchangeable in expressing the idea of a relatively high rate of movement or action, but **fast** more often refers to the person or thing that moves or acts, and **rapid** to the action [a *fast* typist, *rapid* transcription]. **Swift** implies great rapidity, but in addition often connotes smooth, easy movement. **Fleet** suggests a nimbleness or lightness in that which moves swiftly. **Quick** implies promptness of action, or occurrence in a brief space of time, rather than velocity [a *quick* reply]. **Speedy** intensifies the idea of quickness, but may also connote high velocity [a *speedy* recovery, a *speedy* flight]. **Hasty** suggests hurried action and may connote carelessness, rashness, or impatience. —*Antonym:* **slow.**

fasten for synonyms see **bind.**

fastidious for synonyms see **dainty.**

fastidious for antonyms see **slovenly.**

fat, fleshy, obese, plump, stout —**Fat** is the general term applied to someone who is very much overweight and has more fat than muscle [We saw the *fat* man in the sideshow.] **Fleshy** means simply having much flesh [*fleshy* arms]. **Obese** is a more formal word for fat [a diet for *obese* patients]. **Plump** suggests a full, rounded form [a *plump* hen]. **Stout** suggests firmness of flesh [a coat designed for *stout* persons]. **Fleshy, plump,** and **stout** are less pejorative than **fat** and **obese.**

fat for antonyms see **lean.**

fatal, deadly, mortal, lethal —**Fatal** implies the inevitability or actual occurrence of death or disaster [a *fatal* disease, a *fatal* mistake]. **Deadly** is applied to a thing that can and probably (but not inevitably) will cause death [a *deadly* poison]. **Mortal** implies that death has occurred and is applied to the immediate cause of the death [He has received a *mortal* blow.] **Lethal** is applied to that which in its nature or purpose is a cause of death [a *lethal* weapon].

fate, destiny, portion, lot, doom —**Fate** refers to the inevitability of a course of events as supposedly predetermined by a god or other agency beyond human control. **Destiny** also refers to an inevitable succession of events as determined supernaturally or by necessity, but often implies a favorable outcome [It was her *destiny* to become famous.] **Portion** and **lot** refer to what is supposedly distributed in the determining of fate, but **portion** implies an equitable apportionment and **lot** implies a random assignment. **Doom** always connotes an unfavorable or disastrous fate.

fateful for synonyms see **ominous.**

fatigued for synonyms see **tired.**

fatuous for synonyms see **silly.**

fault, failing, weakness, foible, vice —Fault, in this comparison, refers to a definite, although not strongly condemnatory, imperfection in character [Her only *fault* is stubbornness.] **Failing** implies an even less serious shortcoming, usually one of those common to mankind [Tardiness was one of his *failings*.] **Weakness** applies to a minor shortcoming that results from a lack of perfect self-control [Fattening foods are her *weakness*.] **Foible** refers to a slight weakness that is regarded more as an amusing idiosyncrasy than an actual defect in character [Eating desserts first is one of his *foibles*.] **Vice**, although stronger in its implication of moral failure than any of the preceding terms, does not in this connection suggest actual depravity or wickedness [Gambling is his only *vice*.] —*Antonym:* **virtue.**

faultfinding for synonyms see **critical.**

faux pas for synonyms see **error.**

favorable, auspicious, propitious —Favorable applies to that which is distinctly helpful or advantageous in gaining an end [a *favorable* climate for citrus fruits].

Auspicious refers to something regarded as a good omen of some undertaking [He made an *auspicious* debut.] **Propitious** is now usually applied to a circumstance or a time that appears favorable for doing or beginning something [a *propitious* moment]. —*Antonyms:* **adverse, unfavorable.**

faze for synonyms see **embarrass.**

fealty for synonyms see **allegiance.**

fear, dread, fright, alarm, terror, panic —**Fear** is the general term for the anxiety and agitation felt at the presence of danger. **Dread** refers to the fear or depression felt in anticipating something dangerous or disagreeable [to live in *dread* of poverty]. **Fright** applies to a sudden, shocking, usually momentary fear [The mouse gave her a *fright.*] **Alarm** implies the fright felt at the sudden realization of danger [He felt *alarm* at the sight of the pistol.] **Terror** applies to an overwhelming, often paralyzing fear [The *terror* of soldiers in combat.] **Panic** refers to a frantic, unreasoning fear, often one that spreads quickly and leads to irrational, aimless action [The cry of "fire!" created a *panic.*]

fearful for synonyms see **afraid.**

feasible for synonyms see **possible.**

fecund for synonyms see **fertile.**

federation for synonyms see **alliance.**

fee for synonyms see **wage.**

feeble for synonyms see **weak.**

feeling, emotion, passion, sentiment —**Feeling,** when unqualified in the context, refers to any of the subjective reactions, pleasurable or unpleasurable, that one may have to a situation and usually connotes an absence of reasoning [I can't trust my own *feelings.*] **Emotion** implies an intense feeling with physical as well as mental manifestations [Her breast heaved with *emotion.*] **Passion** refers to a strong or overpowering emotion, connoting especially sexual love or intense anger. **Sentiment** applies to a feeling, often a tender one, accompanied by some thought or reasoning [What are your *sentiments* in this matter?]

feign for synonyms see **assume.**

female, feminine, womanly, womanish, effeminate, ladylike —**Female** is the basic term applied to members of the sex that is biologically distinguished from the male sex and is used of animals or plants as well as of human beings. (*See also synonyms at* **woman.**) **Feminine** is now the preferred term for references, other than those basically biological, to qualities characteristic of women or things appropriate to them, as delicacy, gentleness, etc. **Womanly** suggests the noble qualities one associates with a woman, especially one who has maturity of character. **Womanish**, in contrast, suggests the weaknesses and faults that are regarded as characteristic of some women. **Effeminate,** used chiefly in reference to a man, implies delicacy, softness, or lack of virility. **Ladylike** refers to manners, conduct, etc. such as are expected from a refined or well-bred woman.

feminine for synonyms see **female.**

fertile, fecund, fruitful, prolific —**Fertile** implies a producing, or power of producing, fruit or offspring, and may be used figuratively of the mind. **Fecund** implies the abundant production of offspring or fruit, or, figuratively, of creations of the mind. **Fruitful** specifically suggests the bearing of much fruit, but it is also used to imply fertility (of soil), favorable results, profitableness, etc. **Prolific,** a close synonym for **fecund,** more often carries derogatory connotations of overly rapid production or reproduction. —*Antonym:* **barren.** *For other antonyms see* **sterile.**

fervent, fervid for synonyms see **passionate.**

fervor for synonyms see **passion.**

fetch for synonyms see **bring.**

fetid for synonyms see **stinking.**

fetter for synonyms see **hamper.**

fib for synonyms see **lie.**

fictitious, fabulous, legendary, mythical, apocryphal —**Fictitious** refers to that which is invented by the imagination and is therefore not real, true, or actually existent [Gulliver is a *fictitious* character.] **Fabulous** suggests that which is incredible or astounding, but does not necessarily connote nonexistence [The man's wealth is *fabulous.*] **Legendary** refers to something that may have a historical basis in fact but, in popular tradition, has undergone great elaboration and exaggeration [the *legendary* amours of Don Juan]. **Mythical** basically applies to the highly imaginary explanation of natural or historical phenomena by a people and, therefore, connotes that what it qualifies is a product of the imagination. **Apocryphal** suggests that which is of doubtful authenticity or authorship. —*Antonym:* **factual.** *For other antonyms see* **true.**

fickle for synonyms see **inconstant.**

fidelity for synonyms see **allegiance.**

fight for synonyms see **conflict.**

figure for synonyms see **form.**

filch for synonyms see **steal.**

filthy for synonyms see **dirty.**

final for synonyms see **last.**

financial, fiscal, monetary, pecuniary —**Financial** implies reference to money matters, especially where large sums are involved [a *financial* success]. **Fiscal** is used with reference to government revenues and expenditures or the administering of the financial affairs of an organization or corporation [a *fiscal* year]. **Monetary** refers directly to money itself and is used in connection with coinage, circulation, standards, relative values, etc. [the *monetary* unit of a country]. **Pecuniary** is applied to money matters of a practical or personal nature [*pecuniary* motives].

fine for synonyms see **good**.

finish for synonyms see **close²**.

finish for antonyms see **begin**.

firm, hard, solid, stiff —Firm, in referring to material consistency, suggests a compactness that does not yield easily to, or is very resilient under, pressure [*firm* flesh]. **Hard** is applied to that which is so firm that it is not easily penetrated, cut, or crushed [*hard* as rock]. **Solid** suggests a dense consistency throughout a mass or substance that is firm or hard and often connotes heaviness or substantialness [*solid* brick]. **Stiff** implies resistance to bending or stretching [a *stiff* collar].

fiscal for synonyms see **financial**.

fit, suitable, proper, appropriate, fitting, apt —Fit, the broadest term here, means having the qualities or qualifications to meet some condition, circumstance, purpose, or demand [*fit* for a king]. **Suitable** is applied to that which accords with the requirements or needs of the occasion or circumstances [shoes *suitable* for hiking]. **Proper** implies reference to that which naturally or rightfully belongs to something or suggests a fitness or suitability dictated by good judgment [*proper* respect for one's elders]. That is **appropriate** which is especially or distinctively fit or suitable. **Fitting** is applied to that which accords harmoniously with the character, spirit, or tone of something. **Apt**, in this connection, is used of that which is exactly suited to the purpose [an *apt* phrase].

fitting for synonyms see **fit**.

fix for synonyms see **predicament**.

flabbergast for synonyms see **surprise**.

flagrant, glaring, gross, rank —**Flagrant** applies to anything that is so obviously bad or wrong as to be notorious [a *flagrant* violation of the law]. (*See also synonyms at* **outrageous**.) **Glaring** is used of something bad that is even more conspicuous so that it is immediately perceived [a *glaring* error in arithmetic]. **Gross** implies an even greater degree of badness or wrongness, so as to deserve censure [*gross* negligence]. **Rank**, in this connection, is used contemptuously to imply that no exaggeration is intended in the description [It was *rank* folly to send the letter.]

flame for synonyms see **blaze**.

flare for synonyms see **blaze**.

flash, glance, gleam, sparkle, glitter, glisten, shimmer —**Flash** implies a sudden, brief, brilliant light. **Glance** refers to a darting light, especially one that is reflected from a surface at an angle. **Gleam** suggests a steady, narrow ray of light shining through a background of relative darkness. **Sparkle** implies a number of brief, bright, intermittent flashes. **Glitter** implies the reflection of such bright, intermittent flashes. **Glisten** suggests the reflection of a lustrous light, as from a wet surface. **Shimmer** refers to a soft, tremulous reflection, as from a slightly disturbed body of water.

flashy for synonyms see **gaudy**.

flat for synonyms see **insipid** and **level**.

flaunt for synonyms see **show**.

flaw for synonyms see **defect**.

fleet for synonyms see **fast**.

fleeting for synonyms see **transient**.

fleshly for synonyms see **carnal**.

fleshy for synonyms see **fat**.

fleshy for antonyms see **lean**.

flexible for synonyms see **elastic**.

flexible for antonyms see **inflexible**, **strict**.

flicker for synonyms see **blaze**.

flight for synonyms see **group**.

flinch for synonyms see **recoil**.

fling for synonyms see **throw**.

flip for synonyms see **flippant**.

flippant, flip, frivolous —Flippant is applied to whoever or whatever is disrespectful or impertinent [He made *flippant* remarks about the sermon.] **Flip** is a colloquial contraction of **flippant**. **Frivolous** is used of anyone or anything that is silly and light-minded [the *frivolous* life of a playboy].

flippant for antonyms see **serious**.

flirt for synonyms see **trifle**.

flit for synonyms see **fly**.

flock for synonyms see **group**.

flog for synonyms see **beat**.

florid for synonyms see **rosy**.

flourish for synonyms see **succeed**.

flout for synonyms see **scoff**.

flow, pour, gush, squirt —Flow is the broadest term in its application here, meaning to move as a liquid does; stream [The river *flows* to the sea.] (*See also synonyms at* **rise**.) **Pour** means to flow freely in a continuous stream [Rain *poured* off the roof all day.] **Gush** means to flow out suddenly and plentifully [The oil *gushed* from the ground.] **Squirt** means to shoot out in a narrow stream [He *squirted* water from the hose on the garden.]

flowery for synonyms see **bombastic**.

fluctuate for synonyms see **swing**.

fluid for synonym see **liquid**.

flutter for synonyms see **fly**.

fly, flit, hover, soar, flutter —**Fly** is the general word implying movement through the air on wings [Birds, insects, and airplanes *fly*.] **Flit** suggests a series of quick, brief flights from place to place [Sparrows *flitted* about in the trees.] To **hover** is to remain suspended at a point in the air by special movements of the wings [A butterfly *hovered* over the flower.] **Soar** implies a flying high into the air in a straight, almost vertical line [The lark *soared* into the sky.], or it may also describe a gliding on air currents high in the air [eagles *soaring* near the craggy peaks]. **Flutter** suggests a rapid but unsteady flapping of the wings, as in the short flight of a young or injured bird.

foe for synonyms see **opponent**.

fog for synonyms see **mist**.

foible for synonyms see **fault**.

foil for synonyms see **frustrate**.

follow, ensue, succeed, result —**Follow** is the general word meaning to come or occur after, but it does not necessarily imply a causal relationship with what goes before [sunshine *followed* by rain]. **Ensue** implies that what follows comes as a logical consequence of what preceded [Clouds appeared and rain *ensued*.] **Succeed** implies that what follows takes the place of what preceded [Who *succeeded* Polk to the Presidency?] **Result** stresses a definite relationship of cause and effect between what follows and what preceded [Superstition *results* from ignorance.] —*Antonyms:* **precede, guide.**

follower, supporter, adherent, disciple, partisan —**Follower** is the general term for one who follows or believes in the teachings or theories of someone [a *follower* of Freud]. **Supporter** applies to one who upholds or defends opinions or theories that are disputed or under attack [a *supporter* of technocracy]. **Adherent** refers to a close, active follower of some theory, cause, etc. [the *adherents* of a political party]. **Disciple** implies a personal, devoted relationship to the teacher of some doctrine or leader of some movement [Plato was a *disciple* of Socrates.] **Partisan,** in this connection, refers to an unswerving, often blindly devoted, adherent of some person or cause.

foment for synonyms see **incite.**

fondle for synonyms see **caress.**

food, fare, victuals, provisions, ration, rations —**Food** is the general term for all matter that is taken into the body for nourishment. **Fare** refers to the range of foods eaten by a particular organism or available at a particular time and place [the *fare* of horses, a bill of *fare*]. **Victuals** is a dialectal or colloquial word for human fare or diet. **Provisions,** in this connection, refers to a stock of food assembled in advance [*provisions* for the hike]. **Ration** refers to a fixed allowance or allotment of food [the weekly *ration*] and in the plural (**rations**) to food in general [How are the *rations* in this outfit?]

foolish for synonyms see **absurd.**

foolish for antonyms see **wise.**

forbear for synonyms see **refrain.**

forbearance for synonyms see **endurance.** ✓

forbearance for antonyms see **anger.**

forbid, prohibit, interdict, enjoin, ban —**Forbid** is the

basic, direct word meaning to command a person to refrain from some action. **Prohibit** implies a forbidding
by law or official decree. **Interdict** implies legal or ecclesiastical prohibition, usually for a limited time, as an
exemplary punishment or to forestall unfavorable developments. **Enjoin** implies a legal order from a court
prohibiting (or ordering) a given action, under penalty.
Ban implies legal or ecclesiastical prohibition with an
added connotation of strong condemnation or censure.
—*Antonyms:* **permit, allow.**

force, compel, coerce, constrain —**Force** implies the
exertion of power in causing action, movement, or compliance when a person or thing is resisting and may refer
to physical strength or to any impelling motive [Circum-
stances *forced* him to lie.] (*See also synonyms at*
strength.) **Compel** implies a driving irresistibly to some
action, condition, etc. To **coerce** is to compel submission or obedience by the use of superior power, intimidation, threats, etc. **Constrain** implies the operation of a
restricting force and therefore suggests a strained, re-
pressed, or unnatural quality in that which results [a *con-
strained* laugh].

forebode for synonyms see **foretell.**
foreboding for synonyms see **ominous.**
forecast for synonyms see **foretell.**
foregoing for synonyms see **previous.**
foreign for synonyms see **extrinsic.**
foreign for antonyms see **native.**
foreigner for synonyms see **alien.**
foremost for synonyms see **chief.**
forerunner, precursor, herald, harbinger —**Forerunner** and **percursor** both refer to a person or thing that
comes before (and presages the appearance of) another,

precursor more specifically suggesting preparation for the work or achievements of the one that follows. **Herald,** originally applied to one who made public proclamations or carried messages of state, now refers to any person or thing that announces something or bears news. **Harbinger,** originally applied to one sent in advance to secure lodgings as for a royal party, now often applies to something that arrives as the omen or symbol of something to follow.

forestall for synonyms see **prevent.**

foretell, predict, forecast, prophesy, prognosticate, presage, forebode —**Foretell** is the general term for a telling or indicating beforehand and does not in itself suggest the means used [to *foretell* the future]. **Predict,** often interchangeable with **foretell,** more often suggests deduction from facts already known or the use of scientific calculation [The Chaldeans could *predict* eclipses.] **Forecast** comes close to **predict,** now commonly implying estimation of the probable course or future condition of things [to *forecast* the weather]. **Prophesy,** in discriminating use, implies prediction by divine inspiration or occult knowledge [Jeremiah *prophesied* the Captivity.] To **prognosticate** is to foretell by the study of signs or symptoms [to *prognosticate* a depression]. **Presage** and **forebode** are more often used of things than of persons, **presage** referring to either favorable or unfavorable prognostications, and **forebode** to those of an unfavorable nature, based on premonition, presentiment, etc.

foreword for synonyms see **introduction.**

forget for synonyms see **neglect.**

forget for antonyms see **remember.**

forgive for synonyms see **absolve.**

forgo for synonyms see **relinquish.**

forgo for antonyms see **get**.

form, figure, outline, shape, configuration —**Form** denotes the arrangement of the parts of a thing that gives it its distinctive appearance and is the broadest term here, applying also to abstract concepts. (*See also synonyms at* **make**.) **Figure** is applied to physical form as determined by the bounding lines or surfaces. **Outline** is used of the lines bounding the limits of an object and, in an extended sense, suggests an undetailed general plan. **Shape**, although also stressing outline, is usually applied to something that has mass or bulk and may refer to nonphysical concepts. **Configuration** stresses the relative disposition of the inequalities of a surface.

formality for synonyms see **ceremony**.

former for synonyms see **previous**.

forsake for synonyms see **abandon**.

fortitude, grit, backbone, pluck, guts —**Fortitude** refers to the courage that permits one to endure patiently misfortune, pain, etc. [to face a calamity with *fortitude*]. (*See also synonyms at* **endurance**.) **Grit** applies to an obstinate sort of courage that refuses to succumb under any circumstances. **Backbone** refers to the strength of character and resoluteness that permits one to face opposition unflinchingly. **Pluck** and **guts** both refer originally to visceral organs, hence **pluck** implies a strong heart in the face of danger or difficulty and **guts**, a slang word, suggests the sort of stamina that permits one to "stomach" a disagreeable or frightening experience. —*Antonym:* **cowardice**.

fortuitous for synonyms see **accidental**.

fortunate for synonyms see **lucky**.

forward for synonyms see **advance**.

foul for synonyms see **dirty**.

foundation for synonyms see **base¹**.

foxy for synonyms see **sly**.

fraction for synonyms see **part**.

fracture for synonyms see **break**.

fragile, frangible, brittle, crisp, friable —Fragile implies such delicacy of structure as to be easily broken [a *fragile* china teacup]. **Frangible** adds to this the connotation of liability to being broken because of the use to which the thing is put [The handle on this ax seems *frangible*.] **Brittle** implies such inelasticity as to be easily broken or shattered by pressure or a blow [The bones of the body become *brittle* with age.] **Crisp** suggests a desirable sort of brittleness, as of fresh celery or soda crackers. **Friable** is applied to something that is easily crumbled or crushed into powder [*friable* rock]. —*Antonyms:* **tough, sturdy**.

fragment for synonyms see **part**.

fragrance for synonyms see **scent**.

frail for synonyms see **weak**.

frail for antonyms see **healthy**.

frangible for synonyms see **fragile**.

frank, candid, open, outspoken —Frank applies to a person, remark, etc. that is free or blunt in expressing the truth or an opinion, unhampered by conventional reticence [a *frank* criticism]. **Candid** implies a basic honesty that makes deceit or evasion impossible, sometimes to the embarrassment of the listener [a *candid* opinion]. **Open** implies a lack of concealment and often connotes an ingenuous quality [her *open* admiration for him]. **Outspoken** suggests a lack of restraint or reserve in speech, especially when reticence might be preferable.

fraud for synonyms see **deception**.

free, release, liberate, emancipate, discharge —Free

freedom 156

is the general term meaning to set loose from any sort of restraint, entanglement, burden, etc. [to *free* a convict, to *free* one's conscience]. **Release**, more or less interchangeable with **free**, stresses a setting loose from confinement, literally or figuratively [*Release* me from my promise.] **Liberate** emphasizes the state of liberty into which the freed person or thing is brought [to *liberate* prisoners of war]. **Emancipate** refers to a freeing from the bondage of slavery or of social insitutions or conventions regarded as equivalent to slavery [*emancipated* from medieval superstition]. **Discharge**, in this connection, implies a being permitted to leave that which confines or restrains [*discharged* at last from the army]. —*Antonyms:* **bind, confine.** *For other antonyms see* **restrain.**

freedom, liberty, license —**Freedom**, the broadest in scope of these words, implies the absence of hindrance, restraint, confinement, repression, etc. [*freedom* of speech]. **Liberty**, often interchangeable with **freedom**, strictly connotes past or potential restriction, repression, etc. [civil *liberties*]. **License** implies freedom that consists in violating the usual rules, laws, or practices, either by consent [poetic *license*] or as an abuse of liberty [Slander is *license* of the tongue.] —*Antonyms:* **repression, constraint.** *For other antonyms see* **servitude.**

freethinker for synonyms see **atheist**.

frenzy for synonyms see **mania**.

fresh for synonyms see **new**.

fresh for antonyms see **trite**.

friable for synonyms see **fragile**.

friendly, social —**Friendly** is the general term that means showing or having amicable feelings toward other people; willing to be a friend [He spoke to me in a *friendly* manner.] **Social** indicates a willingness to associate with groups of people, as in attending public events or joining clubs or societies [She has an active *social* life.]

friendly for antonyms see **belligerent**.

fright for synonyms see **fear**.

frighten, scare, alarm, terrify, terrorize —Frighten is the broadest of these terms and implies, usually, a sudden, temporary feeling of fear [*frightened* by a mouse] but sometimes, a state of continued dread [She's *frightened* when she's alone.] **Scare**, often equivalent to **frighten**, in stricter use implies a fear that causes one to flee or to stop doing something [I *scared* him from the room.] **Alarm** suggests a sudden fear or apprehension at the realization of an approaching danger [*alarmed* by his warning]. To **terrify** is to cause to feel an overwhelming, often paralyzing fear [*terrified* at the thought of war]. **Terrorize** implies deliberate intention to terrify by threat or intimidation [The gangsters *terrorized* the city.]

frightened for synonyms see **afraid**.

frivolous for synonyms see **flippant**.

frivolous for antonyms see **serious**.

frolic for synonyms see **play**.

frown, scowl, glower —All three of these words denote the making of a wry or gloomy face. **Frown** implies a contracting of the brows in disapproval, annoyance, or deep thought. **Scowl** means a puckering and lowering of the brows in irritation or sullenness. **Glower** is used to describe a staring fiercely in great anger or contempt.

frown for antonyms see **smile**.

frugal for synonyms see **thrifty**.

fruitful for synonyms see **fertile**.

fruitful for antonyms see **futile**.

fruitless for synonyms see **futile**.

frustrate, thwart, foil, baffle, balk —**Frustrate** implies a depriving of effect or a rendering worthless of efforts directed to some end. **Thwart** implies a frustrating by blocking or acting in opposition to a person or thing moving toward some objective. **Foil** implies a throwing something off its course (literally, by confusing the scent or trail) so as to discourage further effort or make it of no avail. To **baffle** is to defeat the efforts of by bewildering or confusing [The crime *baffled* the police.] To **balk** is to frustrate by setting up obstacles or obstructions.

fulfill for synonyms see **perform**.

full for synonyms see **complete**.

full for antonyms see **empty**.

function, office, duty, capacity —**Function** is the broad, general term for the natural, required, or expected activity of a person or thing [the *function* of the liver, the *function* of education]. **Office**, in this connection, refers to the function of a person, as determined by his or her position, profession, or employment [the *office* of a priest]. **Duty** is applied to a task necessary in or appropriate to one's occupation, rank, or status and carries a strong connotation of obligation [the *duties* of a vicar]. **Capacity** refers to a specific function or status, not necessarily the usual or customary one [The judge spoke to him in the *capacity* of a friend.]

funny, laughable, amusing, droll, comic, comical, farcical —**Funny** is the simple, general term for anything that excites laughter or mirth. (*See also synonyms at* **absurd**.) **Laughable** applies to that which is fit to be laughed at and may connote contempt or scorn. That is **amusing** which provokes smiles, laughter, or pleasure by its pleasant, entertaining quality. That is **droll** which amuses one because of its quaintness or strangeness, or its wry or waggish humor. **Comic** is applied to that which contains the elements of comedy (in a dramatic or literary sense) and amuses one in a thoughtful way. **Comical** suggests that which evokes laughter of a more spontaneous, unrestrained kind. **Farcical** suggests a broad comical quality based on nonsense, extravagantly boisterous humor, etc.

furnish, equip, outfit, appoint, arm —**Furnish,** as compared here, implies the provision of all the things requisite for a particular service, action, etc. [to *furnish* a house]. To **equip** is to furnish with what is requisite for efficient action [a car *equipped* with power steering]. To **outfit** is to equip completely with the articles needed for a specific undertaking, occupation, etc. [to *outfit* a hunting expedition]. **Appoint,** a formal word now generally used in the past participle, implies the provision of all the requisites and accessories for proper service [a well-*appointed* studio]. **Arm** literally implies equipment with weapons, etc. for war but, in extended use, connotes provision with what is necessary to meet any circumstance.

further for synonyms see **advance.**

further for antonyms see **hinder.**

furtive for synonyms see **secret.**

fury for synonyms see **anger.**

fuse for synonyms see **mix.**

futile, vain, fruitless, abortive, useless —**Futile** is applied to that which fails completely of the desired end or is incapable of producing any result. **Vain** also implies failure but does not have as strong a connotation of intrinsic inefficacy as **futile.** **Fruitless** stresses the idea of great and prolonged effort that is profitless or fails to yield results. That is **abortive** which fails to succeed or miscarries at an early stage of its development. That is **useless** which has proved to be ineffectual in practice or is theoretically considered to be of no avail. —*Antonym:* **fruitful.** *For other antonyms see* **effective.**

G

gain for synonyms see **get, reach.**
gainsay for synonyms see **deny.**
gale for synonyms see **wind.**
gall for synonyms see **temerity.**
gallant for synonyms see **civil.**
gambol for synonyms see **play.**
gamut for synonyms see **range.**
gape for synonyms see **look.**
garish for synonyms see **gaudy.**
garrulous for synonyms see **talkative.**
gastronome for synonyms see **epicure.**
gather, collect, assemble, muster —**Gather** is the general term for a bringing or coming together [to *gather* scattered objects, people *gathered* at the corners]. (*See also synonyms at* **infer.**) **Collect** usually implies careful choice in gathering from various sources, a bringing into an orderly arrangement, etc. [He *collects* coins.] **Assemble** applies especially to the gathering together of persons for some special purpose [*Assemble* the students in the auditorium.] **Muster** applies to a formal assembling, especially of troops for inspection, roll call, etc.
gather for antonyms see **scatter.**
gaudy, tawdry, garish, flashy, showy —**Gaudy** applies to that which is brightly colored and gay, but inappropriately so or in bad taste [*gaudy* furniture]. **Tawdry** is used

of something cheap and flimsy that is also gaudy [*tawdry* embroidery]. **Garish** implies a glaring brightness of color and excessive ornamentation [*garish* wallpaper]. **Flashy** and **showy** imply a conspicuous brightness and display, but **flashy** connotes that it is offensive to subdued tastes [a *flashy* sport coat], while **showy** does not necessarily connote this [*showy* blossoms]. —*Antonyms:* subdued, quiet.

gauge for synonyms see **standard**.

gaunt for synonyms see **lean**.

gay for synonyms see **lively**.

gaze for synonyms see **look**.

general for synonyms see **common, universal**.

general for antonyms see **special**.

generic for synonyms see **universal**.

generous, bountiful —**Generous** is the basic word in this comparison, meaning unselfish and willing to share or give [Our parents have always been *generous*.] **Bountiful** implies a giving graciously and in great abundance [The foundation was *bountiful* in its help to students.] *See also synonyms at* **profuse**.

generous for antonyms see **stingy**.

genial for synonyms see **amiable**.

genial for antonyms see **sullen**.

genius for synonyms see **talent**.

gentile, Gentile for synonyms see **pagan**.

gentle for synonyms see **soft**.

genuine for synonyms see **authentic**.

genuine for antonyms see **false** and **plausible**.

germane for synonyms see **relevant**.

get, obtain, procure, secure, acquire, gain —**Get** is the word of broadest application meaning to come into possession of, with or without effort or volition [to *get* a job, to *get* an idea, to *get* a headache]. **Obtain** implies that there is effort or desire in the getting [He has *obtained* aid.] **Procure** suggests active effort or contrivance in getting or bringing to pass [to *procure* a settlement of the dispute]. **Secure**, in strict discrimination, implies difficulty in obtaining something and in retaining it [to *secure* a lasting peace]. **Acquire** implies a lengthy process in the getting and connotes collection or accretion [He *acquired* a fine education.] **Gain** always implies effort in the getting of something advantageous or profitable [to *gain* fame]. —*Antonyms:* lose, forgo.

ghastly, grim, grisly, gruesome, macabre —Ghastly suggests the horror aroused by the sight or suggestion of death [a *ghastly* smile on the dead man's face]. **Grim** implies hideously repellent aspects [a *grim* joke]. **Grisly** suggests an appearance that causes one to shudder with horror [the *grisly* sights of Buchenwald]. **Gruesome** suggests the fear and loathing aroused by something horrible and sinister [the *gruesome* details of a murder]. **Macabre** implies concern with the gruesome aspects of death [a *macabre* tale].

gibe for synonyms see **scoff.**

gift for synonyms see **present, talent.**

gigantic for synonyms see **huge.**

giggle for synonyms see **laugh.**

give, grant, present, donate, bestow, confer —Give is the general word meaning to transfer from one's own possession to that of another. **Grant** implies that there has been a request or an expressed desire for the thing given [to *grant* a favor]. **Present** implies a certain formality in the giving and often connotes considerable value in the gift [She *presented* the school with a library.] **Donate** is used especially of a giving to some philanthropic or religious cause. **Bestow** stresses that the thing is given gratuitously and often implies condescension in the giver [to *bestow* charity upon the poor]. **Confer** implies that the giver is a superior and that the thing given is an honor, privilege, etc. [to *confer* a title, to *confer* a college degree].

give for antonyms see **receive**.

glad for synonyms see **happy**.

glance for synonyms see **flash**.

glare for synonyms see **blaze** and **look**.

glaring for synonyms see **flagrant**.

gleam for synonyms see **flash**.

glee for synonyms see **mirth**.

glide for synonyms see **slide**.

glisten, glitter for synonyms see **flash**.

globular for synonyms see **round**.

gloomy for synonyms see **dark**.

glorious for synonyms see **splendid**.

glow for synonyms see **blaze**.

glower for synonyms see **frown**.

glum for synonyms see **sullen**.

glut for synonyms see **satiate**.

glutton for synonyms see **epicure**.

go, depart, leave, quit, withdraw, retire —Go is the general word indicating motion away from the place where one is. **Depart** is a somewhat more formal term and usually suggests a setting out on an expressed or implied journey [She *departed* for France.] **Leave** stresses the separation from a person or thing [I can't *leave* while she's ill.] **Quit** emphasizes a getting rid of by leaving [He *quit* his job yesterday.] **Withdraw** suggests a leaving for a definite, justified, and often unpleasant reason [She *withdrew* from the race because of a strained muscle.]

Retire, often equivalent to the preceding, may imply a permanent withdrawal, a retreat, recession, etc. [He *retired* at 65. She *retired* to a convent.] —Antonyms: **come, arrive.** *For other antonyms see* **stay.**

goal for synonyms see **intention.**

good, fine, excellent —Good, as compared here, is the general term, ranging in implication from merely acceptable to the very best or highest [a *good* boy, a *good* car for short trips, her *good* china]. **Fine** means better than average; superior [a *fine* teacher, *fine* needlework]. **Excellent** is used of that which is outstanding or very good [*excellent* schoolwork, *excellent* weather].

good for antonyms see **bad.**

good-looking for synonyms see **beautiful.**

good-natured for synonyms see **amiable.**

good-natured for antonyms see **sullen.**

gorgeous for synonyms see **splendid.**

gourmand, gourmet for synonyms see **epicure.**

govern, rule, administer —Govern implies the exercise of authority in controlling the actions of the members of a body politic and directing the affairs of state, and generally connotes as its purpose the maintenance of public order and the promotion of the common welfare. **Rule** now usually signifies the exercise of arbitrary or autocratic power. **Administer** implies the orderly management of governmental affairs by executive officials.

grab for synonyms see **take.**

grand, magnificent, imposing, stately, majestic, august, grandiose —Grand is applied to that which makes a strong impression because of its greatness (in size or some favorable quality), dignity, and splendor [the *Grand* Canyon]. **Magnificent** suggests a surpassing beauty, richness, or splendor, or an exalted or glorious quality [a *magnificent* voice]. **Imposing** suggests that which strikingly impresses one by its size, dignity, or excellence of character [an *imposing* array of facts]. **Stately** suggests that which is imposing in dignified grace and may imply a greatness of size [a *stately* mansion]. **Majestic** adds to **stately** the idea of lofty grandeur [the *majestic* Rockies]. **August** suggests an exalted dignity or impressiveness such as inspires awe [an *august* personage]. **Grandiose** is often used disparagingly of a grandeur that is affected or exaggerated [a *grandiose* manner].

grandiloquent for synonyms see **bombastic**.

grandiose for synonyms see **grand**.

grant for synonyms see **give**.

graphic, pictorial, vivid, picturesque —Graphic and **pictorial,** with reference to speech or writing, imply description that calls forth a mental image as sharply defined as the visual impression made by a picture. **Vivid** implies the bringing of strikingly real or lifelike images to the mind. **Picturesque** language is full of unusual or quaint imagery and may achieve interesting pictorial effects at the expense of reality.

grasp for synonyms see **take**.

grasping for synonyms see **greedy**.

gratifying for synonyms see **pleasant**.

gratuity for synonyms see **present**.

grave for synonyms see **serious**.

great for synonyms see **large**.

great for antonyms see **small**.

greedy, avaricious, grasping, acquisitive, covetous —Greedy implies an insatiable desire to possess or acquire something to an amount inordinately beyond what one needs or deserves and is the broadest of the terms compared here. **Avaricious** stresses greed for money or riches and often connotes miserliness. **Grasping** suggests an unscrupulous eagerness for gain that manifests itself in a seizing upon every opportunity to get what one desires. **Acquisitive** stresses the exertion of effort in acquiring or accumulating wealth or material possessions to an excessive amount. **Covetous** implies greed for something that another person rightfully possesses.

grief for synonyms see **sorrow**.

grievance for synonyms see **injustice**.

grim for synonyms see **ghastly**.

grimy for synonyms see **dirty**.

grin for synonyms see **smile**.

grind chop, mince —Grind means to crush into bits or fine particles between two hard surfaces [He *ground* the wheat to make flour.] (*See also synonyms at* **work**.) To **chop**, in this comparison, means to cut something into smaller pieces with a knife, ax, or other sharp implement [*Chop* up the log for firewood.] **Mince** means to cut or chop up into very small pieces [to *mince* celery for a salad].

grisly for synonyms see **ghastly**.

grit for synonyms see **fortitude**.

gross for synonyms see **coarse, flagrant**.

gross for antonyms see **delicate**.

grotesque for synonyms see **fantastic**.

groundwork for synonyms see **base¹**.

group, herd, flock, drove, pack, pride, swarm, school, bevy, covey, flight —Group is the basic, general word expressing the simple idea of an assembly of persons, animals, or things without further connotation. **Herd** is applied to a group of cattle, sheep, or similar large animals feeding, living, or moving together; **flock**, to goats, sheep, or birds; **drove**, to cattle, hogs, or sheep; **pack**, to

hounds or wolves; **pride,** to lions; **swarm,** to insects;
school, to fish, porpoises, whales, or the like; **bevy,** to
quails; **covey,** to partridges or quails; **flight,** to birds
flying together. In extended applications, **flock** connotes
guidance and care, **herd, drove,** and **pack** are used contemptuously of people, **swarm** suggests a thronging, and
bevy and **covey** are used of girls or women.

grudge for synonyms see **malice.**

gruesome for synonyms see **ghastly.**

gruff for synonyms see **blunt.**

guard for synonyms see **defend.**

guess, conjecture, surmise —**Guess** implies the forming of a judgment or estimate (often a correct one)
haphazardly [She *guessed* the number of beans in the
jar.] To **conjecture** is to infer or predict from incomplete or uncertain evidence [I cannot *conjecture* what his
plans are.] **Surmise** implies a conjecturing through mere
intuition or imagination [She *surmised* the truth.]

guest for synonyms see **visitor.**

guffaw for synonyms see **laugh.**

guide, lead, steer, pilot —**Guide** implies the showing of
the way by one who is thoroughly familiar with the
course, and connotes his or her continuous presence or
direction along the way [to *guide* a tourist, to *guide* a
mule, to *guide* one's hand]. **Lead** implies a going ahead
in order to show the way and, figuratively, suggests a
taking of the initiative [She *led* them to victory.] **Steer**
suggests a maneuvering of the controls in order to maintain the correct course [to *steer* a ship]. **Pilot** suggests a
guiding over a difficult course, especially one filled with
obstacles or intricate twists [He *piloted* us through the
maze of tunnels.]

guide for antonyms see **follow.**

gush for synonyms see **flow.**
gushy for synonyms see **sentimental.**
gust for synonyms see **wind.**
guts for synonyms see **fortitude.**
gyrate for synonyms see **turn.**

H

habit, practice, custom, usage, wont —Habit refers to an act repeated so often by an individual that it has become automatic [his *habit* of tugging at his ear in perplexity]. **Practice** also implies the regular repetition of an act but does not suggest that it is automatic [the *practice* of reading in bed]. **Custom** applies to any act or procedure carried on by tradition and often enforced by social disapproval of any violation [the *custom* of dressing for dinner]. **Usage** refers to custom or practice that has become sanctioned through being long established [*Usage* is the only authority in language.] **Wont** is a literary or somewhat archaic equivalent for **practice** [It was her *wont* to rise early.]

habitual for synonyms see **usual.**
hackneyed for synonyms see **trite.**
hale for synonyms see **healthy.**
hallow for synonyms see **devote.**
hallowed for synonyms see **holy.**
hallucination for synonyms see **delusion.**
hamper, fetter, shackle, manacle —Hamper implies an impeding or encumbering so as to keep from moving or acting freely [*hampered* by a heavy load, *hampered* by a lack of cooperation]. **Fetter, shackle,** and **manacle** all imply a checking or restraining so that freedom of move-

ment or progress is curtailed, **fetter**, as if by tying the feet with chains, **shackle**, as if by confining the wrists, ankles, etc. with metal bands, and **manacle**, as if by binding the wrists with handcuffs [a mind *fettered* by superstition, *shackled* to a jealous husband, a *manacled* press].

handsome for synonyms see **beautiful**.
handy for synonyms see **dexterous**.
handy for antonyms see **awkward**.
hanger-on for synonyms see **parasite**.
haphazard for synonyms see **random**.
haphazard for antonyms see **orderly**.
happen, chance, occur, transpire —**Happen** is the general word meaning to take place or come to pass and may suggest either direct cause or apparent accident. **Chance**, more or less equivalent to **happen**, always implies apparent lack of cause in the event. **Occur** is somewhat more formal and usually suggests a specific event at a specific time [What *happened*? The accident *occurred* at four o'clock.] **Transpire** is now frequently used as an equivalent for **happen** or **occur** [What *transpired* at the conference?], apparently by confusion with its sense of to become known, or leak out [Reports on the conference never *transpired*.]
happy, glad, cheerful, optimistic, joyful, joyous —**Happy** generally suggests a feeling of great pleasure, contentment, etc. [a *happy* marriage]. (*See also synonyms at **lucky**.*) **Glad** implies more strongly an exultant feeling of joy [Your letter made her so *glad*.] but both **glad** and **happy** are commonly used in merely polite formulas expressing gratification [I'm *glad*, or *happy*, to have met you.] **Cheerful** implies a steady display of bright spirits, optimism, etc. [He's always *cheerful* in the morning.]

Optimistic implies an attitude, usually habitual, of expecting the best to happen [She is *optimistic* about recovering from her illness.] **Joyful** and **joyous** both imply great elation and rejoicing, the former generally because of a particular event, and the latter as a matter of usual temperament [the *joyful* throngs, a *joyous* family].

happy for antonyms see **sad**.

harbinger for synonyms see **forerunner**.

hard, difficult, arduous, laborious —Hard, in this comparison, is the simple and general word for whatever demands great physical or mental effort [*hard* work, a *hard* problem]. (*See also synonyms at* **firm**.) **Difficult** applies especially to that which requires great skill, intelligence, tact, etc. rather than physical labor [a *difficult* situation]. **Arduous** implies the need for diligent, protracted effort [the *arduous* fight ahead of us]. **Laborious** suggests long, wearisome toil [the *laborious* task of picking fruit].

hard for antonyms see **easy**.

hardened for synonyms see **chronic**.

hardship for synonyms see **difficulty**.

harm for synonyms see **injure**.

harmless, innocuous —Harmless means simply causing or intending to cause no harm [This television program is *harmless*.] **Innocuous** may be used as a synonym for **harmless** [*innocuous* bacteria], but may also mean boring, dull, or of little value [an *innocuous* speech].

harmless for antonyms see **pernicious**.

harmonize for synonyms see **agree**.

harmony for synonyms see **symmetry**.

harmony for antonyms see **conflict, discord, quarrel**.

harsh for synonyms see **rough**.

harsh for antonyms see **soft**.

haste, hurry, speed, expedition, dispatch —Haste implies quick or precipitate movement or action, as from the pressure of circumstances or intense eagerness. **Hurry,** often interchangeable with **haste,** specifically suggests excitement, bustle, or confusion [the *hurry* of city life]. **Speed** implies rapidity of movement, operation, etc., suggesting effectiveness and the absence of excitement or confusion [to increase the *speed* of an assembly line]. **Expedition** adds to **speed** the implication of efficiency and stresses the facilitation of an action or procedure. **Dispatch** comes close to **expedition** in meaning but more strongly stresses promptness in finishing something. —*Antonyms:* **slowness, delay.**

hasten for antonyms see **delay.**

hasty for synonyms see **fast.**

hate, detest, despise, abhor, loathe —To **hate** means to feel great dislike or aversion, and, with persons as the object, connotes the bearing of malice. **Detest** means to have a vehement dislike or antipathy toward someone. **Despise** means to look down with great contempt upon the person or thing one hates. **Abhor** means to feel great repugnance or disgust. **Loathe** implies that one feels utter abhorrence. —*Antonym:* **like.** *For other antonyms see* **love.**

hateful, odious, detestable, obnoxious, repugnant, abhorrent, abominable —**Hateful** is applied to that which provokes extreme dislike or aversion. **Odious** stresses a disagreeable or offensive quality in that which is hateful. **Detestable** refers to that which arouses vehement dislike or antipathy. **Obnoxious** is applied to that which is very objectionable to one and causes great annoyance or discomfort by its presence. That is **repugnant** which is so distasteful or offensive that one offers strong resistance to it. That is **abhorrent** which is regarded with extreme repugnance or disgust. **Abominable** is applied to that which is execrably or degradingly offensive or loathsome.

haughty for synonyms see **proud**.

haul for synonyms see **pull**.

have, hold, own, possess —Have, the broadest term here, predicates the relation between a subject and an object (physical or nonphysical) that belongs to it in any of the various senses in which *belong* is understood [He *had* wealth. The poetry *has* charm. You *have* odd notions.] **Hold** means to have in one's grasp or keeping, or, in extended use, to control as by keeping in a certain place, condition, etc. [to *hold* a book, to *hold* one's attention, etc.] **Own** implies the holding or controlling of something as one's personal property [to *own* lands]. **Possess** is in its basic sense equivalent to **own**, and in extended senses means to have as an attribute, quality, faculty, etc. [to *possess* wisdom].

have for antonyms see **lack**.

havoc for synonyms see **ruin**.

hazard for synonyms see **danger**.

haze for synonyms see **mist**.

heal for synonyms see **cure**.

healthy, sound, hale, robust, well —Healthy implies normal physical and mental vigor and freedom from disease, weakness, disorder, etc. **Sound** implies perfectness of health, suggesting a condition in which there is no sign of disease or defect. **Hale**, closely synonymous with **sound**, is used especially of vigorous elderly people who are free from the infirmities of old age. **Robust** implies a vitality and hardiness that is immediately apparent in muscular build, good color, abundance of energy, etc. **Well** simply implies freedom from illness, without further connotation. —*Antonyms:* **diseased, infirm, frail.** *For other antonyms see* **sick.**

heap for synonyms see **pile.**

heartfelt, hearty for synonyms see **sincere.**

heathen for synonyms see **pagan.**

heavy, weighty, ponderous, massive, cumbersome —**Heavy** implies relatively great density, quantity, intensity, etc. and figuratively connotes a pressing down on the mind, spirits, or senses [*heavy* water, *heavy*-hearted]. **Weighty** suggests heaviness as an absolute rather than a relative quality and figuratively connotes great importance or influence [a *weighty* problem]. **Ponderous** applies to something that is very heavy because of size or bulk and figuratively connotes a labored or dull quality [a *ponderous* dissertation]. **Massive** stresses largeness and solidity rather than heaviness and connotes an impressiveness due to great magnitude [*massive* structures]. **Cumbersome** implies a heaviness and bulkiness that makes for awkward handling and, in extended use, connotes unwieldiness [*cumbersome* formalities]. —*Antonym:* **light.**

heckle for synonyms see **bait.**

hector for synonyms see **bait.**

height, altitude, elevation, stature —**Height** refers to distance from bottom to top [a figurine four inches in *height*] or to distance above a given level [He dropped it from a *height* of ten feet.] **Altitude** and **elevation** refer especially to distance above a given level (usually the surface of the earth) and generally connote great distance [the *altitude* of an airplane, the *elevation* of a mountain]. **Stature** refers especially to the height of a human being standing erect [She was short in *stature*.]

heighten for synonyms see **intensify.**

heinous for synonyms see **outrageous**.

help, aid, assist, succor —**Help** is the simplest and strongest of these words meaning to supply others with whatever is necessary to accomplish their ends or relieve their wants. **Aid** and **assist** are somewhat more formal and weaker, **assist** especially implying a subordinate role in the helper and less need for help [She *assisted* him in his experiments.] **Succor** suggests timely help to one in distress [to *succor* a besieged city].

help for antonyms see **hinder**.

herald for synonyms see **forerunner**.

herd for synonyms see **group**.

hereditary for synonyms see **innate**.

heritage, inheritance, patrimony, birthright —**Heritage**, the most general of these words, applies either to property passed on to an heir, or to a tradition, culture, etc. passed on to a later generation [our *heritage* of freedom]. **Inheritance** applies to property, a characteristic, etc. passed on to an heir. **Patrimony** strictly refers to an estate inherited from one's father, but it is also used of anything passed on from an ancestor. **Birthright**, in its stricter sense, applies to the property rights of a first-born son.

hesitant for synonyms see **reluctant**.

hesitate, waver, vacillate, falter —**Hesitate** implies a pause or delay signifying indecision or reluctance [I *hesitated* to ask him.] **Waver** suggests especially a holding back or hesitating after a course or decision has been adopted [Do not *waver* in your resolution.] **Vacillate** implies a shifting back and forth in a decision, opinion, etc., resulting in continued hesitation [She *vacillates* in her affection.] **Falter** suggests a pausing or slowing down, as in fear or irresolution [They never *faltered* in the counterattack.]

hide, conceal, secrete, cache, bury —**Hide,** the general word, refers to the putting of something in a place where it will not easily be seen or found [*Hide* your money under the mattress.] **Conceal,** a somewhat formal equivalent for **hide,** more often implies deceitful intent [to *conceal* one's face, to *conceal* one's motives]. **Secrete** and **cache** suggest a careful hiding in a secret place [They *secreted,* or *cached,* the loot in the cellar.], but **cache** now often refers merely to a storing for safekeeping [Let's *cache* our supplies in the cave.] **Bury** implies a covering for, or as if for, concealment [Pirates *bury* treasure. The mountain climbers were *buried* in the landslide.]

hide for antonyms see **reveal, show.**

high, tall, lofty, towering —**High** refers to something which has greater extension upward than is normal for its kind, or which is placed at a relatively great distance above the given level [a *high* mountain, *high* clouds], but is never used of persons. **Tall** is more or less equivalent to **high** but specifically implies relatively small breadth or width [a *tall* woman]. **Lofty** and **towering** suggest great, imposing, or conspicuous height [*lofty* peaks, a *towering* castle]. —*Antonyms:* **low, short.**

hilarity for synonyms see **mirth.**

hinder, obstruct, block, impede, bar —**Hinder** implies a holding back of something about to begin and connotes a thwarting of progress [*hindered* by a lack of education]. (*See also synonyms at* **delay.**) **Obstruct** implies a retarding of passage or progress by placing obstacles in the way [to *obstruct* the passage of a bill by a filibuster]. **Block** implies the complete, but not necessarily permanent, obstruction of a passage or progress [The road was *blocked* by a landslide.] **Impede** suggests a slowing up of movement or progress by interfering with the normal action [Tight garters *impede* the circulation of the blood.] **Bar** implies an obstructing as if by means of a barrier [He was *barred* from the club.] —*Antonym:* **further.** *For other antonyms see* **advance, help.**

hindrance for synonyms see **obstacle.**

hint for synonyms see **suggest.**

hire, let, lease, rent, charter —To **hire,** in strict usage, means to get, and **let** means to give, the use of something in return for payment, although **hire,** which is also applied to persons or their services, may be used in either sense [to *hire* a hall, to *hire* a worker, rooms to *let*]. **Lease** implies the letting or the hiring of property (usually real property) by written contract. **Rent** implies payment of a specific amount, usually at fixed intervals, for hiring or letting a house, land, or other property. **Charter** implies the hiring or leasing of a ship, bus, etc.

hit for synonyms see **strike.**

hoax for synonyms see **cheat.**

hoist for synonyms see **lift.**

hold for synonyms see **contain, have.**

hole, hollow, cavity, excavation —**Hole** is the general word for an open space in a thing and may suggest a depression in a surface or an opening from surface to surface [a *hole* in the ground, a *hole* in a sock]. **Hollow** basically suggests an empty space within a solid body, whether or not it extends to the surface, but it may also be applied to a depressed place in a surface [a wooded *hollow*]. **Cavity,** the Latin-derived equivalent of **hollow,** has special application in formal and scientific usage [the thoracic *cavity*]. An **excavation** is a hollow made in or through ground by digging [the *excavations* at Pompeii].

hollow for synonyms see **hole** and **vain.**

holy, sacred, consecrated, hallowed, divine —Holy suggests that which is held in deepest religious reverence or is basically associated with a religion and, in extended use, connotes spiritual purity [the *Holy* Ghost, a *holy* love]. **Sacred** refers to that which is set apart as holy or is dedicated to some exalted purpose and, therefore, connotes inviolability [Parnassus was *sacred* to Apollo. Guarding the church property is a *sacred* trust.] **Consecrated** and **hallowed** describe that which has been made sacred or holy, **consecrated**, in addition connoting solemn devotion or dedication [a life *consecrated* to art], and **hallowed**, inherent or intrinsic holiness [*hallowed* ground]. **Divine** suggests that which is of the nature of, is associated with, or is derived from God or a god [the *divine* right of kings], and, in extended use, connotes supreme greatness [the *Divine* Duse] or, colloquially, great attractiveness. —*Antonyms:* **profane, unholy.**

homage for synonyms see **allegiance, honor.**

honest for synonyms see **upright.**

honest for antonyms see **dishonest.**

honesty, honor, integrity, probity, veracity —Honesty, the most general of these terms, implies freedom from lying, stealing, cheating, etc. [*Honesty* is the best policy.] **Honor** implies faithful adherence to the moral or ethical principles that are expected of one in a given social class, profession, position, etc. [*honor* among thieves]. **Integrity** implies an incorruptible soundness of moral character, especially as displayed in fulfilling trusts [Elect men of *integrity*.] **Probity** suggests honesty or rectitude that is tried and proved. **Veracity** specifically stresses honesty as displayed in habitual truthfulness [a witness of unquestioned *veracity*]. —*Antonyms:* **dishonesty, deceitfulness.**

honor, homage, reverence, deference —Honor, as compared here, implies popular acknowledgment of one's right to great respect as well as any expression of such respect [in *honor* of the martyred dead]. (*See also synonyms at* **honesty.**) **Homage** suggests great esteem shown in praise, tributes, or obeisance [to pay *homage* to the genius of Milton]. **Reverence** implies deep respect together with love [He held her memory in *reverence*.] **Deference** suggests a display of courteous regard for a superior, or for one to whom respect is due, by yielding to his or her claims or wishes [in *deference* to his age].

honor for antonyms see **disgrace.**

honorable for synonyms see **upright.**

hop for synonyms see **skip.**

hope for synonyms see **expect.**

hopeless, despondent, despairing, desperate —**Hopeless** means having no expectation of, or showing no sign of, a favorable outcome [a *hopeless* situation]. **Despondent** implies a being in very low spirits due to a loss of hope and a sense of futility about continuing one's efforts [Her rejection of his suit left him *despondent*.] **Despairing** implies utter loss of hope and may suggest the extreme dejection that results [The *despairing* lover spoke of suicide.] **Desperate** implies such despair as makes one resort to extreme measures [Hunger makes people *desperate*.] —*Antonyms:* **hopeful, optimistic.**

horde for synonyms see **crowd.**

horizontal for synonyms see **level.**

horizontal for antonyms see **vertical.**

horrify for synonyms see **dismay.**

host for synonyms see **crowd.**

hostage for synonyms see **pledge.**

hostility for synonyms see **enmity.**

hound for synonyms see **bait**.

hover for synonyms see **fly**.

hubbub for synonyms see **noise**.

hue for synonyms see **color**.

huge, enormous, immense, gigantic, colossal, mammoth, tremendous —**Huge** usually suggests an immense mass or bulk [a *huge* building, *huge* profits]. **Enormous** implies an exceeding by far what is normal in size, amount, or degree [an *enormous* nose, *enormous* expenses]. **Immense**, basically implying immeasurableness, suggests size beyond the regular run of measurements but does not connote abnormality in that which is very large [Redwoods are *immense* trees.] **Gigantic**, **colossal**, and **mammoth** basically imply a likeness to specific objects of great size (respectively, a giant, the Colossus of Rhodes, and the huge, extinct elephant) and therefore emphasize the idea of great magnitude, force, importance, etc., now often hyperbolically. **Tremendous**, literally suggesting that which inspires awe or amazement because of its great size, is also used loosely as an intensive term.

humane for synonyms see **kind**.

humane for antonyms see **cruel**.

humanitarian for synonyms see **philanthropic**.

humble, lowly, meek, modest —**Humble**, in a favorable sense, suggests an unassuming character in which there is an absence of pride and assertiveness [a *humble* genius] and, unfavorably, connotes an almost abject lack of self-respect. (*See also synonyms at* **degrade**.) **Lowly** is an older equivalent for **humble** but never carries the unfavorable connotation of abjectness [He answered in *lowly* terms.] **Meek** stresses a mildness and patience of disposition which is not easily stirred to anger or resentment and, in an unfavorable sense, connotes spineless submissiveness. **Modest** implies the absence of pretensions, boastfulness, conceit, etc. [to be *modest* about one's achievements]. —*Antonym:* **conceited.** *For other antonyms see* **proud.**

humid for synonyms see **wet.**

humiliate for synonyms see **degrade.**

humiliated for synonyms see **ashamed.**

humor for synonyms see **indulge** and **mood, wit.**

humorous for synonyms see **witty.**

hungry, ravenous, famished, starved —Hungry is the general word expressing any degree of wanting or needing food. **Ravenous** suggests extreme, often frenzied hunger, but may imply mere greediness. **Famished** suggests hunger to the point of actual weakness or suffering. **Starved** implies a continued lack or inadequacy of food resulting in emaciation or death. Both **famished** and **starved** are often used colloquially as hyperbolic equivalents of **hungry.** —*Antonyms:* **sated, satiated.**

hurl for synonyms see **throw.**

hurry for synonyms see **haste.**

hurt for synonyms see **injure.**

hushed for synonyms see **still.**

hypercritical for synonyms see **critical.**

hypothesis for synonyms see **theory.**

hysteria for synonyms see **mania.**

I

idea, concept, conception, thought, notion, impression —**Idea**, the most general of these terms, may be applied to anything existing in the mind as an object of knowledge or thought. **Concept** refers to a generalized idea of a class of objects, based on knowledge of particular instances of the class [his *concept* of a republic]. **Conception**, often equivalent to **concept**, specifically refers to something conceived in the mind, or imagined [my *conception* of how the role should be played]. **Thought** is used of any idea, whether or not expressed, that occurs to the mind in reasoning or contemplation [She rarely speaks her *thoughts*.] **Notion** implies vagueness or incomplete intention [I had a *notion* to go.] **Impression** also implies vagueness of an idea provoked by some external stimulus [I have the *impression* that she's unhappy.]

identical for synonyms see **same**.

identical for antonyms see **opposite**.

idiosyncrasy, eccentricity —**Idiosyncrasy** refers to any personal mannerism or peculiarity and connotes strong individuality [the *idiosyncrasies* of a writer's style]. **Eccentricity** implies considerable deviation from what is normal or customary and connotes whimsicality or even mental aberration [His *eccentricity* of wearing overshoes in the summer.]

idle for synonyms see **inactive** and **loiter**.

idle for antonyms see **busy**.

ignoble for synonyms see **base**[2].

ignominy for synonyms see **disgrace**.

ignorant, illiterate, unlettered, uneducated, untutored, unlearned —Ignorant implies a lack of knowledge, either generally [an *ignorant* man] or on some particular subject [*ignorant* of the reason for their quarrel]. **Illiterate** implies a failure to conform to some standard of knowledge, especially an inability to read or write. **Unlettered**, sometimes a milder term for **illiterate**, often implies unfamiliarity with fine literature [Although a graduate engineer, he is relatively *unlettered*.] **Uneducated** and **untutored** imply a lack of formal or systematic education, as of that acquired in schools [his brilliant, though *uneducated*, mind]. **Unlearned** suggests a lack of learning, either generally or in some specific subject [*unlearned* in science]. —*Antonyms:* **educated, erudite, learned.**

ignore for synonyms see **neglect.**
ill for synonyms see **bad, sick.**
ill for antonyms see **healthy, well.**
illegal, unlawful, illicit —Illegal and unlawful are both applied to actions that are against the law, but **unlawful** may also be used of actions that are immoral or unethical [*illegal* parking, an *unlawful* association]. **Illicit** is applied to actions that are against the law, the customs, or the rules of a society [an *illicit* romance].
illegal for antonyms see **legal.**
illicit for synonyms see **illegal.**
illicit for antonyms see **legal.**
illiterate for synonyms see **ignorant.**
ill-mannered for synonyms see **rude.**
ill-natured for synonyms see **unfeeling.**
ill-natured for antonyms see **amiable.**
illusion for synonyms see **delusion.**
illustration for synonyms see **instance.**

illustrious for synonyms see **famous**.

ill will for synonyms see **malice**.

imaginary, fanciful, visionary, fantastic —**Imaginary** applies to that which exists in the imagination only and is, therefore, unreal [*imaginary* enemies]. **Fanciful** refers to that which has been conceived in the fancy and usually connotes quaintness or whimsicality [*fanciful* tales]. **Visionary** refers to something unreal conceived of in, or as in, a vision and usually connotes impracticality [The airplane was once a *visionary* dream.] **Fantastic** applies to something which seems to be so highly fanciful or odd as to be beyond belief [a *fantastic* scheme for storing energy]. —*Antonyms:* **real, actual**.

imitate, copy, mimic, mock, ape —**Imitate** implies the following of something as an example or model but does not necessarily connote exact correspondence with the original [The child *imitates* the father's mannerisms.] **Copy** implies as nearly exact imitation or reproduction as is possible [to *copy* a painting]. **Mimic** suggests close imitation, often in fun or ridicule [to *mimic* the speech peculiarities of another]. **Mock** implies imitation with the intent to deride or affront ["I can't" she echoed *mockingly.*] **Ape** implies close imitation either in mimicry or in servile emulation [She *aped* the fashions of the court ladies.]

immature, unripe —**Immature** and **unripe** may be used interchangeably in speaking of fruits or vegetables that are not yet ready for harvest, but **immature** is used also of people who have not reached full development physically or emotionally.

immature for antonyms see **ripe**.

immense for synonyms see **huge**.

immigrant for synonyms see **alien**.

immigrate for synonyms see **migrate**.

immoderate for synonyms see **excessive**.

immoral, lewd, wanton —Immoral is the basic word in referring to behavior that is against the moral code of a community, and is sometimes used specifically of sexual behavior that is not in conformity with accepted standards. **Lewd** is used of behavior that is deliberately intended to excite lust, especially in an offensive manner [a *lewd* gesture]. **Wanton** is used of unchaste and unrestrained sexual activity [*wanton* behavior].

immoral for antonyms see **chaste, moral**.

immunity for synonyms see **exemption**.

impair for synonyms see **injure**.

impair for antonyms see **improve**.

impartial for synonyms see **fair**.

impassioned for synonyms see **passionate**.

impassive, apathetic, stoic, stolid, phlegmatic —Impassive means not having or showing any feeling or emotion, although it does not necessarily connote an incapability of being affected [His *impassive* face did not betray his anguish.] **Apathetic** stresses an indifference or listlessness from which one cannot easily be stirred to feeling [an *apathetic* electorate]. **Stoic** implies an austere indifference to pleasure or pain and specifically suggests the ability to endure suffering without flinching [He received the bad news with *stoic* calm.] **Stolid** suggests dullness, obtuseness, or stupidity in one who is not easily moved or excited. **Phlegmatic** is applied to one who by temperament is not easily disconcerted or aroused.

impeach for synonyms see **accuse**.

impecunious for synonyms see **poor**.

impede for synonyms see **delay, hinder**.

impediment for synonyms see **obstacle**.

imperfection for synonyms see **defect**.

imperious for synonyms see **masterful**.

imperious for antonyms see **servile**.

impertinent, impudent, insolent, saucy —**Impertinent** implies a forwardness of speech or action that is disrespectful and oversteps the bounds of propriety or courtesy. **Impudent** implies a shameless or brazen impertinence. **Insolent** implies defiant disrespect as displayed in openly insulting and contemptuous speech or behavior. **Saucy** implies a flippancy and provocative levity toward one to whom respect should be shown.

impetuous for synonyms see **sudden**.

implacable for synonyms see **inflexible**.

implant for synonyms see **instill**.

implement, tool, instrument, appliance, utensil —**Implement** applies to any device used to carry on some work or effect some purpose [agricultural *implements*]. **Tool** is commonly applied to manual implements such as are used in carpentry, plumbing, etc. **Instrument** specifically implies use for delicate work or for scientific or artistic purposes [surgical *instruments*] and may also be applied, as are **tool** and **implement**, to a thing or person serving as a means to an end. **Appliance** specifically suggests a mechanical or power-driven device, especially one for household use. **Utensil** is used of any implement or container for domestic use, especially a pot, pan, etc.

implore for synonyms see **beg**.

imply for synonyms see **suggest**.

impolite for synonyms see **rude**.

import for synonyms see **meaning**.

importance, consequence, moment, weight, significance —**Importance**, the broadest of these terms, implies greatness of worth, meaning, influence, etc. [news of *importance*]. **Consequence**, often interchangeable with the preceding, more specifically suggests importance with regard to outcome or result [a disagreement of no *consequence*]. **Moment** expresses this same idea of importance in effect with somewhat stronger force [affairs of great *moment*]. **Weight** implies an estimation of the relative importance of something [His word carries great *weight* with us.] **Significance** implies an importance or momentousness because of a special meaning that may or may not be immediately apparent [an event of *significance*].

important for antonyms see **petty**.

importune for synonyms see **beg, urge**.

imposing for synonyms see **grand**.

impostor for synonyms see **quack**.

impotent for synonyms see **sterile**.

impoverished for synonyms see **poor**.

imprecate for synonyms see **curse**.

impregnate for synonyms see **soak**.

impress for synonyms see **affect**.

impression for synonyms see **idea**.

improbable for synonym see **unlikely**.

improbable for antonyms see **probable**.

impromptu, extemporaneous, extempore, extemporary, improvised —Impromptu is applied to that which is spoken, made, or done on the spur of the moment to suit the occasion and stresses spontaneity. **Extemporaneous, extempore** (more commonly used as an adverb), and **extemporary** may express the same idea but are now more often used of a speech that has received some preparation, but has not been written out or memorized. **Improvised** applies to something composed

also connotes such harshness or sarcasm as to hurt the feelings [his *cutting* allusion to her inefficiency]. **Biting** implies a caustic or stinging quality that makes a deep impression on the mind [her *biting* satire].

incite, instigate, arouse, foment —**Incite** implies an urging or stimulating to action, either in a favorable or unfavorable sense [*incited* to achievement by rivalry]. **Instigate** always implies responsibility for initiating the action and usually connotes a bad or evil purpose [Who *instigated* the assassination?] **Arouse,** in this connection, means little more than a bringing into being or action [It *aroused* my suspicions.] **Foment** suggests continued incitement over an extended period of time [The unjust taxes *fomented* rebellion.]

incite for antonyms see **restrain.**

inclination, leaning, bent, propensity, proclivity —**Inclination** refers to a more or less vague mental disposition toward some action, practice, or thing [He had an *inclination* to refuse.] **Leaning** suggests a general inclination toward something but implies only the direction of attraction and not the final choice [Dr. Green had always had a *leaning* toward the study of law.] **Bent** and **propensity** imply a natural or inherent inclination, the latter also connoting an almost uncontrollable attraction [She has a *bent* for art. He has a *propensity* for getting into trouble.] **Proclivity** usually suggests strong inclination as a result of habitual indulgence, usually toward something bad or wrong [a *proclivity* to falsehood].

inclined for antonyms see **reluctant.**

include, comprise, comprehend, embrace, involve —**Include** implies a containing as part of a whole. **Comprise,** in discriminating use, means to consist of and takes as its object the various parts that make up the whole [His library *comprises* 2000 volumes and *includes* many first editions.] **Comprehend** suggests that the object is contained within the total scope or range of the subject, sometimes by implication [The word "beauty" *comprehends* various concepts.] **Embrace** stresses the variety of objects comprehended [He had *embraced* a number of hobbies.] **Involve** implies inclusion of an object because of its connection with the subject as a consequence or antecedent [Acceptance of the office *involves* responsibilities.]

include for antonyms see **exclude**.

incognito for synonyms see **pseudonym**.

inconstant, fickle, capricious, unstable —**Inconstant** implies an inherent tendency to change or a lack of steadfastness [an *inconstant* lover]. **Fickle** suggests an even greater instability or readiness to change, especially in affection [spurned by a *fickle* public]. **Capricious** implies an instability or irregularity that seems to be the product of whim or erratic impulse [a *capricious* decision to leave town]. **Unstable**, in this connection, applies to one who is emotionally unsettled or variable [An *unstable* person laughs and cries easily.] —*Antonym:* **constant**. *For other antonyms see* **reliable**.

increase, enlarge, augment, multiply —**Increase**, the general word in this list, means to make or become greater in size, amount, degree, etc. [to *increase* one's weight, to *increase* one's power, to *increase* debts]. **Enlarge** specifically implies a making or becoming greater in size, volume, extent, etc. [to *enlarge* a house, to *enlarge* a business]. **Augment**, a more formal word, generally implies increase by addition, often of something that is already of a considerable size, amount, etc. [to *augment* one's income]. **Multiply** suggests increase in number,

specifically by procreation [Rabbits *multiply* rapidly.]
increase for antonyms see **decrease, wane**.
incredulity for synonyms see **unbelief**.
incredulity for antonyms see **belief**.
inculcate for synonyms see **instill**.
incurious for synonyms see **indifferent**.
incurious for antonyms see **curious**.
indecent, indecorous for synonyms see **improper**.
indelicate for synonyms see **coarse, improper**.
indemnification for synonyms see **reparation**.
indemnify for synonyms see **pay**.
indication for synonyms see **sign**.
indict for synonyms see **accuse**.
indifferent, unconcerned, incurious, detached, disinterested —Indifferent implies either apathy or neutrality, especially with reference to choice [to remain *indifferent* in a dispute]. **Unconcerned** implies a lack of concern, solicitude, or anxiety, as because of callousness, ingenuousness, etc. [to remain *unconcerned* in a time of danger]. **Incurious** suggests a lack of interest or curiosity [*incurious* about the details]. **Detached** implies an impartiality or aloofness resulting from a lack of emotional involvement in a situation [He viewed the struggle with *detached* interest.] **Disinterested** strictly implies a commendable impartiality resulting from a lack of selfish motive or desire for personal gain [a *disinterested* journalist], but it is now often used colloquially to mean not interested, or indifferent.
indigence for synonyms see **poverty**.
indigenous for synonyms see **native**.
indigent for synonyms see **poor**.
indignation for synonyms see **anger**.
indispensable for synonyms see **essential**.

indisposed for synonyms see **sick**.
indisposed for antonyms see **likely, healthy**.
individual for synonyms see **characteristic** and **single**.
indolent for synonyms see **lazy**.
indolent for antonyms see **busy**.
induce for synonyms see **persuade**.
inducement for synonyms see **motive**.
indulge, humor, pamper, spoil, baby —Indulge implies
a yielding to the wishes or desires of oneself or another,
as because of a weak will or an amiable nature. **Humor**
suggests compliance with the mood or whim of another
[They *humored* the dying man.] **Pamper** implies overin-
dulgence or excessive gratification. **Spoil** emphasizes
the harm done to the personality or character by overin-
dulgence or excessive attention [Grandparents often *spoil*
children.] **Baby** suggests the sort of pampering and devoted care lavished on infants and connotes a potential
loss of self-reliance [Because he was sickly, his mother
continued to *baby* him.] —*Antonyms:* **discipline, restrain**.
industrious for synonyms see **busy**.
industry for synonyms see **business**.
inebriated for synonyms see **drunk**.
inelastic for synonyms see **stiff**.
inept for synonyms see **awkward**.
inept for antonyms see **able, dexterous**.
inert for synonyms see **inactive**.
inexpensive for synonym see **cheap**.
infamous for synonyms see **vicious**.
infamy for synonyms see **disgrace**.
infatuation for synonyms see **love**.
infer, deduce, conclude, judge, gather —Infer suggests
the arriving at a decision or opinion by reasoning from

known facts or evidence [From your smile. I *inf* you're pleased.] **Deduce**, in strict discrimination, plies inference from a general principle by logical rea soning [The method was *deduced* from earlier experiments.] **Conclude** strictly implies an inference that is the final logical result in a process of reasoning [I must, therefore, *conclude* that you are wrong.] **Judge** stresses the careful checking and weighing of premises, etc. in arriving at a conclusion. **Gather** is an informal substitute for **infer** or **conclude** [I *gather* that you don't care.]

infertile for synonyms see **sterile**.

infidel for synonyms see **atheist**.

infirm for synonyms see **weak**.

infirm for antonyms see **healthy**.

inflate for synonyms see **expand**.

inflate for antonyms see **contract**.

inflexible, adamant, implacable, obdurate —**Inflexible** implies an unyielding or unshakable firmness in mind or purpose, sometimes connoting stubbornness [his *inflexible* attitude]. (*See also synonyms at* **stiff**.) **Adamant** implies a firm or unbreakable resolve that remains unaffected by temptation or pleading [*adamant* to her entreaties]. **Implacable** suggests the impossibility of pacifying or appeasing [*implacable* in his hatred]. **Obdurate** implies a hardheartedness that is not easily moved to pity, sympathy, or forgiveness [her *obdurate* refusal to help]. —*Antonyms:* **flexible, yielding, compliant.**

influence, authority, prestige, weight —**Influence** implies the power of persons or things (whether or not exerted consciously or overtly) to affect others [He owed his position to *influence*.] (*See also synonyms at* **effect**.) **Authority** implies the power to command acceptance, belief, obedience, etc., based on strength of character, expertness of knowledge, etc. [a statement made on good *authority*]. **Prestige** implies the power to command esteem or admiration, based on brilliance of achievement or outstanding superiority. **Weight** implies influence that is more or less preponderant in its effect [He threw his *weight* to the opposition.]

inform for synonyms see **notify**.

information, knowledge, learning, erudition, wisdom —Information applies to facts that are gathered in any way, as by reading, observation, hearsay, etc. and does not necessarily connote validity [inaccurate *information*]. **Knowledge** applies to any body of facts gathered by study, observation, etc. and to the ideas inferred from these facts, and connotes an understanding of what is known [man's *knowledge* of the universe]. **Learning** is knowledge acquired by study, especially in languages, literature, philosophy, etc. **Erudition** implies profound or abstruse learning beyond the comprehension of most people. **Wisdom** implies superior judgment and understanding based on broad knowledge. —Antonym: **ignorance**.

infrequent for synonyms see **rare**.
infringe for synonyms see **trespass**.
infuse for synonyms see **instill**.
ingenious for synonyms see **clever**.
ingenuous for synonyms see **naive**.
ingredient for synonyms see **element**.
inheritance for synonyms see **heritage**.
inhibit for synonyms see **restrain**.
inhibit for antonyms see **incite**.
inhuman for synonyms see **cruel**.
iniquitous for synonyms see **vicious**.
initiate for synonyms see **begin**.

injure, harm, damage, hurt, impair, spoil —**Injure** implies the marring of the appearance, health, soundness, etc. of a person or thing [*injured* pride]. **Harm** more strongly suggests the pain or distress caused [He wouldn't *harm* a fly.] **Damage** stresses the loss, as in value or usefulness, resulting from an injury [*damaged* goods]. **Hurt** implies a wounding physically or emotionally or a causing of any kind of harm or damage [The rumors *hurt* his business.] To **impair** something is to cause it to deteriorate in quality or to lessen in value, strength, etc. [*impaired* hearing]. **Spoil** implies such serious impairment of a thing as to destroy its value or usefulness [The canned food was *spoiled*.]

injury for synonyms see **injustice**.

injustice, injury, wrong, grievance —**Injustice** implies unjust treatment of another or a violation of his or her rights. **Injury** and **wrong** have special application to injustices for the redress or punishment of which legal action can be taken, both applying to a violation of the private rights of an individual, and **wrong** alone, to crimes and misdemeanors which affect the whole community. A **grievance** is a circumstance considered by the person affected to be unjust and ground for complaint or resentment. —*Antonym:* **justice**.

innate, inborn, inbred, congenital, hereditary —**Innate** and **inborn** are often interchangeable, but **innate** has more extensive connotations, describing that which belongs to something as part of its nature or constitution, and **inborn**, the simpler term, more specifically suggesting qualities so much a part of one's nature as to seem to have been born in or with one [*inborn* modesty]. **Inbred** refers to qualities that are deeply ingrained by breeding [an *inbred* love of learning]. **Congenital** implies existence at or from one's birth, specifically as a result of prenatal environment [*congenital* blindness]. **Hereditary** implies acquirement of characteristics by transmission genetically from parents or ancestors [*hereditary* blondness].

innocuous for synonym see **harmless**.

innocuous for antonyms see **pernicious**.

innumerable for synonyms see **many**.

inordinate for synonyms see **excessive**.

inquest for synonyms see **investigation**.

inquire for synonyms see **ask**.

inquire for antonyms see **answer**.

inquisition for synonyms see **investigation**.

inquisitive for synonyms see **curious**.

insanity, lunacy, dementia, psychosis —**Insanity**, current in popular and legal language but not used technically in medicine, implies mental derangement in one who formerly had mental health. **Lunacy** specifically suggests periodic spells of insanity, but is now most commonly used in its extended sense of extreme folly. **Dementia** is the general term for an acquired mental disorder, now generally one of organic origin, as distinguished from *amentia* (congenital mental deficiency.) **Psychosis** is the psychiatric term for any of various specialized mental disorders, functional or organic, in which the personality is seriously disorganized. —*Antonym:* **sanity**.

inscrutable for synonyms see **mysterious**.

inseminate for synonyms see **instill**.

insert for synonyms see **introduce**.

insinuate for synonyms see **introduce, suggest**.

insipid, vapid, flat, banal —**Insipid** implies a lack of taste or flavor and is, hence, figuratively applied to anything that is lifeless or dull [*insipid* table talk]. **Vapid** and **flat** apply to that which once had, but has since lost, freshness, sharpness, tang, or zest [the *vapid*, or *flat*, epi- grams that had once so delighted him]. **Banal** is used of that which is so trite or hackneyed as to seem highly vapid or flat [her *banal* compliments]. —*Antonym:* **zest- ful.** *For other antonyms see* **pungent.**

insolent for synonyms see **impertinent.**

inspect for synonyms see **scrutinize.**

instance, case, example, illustration —**Instance** refers to a person, thing, or event that is adduced to prove or support a general statement [Here is an *instance* of his sincerity.] **Case** is applied to any happening or condi- tion that demonstrates the general existence or occur- rence of something [a *case* of mistaken identity]. **Ex- ample** is applied to something that is cited as typical of the members of its group [His novel is an *example* of ro- mantic literature.] **Illustration** is used of an instance or example that helps to explain or clarify something [This sentence is an *illustration* of the use of a word.]

instigate for synonyms see **incite.**

instill, implant, inculcate, infuse, inseminate —**In- still,** in this figurative connection, implies a gradual im- parting of knowledge over an extended period of time [He had *instilled* honesty in his children.] **Implant** sug- gests the imparting of knowledge as if by planting it in the mind, with the implication that it will develop there. **Inculcate** implies frequent or insistent repetition so as to impress upon the mind [Prejudice is *inculcated* in one during childhood.] **Infuse** suggests the imparting of qualities as if by pouring [He *infused* life into the play.] **Inseminate** implies the spreading of ideas throughout a group, nation, etc. as if by sowing seeds.

instinctive for synonyms see **spontaneous**.

instruct for synonyms see **command, teach**.

instrument for synonyms see **implement**.

insult for synonyms see **offend**.

insurrection for synonyms see **rebellion**.

intact for synonyms see **complete**.

integrity for synonyms see **honesty**.

intellectual for synonyms see **intelligent**.

intelligent, clever, alert, bright, smart, brilliant, intellectual —Intelligent implies the ability to learn or understand from experience or to respond successfully to a new experience. **Clever** implies quickness in learning or understanding, but sometimes connotes a lack of thoroughness or depth. **Alert** emphasizes quickness in sizing up a situation. **Bright** and **smart** are somewhat informal, less precise equivalents for any of the preceding. **Brilliant** implies an unusually high degree of intelligence. **Intellectual** suggests keen intelligence coupled with interest and ability in the more advanced fields of knowledge. —*Antonym:* **dull**. *For other antonyms see* **silly, stupid.**

intend, mean, design, propose, purpose —Intend implies a having in mind of something to be done, said, etc. [I *intended* to write you.] **Mean**, a more general word, does not connote so clearly a specific, deliberate purpose [He always *means* well.] **Design** suggests careful planning in order to bring about a particular result [Their delay was *designed* to forestall suspicion.] **Propose** implies a clear declaration, openly or to oneself, of one's intention [I *propose* to speak for an hour.] **Purpose** adds to **propose** a connotation of strong determination to effect one's intention [He *purposes* to become a doctor.]

intensify, aggravate, heighten, enhance —Intensify

implies an increasing in the degree of force, vehemence, vividness, etc. [His absence only *intensified* her longing.] **Aggravate** implies a making more serious, unbearable, etc. and connotes something that is unpleasant or troublesome in itself [Your insolence only *aggravates* the offense.] To **heighten** is to make greater, stronger, more vivid, etc. or to raise above the ordinary or commonplace [Music served to *heighten* the effect.] **Enhance** implies the addition of something so as to make more attractive or desirable [She used cosmetics to *enhance* her beauty.] —*Antonyms:* **diminish, mitigate.**

intent for synonyms see **intention.**

intention, intent, purpose, aim, goal, end, object, objective —**Intention** is the general word implying a having something in mind as a plan or design, or referring to the plan had in mind. **Intent,** a somewhat formal term now largely in legal usage, connotes more deliberation [assault with *intent* to kill]. **Purpose** connotes greater resolution or determination in the plan [I have a *purpose* in writing you.] **Aim** refers to a specific intention and connotes a directing of all efforts toward this [His *aim* is to become a doctor.] **Goal** suggests laborious effort in striving to attain something [The presidency was the *goal* of his ambition.] **End** emphasizes the final result one hopes to achieve as distinct from the process of achieving it [Is this *end* justified by the means used?] **Object** is used of an end that is the direct result of a need or desire [The *object* of the discussion was to arouse controversy.] **Objective** refers to a specific end that is capable of being reached [Her immediate *objective* is to pass the course.]

intentional for synonyms see **voluntary.**

intercede for synonyms see **interpose.**

interdict for synonyms see **forbid**.

interfere for synonyms see **interpose**.

interject for synonyms see **introduce**.

interlope for synonyms see **intrude**.

itermittent, recurrent, periodic, alternate —**Intermittent** and **recurrent** both apply to something that stops and starts, or disappears and reappears, from time to time, but the former usually stresses the breaks or pauses, and the latter, the repetition or return [an *intermittent* fever, *recurrent* attacks of the hives]. **Periodic** refers to something that recurs at more or less regular intervals [*periodic* economic crises]. **Alternate** is usually used of two recurrent things that follow each other in regular order [a life of *alternate* sorrow and joy]. —*Antonym:* **continued.** *For other antonyms see* **continual**.

interpolate for synonyms see **introduce**.

interpose, intervene, interfere, intercede, mediate —**Interpose**, in this comparison, is the general word, meaning no more than to introduce action, a remark, etc. in some conversation or affair, with no further implication of motive or effect. (*See also synonyms at* **introduce**.) **Intervene** implies an interposing in order to modify action, adjust differences, etc. [to *intervene* in the internal affairs of another country]. **Interfere** implies an interposing actively in order to hinder action or effect certain results [Don't *interfere* in their decision to move.] **Intercede** suggests an intervening in order to plead or argue on behalf of another [He *interceded* for the accused.] **Mediate** implies intervention by someone in order to reconcile, or effect a compromise between, opposing parties [to *mediate* a labor dispute].

interpret for synonyms see **explain**.

interrogate for synonyms see **ask**.

intervene for synonyms see **interpose**.

intimate for synonyms see **familiar** and **suggest**.

intoxicated for synonyms see **drunk**.

intractable for synonyms see **unruly**.

intrepid for synonyms see **brave**.

intricate for synonyms see **complex**.

intrigue for synonyms see **conspiracy**.

introduce, insert, insinuate, interpolate, interpose, interject —Introduce implies the bringing or putting of someone or something into a place, position, notice, etc., sometimes stressing this as an innovation [to *introduce* a new song to the public]. **Insert** suggests the putting of something into a hole or gap or between two things [*Insert* the candle into the holder.] **Insinuate** implies the slow, indirect, but skillful introduction of something [He *insinuated* himself into her trust.] **Interpolate** refers to the introduction of new words or passages, especially of spurious copy, into a writing [Certain phrases in his book were *interpolated* by the editor.] **Interpose**, in this connection, and **interject** imply the introduction of a comment or opinion that serves to interrupt [if I may *interpose*, or *interject*, a few remarks at this point]. —*Antonyms:* **withdraw, remove.**

introduction, preface, foreword, preamble, prologue —Introduction, in strict usage, refers to the preliminary section of a book or other writing that explains and leads into the subject proper. **Preface** strictly refers to a statement preliminary to, and distinct from, a book, etc. written by the author or someone else and explaining the purpose, plan, or preparation of the work. **Foreword** is usually used for a very brief or simple preface. **Preamble** refers to a formal, but usually brief, introduction to a constitution, treaty, etc. **Prologue** applies to the preliminary section of a play, poem, etc., serving as an introduction and, in the play, frequently spoken by one of the characters. —*Antonyms:* **conclusion, epilogue.**

intrude, obtrude, interlope, butt in —**Intrude** implies the forcing of oneself or something upon another without invitation, permission, or welcome [to *intrude* upon another's privacy]. (*See also synonyms at* **trespass.**) **Obtrude** connotes even more strongly the distractive nature or the undesirability of the invasion [Side issues keep *obtruding.*] **Interlope** implies an intrusion upon the rights or privileges of another to the disadvantage or harm of the latter [The *interloping* merchants have ruined our trade.] **Butt in** (or **into**) is a slang term implying intrusion in a meddling or officious way [Stop *butting into* my business.]

invade for synonyms see **trespass.**

invalidate for synonyms see **nullify.**

invaluable for synonyms see **costly.**

inveigle for synonyms see **lure.**

inventory for synonyms see **list.**

invert for synonyms see **reverse.**

investigation, probe, inquest, inquisition, research —**Investigation** refers to a detailed examination or search, often formal or official, to uncover facts and determine the truth [the *investigation* of a crime]. **Probe** applies to an extensive, searching investigation, as by an appointed committee, of alleged corrupt practices, etc. **Inquest** now refers to a judicial inquiry, especially one conducted by a coroner to determine the cause of a suspicious death. **Inquisition** strictly refers to any penetrating investigation, but because of its application to the ecclesiastical inquiries for the suppression of heresy, it now usually connotes ruthless, hounding persecution. **Re-**

search implies careful, patient study and investigation from original sources of information, as by scientists or scholars.

inveterate for synonyms see **chronic.**

invigorate for synonyms see **animate.**

invite for synonyms see **call.**

involuntary for synonyms see **spontaneous.**

involved for synonyms see **complex.**

irascible for synonyms see **irritable.**

ire for synonyms see **anger.**

irk for synonyms see **annoy.**

ironical for synonyms see **sarcastic.**

irony for synonyms see **wit.**

irrational, unreasonable —**Irrational** implies mental unsoundness or may be used to stress the utterly illogical nature of that which is directly contrary to reason [He had an *irrational* belief that everybody was his enemy.] **Unreasonable** implies bad judgment, willfulness, prejudice, etc. as responsible for that which is not justified by reason [She made *unreasonable* demands on her friends.]

irrational for antonyms see **rational.**

irregular, abnormal, anomalous, unnatural —**Irregular** implies deviation from the customary or established rule, procedure, etc. [an *irregular* marriage]. **Abnormal** and **anomalous** imply deviation from the normal condition or from the ordinary type, **abnormal** stressing atypical form or character [a man of *abnormal* height], and **anomalous**, an exceptional condition or circumstance [in the *anomalous* position of a leader without followers]. **Unnatural** applies to that which is contrary to the order of nature or to natural laws [an *unnatural* appetite for chalk].

irregular for antonyms see **normal.**

irritable, irascible, choleric, splenetic, touchy, cranky, cross —**Irritable** implies quick excitability to annoyance or anger, usually resulting from emotional tension, restlessness, physical indisposition, etc. **Irascible** and **choleric** are applied to persons who are hot-tempered and can be roused to a fit of anger at the slightest irritation. **Splenetic** suggests a peevish moroseness in one quick to vent his or her malice or spite. **Touchy** applies to one who is acutely irritable or sensitive and is too easily offended. **Cranky** and **cross** suggest moods in which one cannot be easily pleased or satisfied, **cranky** because of stubborn notions or whims, and **cross** because of ill humor.

irritate, provoke, nettle, exasperate, peeve —**Irritate,** the broadest in scope of these terms, may suggest temporary superficial impatience, constant annoyance, or an outburst of anger in the person stirred to feeling [Their smugness *irritated* him.] To **provoke** is to arouse strong annoyance or resentment, or, sometimes, vindictive anger [*provoked* by an insult]. **Nettle** implies irritation that stings or piques rather than infuriates [sly, *nettling* remarks]. **Exasperate** implies intense irritation such as exhausts one's patience or makes one lose one's self-control [*exasperating* impudence]. **Peeve,** an informal word, means to cause to be annoyed, cross, or fretful [He seems *peeved* about something.]

isolation for synonyms see **solitude.**

issue for synonyms see **effect** and **rise.**

iterate for synonyms see **repeat.**

itinerant, ambulatory, peripatetic, nomadic, vagrant —**Itinerant** applies to persons whose work or profession requires them to travel from place to pace [*itinerant* la-

borers, an *itinerant* preacher]. **Ambulatory** specifically
implies ability to walk about [an *ambulatory* patient].
Peripatetic implies a walking or moving about in carrying on some activity and is applied humorously to persons who are always on the go. **Nomadic** is applied to
tribes or groups of people who have no permanent home,
but move about constantly in search of food for themselves, pasture for the animals they herd, etc. **Vagrant** is
applied to individuals, specifically hobos or tramps, who
wander about without a fixed home, and implies shiftlessness, disorderliness, etc.

J

jagged for synonyms see **rough**.
jargon for synonyms see **dialect**.
jaunt for synonyms see **trip**.
jeer for synonyms see **scoff**.
jeopardy for synonyms see **danger**.
jest for synonyms see **joke**.
job for synonyms see **position, task**.
jocose, jocular for synonyms see **witty**.
**join, combine, unite, connect, link, associate, con-
solidate** —Join is the general term implying a bringing
or coming together of two or more things and may suggest direct contact, affiliation, etc. **Combine** implies a
mingling together of things, often with a loss of distinction of elements that completely merge with one another
[to *combine* milk and water]. **Unite** implies a joining or
combining of things to form a single whole [the *United*
States]. **Connect** implies attachment by some fastening
or relationship [roads *connected* by a bridge, the duties

connected with a job]. **Link** stresses firmness of a connection [*linked* together in a common cause]. **Associate** implies a joining with another or others as a companion, partner, etc. and, in extended use, suggests a connection made in the mind [to *associate* Freud's name with psychoanalysis]. **Consolidate** implies a merger of distinct and separate units into a single whole for resulting compactness, strength, efficiency, etc. [to *consolidate* one's debts].

join for antonyms see **separate**.

joke, jest, quip, sally, witticism, wisecrack —Joke is the simple, basic word for anything said or done in fun or to excite laughter and may apply to remarks, anecdotes, pranks, etc. **Jest**, the more formal equivalent, usually is applied to joking language and suggests banter or light, good-natured ridicule. **Quip** and **sally** suggest a smart, neatly turned jest. A **witticism** is a witty or amusingly clever saying or remark. **Wisecrack**, a slang term, applies to a witty remark that is flippant or facetious.

jollity for synonyms see **mirth**.

journey for synonyms see **trip**.

joy for synonyms see **pleasure**.

joy for antonyms see **sorrow**.

joyful, joyous for synonyms see **happy**.

judge, arbiter, referee, umpire —Judge is applied to one who, by the authority vested in him or her or by expertness of knowledge, is qualified to settle a controversy or decide on the relative merit of things [a *judge* of a beauty contest]. (*See also* synonyms at **infer**.) **Arbiter** emphasizes the authoritativeness of decision of one whose judgment in a particular matter is considered indisputable [an *arbiter* of the social graces]. **Referee** and umpire both apply to a person to whom anything is referred for decision or settlement [a *referee* in bankruptcy] and, in sports, to officials charged with the regulation of a contest, ruling on the plays in a game, etc. [a *referee* in boxing, basketball, etc., an *umpire* in baseball, cricket, etc.]

judicious for synonyms see **wise**.
jumble for synonyms see **confusion**.
jurisdiction for synonyms see **power**.
just for synonyms see **fair, upright**.
juvenile for synonyms see **young**.

K

keen for synonyms see **cry** and **eager, sharp**.
keen for antonyms see **dull**.
keep, retain, withhold, reserve —**Keep**, a general word of broad application, in its simplest sense implies merely a continuing to have or hold. (*See also synonyms at* **celebrate**.) **Retain**, a more formal equivalent, often stresses the possibility of loss or seizure [He has managed to *retain* most of his fortune.] **Withhold** implies a keeping or holding back and connotes refusal to release [to *withhold* information]. **Reserve** implies a keeping or holding back for some time or for some future use [Is this table *reserved* for us?] —*Antonym:* **release**. *For other antonyms see* **relinquish**.
kill, slay, murder, assassinate, execute, dispatch —**Kill** is the general word in this list, meaning to cause the death of in any way and may be applied to persons, animals, or plants. **Slay**, now largely a literary word, implies deliberate and violent killing. **Murder** applies to

an unlawful and malicious or premeditated killing. **Assassinate** implies specifically the sudden killing of a politically important person by someone hired or delegated to do this. **Execute** denotes a killing in accordance with a legally imposed sentence. **Dispatch** suggests a killing by direct action, such as stabbing or shooting, and emphasizes speed or promptness.

kind, kindly, benign, benevolent, humane —Kind implies the possession of sympathetic or generous qualities, either habitually or specifically, or is applied to actions manifesting these [He is *kind* to his mother. Thank you for your *kind* remarks.] (*See also synonyms at* **type**.) **Kindly** usually implies a characteristic nature or general disposition marked by such qualities [his *kindly* old uncle]. **Benign** suggests a mild or kindly nature and is applied especially to a gracious superior [a *benign* employer]. **Benevolent** implies a charitable or altruistic inclination to do good [his *benevolent* interest in orphans]. **Humane** is used in describing one who has or shows the best qualities of humankind, such as kindness, sympathy, and mercy [a *humane* ruler].

kind for antonyms see **cruel, unkind.**

kindly for synonyms see **kind.**

kindred for synonyms see **related.**

knack for synonyms see **talent.**

knock for synonyms see **strike.**

knowledge for synonyms see **information.**

L

labor for synonyms see **work**.

laborious for synonyms see **hard**.

lack, want, need, require —**Lack** implies an absence or insufficiency of something essential or desired [She *lacks* experience.] **Want** (in this sense, chiefly British) and **need** stress the urgency of supplying what is lacking [This matter *needs*, or *wants*, immediate attention.] **Require** emphasizes even more strongly imperative need, connoting that what is needed is indispensable [His work *requires* great powers of concentration.]

lack for antonyms see **have**.

laconic for synonyms see **concise**.

lady for synonyms see **woman**.

ladylike for synonyms see **female**.

lampoon for synonyms see **caricature**.

languor for synonyms see **lethargy**.

lanky for synonyms see **lean**.

larceny for synonyms see **theft**.

large, big, great —These three words are often interchangeable in meaning of more than usual size, extent, etc. [a *large*, *big*, or *great* oak]. But in strict discrimination, **large** is used with reference to dimensions or quantity [a *large* studio, a *large* amount], **big**, to bulk, weight, or extent [a *big* baby, *big* business], and **great**, to size or extent that is impressive, imposing, surprising, etc. [a *great* river, *great* success].

large for antonyms see **small**.

lassitude for synonyms see **lethargy**.

last, final, terminal, ultimate —**Last** implies a coming after all others in a series or sequence and connotes that nothing else follows [He was the *last* one to enter.] (*See also synonyms at* **continue**.) **Final** implies a coming at the end so as to terminate or conclude and connotes decisiveness [That's my *final* offer.] **Terminal** applies to that which marks an end, limit, or extremity [the *terminal* outpost of a settlement]. **Ultimate** applies to a concluding point or result beyond which it is impossible to go [His *ultimate* fate is death.] —*Antonym:* **first**.

lasting for synonym see **permanent**.

lasting for antonyms see **dead**, **transient**.

late for synonyms see **dead**, **tardy**.

latent, potential, dormant, quiescent —**Latent** applies to that which exists but is as yet concealed or unrevealed [his *latent* ability]. **Potential** applies to that which exists in an undeveloped state but which can be brought to development in the normal course of events [a *potential* concert pianist]. **Dormant** suggests a lack of visible activity, as of something asleep [a *dormant* volcano]. **Quiescent** implies a stopping of activity, usually only temporarily [The raging sea had become *quiescent*.] —*Antonyms:* **actual, operative**. *For other antonyms see* **active**.

laud for synonyms see **praise**.

laugh, chuckle, giggle, titter, snicker, guffaw —**Laugh** is the general word for the sounds or exhalation made in expressing mirth, amusement, etc. **Chuckle** describes soft laughter in low tones, expressive of mild amusement or inward satisfaction. **Giggle** and **titter** both refer to a half-suppressed laugh consisting of a series of rapid, high-pitched sounds, suggesting embarrassment, silliness, etc., but **titter** is also used of a laugh of mild amusement suppressed in affected politeness. **Snicker** is used of a sly, half-suppressed laugh, as at another's discomfiture or a bawdy story. **Guffaw** refers to loud, coarse laughter.

laughable for synonyms see **funny**.

lavish for synonyms see **profuse**.

lavish for antonyms see **thrifty**.

law, rule, regulation, statute, ordinance, canon —**Law**, in its specific application, implies prescription and enforcement by a ruling authority [the *law* of the land]. (*See also synonyms at* **theory**.) A **rule** may not be authoritatively enforced, but it is generally observed in the interests of order, uniformity, etc. [the *rules* of golf]. **Regulation** refers to a rule of a group or organization, enforced by authority [military *regulations*]. A **statute** is a law enacted by a legislative body. An **ordinance** is a local, generally municipal, law. A **canon** is, strictly, a law of a church, but the term is also used of any rule or principle regarded as true or in conformity with good usage [the *canons* of taste].

lawful for synonyms see **legal**.

lawyer, counselor, barrister, attorney, solicitor, counsel —**Lawyer** is the general term for a person trained in the law and authorized to advise or represent others in legal matters. **Counselor** and its British equivalent, **barrister**, refer to a lawyer who conducts cases in court. **Attorney**, usually, and its British equivalent, **solicitor**, always, refer to a lawyer legally empowered to act for a client, as in drawing up a contract or will, settling property, etc. **Counsel**, often equivalent to **counselor**, is frequently used collectively for a group of counselors.

lax for synonyms see **remiss**.

lax for antonyms see **careful, severe, strict, tight**.

laxative for synonyms see **physic**.

lazy, slothful, indolent —**Lazy** is the more common

word and **slothful** the less common word for those who are neither eager nor willing to work or exert themselves [I was too *lazy* to help in the kitchen. Our *slothful* guest slept all day.] **Indolent** is used of those who dislike or avoid work [The *indolent* workers slowed down production.]

lazy for antonyms see **busy**.

lead for synonyms see **guide**.

leading for synonyms see **chief**.

league for synonyms see **alliance**.

lean, spare, lanky, skinny, scrawny, gaunt —Lean implies a healthy, natural absence of fat or fleshiness. **Spare** suggests a sinewy frame without any superfluous flesh. **Lanky** implies an awkward tallness and leanness, and, often, loose-jointedness. **Skinny** and **scrawny** imply extreme thinness that is unattractive and indicative of a lack of vigor. **Gaunt** implies a bony thinness such as that caused by a wasting away of the flesh from hunger or suffering. *See also synonyms at* **thin**.

lean for antonyms see **fat**.

leaning for synonyms see **inclination**.

learn, ascertain, determine, discover, unearth —Learn, as considered here, implies a finding out of something without conscious effort [I *learned* of his marriage from a friend.] **Ascertain** implies a finding out with certainty by careful inquiry, experimentation, research, etc. [He *ascertained* the firm's credit rating.] **Determine** stresses intention to establish the facts exactly, often so as to settle something in doubt [to *determine* the exact denotation of a word]. **Discover** implies a finding out, by chance, exploration, etc., of something already existing or known to others [to *discover* a plot, to *discover* a star]. **Unearth**, in its figurative sense, implies a bringing to light, as by diligent search, of something that has been concealed, lost, forgotten, etc. [to *unearth* old documents, to *unearth* a secret].

learned for synonyms see **profound, wise**.

learned for antonyms see **ignorant**.

learning for synonyms see **information**.

lease for synonyms see **hire**.

leave for synonyms see **go**.

leave for antonyms see **stay**.

lecture for synonyms see **speech**.

leech for synonyms see **parasite**.

left for synonyms see **liberal**.

legal, lawful, legitimate, licit —**Legal** implies literal connection or conformity with statute or common law or its administration [*legal* rights]. **Lawful**, a more general word, may suggest conformity to the principle rather than to the letter of the law or may broadly refer to that which is not contrary to the law [a *lawful* but shady enterprise]. **Legitimate** implies a legality of a claim to a title or right [a *legitimate* heir] or accordance with what is sanctioned or accepted as lawful, reasonable, etc. [a *legitimate* argument]. **Licit** implies strict conformity to the law, especially in trade, commerce, or personal relations [*licit* marriage].

legal for antonyms see **illegal**.

legendary for synonyms see **fictitious**.

legitimate for synonyms see **legal**.

lengthen for synonyms see **extend**.

lengthen for antonyms see **shorten**.

lenity for synonyms see **mercy**.

lessen for synonyms see **decrease**.

lessen for antonyms see **increase**.

let, allow, permit, suffer —**Let** may imply positive consent but more often stresses the offering of no opposition or resistance, sometimes connoting negligence, lack of power, etc. [Don't *let* this happen again.] (*See also synonyms at* hire.) **Allow** and **permit** imply power or authority to give or deny consent, **allow** connoting a refraining from the enforcement of usual requirements [Honor students were *allowed* to miss the examinations.], and **permit** more positively suggesting formal consent or authorization [He was *permitted* to talk to the prisoner.] **Suffer,** now somewhat rare in this sense, is closely synonymous with **allow** and may connote passive consent or reluctant tolerance.

lethal for synonyms see fatal.

lethargy, languor, lassitude, stupor, torpor —**Lethargy** implies a dull, sluggish state brought on by illness, great fatigue, overeating, etc. **Languor** now generally suggests an inertia or limpness that results from indolence, enervating weather, a dreamy, tender mood, etc. **Lassitude** suggests a listlessness or spiritlessness resulting from overwork, dejection, etc. **Stupor** suggests a state in which the faculties and senses are deadened, as by emotional shock, alcohol, or narcotics. **Torpor** implies a temporary loss of all or part of the power of sensation or motion.

level, horizontal, flat, plane, even —**Level** and **horizontal** are applied to a surface that is parallel to, or conforms with, the horizon. **Flat** implies the absence to any marked degree of depressions or elevations in a surface, in whatever direction it lies. **Plane** describes a real or imaginary surface that is absolutely flat and wholly contains every straight line joining any two points lying in it. **Even** is applied to a surface that is uniformly level or flat, or to a surface that is in the same plane with, or a parallel plane to, another.

lewd for synonyms see **immoral**.

lewd for antonyms see **chaste**.

liable for synonyms see **likely**.

liberal, progressive, advanced, radical, left —Liberal implies tolerance of others' views as well as openmindedness to ideas that challenge tradition, established institutions, etc. **Progressive**, a relative term as opposed to *reactionary* or *conservative*, is applied to persons favoring progress and reform in politics, education, etc. and connotes an inclination to more direct action than **liberal**. **Advanced** specifically implies a being ahead of the times, as in science, the arts, philosophy, etc. **Radical** implies a favoring of fundamental or extreme change, specifically of the social structure. **Left,** originally referring to the position in legislatures of the seats occupied by parties holding such views, implies political liberalism or radicalism.

liberate for synonyms see **free**.

liberty for synonyms see **freedom**.

liberty for antonyms see **servitude**.

license for synonyms see **authorize** and **freedom**.

licit for synonyms see **legal**.

lie, prevaricate, equivocate, fabricate, fib —Lie is the simple direct word meaning to make a deliberately false statement. **Prevaricate** strictly means to quibble or confuse the issue in order to evade the truth, but it is loosely used as a formal or affected substitute for **lie**. **Equivocate** implies the deliberate use of ambiguity in order to deceive or mislead. **Fabricate** suggests the invention of a false story, excuse, etc. intended to deceive and is, hence, sometimes used as a somewhat softer equivalent for **lie**. **Fib** implies the telling of a falsehood about something unimportant and is sometimes a euphemism for **lie**.

lifeless for synonyms see **dead**.

lift, raise, elevate, rear, hoist, boost —**Lift**, in its general literal sense, implies the use of some effort in bringing something up to a higher position [Help me *lift* the table.] (*See also synonyms at* **steal**.) **Raise**, often interchangeable with **lift**, specifically implies a bringing into an upright position by lifting one end [to *raise* a flagpole]. **Elevate** is now a less frequent synonym for **lift** or **raise** [The balloon had been *elevated* 500 feet.] **Rear** is a literary equivalent of **raise** [The giant trees *reared* their branches to the sky.] **Hoist** implies the lifting of something heavy, usually by some mechanical means, as a block and tackle, crane, etc. [to *hoist* bales of cotton into a ship]. **Boost** is a colloquial term implying a lifting by or as by a push from behind or below [*Boost* me into the tree.] All these terms are used figuratively to imply a bringing into a higher or better state [to *lift*, or *hoist*, one's spirits, to *raise* one's hopes, to *elevate* one's mind, to *rear* children, to *boost* sales]. —*Antonym:* **lower**.

lighten for synonyms see **relieve**.

likely, liable, apt, prone —**Likely** suggests probability or an eventuality that can reasonably be expected [He's not *likely* to win.] (*See also synonyms at* **probable**.) **Liable** and **apt** are loosely or informally used as equivalents of **likely**, but in strict discrimination, **liable** implies exposure or susceptibility to something undesirable [He's *liable* to be killed if he plays with firearms.] and **apt** suggests a natural or habitual inclination or tendency [Such people are always *apt* to be fearful.] **Prone** also suggests a propensity or predisposition to something that seems almost inevitable [He's *prone* to have accidents.] —*An-*

tonym: **indisposed.** *For other antonyms see* **unlikely.**

likeness, similarity, resemblance, analogy —**Likeness** implies close correspondence in appearance, qualities, nature, etc. [his remarkable *likeness* to his brother]. **Similarity** suggests only partial correspondence [Your problem bears a certain *similarity* to mine.] **Resemblance** usually implies correspondence in appearance or in superficial aspects [the *resemblance* between a diamond and zircon]. **Analogy** refers to a correspondence between attributes or circumstances of things that are basically unlike [the *analogy* between a computer and the human brain]. —*Antonyms:* **unlikeness, difference.**

limit, bound, restrict, circumscribe, confine —**Limit** implies the prescribing of a point in space, time, extent, etc. beyond which it is impossible or forbidden to go [*Limit* your slogan to 25 words.] **Bound** implies an enclosing in boundaries or borders [a meadow *bounded* by hills]. **Restrict** implies a boundary that completely encloses and connotes a restraining within these bounds [The soldier was *restricted* to the camp area.] **Circumscribe** emphasizes more strongly the cutting off or isolation of that which is within the bounds [He leads the *circumscribed* life of a monk.] **Confine** stresses the restraint or hampering of enclosing limits [*confined* in jail]. —*Antonyms:* **widen, expand.**

linger for synonyms see **stay.**

lingo for synonyms see **dialect.**

link for synonyms see **join.**

liquefy for synonyms see **melt.**

liquid, fluid —**Liquid** refers to a substance that flows readily and assumes the form of its container but retains its independent volume [Water that is neither ice nor steam is a *liquid.*] **Fluid** applies to any substance that flows [All liquids, gases, and viscous substances are *fluids.*] —*Antonym:* **solid.**

list, catalog, inventory, register, roll —**List,** the broadest in scope of these terms, applies to a series of items of any kind, no matter what the arrangement or purpose. **Catalog** implies methodical arrangement, usually alphabetical, and is used of lists of articles for sale or on exhibit, library card files, etc. An **inventory** is an itemized list of goods, property, etc., especially one made annually in business. A **register** is a book, etc. in which names, events, or other items are formally or officially recorded [a *register* of voters]. A **roll** is an official list of the members of an organization, especially as used for checking attendance.

little for synonyms see **small.**

little for antonyms see **large.**

lively, animated, vivacious, sprightly, gay —**Lively** implies a being full of life and energy and suggests an active or vigorous quality in something [a *lively* dance, talk *lively*]. **Animated** is applied to that which is made alive or bright and suggests a spirited quality [an *animated* face, an *animated* discussion]. **Vivacious** and, more emphatically, **sprightly** suggest buoyancy of spirit or sparkling brightness [a *vivacious* manner, a *sprightly* tune]. **Gay** suggests lightheartedness and unrestrained good spirits [a *gay* life]. —*Antonym:* **dull.** *For other antonyms see* **inactive.**

livid for synonyms see **pale.**

living, alive, animate, animated, vital —**Living** and **alive,** the latter usually a predicate adjective, are the simple, basic terms for organisms having life or existence, **living** figuratively connoting continued existence or activity [a *living* faith] and **alive,** full force or vigor [prejudices kept *alive* by ignorance]. **Animate**, opposed to *inanimate*, is applied to living organisms as distinguished from lifeless ones or inorganic objects. **Animated** is applied to inanimate things to which life or, in extended use, motion has been imparted [*animated* cartoons]. **Vital** is applied to that which is essential to organic life [*vital* functions] or to the energy, force, etc. manifested by living things.

living for antonyms see **dead**.

loath for synonyms see **reluctant**.

loathe for synonyms see **hate**.

loathing for synonyms see **aversion**.

lofty for synonyms see **high**.

loiter, dawdle, dally, idle —Loiter implies aimlessness or slowness of movement and may suggest a wasting of time in lingering or lagging [to *loiter* around street corners]. **Dawdle** implies a wasting of time over trifles or a frittering away of time that makes for slow progress [to *dawdle* over a cup of tea]. **Dally** suggests a spending of time in trifling or frivolous pursuit. **Idle** suggests habitual avoidance of work, or inactivity, indolence, etc. [to *idle* away the hours].

lone, lonely, lonesome for synonyms see **alone**.

look, gaze, stare, gape, glare, peek, peer —Look is the general term meaning to direct the eyes in order to see [Don't *look* now.] (*See also synonyms at* **appearance**.) **Gaze** implies a looking intently and steadily, as in wonder, delight, or interest [to *gaze* at the stars]. To **stare** is to look fixedly with wide-open eyes, as in surprise, curiosity, abstraction, etc. [It is rude to *stare* at people.] To **gape** is to stare with the mouth open in ignorant or naive wonder or curiosity [The child stood *gaping* at the elephant.] To **glare** is to stare fiercely or angrily [He *glared* at her for talking.] To **peek** is to take a quick, furtive look, as through a hole or from behind a barrier, at something not supposed to be seen. To **peer** is to look searchingly with the eyes narrowed [She *peered* down the well.]

loot for synonyms see **spoil**.

loquacious for synonyms see **talkative**.

lot for synonyms see **fate**.

love, affection, attachment, infatuation —**Love** implies intense fondness or deep devotion and may apply to various relationships or objects [sexual *love*, brotherly *love*, *love* of one's work]. **Affection** suggests warm, tender feelings, usually not as powerful or deep as those implied by **love** [He has no *affection* for children.] **Attachment** implies connection by ties of affection, attraction, devotion, etc. and may be felt for inanimate things as well as for people [an *attachment* to an old hat]. **Infatuation** implies a foolish or unreasoning passion or affection, often a transient one [an elderly man's *infatuation* for a young girl].

love for antonyms see **hate**.

lovely for synonyms see **beautiful**.

low for synonyms see **base¹**.

lowly for synonyms see **humble**.

loyal for synonyms see **faithful**.

loyalty for synonyms see **allegiance**.

lucky, fortunate, providential, happy —**Lucky** implies a favorable or advantageous event happening by mere chance, often unexpectedly, and not as the result of effort or merit [a *lucky* find, a *lucky* guess]. **Fortunate**, a more formal word, is usually used of more important or serious matters [She made a *fortunate* choice of profession]. **Providential** connotes the intervention of God or some higher agency in bringing about the favorable event [a *providential* escape from death]. **Happy** emphasizes the pleasure felt by the person affected by the lucky event [Marriage resulted from that *happy* encounter.] —*Antonyms:* **unlucky, disastrous.**

ludicrous for synonyms see **absurd.**

luminous for synonyms see **bright.**

lunacy for synonyms see **insanity.**

lure, entice, inveigle, decoy, beguile, tempt, seduce —**Lure** suggests an irresistible force, as desire, greed or curiosity in attracting someone, especially to something harmful or evil [*lured* on by false hopes]. **Entice** implies a crafty or skillful luring [He *enticed* the squirrel to eat from his hand.] **Inveigle** suggests the use of deception or cajolery in enticing someone [They *inveigled* him with false promises.] **Decoy** implies the use of deceptive appearances in luring into a trap [Artificial birds are used to *decoy* wild ducks.] **Beguile** suggests the use of subtly alluring devices in leading someone on [*beguiled* by her sweet words]. **Tempt** suggests the influence of a powerful attraction that tends to overcome scruples or judgment [I'm *tempted* to accept your offer.] **Seduce** implies enticement to a wrongful or unlawful act, especially to loss of chastity. —*Antonym:* **repel.**

lurk, skulk, sneak, slink, prowl —**Lurk** implies a waiting in concealment or in the background, especially with sinister or menacing intentions. **Skulk** implies a lurking or moving about in a stealthy, sinister way, and also connotes cowardliness. **Sneak** and **slink** suggest stealthy movement to avoid being seen or heard, but **sneak** more often implies an underhanded or cowardly purpose and **slink** suggests merely fear, guilt, etc. **Prowl** suggests a furtive, watchful roaming about, as in searching for prey or loot.

lush for synonyms see **profuse**.

lustrous for synonyms see **bright**.

luxuriant for synonyms see **profuse**.

luxurious for synonyms see **sensuous**.

lying for synonyms see **dishonest**.

M

macabre for synonyms see **ghastly**.

machination for synonyms see **conspiracy**.

magic, sorcery, witchcraft, wizardry —**Magic** is the general term for any of the supposed arts of producing marvelous effects by supernatural or occult power and is figuratively applied to any extraordinary, seemingly inexplicable power. **Sorcery** implies magic in which spells are cast or charms are used, usually for a harmful or sinister purpose. **Witchcraft** (of women) and **wizardry** (of men) imply the possession of supernatural power by compact with evil spirits, **witchcraft** figuratively suggesting the use of womanly wiles, and **wizardry**, remarkable skill, cleverness, etc.

magisterial for synonyms see **masterful**.

magnificent for synonyms see **grand**.

maim, cripple, mutilate, mangle, disable —**Maim** implies an injuring of a person's body so as to deprive him or her of some member or its use [*maimed* in an auto accident]. To **cripple** is to cause to be lame in a way that prevents normal motion of a limb or limbs [*crippled* by rheumatism]. To **mutilate** is to remove or severely damage a part of a person or thing essential to completeness [a speech *mutilated* by censors]. **Mangle** implies mutilation or disfigurement by or as by repeated tearing, hacking, or crushing [His arm was *mangled* in the press.] To **disable** is to make incapable of normal physical activity, as by crippling [*disabled* war veterans].

main for synonyms see **chief**.

maintain for synonyms see **support**.

majestic for synonyms see **grand**.

make, form, shape, fashion, construct, manufacture, fabricate —**Make** is the general term meaning to bring into being and may imply a producing of something physically or mentally. **Form** suggests a definite contour, structure, or design in the thing made. **Shape** suggests the imparting of a specific form as by molding, cutting, hammering, etc. **Fashion** implies inventiveness, cleverness of design, and the use of skill. **Construct** implies a putting of parts together systematically according to some design. **Manufacture** implies a producing from raw materials, now especially by machinery and on a large scale. **Fabricate** implies a building or manufacturing, often by assembling standardized parts, and, in extended use, connotes fictitious invention.

makeshift for synonyms see **resource**.

maladroit for synonyms see **awkward**.

malady for synonyms see **disease**.

male, masculine, manly, mannish, virile —**Male** is the basic term applied to members of the sex that is biologically distinguished from the female sex and is used of animals and plants as well as of human beings. **Masculine** is applied to qualities, such as strength and vigor, characteristic of men, or to things appropriate to men. **Manly** suggests the noble qualities, such as courage and independence, that one associates with a man who has maturity of character. **Mannish,** used chiefly of women, implies the possession or adoption of the traits and manners of a man.   **Virile** stresses qualities such as robustness, vigor, and, specifically, sexual potency, that belong to a physically mature man.

malevolence for synonyms see **malice**.

malice, ill will, malevolence, spite, rancor, malignity, grudge —Malice implies a deep-seated animosity that delights in causing others to suffer or in seeing them suffer.   **Ill will** and the more formal **malevolence** imply hostile or unfriendly feelings such as dispose one to wish evil to others.   **Spite** suggests a mean desire to hurt, annoy, or frustrate others, usually as displayed in petty, vindictive acts.   **Rancor** implies an intensely bitter ill will that rankles.   **Malignity** suggests extreme and virulent malevolence that is relentless in expressing itself.   **Grudge** implies ill will inspired by resentment over a grievance.

malign for synonyms see **sinister**.
malignity for synonyms see **malice**.
malleable for synonyms see **pliable**.
malodorous for synonyms see **stinking**.
mammoth for synonyms see **huge**.
manacle for synonyms see **hamper**.
manage for synonyms see **conduct**.
maneuver for synonyms see **trick**.
mangle for synonyms see **maim**.

mania, delirium, frenzy, hysteria —Mania in its basic sense (wild behavior characterized by abnormal excitability, exaggerated feelings of well-being, and flight of ideas) describes the phase of manic-depressive psychosis that is distinguished from *depression*.   **Delirium** denotes a temporary state of extreme mental disturbance (marked by restlessness, incoherence, and hallucinations) that occurs during fevers, in alcoholic psychosis, etc. **Frenzy**, not used technically in psychiatry, implies extreme emotional agitation in which self-control is lost. **Hysteria** is applied in psychiatry to certain psychogenic disorders characterized by excitability, anxiety, sensory and motor disturbances, and the involuntary simulation of blindness, deafness, etc. In extended use, **mania** suggests a craze for something [a *mania* for surfing], **delirium**, rapturous excitement [a *delirium* of joy], and **hysteria**, an outburst of wild, uncontrolled feeling [She laughed and cried in her *hysteria*.]

manifest for synonyms see **evident**.

manifold for synonyms see **many**.

manly for synonyms see **male**.

manly for antonyms see **female**.

manner for synonyms see **bearing** and **method**.

mannerism for synonyms see **pose**.

mannish for synonyms see **male**.

mannish for antonyms see **female**.

manufacture for synonyms see **make**.

many, numerous, manifold, multifarious, innumerable —Many is the simple, common word implying a relatively large number of units [*many* children, *many* excuses, *many* bacteria]. **Numerous**, a more formal equivalent for **many**, sometimes connotes a crowding of one unit upon another [*Numerous* complaints have come in.] **Manifold** adds the connotation of great variety [*manifold* problems] or, in modifying a singular noun, great complexity in the component parts of the whole [her *manifold* sorrow]. **Multifarious** adds the connotation of great diversity, or even incongruity, in the variety [*multifarious* interests]. **Innumerable** implies a number too great to count and is often used hyperbolically [*innu-*

merable instances of his kindness]. —*Antonym:* **few.**

margin for synonyms see **border.**

mark for synonyms see **sign.**

marriage, matrimony, wedlock, wedding, nuptials
—**Marriage** refers to the state of, or relation between, a man and woman who have become husband and wife or to the ceremony marking this union. **Matrimony**, a formal word, applies specifically to the religious sacrament of marriage and stresses the rights and obligations of the marriage state [the bonds of holy *matrimony*]. **Wedlock** now applies specifically to marriage as a legal relationship [a child born out of *wedlock*]. **Wedding** refers specifically to the marriage ceremony and connotes festivities of one sort or another. **Nuptials** is a highly formal, sometimes affected, term implying an elaborate ceremony and pomp.

martial for synonyms see **warlike.**

masculine for synonyms see **male.**

masculine for antonyms see **female.**

mass for synonyms see **bulk.**

massacre for synonyms see **slaughter.**

massive for synonyms see **heavy.**

masterful, domineering, imperious, magisterial
—**Masterful** implies such strength of personality as enables one to impose his or her will on others [a *masterful* orchestral conductor]. **Domineering** implies the arrogant, tyrannical manner of one who openly tries to dominate another [a *domineering* mother]. **Imperious** suggests the arbitrary ruling of an emperor, but connotes less arrogance than **domineering** [the *imperious* old dean of the college]. **Magisterial**, while not suggesting an assumption of arbitrary powers, implies an excessive use or display of such inherent powers as a magistrate might

have [She dismissed me with a *magisterial* air.]

material, physical, corporeal, sensible —**Material** is applied to anything that is formed of matter and has substance [*material* objects, *material* possessions]. **Physical** applies either to material things as they are perceivable by the senses or to forces that are scientifically measurable [the *physical* world, the *physical* properties of sound]. **Corporeal** applies only to such material objects as have bodily form and are tangible [*corporeal* property]. **Sensible** is specifically applied to anything that can be known through the senses rather than through the intellect [a *sensible* phenomenon]. —*Antonyms:* **spiritual, mental, psychical.**

matrimony for synonyms see **marriage.**

mature for synonyms see **ripe.**

mature for antonyms see **young.**

maudlin for synonyms see **sentimental.**

maul for synonyms see **beat.**

mawkish for synonyms see **sentimental.**

maxim for synonyms see **saying.**

may for synonym see **can.**

meager, scanty, scant, spare, sparse —**Meager** literally implies an emaciated thinness and, hence, connotes a lack of those qualities which give something richness, vigor, or strength [*meager* cultural resources]. **Scanty** implies an inadequacy in amount, number, or quantity of something essential [a *scanty* income]. **Scant** is applied to a barely sufficient amount or a stinted quantity [the *scant* attendance at the concert]. **Spare** implies less than a sufficient amount but does not necessarily connote great hardship [to live on *spare* rations]. **Sparse** applies to a scanty quantity that is thinly distributed over a wide area [his *sparse* hair].

meager for antonyms see **plentiful**.

mean for synonyms see **average**, **base²**, and **intend**.

meander for synonyms see **roam**.

meaning, sense, import, purport, signification, significance —**Meaning** is the general word for what is intended to be expressed or understood by something [the *meaning* of a sentence]. **Sense**, in this connection, refers especially to any of the various meanings conveyed by a word or phrase [This word has several slang *senses*.] **Import** refers to the total implication of something said or done, including the subtle connotations [I didn't get the full *import* of his remark.] **Purport** refers to the general meaning, or gist, of something [What was the *purport* of her letter?] **Signification** is applied especially to the meaning conventionally understood by a sign, symbol, character, etc. [the *signification* of the ace of spades in fortunetelling]. **Significance** refers to the subtle, hidden implications of something as distinguished from its openly expressed meaning [His "no!" had a special *significance* for us.]

meddlesome for synonyms see **curious**.

median for synonyms see **average**.

mediate for synonyms see **interpose**.

meditate for synonyms see **ponder**.

meditative for synonyms see **pensive**.

meek for synonyms see **humble**.

melancholy for synonyms see **sad**.

melancholy for antonyms see **mirth**.

mellow for synonyms see **ripe**.

melody, air, tune —**Melody** refers to the rhythmic arrangement of tones in sequence to express a musical idea. **Air**, in strict application, refers to the principal, or leading, melody of a harmonized composition, but it is sometimes used as an equivalent of **tune**, which is the popular term for any easily remembered melody that identifies a song, dance, etc.

melt, dissolve, liquefy, thaw —**Melt** implies the bringing of a substance from its solid to its liquid state, usually by heat [to *melt* butter]. **Dissolve** refers specifically to the reduction of a solid to a liquid by placing it in another liquid so that its particles are evenly distributed among those of the solvent [to *dissolve* sugar in water]. **Liquefy** is the general term meaning to change to a liquid state and may be applied to gases as well as solids. **Thaw** implies the reducing of a frozen substance to its normal state, usually to a liquid or a semiliquid, by raising its temperature [The ice has *thawed*.] —*Antonyms:* **solidify, freeze.**

memory, remembrance, recollection, reminiscence —**Memory** refers specifically to the ability or power for retaining or reviving in the mind past thoughts, images, ideas, etc. [to have a good *memory*]. **Remembrance** applies to the act or process of having such events or things come to mind again [the *remembrance* of things past]. **Recollection** implies the voluntary and detailed remembering of a half-forgotten event [His *recollection* of the campaign is not too clear.] **Reminiscence** implies the pensive or wistful recollection of long-past, usually pleasurable, events, or the narration of these [He entertained us with *reminiscences* of his childhood.] —*Antonyms:* **forgetfulness, oblivion.**

menace for synonym see **threaten.**

mend, repair, patch, darn —**Mend** is the general word implying a making whole again something that has been broken, torn, etc. [to *mend* a toy, to *mend* a dress]. **Repair**, often equivalent to **mend**, is preferred when the object is a relatively complex one that has become damaged or decayed through use, age, exhaustion, etc. [to *repair* an automobile, to *repair* a radio]. **Patch** and **darn** imply the mending of a hole or tear, the former by inserting or applying a piece of similar material [to *patch* a coat, to *patch* a tire], the latter by sewing a network of stitches across the gap [to *darn* a sock].

menial for synonyms see **servile**.

mercy, clemency, lenity, charity —Mercy implies a kindness or forbearance, as in punishing offenders, in excess of what may be demanded by fairness, or it may connote kindness and sympathy to those in distress. **Clemency** refers to a tendency toward mercy in one whose duty it is to punish offenders. **Lenity** usually implies excessive mercy or mildness toward offenders where greater strictness might be preferable. **Charity**, in this connection, implies a kindly understanding and tolerance in judging others. —*Antonyms:* **severity, cruelty.**

merge for synonyms see **mix**.

merriment for synonyms see **mirth**.

metamorphose for synonyms see **transform**.

method, manner, mode, way, fashion, system —Method implies a regular, orderly, logical procedure for doing something [a *method* of vulcanizing rubber]. **Manner** applies to a distinctive, often personal, procedure or course [her *manner* of speech]. **Mode** refers to a customary, established, or usual method or manner [their *mode* of dress]. **Way** is a simple, common, but less explicit synonym for any of the preceding words [a *way* of talking, a *way* of preparing something]. **Fashion**, also a general term, often emphasizes currency of mode [It is the *fashion* to wear bright colors.] **System**, in this comparison, implies a carefully developed, relatively complex method [a *system* of government].

methodical for synonyms see **orderly**.

meticulous for synonyms see **careful**.

middle, center, midst —**Middle** refers to the point or part equally distant from either or all sides or extremities and may apply to space, time, etc. [the *middle* of the stage, the *middle* of the day]. **Center** more precisely stresses the point equidistant from the bounding lines or surfaces of any plane or solid figure [the *center* of a circle, the *center* of a globe] and is sometimes used figuratively [the *center* of town, a trade *center*]. **Midst**, usually used in prepositional phrases, denotes a middle part that is surrounded by persons or things or a middle point in some action [in the *midst* of a crowd, in the *midst* of one's work].

midget for synonyms see **dwarf**.

midst for synonyms see **middle**.

mien for synonyms see **bearing**.

might for synonyms see **strength**.

migrate, emigrate, immigrate —**Migrate** denotes a moving from one region or country to another and may imply, of people, intention to settle in a new land, or, of animals, a periodical movement influenced by climate, food supply, etc. **Emigrate** and **immigrate** are used only of people, **emigrate** specifically denoting the leaving of a country to settle in another, and **immigrate**, the coming into the new country.

mild for synonyms see **soft**.

mild for antonyms see **severe**.

militant for synonyms see **aggressive**.

military for synonyms see **warlike**.

mimic for synonyms see **imitate**.

mince for synonyms see **grind**.

mingle for synonyms see **mix**.

miniature for synonyms see **small**.

minimize for synonyms see **disparage**.

minute for synonyms see **small**.

mirage for synonyms see **delusion**.

mirth, glee, jollity, merriment, hilarity —Mirth implies gaiety, gladness, or great amusement, especially as expressed by laughter. **Glee** implies exultant and demonstrative joy or it may suggest malicious delight over another's misfortunes. **Jollity** and **merriment** imply exuberant mirth or joy and usually suggest convivial merrymaking. **Hilarity** implies boisterous merriment and sometimes suggests an excessively noisy display of high spirits. —Antonyms: **sadness, melancholy**.

misanthropic for synonyms see **cynical**.

miserly for synonyms see **stingy**.

misfortune for synonyms see **affliction**.

misgiving for synonyms see **qualm**.

mislead for synonyms see **deceive**.

mist, haze, fog, smog —Mist, in this comparison, applies to a visible atmospheric vapor of rather fine density, that blurs the vision. **Haze** suggests a thin dispersion of smoke, dust, etc. that makes objects indistinct. **Fog** is applied to a greater density of moisture particles than **mist**, sometimes suggesting a thickness impenetrable by the vision. **Smog** is applied to a mixture of fog and smoke of a kind that sometimes appears in industrial centers. The first three terms are also used figuratively [lost in the *mists* of the past, a mellow *haze* of intoxication, in a *fog* of doubt].

mistake for synonyms see **error**.

mitigate for synonyms see **relieve**.

mitigate for antonyms see **intensify**.

mix, mingle, blend, merge, coalesce, fuse —**Mix** implies a combining of things so that the resulting substance is uniform in composition, whether or not the separate elements can be distinguished [to *mix* paints]. **Mingle** usually implies that the separate elements can be distinguished [*mingled* feelings of joy and sorrow]. **Blend** implies a mixing of different varieties to produce a desired quality [a *blended* tea, *blended* whiskey] or the mingling of different elements to form a harmonious whole [a novel *blending* fact and fiction]. **Merge** stresses the loss of distinction of elements by combination or may suggest the total absorption of one thing in another [The companies *merged* to form a large corporation.] **Coalesce** implies a union or growing together of things into a single body or mass [The factions *coalesced* into a party of opposition.] **Fuse** means to unite by melting together and stresses the indissoluble nature of the union.

moan for synonyms see **cry**.

mob for synonyms see **crowd**.

mock for synonyms see **imitate, ridicule**.

mode for synonyms see **fashion, method**.

model, example, pattern, paradigm, archetype, standard —**Model** refers to a representation made to be copied or, more generally, to any person or thing to be followed or imitated because of excellence or worth. **Example** suggests that which is presented as a sample, or that which sets a precedent for imitation, whether good or bad. A **pattern** is a model, guide, plan, etc. to be strictly followed. **Paradigm** is common now only in its grammatical sense of an example of a declension or conjugation, giving all the inflectional forms of a word. **Ar-**

chetype applies to the original pattern serving as the model for all later things of the same kind. **Standard** refers to something established for use as a rule or a basis of comparison in judging quality or value.

moderate, temperate —These two words are often interchangeable as used to denote a staying within reasonable limits, but in strict discrimination, **moderate** implies merely an absence of excesses or extremes, while **temperate** suggests deliberate self-restraint [*moderate* demands, a *temperate* reply]. —*Antonym:* **extreme**. *For other antonyms see* **excessive**.

modern for synonyms see **new**.

modern for antonyms see **old**.

modernistic for synonyms see **new**.

modest for synonyms see **chaste, humble, shy**.

modify for synonyms see **change**.

moist for synonyms see **wet**.

moist for antonyms see **dry**.

molder for synonyms see **decay**.

mollify for synonyms see **pacify**.

moment for synonyms see **importance**.

momentary for synonyms see **transient**.

monastery for synonyms see **cloister**.

monetary for synonyms see **financial**.

monopoly,   trust,   cartel,   syndicate,   corner —**Monopoly** applies to the exclusive control of a commodity or service that makes possible the fixing of prices and the virtual elimination of competition. A **trust** is a combination of corporations, organized for the purpose of gaining a monopoly, in which stock is turned over to trustees who issue stock certificates to the stockholders: trusts are now illegal in the U.S. **Cartel,** the European term for a trust, now usually implies an international trust. A **syndicate** is now usually a group of bankers, corporations, etc. organized to buy large blocks of securities, afterwards selling them in small parcels to the public at a profit. A **corner** is a temporary speculative monopoly of some stock or commodity for the purpose of raising the price.

monstrous for synonyms see **outrageous**.

mood, humor, temper, vein —Mood is the broadest of these terms referring to a temporary state of mind and emphasizes the constraining or pervading quality of the feeling [She's in a merry *mood*.] **Humor** emphasizes the variability or capriciousness of the mood [He wept and laughed as his *humor* moved him.] **Temper**, in this comparison, applies to a mood characterized by a single, strong emotion, especially that of anger [My, he's in a nasty *temper!*] **Vein** stresses the transient nature of the mood [if I may speak in a serious *vein* for a moment.]

moral, ethical, virtuous, righteous —Moral implies conformity with the generally accepted standards of goodness or rightness in conduct or character, sometimes, specifically, in sexual conduct [a *moral* woman]. **Ethical** implies conformity with an elaborated, ideal code of moral principles, sometimes, specifically, with the code of a particular profession [an *ethical* lawyer]. **Virtuous** implies a morally excellent character, connoting justice, integrity, and often, specifically, chastity. **Righteous** implies a morally blameless or justifiable [*righteous* anger]. —*Antonym:* **immoral.** *For other antonyms see* **bad** *and* **base**[2].

morose for synonyms see **sullen**.

mortal for synonyms see **fatal**.

mortified for synonyms see **ashamed**.

motive, incentive, inducement, spur —Motive refers

to any impulse, emotion, or desire that moves one to action [Greed was his only *motive* for stealing.] (*See also synonyms at* **cause**.) **Incentive** applies to a stimulus, often a reward, that encourages or inspires one to action [He needs no *incentive* other than the desire to be useful.] **Inducement** always refers to an outer stimulus, rather than an inner urge, that tempts or entices one to do something [The money was an added *inducement*.] A **spur** is an impulse or incentive that pricks one on to greatly increased activity or endurance [Security for his family was the *spur* that drove him on.]

motto for synonyms see **saying**.

mountebank for synonyms see **quack**.

move, remove, shift, transfer —**Move,** the broadest in scope of these terms, means merely to change from one place or position to another [to *move* a rock, to *move* one's foot, to *move* a house]. (*See also synonyms at af-fect*.) **Remove** stresses the departure of the thing moved from its original or usual place or position [to *remove* one's hat, to *remove* a cause of strife]. **Shift** emphasizes the change in position or location and, hence, often connotes instability, unrest, etc. [to *shift* in one's opinions]. **Transfer** implies a change from one container, vehicle, ownership, etc. to another [We *transferred* to a cross-town bus.]

moving, poignant, affecting, touching, pathetic —**Moving** implies a general arousing or stirring of the emotions or feelings, sometimes, specifically, of pathos [her *moving* plea for help]. **Poignant** is applied to that which is sharply painful to the feelings [the *poignant* cry of a lost child]. **Affecting** applies to that which stirs the emotions, as to tears [the *affecting* scene of their reunion]. **Touching** is used of that which arouses tender feelings, as of sympathy, gratitude, etc. [her *touching* little gift to me]. **Pathetic** applies to that which arouses pity or compassion, sometimes pity mingled with contempt [his *pathetic* attempt at wit].

muddle for synonyms see **confusion**.

multifarious for synonyms see **many**.

multiply for synonyms see **increase**.

multitude for synonyms see **crowd**.

mumble for synonyms see **murmur**.

mundane for synonyms see **earthly**.

murder for synonyms see **kill**.

murky for synonyms see **dark**.

murmur, mutter, mumble —**Murmur** implies a continuous flow of words or sounds in a low, indistinct voice and may apply to utterances of satisfaction or dissatisfaction [to *murmur* a prayer]. **Mutter** usually suggests angry or discontented words or sounds of this kind [to *mutter* curses]. To **mumble** is to utter almost inaudible or inarticulate sounds in low tones, with the mouth nearly closed [an old woman *mumbling* to herself].

muse for synonyms see **ponder**.

muster for synonyms see **gather**.

musty for synonyms see **stinking**.

mute for synonyms see **voiceless**.

mutilate for synonyms see **maim**.

mutiny for synonyms see **rebellion**.

mutter for synonyms see **murmur**.

mutual, reciprocal, common —**Mutual** may be used for an interchange of feeling between two persons [John and Joe are *mutual* enemies.] or may imply a sharing jointly with others [the *mutual* efforts of a group]. **Reciprocal** implies a return in kind or degree by each of two sides of what is given or demonstrated by the other [a *reciprocal* trade agreement], or it may refer to any inversely corresponding relationship [the *reciprocal* functions of two machine parts]. **Common** simply implies a being shared by others or by all the members of a group [our *common* interests].

mysterious, inscrutable, mystical —Mysterious is applied to that which excites curiosity or wonder, but is impossible or difficult to explain or solve [a *mysterious* murder]. That is **inscrutable** which is completely mysterious and is altogether incapable of being searched out, interpreted, or understood [the *inscrutable* ways of God]. **Mystical** applies to that which is occult or esoteric in connection with religious rites or spiritual experience.

mystery, enigma, riddle, puzzle, conundrum —Mystery is applied to something beyond human knowledge or understanding, or it merely refers to any unexplained or seemingly inexplicable matter. **Enigma** specifically applies to that whose meaning is hidden by cryptic or ambiguous allusions, and generally, to anything very difficult to explain. A **riddle** is an enigma (usually in the form of a question in guessing games) that involves paradoxes. A **puzzle** is a situation, problem, or, often, a contrivance, that requires some ingenuity to solve or explain. **Conundrum** is specifically applied to a riddle whose answer is a pun, and generally, to any puzzling question or problem.

mystical for synonyms see **mysterious**.
mythical for synonyms see **fictitious**.

N

nab for synonyms see **catch.**

naive, ingenuous, artless, unsophisticated —**Naive** implies a genuine, innocent simplicity or lack of artificiality but sometimes connotes an almost foolish lack of worldly wisdom [She has a *naive* belief in the kindness of others.] **Ingenuous** implies a frankness or straightforwardness that suggests the simplicity of a child [her *ingenuous* smile at my discomfiture]. **Artless** suggests a lack of artificiality or guile that derives from indifference to the effect one has upon others [her *artless* beauty]. **Unsophisticated,** like **naive,** implies a lack of worldly wisdom but connotes that this is the result merely of a lack of experience [an *unsophisticated* freshman]. —*Antonyms:* **sophisticated, artful.**

naked for synonyms see **bare.**

narrate for synonyms see **tell.**

narrative for synonyms see **story.**

national for synonyms see **citizen.**

national for antonyms see **alien.**

native, indigenous, aboriginal, endemic —**Native** applies to a person born, or thing originating, in a certain place or country [a *native* Italian, *native* fruits]. **Indigenous,** which also suggests natural origin in a particular region, is applied to races or species rather than to individuals [The potato is *indigenous* to South America.] **Aboriginal** applies to the earliest known inhabitants (or, rarely, animals or plants) of a region [The Indians are the *aboriginal* Americans.] **Endemic,** applied especially to plants and diseases, implies prevalence in or restriction to a particular region [Typhus is *endemic* in various countries.] —*Antonyms:* **alien, foreign.**

natural for synonyms see **normal.**

natural for antonyms see **artificial, irregular.**

nature for synonyms see **type.**

naughty for synonyms see **bad.**

neat, tidy, trim —**Neat** suggests cleanness and orderliness and, hence, connotes a lack of superfluous or confusing details [a *neat* house and yard, a *neat* design]. **Tidy** emphasizes painstaking, orderly arrangement rather than cleanliness [a *tidy* closet]. **Trim** adds to the sense of **neat** connotations of smartness, dapperness, good proportion, etc. [a *trim* figure, a *trim* ship].

neat for antonyms see **slovenly.**

necessary for synonyms see **essential.**

necessity for synonyms see **need.**

need, necessity, exigency, requisite —**Need** refers to an urgent requirement of something essential or desirable that is lacking. (*See also synonyms at* **lack.**) **Necessity,** a more formal word, suggests an imperative need for something indispensable but lacks the emotional connotations of **need** [They are in *need* of food. Food is a *necessity* for all living things.] **Exigency** refers to a necessity that is created by some emergency, crisis, or compelling circumstances [the *exigencies* created by the flood]. **Requisite** applies to something that is indispensable to a particular end or goal [A sense of rhythm is a *requisite* in a dancer.]

nefarious for synonyms see **vicious.**

negate for synonyms see **nullify.**

neglect, omit, overlook, disregard, ignore, slight, forget —**Neglect** implies a failure to carry out some expected or required action, either through carelessness or by intention [I *neglected* to wind the clock.] **Omit**, in this connection, implies a neglecting through oversight, absorption, etc. [She should not *omit* to visit the Louvre.] **Overlook** suggests a failure to see or to take action, either inadvertently or indulgently [I'll *overlook* your errors this time.] **Disregard** implies inattention or neglect, usually intentional [She always *disregards* his wishes.] **Ignore** suggests a deliberate disregarding, sometimes through stubborn refusal to face the facts [But you *ignore* the necessity for action.] **Slight** implies a disregarding or neglecting in an indifferent or disdainful way [He seems to *slight* the newer writers.] **Forget**, in this connection, implies an intentional disregarding or omitting [After his election he *forgot* the wishes of the voters.]

neglectful for synonyms see **remiss**.

negligent for synonyms see **remiss**.

negligent for antonyms see **careful**.

neighboring for synonyms see **adjacent**.

neophyte for synonyms see **amateur**.

nerve for synonyms see **temerity**.

nettle for synonyms see **irritate**.

new, fresh, novel, modern, modernistic, original —**New** is applied to that which has never existed before or which has only just come into being, possession, use, etc. [a *new* coat, a *new* plan]. **Fresh** implies such newness that the original appearance, quality, or vigor have not been affected by time or use [*fresh* eggs, a *fresh* start]. **Novel** implies a newness that is strikingly unusual or strange [a *novel* idea, a *novel* combination]. **Modern** and **modernistic** apply to that which is of the present time, as distinguished form earlier periods, and connotes up-to-dateness, **modernistic**, sometimes, with derogatory implications. **Original** is used of that which is not only new but is also the first of its kind [an *original* plan, an *original* melody].

new for antonyms see **old**.

nice for synonyms see **dainty**.

niggardly for synonyms see **stingy**.

nimble for synonyms see **agile**.

noise, din, uproar, clamor, hubbub, racket —Noise is the general word for any loud, unmusical, or disagreeable sound. (*See also synonyms at* **sound**[1].) **Din** refers to a loud, prolonged, deafening sound, painful to the ears [the *din* of the steeple bells]. **Uproar** applies to a loud, confused sound, as of shouting or laughing, and connotes commotion or disturbance [His remarks threw the audience into an *uproar*.] **Clamor** suggests loud, continued, excited shouting, as in protest or demand [the *clamor* of an aroused people]. **Hubbub** implies the confused mingling of many voices [the *hubbub* of a subway station]. **Racket** refers to a loud, clattering combination of noises regarded as annoyingly excessive [She couldn't work for the *racket* next door.] —*Antonym:* quiet.

noiseless for synonyms see **still**.

noisome for synonyms see **stinking**.

nomadic for synonyms see **itinerant**.

nom de plume for synonyms see **pseudonym**.

nonchalance for synonyms see **equanimity**.

nonchalant for synonyms see **cool**.

nonplus for synonyms see **bewilder**.

nonsocial for synonyms see **unsocial**.

norm for synonyms see **average**.

normal, regular, typical, natural, usual, average —Normal implies conformity with the established norm or standard for its kind [*normal* intelligence]. **Regular** implies conformity with the prescribed rule or accepted pattern for its kind [the *regular* working day]. **Typical** applies to that which has the representative characteristics of its type or class [a *typical* Southern town]. **Natural** implies behavior, operation, etc. that conforms with the nature or innate character of the person or thing [a *natural* comedian]. **Usual** applies to that which conforms to the common or ordinary use or occurrence [the *usual* price]. **Average**, in this connection, implies conformity with what is regarded as normal or ordinary [the *average* man]. —*Antonym:* **unusual**. *For other antonyms see* **irregular**.

noted for synonyms see **famous**.

notice for synonyms see **discern**.

noticeable, remarkable, prominent, outstanding, conspicuous, striking —**Noticeable** is applied to that which must inevitably be noticed [a *noticeable* coolness in his manner]. **Remarkable** applies to that which is noticeable because it is unusual or exceptional [*remarkable* beauty]. **Prominent** refers to that which literally or figuratively stands out from its background [a *prominent* nose, a *prominent* author]. An **outstanding** person or thing is remarkable as compared with others of its kind [an *outstanding* sculptor]. **Conspicuous** applies to that which is so obvious or manifest as to be immediately perceptible [*conspicuous* gallantry]. **Striking** is used of something so out of the ordinary that it leaves a sharp impression on the mind [a *striking* epigram].

notify, inform, acquaint, apprise —**Notify** implies a sending of a formal notice imparting required or pertinent information [*Notify* me when you are ready.] **Inform** implies a making aware of something by giving knowledge of it [He *informed* me of your decision to join us.] **Acquaint** suggests a making familiar with something hitherto unknown to one [She *acquainted* me with her problems.] **Apprise** implies a notifying someone of something that has particular interest for him or her [I have *apprised* him of your arrival.]

notion for synonyms see **idea**.

notorious for synonyms see **famous**.

novel for synonyms see **new**.

novice for synonyms see **amateur**.

noxious for synonyms see **pernicious**.

nude for synonyms see **bare**.

nullify, invalidate, void, negate —To **nullify** is literally to bring to nought, as by depriving of effectiveness, validity, etc. [The bad weather *nullified* whatever advantage we'd had.] **Invalidate** and **void** specifically imply a depriving of legal force or authority [to *invalidate*, or *void*, a contract]. **Negate** implies a bringing to a state of nonexistence, as by destroying or denying [good *negates* evil].

numerous for synonyms see **many**.

nunnery for synonyms see **cloister**.

nuptials for synonyms see **marriage**.

O

obdurate for synonyms see **inflexible**.

obedient, docile, tractable, compliant, amenable —**Obedient** suggests a giving in to the orders or instructions of one in authority or control [an *obedient* child]. **Docile** implies a temperament that submits easily to control or that fails to resist domination [a *docile* wife]. **Tractable** implies ease of management or control but does not connote the submissiveness of **docile** and applies to things as well as people [Silver is a *tractable*, that is, malleable, metal.] **Compliant** suggests a weakness of character that allows one to yield meekly to another's request or demand [Army life had made him *compliant*.] **Amenable** suggests such amiability or desire to be agreeable as would lead one to submit readily [He is *amenable* to discipline.] —*Antonyms:* **disobedient, refractory.**

obese for synonyms see **fat.**

object, protest, remonstrate, expostulate, demur —Object implies opposition to something because of strong dislike or disapproval [I *object* to her meddling.] (*See also synonyms at* **intention.**) **Protest** implies the making of strong, formal, often written objection to something [They *protested* the new tax increase.] **Remonstrate** implies protest and argument in demonstrating to another that he or she is wrong or blameworthy [He *remonstrated* against her hostile attitude.] **Expostulate** suggests strong, earnest pleading or argument to change another's views or actions [I *expostulated* with him about his self-sacrifice.] **Demur** implies the raising of objections or the taking of exception so as to delay action [I *demurred* at her proposal to dine out.]

object for antonyms see **agree, consent.**

objective for synonyms see **fair** and **intention.**

obligation for synonyms see **duty.**

obliging for synonyms see **amiable.**

obliterate for synonyms see **erase.**

obnoxious for synonyms see **hateful.**

obscene for synonyms see **coarse.**

obscure, vague, enigmatic, cryptic, ambiguous, equivocal —Obscure applies to that which is perceived with difficulty either because it is concealed or veiled or because of obtuseness in the perceiver [Her reasons remain *obscure*.] **Vague** implies such a lack of precision or exactness as to be indistinct or unclear [a *vague* idea]. **Enigmatic** and **cryptic** are used of that which baffles or perplexes, the word implying deliberate intention to puzzle [his *enigmatic* behavior, a *cryptic* warning]. **Ambiguous** applies to that which puzzles because it allows of more than one interpretation [an *ambiguous* title]. **Equivocal** is used of something ambiguous that is deliberately used to mislead or confuse [an *equivocal* answer]. —*Antonyms:* **clear, distinct, obvious.** *For other antonyms see* **evident.**

obsequious for synonyms see **servile.**

observation for synonyms see **remark.**

observe for synonyms see **celebrate, discern.**

obsolete for synonyms see **old.**

obstacle, impediment, obstruction, hindrance, barrier —**Obstacle** is used of anything which literally or figuratively stands in the way of one's progress [Her father's opposition remained their only *obstacle*.] **Impediment** applies to anything that delays or retards progress by interfering with the normal action [a speech *impediment*]. **Obstruction** refers to anything that blocks progress or some activity as if by stopping up a passage [Your interference is an *obstruction* of justice.] **Hindrance** applies to anything that thwarts progress by holding back or delaying [Lack of supplies is the greatest *hindrance* to my experiment.] **Barrier** applies to any apparently insurmountable obstacle that prevents progress or keeps separate and apart [Language differences are often a *barrier* to understanding.]

obstinate for synonyms see **stubborn.**

obstreperous for synonyms see **vociferous.**

obstruct for synonyms see **hinder.**

obstruction for synonyms see **obstacle**.

obtain for synonyms see **get**.

obtrude for synonyms see **intrude**.

obtuse for synonyms see **dull**.

obviate for synonyms see **prevent**.

obvious for synonyms see **evident**.

obvious for antonyms see **obscure**, **secret**.

occasion for synonyms see **cause**.

occur for synonyms see **happen**.

occurrence, event, incident, episode, circumstance —**Occurrence** is the general word for anything that happens or takes place [an unforeseen *occurrence*]. An **event** is an occurrence of relative significance, especially one growing out of earlier happenings or conditions [the *events* that followed the surrender]. An **incident** is an occurrence of relatively minor significance, often one connected with a more important event [The award was just another *incident* in his career.] An **episode** is a distinct event that is complete in itself but forms part of a larger event or is one of a series of events [an *episode* of his childhood]. A **circumstance** is an event that is either incidental to, or a determining factor of, another event [the *circumstances* surrounding my decision].

odd for synonyms see **strange**.

odious for synonyms see **hateful**.

odium for synonyms see **disgrace**.

odor for synonyms see **smell**.

offend, affront, insult, outrage —**Offend** implies a causing displeasure or resentment, intentionally or unintentionally, by wounding another's feelings or by a breach of his or her sense of propriety [He will be *offended* if he is not invited.] **Affront** implies open and deliberate disrespect or offense [to *affront* one's modesty]. **Insult** implies an affront so insolent or contemptuously rude as to cause deep humiliation and resentment [She *insulted* me by calling me a liar.] **Outrage** implies an extreme offense against one's sense of right, justice, propriety, etc. [The judge was *outraged* by the offer of a bribe.]

offense, resentment, umbrage, pique, displeasure —**Offense** implies displeased or hurt feelings as the result of a slight or insult [Don't take *offense* at my criticism.] **Resentment** adds implications of indignation, a brooding over an injury, and ill will toward the offender [a *resentment* cherished for days]. **Umbrage** implies offense or resentment at being slighted or having one's pride hurt [He took *umbrage* at the tone of her letter.] **Pique** suggests a passing feeling of ruffled pride, usually over a trifle. **Displeasure** may describe a feeling varying from dissatisfaction or disapproval to anger and indignation.

offer, proffer, tender, present —**Offer** is the general term meaning to hold out before one for acceptance or refusal [to *offer* money, to *offer* help]. **Proffer**, a literary term, is usually used of something intangible [She accepted the *proffered* assistance.] **Tender** is a formal or polite synonym [to *tender* one's thanks, to *tender* one's resignation] and is specifically applied to something offered in payment of an obligation. **Present** often adds to *offer* the idea of outward show, formality, or ceremony [to *present* a petition to Congress, to *present* a new play].

office for synonyms see **function, position.**

old, ancient, antique, antiquated, archaic, obsolete —**Old** implies a having been in existence or use for a relatively long time [old shoes, old civilizations]. **Ancient**

specifically implies reference to times long past [*ancient* history]. **Antique** is applied to that which dates from ancient times, or, more commonly, from a former period [*antique* furniture]. **Antiquated** is used to describe that which has become old-fashioned or outdated [*antiquated* notions of decorum]. **Archaic**, in this connection, applies to that which is marked by the characteristics of an earlier period [An *archaic* iron fence surrounded the house.] **Obsolete** is applied to that which has fallen into disuse or is out-of-date [*obsolete* weapons].

old for antonyms see **new, young.**

ominous, portentous, fateful, foreboding —**Ominous** implies a threatening character but does not necessarily connote a disastrous outcome [His request was met by an *ominous* silence.] **Portentous** literally implies a foreshadowing, especially of evil, but is now more often used of that which arouses awe or amazement because of its prodigious or marvelous character [a *portentous* event]. **Fateful** may imply a fatal character or control by fate, but is now usually applied to that which is of momentous or decisive significance [a *fateful* truce conference]. **Foreboding** implies a portent or presentiment of something evil or harmful [a *foreboding* anxiety].

omit for synonyms see **neglect.**

omnipresent, ubiquitous —**Omnipresent**, strictly applicable only to the Deity in its implication of presence in all places at the same time, is loosely used of anything that is always present within a given sphere [The spirit of competition is *omnipresent* in business.] **Ubiquitous** implies a being present, or seeming to be present, everywhere but not always at the same time or place [The trillium is a *ubiquitous* spring wildflower.]

onerous, burdensome, oppressive, exacting —Onerous applies to that which is laborious or troublesome, often because of its annoying or tedious character [the *onerous* duties of a janitor]. **Burdensome** applies to that which is wearisome or oppressive to the mind or spirit as well as to the body [*burdensome* responsibilities]. **Oppressive** stresses the overbearing cruelty of the person or thing that inflicts hardship, or emphasizes the severity of the hardship itself [*oppressive* weather, an *oppressive* king]. **Exacting** suggests the making of great demands on one's attention, skill, or care [an *exacting* supervisor, *exacting* work].

opaque, cloudy, turbid —Opaque means impervious to the transmission of light; not transparent or translucent [The oil made an *opaque* film on the water.] **Cloudy**, in this comparison, is used in describing a liquid that contains sediment or any glass, plastic, etc. through which one cannot see clearly [The aquarium was *cloudy*.] **Turbid** means muddy or cloudy from having sediment stirred up [The lake was *turbid* after the storm.]

opaque for antonyms see **clear**.

open for synonyms see **frank**.

open for antonyms see **close**[1], **secret**.

opinion, belief, view, conviction, sentiment, persuasion —Opinion applies to a conclusion or judgment which, while it remains open to dispute, seems true or probable to one's own mind [It's my *opinion* that he'll agree.] **Belief** refers to the mental acceptance of an idea or conclusion, often a doctrine or dogma proposed to one for acceptance [religious *beliefs*]. A **view** is an opinion affected by one's personal manner of looking at things [She gave us her *views* on life.] A **conviction** is a strong belief about whose truth one has no doubts [I have a *conviction* of his innocence.] **Sentiment** refers to an opinion that is the result of deliberation but is colored with emotion. **Persuasion** refers to a strong belief that is unshakable because one wishes to believe in its truth.

opponent, antagonist, adversary, enemy, foe —**Opponent**, an unemotional word, refers to anyone who is opposed to one, as in a fight, game, or debate. **Antagonist** implies more active opposition, especially in a struggle for control or power. **Adversary** usually suggests actual hostility in the conflict. **Enemy** may imply actual hatred in the opponent and a desire to injure, or it may simply refer to any member of the opposing group, nation, etc., whether or not there is personal animosity or hostility involved. **Foe**, now a somewhat literary synonym for **enemy**, connotes more active hostility.

opponent for antonyms see **associate**.

opportune for synonyms see **timely**.

oppose, resist, withstand —**Oppose** implies offensive action taken against something that threatens or interferes with one. **Resist** implies defensive action taken against something that is already in active opposition to one [One *opposes* legislative action under consideration, one *resists* a measure already passed by refusing to comply with it.] **Withstand** usually implies resistance that successfully thwarts or frustrates the attack [Can they *withstand* the new onslaught?] —*Antonyms:* **submit, succumb, comply**.

opposite, contrary, antithetical, reverse, antonymous —**Opposite** is applied to things that are symmetrically opposed in position, direction, etc. [They sat at *opposite* ends of the table.] **Contrary** adds to this connotations of conflict or antagonism [They hold *contrary* views.] **Antithetical** implies diametrical opposition so that the contrasted things are as far apart or as different as is possible [Our interests are completely *antithetical.*] **Reverse** applies to that which moves or faces in the opposite direction [the *reverse* side of a fabric]. **Antonymous** is used specifically of words that are so opposed in meaning that each contradicts, reverses, or negates the other [Good and bad are *antonymous* terms.] —*Antonym:* **like.** *For other antonyms see* **same.**

oppress for synonyms see **wrong.**

oppressive for synonyms see **onerous.**

optimistic for synonyms see **happy.**

optimistic for antonyms see **cynical, hopeless.**

option for synonyms see **choice.**

opulent for synonyms see **rich.**

oral, verbal —Oral refers to that which is spoken, as distinguished from that which is written or otherwise communicated [an *oral* promise, an *oral* request]. **Verbal,** though sometimes synonymous with *oral,* in strict discrimination refers to anything using words, either written or oral, to communicate an idea or feeling [a *verbal* image, a *verbal* illustration].

oration for synonyms see **speech.**

order for synonyms see **command.**

order for antonyms see **confusion.**

orderly, methodical, systematic —Orderly implies freedom from disorder or confusion as by observing a proper arrangement, a set rule, etc. [an *orderly* desk, an *orderly* crowd, an *orderly* meeting]. **Methodical** implies a following closely and regularly a definite procedure that is carefully planned in detail [a *methodical* investigation, a *methodical* worker]. **Systematic** often adds the implications of thoroughness and elaborateness and stresses the overall purpose, design, pattern, etc. [a *systematic* suppression of the opposition, a *systematic* study of consumers' preferences]. —*Antonyms:* **disorderly, haphazard, chaotic.**

ordinance for synonyms see **law.**

ordinary for synonyms see **common.**

ordinary for antonyms see **strange.**

origin, source, beginning, inception, root —**Origin** is applied to that from which a person or thing has its very beginning [the *origin* of a word]. **Source** is applied to the point or place from which something arises, comes, or develops [The sun is our *source* of energy]. **Beginning** is the basic general term for a starting point or place [the *beginning* of a quarrel]. **Inception** is specifically applied to the beginning of an undertaking, organization, etc. [Smith headed the business from its *inception.*] **Root** suggests an origin so deep and basic as to be the ultimate cause from which something stems [to go to the *root* of the matter].

original for synonyms see **new.**

original for antonyms see **trite.**

originate for synonyms see **rise.**

ornament for synonyms see **adorn.**

oscillate for synonyms see **swing.**

ostracize for synonyms see **banish.**

otiose for synonyms see **vain.**

oust for synonyms see **eject.**

outcome for synonyms see **effect.**

outdo for synonyms see **excel.**

outfit for synonyms see **furnish.**

outlandish for synonyms see **strange.**

outlast for synonyms see **outlive.**

outline, contour, profile, silhouette —**Outline** is used of the line bounding the limits of an object [The sketch shows only the *outline* of the skyscrapers.] (*See also* synonyms at **form**.) **Contour**, specifically applied to the configuration of a land mass, in extension stresses the shape of an object or mass as determined by its outline [the soft *contour* of her waist]. **Profile** is used of the outline or contour of the face in a side view or of the outline of any object as it is seen against a background [the *profile* of the trees against the sky]. **Silhouette** applies to a profile protrait, especially of the head and usually in solid black, or it may be used of any dark shape seen against a light background [the *silhouette* of a house against the moonlight].

outlive, outlast, survive —All three of these words imply a continuing to exist longer than others or after a specified occasion. **Outlive** stresses one's power to endure, as in competition with others or in overcoming a difficulty [to *outlive* one's enemies, to *outlive* a disgrace]. **Outlast** means to remain existent for a longer time [to *outlast* one's usefulness]. **Survive** means to remain alive after another's death [Two sons *survive* the deceased.] or after a perilous incident [They *survived* the tornado.]

outrage for synonyms see **offend**.

outrageous, flagrant, monstrous, atrocious, heinous —**Outrageous** applies to that which so exceeds all bounds of right, morality, or decency as to be intolerable [an *outrageous* insult]. **Flagrant** implies a glaringly bad or openly evil character in persons or their acts [a *flagrant* sinner, a *flagrant* violation]. **Monstrous** and **atrocious** are applied to that which is extremely or shockingly wrong, bad, evil, cruel, etc. [a *monstrous* vice, a *monstrous* lie, *atrocious* cruelty, *atrocious* manners]. **Heinous** implies such exteme wickedness as to arouse the strongest hatred and revulsion [a *heinous* crime].

outspoken for synonyms see **frank**.

outstanding for synonyms see **noticeable**.
overbearing for synonyms see **proud**.
overcome for synonyms see **conquer**.
overdue for synonyms see **tardy**.
overlook for synonyms see **neglect**.
overthrow for synonyms see **conquer**.
overturn for synonyms see **upset**.
own for synonyms see **acknowledge** and **have**.

P

**pacify, appease, mollify, placate, propitiate, concili-
ate** —Pacify implies a making quiet and peaceful that
which has become noisy or disorderly [to *pacify* a crying
child]. **Appease** suggests a pacifying by gratifying or
giving in to the demands of [to *appease* one's hunger].
Mollify suggests a soothing of wounded feelings or an allaying of indignation [His compliments failed to *mollify*
her.] **Placate** implies the changing of a hostile or angry
attitude to a friendly or favorable one [to *placate* an offended colleague]. **Propitiate** is used to mean an allaying or forestalling of hostile feeling by winning the good
will of [to *propitiate* a deity]. **Conciliate** implies the use
of arbitration, concession, persuasion, etc. in an attempt
to win over. —*Antonyms:* **anger, enrage**.
pack for synonyms see **bundle, group**.
package for synonyms see **bundle**.
pagan, heathen, gentile —Pagan and heathen are both
applied to nonmonotheistic peoples, but **pagan** specifically refers to one of the ancient polytheistic peoples,
especially the Greeks and Roman. **Heathen** is applied
to any of the peoples regarded as primitive idolaters;

gentile (often **Gentile**) is applied to one who is not a Jew, or, among Mormons, to one who is not a Mormon.

pains for synonyms see **effort**.

pair for synonyms see **couple**.

pale, pallid, wan, ashen, livid —**Pale**, in this comparison the least connotative of these words, implies merely an unnatural whiteness or colorlessness, often temporary, of the complexion of a person with fair skin. **Pallid** suggests a paleness resulting from exhaustion, faintness, or emotional strain. **Wan** suggests the paleness resulting from an emaciating illness. **Ashen** implies the grayish paleness of the skin as in death. **Livid** refers to a grayish-blue (now sometimes misunderstood as white or red) complexion, as of one in great rage or fear.

pale for antonyms see **rosy**.

pallid for synonyms see **pale**.

palpable for synonyms see **evident, perceptible**.

paltry for synonyms see **petty**.

pamper for synonyms see **indulge**.

panegyric for synonyms see **tribute**.

panic for synonyms see **fear**.

paradigm for synonyms see **model**.

paralyze for synonyms see **shock**.

paramount for synonyms see **dominant**.

paraphrase for synonyms see **translation**.

parasite, sycophant, toady, hanger-on, leech, sponge, sponger —**Parasite** refers to one who derives advantage or sustenance from another and gives nothing in return. A **sycophant** is one who seeks advantage or favor from the wealthy or powerful by flattery and fawning. **Toady** suggests the servility and snobbery of one who seeks familiarity with those whom he or she regards as superiors. **Hanger-on** is applied to anyone regarded contemptuously for close adherence to and dependence on another. **Leech** is applied to a parasite who clings closely to another and extracts whatever can be taken for his or her own advantage. **Sponge** (or **sponger**) is a colloquial term for a parasite and stresses total dependence and disinclination to work.

parcel for synonyms see **bundle**.

pardon for synonyms see **absolve**.

parody for synonyms see **caricature**.

parsimonious for synonyms see **stingy**.

part, portion, piece, division, section, segment, fraction, fragment —Part is the general word for any of the components of a whole [a *part* of one's life]. (*See also synonyms at* **separate**.) A **portion** is specifically a part allotted to someone or something [his *portion* of the inheritance]. A **piece** is either a part separated from the whole [a *piece* of pie] or a single standardized unit of a collection [a *piece* of statuary]. A **division** is a part formed by cutting, partitioning, classifying, etc. [the fine-arts *division* of a library]. **Section** is equivalent to **division** but usually connotes a smaller part [a *section* of a bookcase]. **Segment** implies a part separated along natural lines of division [a *segment* of a tangerine]. A **fraction** is strictly a part contained by the whole an integral number of times, but generally it connotes an insignificant part [He received only a *fraction* of the benefits.] A **fragment** is a relatively small part separated by or as by breaking [a *fragment* of rock].

part for antonyms see **complete, join, stick, tie**.

partial for antonyms see **complete**.

partiality for synonyms see **prejudice**.

particular for synonyms see **dainty, single, special**.

partisan for synonyms see **follower**.

pass away or **pass on** for synonyms see **die**.

passion, fervor, ardor, enthusiasm, zeal —Passion usually implies a strong emotion that has an overpowering or compelling effect [His *passions* overcame his reason.] (*See also synonyms at* **feeling**.) **Fervor** and **ardor** both imply emotion of burning intensity, **fervor** suggesting a constant glow of feeling [religious *fervor*], and **ardor**, a restless, flamelike emotion [the *ardors* of youth]. **Enthusiasm** implies strongly favorable feelings for an object or cause and usually suggests eagerness in the pursuit of something [his *enthusiasm* for golf]. **Zeal** implies intense enthusiasm for an object or cause, usually as displayed in vigorous and untiring activity in its support [a *zeal* for reform].

passionate, impassioned, ardent, fervent, fervid —Passionate implies strong or violent emotion, often of an impetuous kind [a *passionate* rage]. **Impassioned** suggests an expression of emotion that is deeply and sincerely felt [an *impassioned* plea for tolerance]. **Ardent** and **fervent** suggest a fiery or glowing feeling of eagerness, enthusiasm, devotion, etc. [an *ardent* pursuit of knowledge, a *fervent* prayer]. **Fervid** differs from **fervent** in often suggesting an outburst of intense feeling that is at a fever pitch [a vengeful, *fervid* hatred].

passive for synonyms see **inactive**.

pastoral for synonyms see **rural**.

patch for synonyms see **mend**.

pathetic for synonyms see **moving**.

pathos, bathos, poignancy —Pathos names that quality, in a real situation or in a literary or artistic work, which evokes sympathy and a sense of sorrow or pity. **Bathos** applies to a false or overdone pathos that is absurd in its effect. **Poignancy** implies an emotional quality that is keenly felt, often to the point of being sharply painful.

patience for synonyms see **endurance**.

patrimony for synonyms see **heritage**.

patron for synonyms see **sponsor**.

pattern for synonyms see **model**.

pawn for synonyms see **pledge**.

pay, compensate, remunerate, reimburse, indemnify, repay, recompense —**Pay** is the simple, direct word meaning to give money, etc. due for services rendered, goods received, etc. (*See also synonyms at* **wage**.) **Compensate** implies a return, whether monetary or not, thought of as equivalent to the service given, the effort expended, or the loss sustained [He could never be *compensated* for the loss of his son.] **Remunerate** stresses the idea of payment for a service rendered, but it often also carries an implication of reward [A bumper crop *remunerated* the farmer for his labors.] To **reimburse** is to pay back what has been expended [The salesman was *reimbursed* for his traveling expenses.] To **indemnify** is to pay for what has been lost or damaged [They were *indemnified* for the war destruction.] **Repay** implies a paying back of money given to one or it may refer to a doing or giving of anything in requital [How can I *repay* you for your kindness?] **Recompense** stresses the idea of compensation or requital.

peaceful for synonyms see **calm**.

peaceful for antonyms see **belligerent, warlike**.

peak for synonyms see **summit**.

peculiar for synonyms see **strange**.

pecuniary for synonyms see **financial**.

peek for synonyms see **look**.

peer for synonyms see **look**.

peeve for synonyms see **irritate.**

pellucid for synonyms see **clear.**

penitence, repentance, contrition, compunction, remorse, regret —**Penitence** implies sorrow over having sinned or done wrong. **Repentance** implies full realization of one's sins or wrongs and a will to change one's ways. **Contrition** implies a deep, crushing sorrow for one's sins, with a true purpose of amendment. **Compunction** implies a pricking of the conscience and therefore suggests a sharp but passing feeling of uneasiness about wrongdoing. **Remorse** implies a deep and torturing sense of guilt. **Regret** may refer to sorrow over any unfortunate occurrence as well as over a fault or act of one's own.

pen name for synonyms see **pseudonym.**

pensive, contemplative, reflective, meditative —**Pensive** suggests a dreamy, often somewhat sad or melancholy concentration of thought [the *pensive* look in her eyes]. **Contemplative** implies intent concentration of thought as on some abstract matter, often connoting this as a habitual practice [a *contemplative* scholar]. **Reflective** suggests an orderly, often analytical turning over in the mind with the aim of reaching some definite understanding [After a *reflective* pause he answered.] **Meditative**, on the other hand, implies a quiet and sustained musing, but with no definite intention of understanding or reaching a conclusion [a *meditative* walk in the cloister].

penurious for synonyms see **stingy.**

penury for synonyms see **poverty.**

perceive for synonyms see **discern.**

perceptible, sensible, palpable, tangible, appreciable —**Perceptible** is applied to anything that can be apprehended by the senses but often connotes that the thing is just barely visible, audible, etc. [a *perceptible* smell of coffee]. **Sensible** applies to that which can clearly be perceived [a *sensible* difference in their size]. **Palpable** refers to anything that can be perceived by or as by the sense of touch [a *palpable* fog]. **Tangible** applies to that which can be grasped, either with the hand or the mind [*tangible* property, *tangible* ideas]. **Appreciable** is used of that which is sufficiently perceptible to be measured or estimated, or to have significance [an *appreciable* amount]. —*Antonym:* **imperceptible**.

perfidious for synonyms see **faithless**.

perform, do, execute, accomplish, achieve, effect, fulfill —Perform, often a mere formal equivalent for **do**, is usually used of a more or less involved process rather than a single act [to *perform* an experiment]. **Execute** implies a putting into effect or completing that which has been planned or ordered [to *execute* a law]. **Accomplish** suggests effort and perseverance in carrying out a plan or purpose [to *accomplish* a mission]. **Achieve** implies the overcoming of obstacles in accomplishing something of worth or importance [to *achieve* a lasting peace]. **Effect** also suggests the conquering of difficulties but emphasizes what has been done to bring about the result [His cure was *effected* by the use of certain drugs.] **Fulfill**, in strict discrimination, implies the full realization of what is expected or demanded [to *fulfill* a promise].

perfume for synonyms see **scent**.

peril for synonyms see **danger**.

perimeter for synonyms see **circumference**.

period, epoch, era, age, eon —Period is the general term for any portion of time. **Epoch** and **era** are often used interchangeably, but in strict discrimination **epoch** applies to the beginning of a new period marked by radical changes, new developments, etc. and **era**, to the entire period [The steam engine marked an *epoch* in transportation. Our forefathers lived in an *era* of revolution.] **Age** is applied to period identified with some dominant personality or distinctive characteristic [the Stone *Age*]. **Eon** refers to an indefinitely long period [It all happened *eons* ago.]

periodic for synonyms see **intermittent**.

peripatetic for synonyms see **itinerant**.

periphery for synonyms see **circumference**.

perish for synonyms see **die**.

permanent, lasting —**Permanent** means lasting or expected to last indefinitely without change [The Sphinx is a *permanent* structure.] **Lasting** means enduring for a very long time [a *lasting* peace]. *See also synonyms at* **continual**.

permanent for antonyms see **temporary, transient**.

permit for synonyms see **let**.

permit for antonyms see **forbid, prevent**.

pernicious, baneful, noxious, deleterious, detrimental —**Pernicious** applies to that which does great harm by insidiously undermining or weakening [*pernicious* anemia, a *pernicious* dogma]. **Baneful** implies a harming by or as by poisoning [a *baneful* superstition]. **Noxious** refers to anything that is injurious to physical or mental health [*noxious* fumes]. **Deleterious** implies slower, less irreparable injury to the health [the *deleterious* effects of an unbalanced diet]. **Detrimental** implies a causing of damage, loss, or disadvantage to something specified [His error was *detrimental* to our cause.] —*Antonyms:* **harmless, innocuous**.

perpendicular for synonyms see **vertical**.

perpetual for synonyms see **continual**.

perplex for synonyms see **bewilder**.

persecute for synonyms see **wrong**.

perseverance, persistence, tenacity, pertinacity
—**Perseverance** implies a continuing to do something in spite of difficulties, obstacles, etc. **Persistence**, in a favorable sense, implies steadfast perseverance; in an unfavorable sense, annoyingly stubborn continuance. **Tenacity** and **pertinacity** imply firm adherence to some purpose, action, belief, etc., the former word in a favorable sense, and the latter with the unfavorable connotation of annoying obstinacy.

persist for synonyms see **continue**.

persistence for synonyms see **perseverance**.

personality for synonyms see **disposition**.

perspicacious for synonyms see **shrewd**.

persuade, induce, prevail on —**Persuade** implies an influencing to an action or belief by an overt appeal to a person's reason or emotions [After some coaxing, pleading, and arguing, we *persuaded* her to go.] **Induce** suggests a subtler leading of a person to a course of action so that the decision seems finally to come from him or her [She was *induced* to accept the position.] **Prevail on**, interchangeable with either of the preceding, often suggests stronger resistance overcome only after considerable argument, etc. [He could not be *prevailed on* to change his mind.]

persuasion for synonyms see **opinion**.

pertinacious for synonyms see **stubborn**.

pertinacity for synonyms see **perseverance**.

pertinent for synonyms see **relevant**.

perturb for synonyms see **disturb**.

perverse for synonyms see **contrary**.

pervert for synonyms see **debase**.

pessimistic for synonyms see **cynical**.

pet for synonyms see **caress**.

petite for synonyms see **small**.

petition for synonyms see **appeal**.

petty, trivial, trifling, paltry, picayune —**Petty** is applied to that which is comparatively small, minor, or unimportant of its kind, and it is often used to imply small-mindedness [*petty* cash, a *petty* grudge]. **Trivial**, in strict usage, applies to that which, because it is both petty and commonplace, is quite insignificant [a *trivial* remark]. **Trifling** applies to something so small and unimportant as to be negligible or of very little account [a *trifling* matter]. **Paltry** is applied to something contemptibly small or worthless [a *paltry* wage]. **Picayune** is used of a person or thing considered small, mean, or insignificant [a *picayune* objection]. —*Antonyms:* **important, significant.**

phase, aspect, facet, angle —**Phase** applies to any of the ways in which something may be observed, considered, or presented, and often refers to a state in development or in a cycle of changes [the *phases* of the moon]. **Aspect** emphasizes the appearance of a thing as seen or considered from a particular point of view [to consider a problem from all *aspects*]. **Facet** literally or figuratively applies to any of the faces of a many-sided thing [the many *facets* of a diamond, the *facets* of a personality]. **Angle** suggests a specific aspect seen from a point of view sharply limited in scope, or, sometimes, an aspect seen only by a sharply acute observer [He knows all the *angles*.]

philanthropic, humanitarian, charitable, altruistic

—**Philanthropic** implies interest in the general human welfare, especially as shown in large-scale gifts to charities or the endowment of institutions for human advancement. **Humanitarian** implies more direct concern with promoting the welfare of humanity, especially through reducing pain and suffering. **Charitable** implies the giving of money or other help to those in need. **Altruistic** implies a putting of the welfare of others before one's own interests and therefore stresses freedom from selfishness.

phlegmatic for synonyms see **impassive**.

physic, laxative, aperient, purgative, cathartic —**Physic** is the general word for anything taken to relieve constipation or to effect a bowel movement. **Laxative** and **aperient** usually refer to milder physics of a kind that are ordinarily taken to promote discharge from the bowels, such as mineral oil, agar-agar, certain fruit juices, etc. **Purgative** and **cathartic** apply to stronger physics, such as castor oil, Epsom salts, calomel, etc., that are more drastic in their action.

physical for synonyms see **bodily, material**.

physiognomy for synonyms see **face**.

picayune for synonyms see **petty**.

pick for synonyms see **choose**.

pickle for synonyms see **predicament**.

pictorial for synonyms see **graphic**.

picturesque for synonyms see **graphic**.

piece for synonyms see **part**.

pile, heap, stack —**Pile** is usually used of a mass of things gathered together [a *pile* of dishes in the sink]. (*See also synonyms at* **building**.) **Heap** refers to a mass or mound of things that are jumbled together [a *heap* of dirty clothes on the chair]. **Stack** is used of a somewhat orderly pile [a *stack* of hay, a *stack* of books].

pilfer for synonyms see **steal**.

pillage for synonyms see **ravage**, **spoil**.

pilot for synonyms see **guide**.

pinch for synonyms see **steal**.

pinnacle for synonyms see **summit**.

pious, devout, religious, sanctimonious —**Pious** suggests scrupulous adherence to the forms of one's religion but may, in derogatory usage, connote hypocrisy [The *pious* burghers defrauded their tenants.] **Devout** implies sincere, worshipful devotion to one's faith or religion [a *devout* nun]. **Religious** stresses faith in a particular religion and constant adherence to its tenets [to lead a *religious* life]. **Sanctimonious** in current usage implies a hypocritical pretense of piety or devoutness and often connotes smugness or haughtiness [his *sanctimonious* disapproval of dancing]. —*Antonym:* **impious**.

piquant for synonyms see **pungent**.

pique for synonyms see **offense** and **provoke**.

pitch for synonyms see **throw**.

piteous for synonyms see **pitiful**.

pitfall for synonyms see **trap**.

pithy for synonyms see **concise**.

pithy for antonyms see **wordy**.

pitiable for synonyms see **pitiful**.

pitiful, pitiable, piteous —**Pitiful** applies to that which arouses or deserves pity because it is sad or pathetic [The suffering of the starving natives was *pitiful.*] **Pitiable** is the preferred term when a greater or lesser degree of contempt is mingled with commiseration [The opposition shrank to a *pitiable* minority.] **Piteous** stresses the nature of the thing calling for pity rather than its influence on the observer [*piteous* groans].

pitiless for synonyms see **cruel**.

pity, compassion, commiseration, sympathy, condolence —**Pity** implies sorrow felt for another's suffering or misfortune, sometimes connoting slight contempt because the object is regarded as weak or inferior [He felt *pity* for a man so ignorant.] **Compassion** implies pity accompanied by an urge to help or spare [Moved by *compassion*, I did not press for payment.] **Commiseration** implies deeply felt and openly expressed feelings of pity [She wept with her friend in *commiseration*.] **Sympathy**, in this connection, implies such kinship of feeling as enables one to really understand or even to share the sorrow, etc. of another [He always turned to his wife for *sympathy*.] **Condolence** now usually implies a formal expression of sympathy with another in sorrow [a letter of *condolence*].

placate for synonyms see **pacify**.

placid for synonyms see **calm**.

plague for synonyms see **annoy**.

plain for synonyms see **evident**.

plan, design, project, scheme —**Plan** refers to any detailed method, formulated beforehand, for doing or making something [vacation *plans*]. **Design** stresses the final outcome of a plan and implies the use of skill or craft, sometimes in an unfavorable sense, in executing or arranging this [It was his *design* to separate us.] **Project** implies the use of enterprise or imagination in formulating an ambitious or extensive plan [a housing *project*]. **Scheme**, a less definite term than the preceding, often connotes either an impractical, visionary plan or an underhanded intrigue [a *scheme* to embezzle the funds].

plane for synonyms see **level**.

plastic for synonyms see **pliable**.

platitude, commonplace, truism, cliché, bromide —A **platitude** is a trite remark or idea, especially one uttered as if it were novel or momentous. A **commonplace** is any obvious or conventional remark or idea. A **truism** is a statement whose truth is widely known and whose utterance, therefore, seems superfluous. A **cliché** is an expression or idea which, though once fresh and forceful, has become hackneyed and weak through much repetition. **Bromide** is an informal term for a platitude that is especially dull, tiresome, or annoying.

plausible, credible, specious —**Plausible** applies to that which at first glance appears to be true, reasonable, and valid, but which may or may not be so, although there is no connotation of deliberate deception [a *plausible* argument]. **Credible** is used of that which is believable because it is supported by evidence, sound logic, etc. [a *credible* account]. **Specious** applies to that which is superficially reasonable or valid, but is actually not so, and it connotes intention to deceive [a *specious* excuse]. —*Antonyms:* **genuine, actual.**

play, sport, frolic, romp, gambol —**Play**, the general verb, implies activity, physical or mental, whose sole aim is diversion or amusement. **Sport**, in this connection now somewhat literary, implies active physical play out-of-doors [children *sporting* in the woods]. **Frolic** implies lighthearted, carefree gaiety in playing [*frolicking* at a New Year's Eve party]. **Romp** suggests active, boisterous play that involves running about and jumping [Young people were *romping* on the beach.] **Gambol** suggests the skipping about of lambs or young children in play [Let them *gambol* on the lawn.]

play for antonyms see **work.**

plead for synonyms see **appeal.**

pleasant, pleasing, agreeable, enjoyable, gratifying
—**Pleasant** and **pleasing** both imply the producing of an agreeable effect upon the mind or senses, but the former word stresses the effect produced [a *pleasant* smile] and the latter, the ability to produce such an effect [her *pleasing* ways]. **Agreeable** is used of that which is in accord with one's personal likes, mood, etc. [*agreeable* music]. **Enjoyable** implies the ability to give enjoyment or pleasure [an *enjoyable* picnic]. **Gratifying** implies the ability to give satisfaction or pleasure by indulging a person's wishes, hopes, or dreams [a *gratifying* experience]. —*Antonyms:* **unpleasant, disagreeable.**

pleasure, delight, joy, enjoyment —**Pleasure** is the general term for an agreeable feeling of satisfaction, ranging from a quiet sense of gratification to a positive sense of happiness. **Delight** implies a high degree of obvious pleasure, openly and enthusiastically expressed [a child's *delight* with a new toy]. **Joy** describes a keenly felt, exuberant, often demonstrative happiness [their *joy* at his safe return]. **Enjoyment** suggests a somewhat more quiet feeling of satisfaction with that which pleases [our *enjoyment* of the recital]. —*Antonyms:* **displeasure, vexation.** *For other antonyms see* **sorrow.**

pledge, earnest, token, pawn, hostage —**Pledge** applies to anything given as security for the performance of an act or contract or for the payment of a debt [He gave her a ring as a *pledge*.] **Earnest**, in current usage, applies to anything given or done as an indication, promise, or assurance of more to follow [His early triumphs are an *earnest* of his success.] **Token** is used of anything serving or given as evidence of authority, genuineness, or good faith [This watch is a *token* of our gratitude.] **Pawn** now usually refers to an article left as security for the money lent on it by a pawnbroker. **Hostage** is applied to a person handed over as a pledge for the fulfillment of certain terms or one seized and kept to force others to comply with demands.

✓ **plentiful, abundant, copious, profuse, ample** —**Plentiful** implies a large or full supply [a *plentiful* supply of food]. **Abundant** implies a very plentiful or very large supply [a forest *abundant* in wild game]. **Copious**, now used chiefly with reference to quantity produced or used, implies a rich or flowing abundance [a *copious* harvest, a *copious* discharge]. **Profuse** implies a giving or pouring forth abundantly or lavishly, often to excess [*profuse* in his thanks]. **Ample** applies to that which is large enough to meet all demands [Her savings are *ample* to see her through this crisis.] —*Antonym:* **scarce.** *For other antonyms see* **meager.**

✓ **pliable, pliant, plastic, ductile, malleable** —**Pliable** and **pliant** both imply capability of being easily bent, suggesting the suppleness of a wooden switch and, figuratively, a yielding nature or adaptability. **Plastic** is used of substances, such as plaster or clay, that can be molded into various forms which are retained upon hardening, and figuratively suggests an impressionable quality. **Ductile** literally and figuratively suggests that which can be finely drawn or stretched out [Copper is a *ductile* metal]. **Malleable** literally or figuratively suggests that which can be hammered, beaten, or pressed into various forms [Copper is *malleable* as well as ductile.] —*Antonyms:* **inflexible, rigid, brittle.** *For other antonyms see* **stiff.**

pliant for synonyms see **pliable.**

plight for synonyms see **predicament.**

plot for synonyms see **conspiracy.**

pluck for synonyms see **fortitude**.

plucky for synonyms see **brave**.

plumb for synonyms see **vertical**.

plump for synonyms see **fat**.

plunder for synonyms see **ravage, spoil**.

poet, rhymer, rhymester, versifier, poetaster —Poet, the general term for a writer of poems or verses, is sometimes used specifically to designate a writer of verse, or, in extended use, of elevated prose, who has great powers of imagination, intuition, and expression. **Rhymer, rhymester,** and **versifier** do not in themselves carry the special favorable connotations of **poet** and, when used in contrast to it, specifically suggest a lack of true poetic powers. **Poetaster** is always a term of contempt for a writer of inferior or trashy verse.

poetaster for synonyms see **poet**.

pogrom for synonyms see **slaughter**.

poignancy for synonyms see **pathos**.

poignant for synonyms see **moving**.

poise for synonyms see **tact**.

polish, burnish, buff, shine —Polish implies a rubbing, as with a cloth or tool and, often, an abrasive, paste, etc., to produce a smooth or glossy surface [to *polish* silver, to *polish* glass, to *polish* furniture]. **Burnish** specifically suggests a rubbing of metals to make them bright and lustrous [*burnished* steel]. **Buff** implies polishing with a stick or tool covered with specially treated leather (originally buffalo hide) or other material [to *buff* the fingernails]. **Shine** implies a making bright and clean by polishing [to *shine* shoes].

polite for synonyms see **civil**.

polite for antonyms see **rude**.

politic for synonyms see **suave**.

pollute for synonyms see **contaminate**.

ponder, meditate, muse, ruminate —Ponder implies a weighing mentally and suggests careful consideration of a matter from all sides [to *ponder* over a problem]. **Meditate**, in intransitive use, suggests quiet, deep contemplation [He *meditated* on the state of the world] and, transitively, deliberate consideration of some plan [to *meditate* revenge]. **Muse** implies such contemplation or reflection as seems to absorb one completely [to *muse* over the past]. **Ruminate** suggests turning a matter over and over in the mind.

ponderous for synonyms see **heavy**.

poor, impoverished, destitute, impecunious, indigent —Poor is the simple, direct term for one who lacks the resources for reasonably comfortable living. **Impoverished** is applied to one who having once had plenty is now reduced to poverty [an *impoverished* aristocrat]. **Destitute** implies such great poverty that the means for mere subsistence, such as food and shelter, are lacking [left *destitute* by the war]. **Impecunious** applies to one in a habitual state of poverty and suggests that this results from his or her own practices [an *impecunious* gambler]. **Indigent** implies such relative poverty as results in a lack of luxuries and the endurance of hardships [books for *indigent* children].

poor for antonyms see **rich**.

popular for synonyms see **common**.

portentous for synonyms see **ominous**.

portion for synonyms see **fate, part**.

pose, affectation, mannerism, airs —Pose refers to an attitude or manner that is assumed for the effect that it will have on others [Her generosity is a mere *pose*.] *(See also synonyms at* **posture**.) **Affectation** is used of a specific instance of artificial behavior intended obviously to impress others [an *affectation* of speech]. A **mannerism** is a peculiarity in behavior, speech, etc. (often originally an affectation) that has become habitual and unconscious [his *mannerism* of raising one eyebrow in surprise]. **Airs** is used of an affected pretense of superior manners and graces [She's always putting on *airs.*]

position, situation, office, post, job —Position applies to any specific employment for salary or wages, but often connotes white-collar or professional employment. **Situation** now usually refers to a position that is open or to one that is desired [*situation* wanted as instructor]. **Office** refers to a position of authority or trust, especially in government, a corporation, etc. A **post** is a position or office that carries heavy responsibilities, especially one to which a person is appointed. **Job** is now the common, comprehensive equivalent for any of the preceding terms.

positive for synonyms see **sure.**

possess for synonyms see **have.**

possess for antonyms see **lack.**

possible, practicable, feasible —Possible is used of anything that may exist, occur, or be done, depending on circumstances [a *possible* solution to a problem]. (*See also synonyms at* **probable.**) **Practicable** applies to that which can readily be effected under the prevailing conditions or by the means available [a *practicable* plan]. **Feasible** is used of that which is likely to be carried through to a successful conclusion and, hence, connotes the desirability of doing so [a *feasible* enterprise].

post for synonyms see **position.**

postpone for synonyms see **adjourn.**

postulate for synonyms see **presume.**

posture, attitude, pose, stance —Posture refers to the habitual or assumed disposition of the parts of the body in standing, sitting, etc. [erect *posture*]. Attitude refers to a posture assumed either unconsciously, as in manifesting a mood or emotion, or intentionally for carrying out a particular purpose [an *attitude* of watchfulness]. **Pose** suggests a posture assumed, usually deliberately, as for artistic effect [to hold a *pose* for a photographer]. **Stance** refers to a particular way of standing, especially with reference to the position of the feet, as in certain sports [the *stance* of a golfer].

potency for synonyms see **strength.**

potential for synonyms see **latent.**

pound for synonyms see **beat.**

pour for synonyms see **flow.**

poverty, destitution, indigence, penury —Poverty, the broadest of these terms, implies a lack of the resources for reasonably comfortable living. **Destitution** and **want** imply such great poverty that the means for mere subsistence, such as food and shelter, are lacking. **Indigence**, a somewhat euphemistic term, implies a lack of luxuries to which one was formerly accustomed. **Penury** suggests such severe poverty as to cause abjectness, or a loss of self-respect. —Antonyms: **wealth, affluence.**

power, authority, jurisdiction, dominion, sway, control, command —Power denotes the inherent ability or the admitted right to rule, govern, determine, etc. [the strictly limited *power* of a president]. (*See also synonyms at* **strength.**) Authority refers to the power, because of rank or office, to give commands, enforce obedience, make decisions, etc. [the *authority* of a teacher]. **Jurisdiction** refers to the power to rule or decide within certain defined limits [the *jurisdiction* of the courts]. **Do-**

minion implies sovereign or supreme authority [*dominion* over a dependent state]. **Sway** stresses the predominance or sweeping scope of power [The Romans held *sway* over the ancient world.] **Control**, in this connection, implies authority to regulate, restrain, or curb [under the *control* of a guardian]. **Command** implies such authority that enforces obedience to one's orders [in *command* of a regiment].

practicable for synonyms see **possible, practical.**

practical, practicable —**Practical** stresses effectiveness as tested by actual experience or as measured by a completely realistic approach to life or the particular circumstances involved. **Practicable** is used of something that appears to be capable of being put into effect, but has not yet been developed or tried [Before the era of electronics, television did not seem *practicable;* today it is but one of the *practical* applications of the science.] —*Antonyms:* **impractical, impracticable.**

practice for synonyms see **habit.**

praise, laud, acclaim, extol, eulogize —**Praise** is the simple, basic word implying an expression of approval, esteem, or commendation [to *praise* one's performance]. **Laud** implies great, sometimes extravagant praise [The critics *lauded* the actor to the skies.] **Acclaim** suggests an outward show of strong approval, as by loud applause and cheering [He was *acclaimed* the victor.] **Extol** implies exalting or lofty praise [The scientist was *extolled* for his work.] **Eulogize** suggests formal praise in speech or writing, as on a special occasion [The minister *eulogized* the exemplary life of the deceased.]

praise for antonyms see **criticize, disparage.**

pray for synonyms see **appeal.**

preamble for synonyms see **introduction.**

preceding for synonyms see **previous**.

precept for synonyms see **doctrine**.

precipitate for synonyms see **sudden**.

precipitous for synonyms see **steep**.

precise for synonyms see **correct**.

preclude for synonyms see **prevent**.

precursor for synonyms see **forerunner**.

predicament, dilemma, quandary, plight, fix, pickle
—**Predicament** implies a complicated, perplexing situation from which it is difficult to disentangle oneself.
Dilemma implies a predicament necessitating a choice
between equally disagreeable alternatives. **Quandary**
emphasizes a state of great perplexity and uncertainty.
Plight emphasizes a distressing or unfortunate situation.
Fix and **pickle** are both colloquial terms loosely interchangeable with any of the preceding, although more
precisely **fix** is equivalent to **predicament** and **pickle**, to
plight.

predict for synonyms see **foretell**.

predilection for synonyms see **prejudice**.

predominant for synonyms see **dominant**.

preeminent for synonyms see **dominant**.

preface for synonyms see **introduction**.

prefer for synonyms see **choose**.

preference for synonyms see **choice**.

prejudice, bias, partiality, predilection —**Prejudice**
implies a preconceived and unreasonable judgment or
opinion, usually an unfavorable one marked by suspicion, fear, intolerance, or hatred [The murder was
motivated by race *prejudice*.] **Bias** implies a mental leaning in favor of or against someone or something [Few of
us are without *bias* of any kind.] **Partiality** implies an
inclination to favor a person or thing because of strong

fondness or attachment [The conductor has a *partiality* for the works of Brahms.]   **Predilection** implies a preconceived liking, formed as a result of one's background or temperament, that inclines one to a particular preference [She has a *predilection* for murder mysteries.]

prejudiced for antonyms see **fair**.

premise for synonyms see **presume**.

premium for synonyms see **bonus, reward**.

preoccupied for synonyms see **absent-minded**.

preponderant for synonyms see **dominant**.

preposterous for synonyms see **absurd**.

presage for synonyms see **foretell**.

present, gift, donation, gratuity —**Present** and **gift** both refer to something given as an expression of friendship, affection, or esteem, but **gift**, in current use, more often suggests formal bestowal [Christmas *presents*, the painting was a *gift* to the museum]. (*See also synonyms at* **give, offer**.)   **Donation** applies to a gift of money, etc. for a philanthropic, charitable, or religious purpose, especially as solicited in a public drive for funds [a *donation* to the orchestra fund].   **Gratuity** usually applies to a gift of money for services rendered, such as a tip to a waiter.

preserve for synonyms see **defend**.

press for synonyms see **urge**.

prestige for synonyms see **influence**.

presume, presuppose, assume, postulate, premise —**Presume** implies a taking something for granted or accepting it as true, usually on the basis of probable evidence in its favor and the absence of proof to the contrary [The man is *presumed* to be of sound mind.]   **Presuppose** is the broadest term here, sometimes suggesting a taking something for granted unwarrantedly

[This writer *presupposes* a too extensive vocabulary in children.] and, in another sense, implying that something is required as a preceding condition [Brilliant technique in piano playing *presupposes* years of practice.] **Assume** implies the supposition of something as the basis for argument or action [Let us *assume* his motives were good.] **Postulate** implies the assumption of something as an underlying factor, often one that is incapable of proof [His argument *postulates* the inherent goodness of human beings.] **Premise** implies the setting forth of a proposition on which a conclusion can be based.

presuppose for synonyms see **presume.**

pretend for synonyms see **assume.**

pretty for synonyms see **beautiful.**

prevail for synonyms see **persuade.**

prevailing, current, prevalent, rife —**Prevailing** applies to that which leads all others in acceptance, usage, belief, etc. at a given time and in a given place [a *prevailing* practice]. **Current** refers to that which is commonly known or accepted or in general usage at the time specified or, if unspecified, at the present time [That pronunciation was *current* in the 18th century.] **Prevalent** implies widespread occurrence or acceptance but does not now connote the predominance of **prevailing** [a *prevalent* belief]. **Rife** implies rapidly increasing prevalence and often connotes excitement or commotion [Rumors about the plague were *rife.*]

prevalent for synonyms see **prevailing.**

prevaricate for synonyms see **lie.**

prevent, forestall, preclude, obviate, avert —**Prevent** implies a stopping or keeping from happening, as by some prior action or by interposing an obstacle or impediment [to *prevent* disease]. **Forestall** suggests advance action to stop something in its course and thereby make it ineffective [Try to *forestall* their questions.] **Preclude** implies a making impossible by shutting off every possibility of occurrence [Locked doors *precluded* his escape.] **Obviate** suggests the preventing of some unfavorable outcome by taking the necessary anticipatory measures [His frankness *obviated* objections.] **Avert** suggests a warding off of imminent danger or misfortune [Diplomacy can *avert* war.] —*Antonyms:* **permit, allow.**

previous, prior, preceding, antecedent, foregoing, former —**Previous** generally implies a coming before in time or order [a *previous* encounter]. **Prior** adds to this a connotation of greater importance or claim as a result of being first [a *prior* commitment]. **Preceding**, especially when used with the definite article, implies a coming immediately before [the *preceding* night]. **Antecedent** adds to the meaning of **previous** a connotation of direct causal relationship with what follows [events *antecedent* to the war]. **Foregoing** applies specifically to something previously said or written [the *foregoing* examples]. **Former** always connotes comparison, stated or implied, with what follows (termed *latter*). —*Antonym:* **following.**

pride, conceit, vanity, vainglory, self-esteem —**Pride** refers either to a justified or excessive belief in one's own worth, merit, or superiority [He takes *pride* in his accuracy.] (*See also synonyms at* **group.**) **Conceit** always implies an exaggerated opinion of oneself, one's achievements, etc. [blinded by his overweening *conceit*]. **Vanity** suggests an excessive desire to be admired by others for one's achievements, appearance, etc. [Her *vanity* is wounded by criticism.] **Vainglory** implies extreme conceit as manifested by boasting, swaggering, or arrogance [the *vainglory* of a conquering general]. **Self-esteem** implies a high opinion of oneself, sometimes a higher opinion than is held by others. —*Antonym:* humility.

principal for synonyms see **chief.**

prior for synonyms see **previous.**

priory for synonyms see **cloister.**

prize for synonyms see **appreciate, reward, spoil.**

probable, possible, likely —**Probable** applies to that which appears reasonable on the basis of evidence or logic but is neither certain nor proved. **Possible** applies to that which, although not probable, can conceivably exist, occur, be done, etc. **Likely** suggests greater probability than **possible**, but less credibility than **probable**. —*Antonyms:* improbable, unlikely.

probe for synonyms see **investigation.**

probity for synonyms see **honesty.**

problematical for synonyms see **doubtful.**

proclaim for synonyms see **declare.**

proclivity for synonyms see **inclination.**

procure for synonyms see **get.**

prodigal for synonyms see **profuse.**

prodigal for antonyms see **thrifty.**

profanation for synonyms see **sacrilege.**

profane for antonyms see **holy.**

profanity for synonyms see **blasphemy.**

professional, expert —A **professional** is a person who has a vocation requiring advanced education, such as medicine, law, teaching, engineering, theology, etc. An **expert** is one who has much knowledge or training in a special field [He is an *expert* in appraising antiques.]

professional for antonyms see **amateur.**

proffer for synonyms see **offer.**

profile for synonyms see **outline.**

profound, learned, erudite —**Profound** denotes something that is marked by intellectual depth [We had a *profound* discussion about death.] **Learned** means having or showing much learning, especially that which is acquired by extensive study [a *learned* doctor]. **Erudite** means having a deep learning gained by reading, and implies learning that is beyond the grasp of the ordinary mind [an *erudite* scholar]. *See also synonyms at* **wise**.

profound for antonyms see **superficial**.

profuse, lavish, extravagant, prodigal, luxuriant, lush —**Profuse** implies a pouring or giving forth freely, often to the point of excess [*profuse* apologies]. (*See also synonyms at* **plentiful**.) **Lavish** implies an unstinted, generous, sometimes unreasonably liberal, giving [*lavish* attentions]. **Extravagant** always suggests unreasonably excessive, wasteful spending or giving [*extravagant* living]. **Prodigal** implies such reckless extravagance as to suggest eventual impoverishment [the *prodigal* heirs to a fortune]. **Luxuriant** suggests production in great and rich abundance [*luxuriant* foliage]. **Lush** implies such great luxuriance as to seem excessive [a *lush* jungle]. —*Antonyms:* **limited, scant, spare**.

prognosticate for synonyms see **foretell**.

progressive for synonyms see **liberal**.

prohibit for synonyms see **forbid**.

project for synonyms see **plan**.

projection, protrusion, protuberance, bulge —**Projection** implies a jutting out abruptly beyond the rest of the surface [the *projection* of the eaves beyond the sides of a house]. **Protrusion** suggests a thrusting or pushing out that is of an abnormal or disfiguring nature [*protrusion* of the eyeballs]. **Protuberance** suggests a swelling out, usually in rounded form [The tumor on his arm formed a *protuberance*.] **Bulge** suggests an outward swelling of a kind that may result from internal pressure [The *bulge* in the can resulted from the fermentation of its contents.]

prolific for synonyms see **fertile**.

prolix for synonyms see **wordy**.

prolix for antonyms see **concise**.

prologue for synonyms see **introduction**.

prolong for synonyms see **extend**.

prolonged for antonyms see **brief**.

prominent for synonyms see **noticeable**.

promote for synonyms see **advance**.

prompt for synonyms see **quick**.

prone, supine, prostrate, recumbent —**Prone**, in strict use, implies a position in which the front part of the body lies upon or faces the ground [He fell *prone* upon the ground and drank from the brook.] (*See also synonyms at* **likely**.) **Supine** implies a position in which a person lies on his or her back [He snores when he sleeps in a *supine* position.] **Prostrate** implies the position of one thrown or lying flat in a prone or supine position, as in great humility or complete submission, or because laid low [The victim lay *prostrate* at the murderer's feet.] **Recumbent** suggests a lying down or back in any position one might assume for rest or sleep [She was *recumbent* on the chaise longue.] —*Antonym:* **erect**.

proof, evidence, testimony, exhibit —**Proof**, as compared here, applies to facts, documents, etc. that are so certain or convincing as to demonstrate the validity of a conclusion beyond reasonable doubt. **Evidence** applies to something presented before a court, as a witness's statement, an object, etc. which bears on or establishes a fact. **Testimony** applies to verbal evidence given by a witness under oath. **Exhibit** applies to a document or object produced as evidence in a court of law.

propel for synonyms see **push**.

propensity for synonyms see **inclination**.

proper for synonyms see **fit**.

proper for antonyms see **improper**.

property for synonyms see **quality**.

prophesy for synonyms see **foretell**.

propitiate for synonyms see **pacify**.

propitious for synonyms see **favorable**.

proportion for synonyms see **symmetry**.

proportional for synonyms see **proportionate**.

proportionate, proportional, commensurable, commensurate —**Proportionate** and **proportional** both imply a being in due proportion, the former usually being preferred with reference to two things that have a reciprocal relationship to each other [The output was *proportionate* to the energy expended.] and the latter with reference to a number of similar or related things [*proportional* representation]. **Commensurable** applies to things measurable by the same standard or to things properly proportioned. **Commensurate**, in addition, implies equality in measure or size of things that are alike or somehow related to each other [a reward *commensurate* with his heroism]. —*Antonym:* **disproportionate**.

proposal, proposition —**Proposal** refers to a plan, offer, etc. presented for acceptance or rejection [His *proposal* for a decrease in taxes was approved.] **Proposition**, commonly used in place of **proposal** with reference to business dealings and the like, in a strict sense applies to a statement, theorem, etc. set forth for argument, demonstration, or proof [We had a debate on the *proposition* that all men are created equal.]

propose for synonyms see **intend**.

proposition for synonym see **proposal**.

propriety for synonyms see **decorum**.

prorogue for synonyms see **adjourn**.

prospect for synonyms see **view**.

prosper for synonyms see **succeed**.

prostrate for synonyms see **prone**.

protect for synonyms see **defend**.

protest for synonyms see **object**.

protract for synonyms see **extend**.

protrusion for synonyms see **projection**.

protuberance for synonyms see **projection**.

proud, arrogant, haughty, insolent, overbearing, supercilious, disdainful —**Proud** is the broadest term in this comparison, ranging in implication from proper self-esteem or pride to an overweening opinion of one's importance [too *proud* to ask for help, *proud* as a peacock]. **Arrogant** implies an aggressive, unwarranted assertion of superior importance or privileges [the *arrogant* colonel]. **Haughty** implies such consciousness of high station or rank as is displayed in scorn of those one considers beneath one [a *haughty* dowager]. **Insolent,** in this connection, implies both haughtiness and great contempt, especially as manifested in behavior or speech that insults or affronts others [She has an *insolent* disregard for her servant's feelings.] **Overbearing** implies extreme, domineering insolence [an *overbearing* supervisor]. **Supercilious** stresses an aloof, scornful manner toward others [a *supercilious* intellectual snob]. **Disdainful** implies even stronger and more overt feelings of scorn for that which is regarded as beneath one.

proud for antonyms see **ashamed, humble**.

proverb for synonyms see **saying**.

provident for synonyms see **thrifty**.

providential for synonyms see **lucky**.
provisional for synonyms see **temporary**.
provisions for synonyms see **food**.
provoke, excite, stimulate, pique —**Provoke**, in this connection, implies rather generally an arousing to some action or feeling [thought-*provoking*]. *(See also synonyms at* **irritate**.) **Excite** suggests a more powerful or profound stirring or moving of the thoughts or emotions [The story *excites* my imagination.] **Stimulate** implies an arousing as if by goading or pricking and, hence, often connotes a bringing out of a state of inactivity or indifference [to *stimulate* one's enthusiasm]. **Pique** suggests a stimulating as if by irritating [to *pique* one's curiosity].
prowl for synonyms see **lurk**.
prudent for synonyms see **careful, wise**.
prying for synonyms see **curious**.
pseudonym, pen name, nom de plume, alias, incognito —A **pseudonym** is a fictitious name assumed, especially by a writer, as for anonymity, for effect, etc. **Pen name** and **nom de plume** are applied specifically to the pseudonym of a writer. **Alias** also refers to an assumed name and, in popular use, is specifically applied to one taken by a criminal to disguise his or her identity. **Incognito** is usually applied to a fictitious name temporarily assumed by a famous person, as in traveling, to avoid being recognized.
psychosis for synonyms see **insanity**.
publish for synonyms see **declare**.
puerile for synonyms see **young**.
pugnacious for synonyms see **belligerent**.
pull, draw, drag, tug, haul, tow —**Pull** is the broad, general term of this list, meaning to exert force on so as

to cause to move. **Draw** suggests a smoother, more even motion than **pull** [He *drew* his sword from its scabbard.] **Drag** implies the slow pulling of something heavy, connoting great resistance in the thing pulled [They *dragged* the desk across the floor.] **Tug** suggests strenuous, persistent effort in pulling but does not necessarily connote success in moving the object [He *tugged* at the rope to no avail.] **Haul** implies sustained effort in transporting something heavy, often mechanically [to *haul* furniture in a truck]. **Tow** implies pulling by means of a rope or cable [to *tow* a stalled automobile].

pull for antonyms see **push**.

pummel for synonyms see **beat**.

punch for synonyms see **strike**.

pungent, piquant, racy, spicy —**Pungent** literally applies to taste or smell, suggesting a sharp, stinging quality [*pungent* spices], and figuratively implies a penetrating or stimulating quality [*pungent* humor]. **Piquant** implies an agreeable pungency, tartness, or zest [a *piquant* salad dressing, *piquant* wit]. **Racy** suggests the piquancy and tang of something in its natural and freshest condition [a *racy* flavor] and, in its now more usual figurative use, implies a spirited, vigorous quality [*racy* slang]. **Spicy** suggests the pungent taste or fragrant aroma of spices [a *spicy* drink] and, figuratively, an exciting, often risqué quality [*spicy* stories]. —*Antonym:* **bland**. *For other antonyms see* **insipid**.

punish, discipline, correct, chastise, castigate, chasten —**Punish** implies the infliction of some penalty on a wrongdoer and generally connotes retribution rather than correction [to *punish* a murderer by hanging him]. **Discipline** suggests punishment that is intended to control or to establish habits of self-control [to *discipline* a naughty child]. **Correct** suggests punishment for the purpose of overcoming faults [to *correct* unruly pupils]. **Chastise** implies usually corporal punishment and connotes both retribution and correction. **Castigate** now implies punishment by severe public criticism or censure [to *castigate* a corrupt official]. **Chasten** implies the infliction of tribulation in order to make obedient, meek, etc. and is used especially in a theological sense ["He *chastens* and hastens His will to make known."]

pupil, student, scholar —**Pupil** is applied either to a child in school or to a person who is under the personal supervision of a teacher [Heifetz was a *pupil* of Leopold Auer.] **Student** is applied either to one attending an institution above the elementary level or to one who is making a study of a particular problem [a *student* of social problems]. **Scholar**, originally equivalent to **pupil**, is now usually applied to one who has general erudition or who is highly versed in a particular branch of learning [a linguistics *scholar*].

pure for synonyms see **chaste**.

purgative for synonyms see **physic**.

purloin for synonyms see **steal**.

purport for synonyms see **meaning**.

purpose for synonyms see **intend** and **intention**.

push, shove, thrust, propel —**Push** implies the exertion of force or pressure by a person or thing in contact with the object to be moved ahead, aside, etc. [to *push* a baby carriage]. **Shove** implies a pushing of something so as to force it to slide along a surface, or it suggests roughness in pushing [*Shove* the box into the corner.] To **thrust** is to push with sudden, often violent force, sometimes so as to penetrate something [He *thrust* his hand into the water.] **Propel** implies a driving forward by a force that

imparts motion [The wind *propelled* the sailboat.]
push for antonyms see **pull**.
pushy for synonyms see **aggressive**.
pusillanimous for synonyms see **cowardly**.
putrefy for synonyms see **decay**.
putrid for synonyms see **stinking**.
puzzle for synonyms see **bewilder**.
Pygmy or **pygmy** for synonyms see **dwarf**.

Q

quack, charlatan, mountebank, impostor, faker —**Quack** and **charlatan** both apply to a person who unscrupulously pretends to knowledge or skill he or she does not possess, but **quack** almost always is used of a fraudulent or incompetent practitioner of medicine. **Mountebank**, in modern use, applies to a person who resorts to cheap and degrading methods in some activity. **Impostor** applies especially to a person who fraudulently impersonates another and, more generally, to anyone who is inclined to fraud, deception, etc. **Faker** is a colloquial term for a person who gives a false representation of his or her character, work, etc.
quail for synonyms see **recoil**.
quaint for synonyms see **strange**.
quake for synonyms see **shake**.
qualified for synonyms see **able**.
quality, property, character, attribute, trait —**Quality**, the broadest in scope of these terms, refers to a characteristic (physical or nonphysical, individual or typical) that constitutes the basic nature of a thing or is one of its distinguishing features [the *quality* of mercy]. **Property**

applies to any quality that belongs to a thing by reason of the essential nature of the thing [Elasticity is a *property* of rubber.] **Character** is the scientific or formal term for a distinctive or peculiar quality of an individual or of a class, species, etc. [a hereditary *character*]. An **attribute** is a quality assigned to a thing, especially one that may reasonably be deduced as appropriate to it [Omnipotence is an *attribute* of God.] **Trait** specifically applies to a distinguishing quality of a personality [Enthusiasm is one of his outstanding *traits*.]

qualm, scruple, compunction, misgiving —Qualm implies a painful feeling of uneasiness arising from a consciousness that one is or may be acting wrongly [He had *qualms* about having cheated on the test.] **Scruple** implies doubt or hesitation arising from difficulty in deciding what is right, proper, just, etc. [to break a promise without *scruple*]. **Compunction** implies a twinge of conscience for wrongdoing, now often for a slight offense [to have no *compunctions* about telling a white lie]. **Misgiving** implies a disturbed state of mind resulting from a loss of confidence as to whether one is doing what is right [*misgiving* of conscience].

quandary for synonyms see **predicament**.

quarrel, wrangle, altercation, squabble, spat —Quarrel implies heated verbal strife marked by anger and resentment and often suggests continued hostility as a result. **Wrangle** suggests a noisy dispute in which each person is vehemently insistent on his or her views. **Altercation** implies verbal contention which may or may not be accompanied by blows. **Squabble** implies undignified, childish wrangling over a small matter. **Spat** is the colloquial term for a petty quarrel and suggests a brief outburst that does not have a significant effect on a relationship. —*Antonyms:* **agreement, harmony.**

quarrelsome for synonyms see **belligerent.**

queer for synonyms see **strange.**

query for synonyms see **ask.**

question for synonyms see **ask.**

question for antonyms see **answer.**

questionable for synonyms see **doubtful.**

quick, prompt, ready, apt —**Quick** implies ability to respond rapidly as an innate rather than a developed faculty [a *quick* mind]. (*See also synonyms at* **agile, fast.**) **Prompt** stresses immediate response to a demand as resulting from discipline, practice, etc. or from willingness [*prompt* to obey, a *prompt* acceptance]. **Ready** also implies preparation or willingness and, in another sense, connotes fluency, expertness, etc. [a *ready* sympathy, a *ready* jest]. **Apt,** in this connection, implies superior intelligence or a special talent as the reason for quickness of response [an *apt* pupil]. —*Antonym:* **slow.**

quicken for synonyms see **animate.**

quiescent for synonyms see **latent.**

quiet for synonyms see **still.**

quiet for antonyms see **gaudy** and **noise.**

quip for synonyms see **joke.**

quit for synonyms see **abandon, go, stop.**

quiver for synonyms see **shake.**

quiz for synonyms see **ask.**

R

rack for synonyms see **torment**.

racket for synonyms see **noise**.

racy for synonyms see **pungent**.

radiant for synonyms see **bright**.

radical for synonyms see **liberal**.

rage for synonyms see **anger** and **fashion**.

raise for synonyms see **lift**.

rally for synonyms see **stir**.

ramble for synonyms see **roam**.

rancid for synonyms see **stinking**.

rancor for synonyms see **malice**.

random, haphazard, casual, desultory, chance —**Random** applies to that which occurs or is done without careful choice, aim, plan, etc. [a *random* remark]. **Haphazard** applies to that which is done, made, or said without regard for its consequences or relevancy, and therefore stresses the implication of accident or chance [a *haphazard* selection of books]. **Casual** implies a happening or seeming to happen by chance without intention or purpose and often connotes nonchalance or indifference [a *casual* acquaintance]. **Desultory** suggests a lack of method or system, as in jumping from one thing to another [his *desultory* reading in the textbook]. **Chance** emphasizes accidental occurrence without prearrangement or planning [a *chance* encounter]. —*Antonym:* **deliberate**.

range, reach, scope, compass, gamut —**Range** refers to the full extent over which something is perceivable, effective, etc. [the full *range* of his knowledge]. (*See also synonyms at* **roam**.) **Reach** refers to the furthest limit of effectiveness, influence, etc. [beyond the *reach* of my understanding]. **Scope** implies considerable room and freedom of range, but within prescribed limits [Does it fall within the *scope* of this dictionary?] **Compass** also suggests completeness within limits regarded as a circumference [He did all within the *compass* of his power.] **Gamut**, in this connection, refers to the full range of shades or tones between the limits of something [the full *gamut* of emotions].

rank for synonyms see **flagrant, stinking.**

ransom for synonyms see **rescue.**

rapid for synonyms see **fast.**

rapture for synonyms see **ecstasy.**

rare, infrequent, uncommon, unusual, scarce —**Rare** is applied to something of which there are not many instances or specimens and usually connotes, therefore, great value [a *rare* gem]. **Infrequent** applies to that which occurs only at long intervals [his *infrequent* trips]. **Uncommon** and **unusual** refer to that which does not ordinarily occur and is therefore exceptional or remarkable [her *uncommon* generosity, this *unusual* heat]. **Scarce** applies to something of which there is, at the moment, an inadequate supply [Potatoes are *scarce* these days.] —*Antonyms:* **frequent, abundant.** *For other antonyms see* **common.**

rate for synonyms see **estimate.**

ratify for synonyms see **approve.**

ration for synonyms see **food.**

rational, reasonable, sensible —**Rational** implies the ability to reason logically, as by drawing conclusions from inferences, and often connotes the absence of emotionalism [Human beings are *rational* creatures.] **Reasonable** is a less technical term and suggests the use of practical reason in making decisions, choices, etc. [a *reasonable* solution to a problem]. **Sensible,** also a nontechnical term, implies the use of common sense or sound judgment [You made a *sensible* decision.]

rational for antonyms see **absurd, irrational.**

rations for synonyms see **food.**

rattle for synonyms see **embarrass.** ✓

ravage, devastate, plunder, sack, pillage, despoil —Ravage implies violent destruction, usually in a series of depredations or over an extended period of time, as by an army, a plague, etc. **Devastate** stresses the total ruin and desolation resulting from a ravaging. **Plunder** refers to the forcible taking of loot by an invading or conquering army. **Sack** and **pillage** both specifically suggest violent destruction and plunder by an invading or conquering army, **sack** implying the total stripping of all valuables in a city or town. **Despoil** is equivalent to **sack** but is usually used with reference to buildings, institutions, etc.

ravenous for synonyms see **hungry.**

raze for synonyms see **destroy.**

reach, gain, achieve, attain, accomplish —Reach, the broadest of these terms, implies an arriving at some goal, destination, point in development, etc. [He's *reached* the age of 60.] (*See also synonyms at* **range.**) **Gain** suggests the exertion of considerable effort to reach some goal [They've *gained* the top of the hill.] **Achieve** suggests the use of skill in reaching something [We've *achieved* a great victory.] **Attain** suggests a being goaded on by great ambition to gain an end regarded as beyond the reach of most people [He has *attained* fame in his profession.] **Accomplish** implies success in completing an assigned task [to *accomplish* an end].

ready for synonyms see **quick.**

real for synonyms see **true.**

real for antonyms see **false, fictitious, imaginary.**

rear for synonyms see **lift.**

reason for synonyms see **cause, think.**

reasonable for synonyms see **rational.**

reasonable for antonyms see **irrational.**

rebellion, revolution, insurrection, revolt, mutiny, uprising —**Rebellion** implies organized, armed, open resistance to the authority or government in power, and, when applied historically, connotes failure [Shay's *Rebellion*]. **Revolution** applies to a rebellion that succeeds in overthrowing an old government and establishing a new one [the American *Revolution*] or to any movement that brings about a drastic change in society [the Industrial *Revolution*]. **Insurrection** suggests a less extensive or less organized outbreak than **rebellion** [the Philippine *Insurrection*]. **Revolt** stresses a casting off of allegiance or a refusal to submit to established authority [the *revolt* of the angels led by Lucifer]. **Mutiny** applies to a forcible revolt of soldiers, or especially sailors, against their officers [*mutiny* on the Bounty]. **Uprising** is a simple, direct term for any outbreak against a government and applies to small limited actions or to initial indications of a general rebellion [local *uprisings* against the Stamp Act].

rebut for synonyms see **disprove.**

recalcitrant for synonyms see **unruly.**

recall for synonyms see **remember.**

recapitulate for synonyms see **repeat.**

receive, accept, admit, take —**Receive** means to get by having something given, told, absorbed, etc. and may or may not imply the consent of the recipient [to *receive* a gift, to *receive* a blow]. **Accept** means to receive willingly or favorably, but it sometimes connotes acquiescence rather than explicit approval [He was *accepted* as a member. She *accepted* the inevitable.] **Admit** stresses permission or concession on the part of the one that receives [I will not *admit* him in my home.] **Take**, in this connection, means to accept something that is offered or presented [We can't *take* money from you.]

receive for antonyms see **give**.

reciprocal for synonyms see **mutual**.

reckon for synonyms see **compute, rely**.

reclaim for synonyms see **recover**.

reclaim for antonyms see **abandon**.

recoil, shrink, flinch, wince, quail —Recoil implies a startled reaction or movement in fear, surprise, disgust, etc. [She *recoiled* in horror.] **Shrink** implies a drawing back, literally or figuratively, from that which is distressing, terrifying, etc. [She *shrank* from telling him.] **Flinch** implies a show of weakness or faintheartedness in shrinking from anything difficult, dangerous, or painful [He will not *flinch* from duty.] **Wince** suggests an involuntary manifestation of pain or distress, as by facial distortion [She *winced* at the blow.] **Quail** suggests a cowering abjectly in the face of anything that menaces one [He *quailed* as the bully approached.]

recollect for synonyms see **remember**.

recollection for synonyms see **memory**.

recompense for synonyms see **pay**.

recount for synonyms see **tell**.

recoup for synonyms see **recover**.

recover, regain, retrieve, recoup, reclaim —Recover implies a finding or getting back something that one has lost in any manner [to *recover* stolen property, to *recover* one's self-possession]. **Regain** more strongly stresses a winning back of something that has been taken from one [to *regain* a military objective]. **Retrieve** suggests diligent effort in regaining something [He was determined to *retrieve* his honor.] **Recoup** implies recovery of an equivalent in compensation [I tried to *recoup* my losses.] **Reclaim** implies recovery or restoration to a better or useful state [to *reclaim* wasteland].

recumbent for synonyms see **prone**.

recur for synonyms see **return**.

recurrent for synonyms see **intermittent**.

redeem for synonyms see **rescue**.

redolence for synonyms see **scent**.

redress for synonyms see **reparation**.

reduce for synonyms see **decrease**.

redundant for synonyms see **wordy**.

redundant for antonyms see **concise**.

reef for synonyms see **shoal**.

reel for synonyms see **stagger**.

refer, allude —**Refer** implies deliberate, direct, and open mention of something [The speaker *referred* in detail to their corrupt practice.] **Allude** implies indirect, often casual mention, as by a hint, a figure of speech, etc. [Although he used different names, he was *alluding* to his family.]

referee for synonyms see **judge**.

reflect for synonyms see **consider, think**.

reflective for synonyms see **pensive**.

refractory for synonyms see **unruly**.

refractory for antonyms see **obedient**.

refrain, abstain, forbear —**Refrain** usually suggests the curbing of a passing impulse in keeping oneself from saying or doing something [Although provoked, he *refrained* from answering.] **Abstain** implies voluntary self-denial or the deliberate giving up of something [to *abstain* from liquor]. **Forbear** suggests self-restraint manifesting a patient endurance under provocation [to *forbear* venting one's wrath].

refresh for synonyms see **renew**.

refuge for synonyms see **shelter**.

refuse for synonyms see **decline**.

refuse for antonyms see **consent**.

refute for synonyms see **disprove**.

regain for synonyms see **recover**.

regard, respect, esteem, admire —**Regard** is the most neutral of the terms here, in itself usually implying evaluation of worth rather than recognition of it [The book is highly *regarded* by authorities.] **Respect** implies high valuation of worth, as shown in deference or honor [a jurist *respected* by lawyers]. **Esteem**, in addition, suggests that the person or object is highly prized or cherished [a friend *esteemed* for his loyalty]. **Admire** suggests a feeling of enthusiastic delight in the appreciation of that which is superior [One must *admire* such courage.]

register for synonyms see **list**.

regret for synonyms see **penitence**.

regular for synonyms see **normal, steady**.

regular for antonyms see **irregular**.

regulation for synonyms see **law**.

reimburse for synonyms see **pay**.

reiterate for synonyms see **repeat**.

reject for synonyms see **decline**.

reject for antonyms see **approve, choose**.

rejoin for synonyms see **answer**.

rejuvenate for synonyms see **renew**.

relate for synonyms see **tell**.

related, kindred, cognate, allied, affiliate —**Related,**

applied to persons, implies close connection through consanguinity or, less often, through marriage [We are *related* through our mothers.], applied to things, close connection through common origin, interdependence, etc. [*related* subjects]. **Kindred** basically suggests blood relationship but in extension connotes close connection as because of similar nature, tastes, goals, etc. [We are *kindred* souls.] **Cognate** now usually applies to things and suggests connection because of a common source [*cognate* languages]. **Allied**, applied to persons, suggests connection through voluntary association; applied to things, connection through inclusion in the same category [*allied* sciences]. **Affiliate** usually suggests alliance of a smaller or weaker party with a larger or stronger one as a branch or dependent [Several companies are *affiliated* with this corporation.]

release for synonyms see **free**.

release for antonyms see **keep**.

relegate for synonyms see **commit**.

relent for synonyms see **yield**.

relevant, germane, pertinent, apposite, applicable, apropos —**Relevant** implies close logical relationship with, and importance to, the matter under consideration [*relevant* testimony]. **Germane** implies such close natural connection as to be highly appropriate or fit [Your reminiscences are not truly *germane* to this discussion.] **Pertinent** implies an immediate and direct bearing on the matter in hand [a *pertinent* suggestion]. **Apposite** applies to that which is both relevant and happily suitable or appropriate [an *apposite* analogy]. **Applicable** refers to that which can be brought to bear upon a particular matter or problem [Your description is *applicable* to several people.] **Apropos** is used of that which is opportune as well as relevant [an *apropos* remark]. —*Antonyms:* **inappropriate, extraneous.**

reliable for synonyms see **dependable.**

reliable for antonyms see **inconstant.**

relieve, alleviate, lighten, assuage, mitigate, allay —**Relieve** implies the reduction of misery, discomfort, or tediousness sufficiently to make it bearable [They played a game to *relieve* the monotony of the trip.] (*See also synonyms at* **comfort.**) **Alleviate** implies temporary relief, suggesting that the source of the misery remains unaffected [drugs to *alleviate* the pain]. **Lighten** implies a cheering or gladdening as by reducing the weight of oppression or depression [Nothing can *lighten* the burden of her grief.] **Assuage** suggests a softening or pacifying influence in lessening pain, calming passion, etc. [Her kind words *assuaged* his resentment.] **Mitigate** implies a moderating or making milder of that which is likely to cause pain [to *mitigate* a punishment]. **Allay** suggests an effective, although temporary or incomplete, calming or quieting [We've *allayed* his suspicions.]

religious for synonyms see **pious.**

relinquish, abandon, waive, forgo —**Relinquish** implies a giving up of something desirable and connotes compulsion or the force of necessity [He will not *relinquish* his advantage.] (*See also synonyms at* **surrender.**) **Abandon,** in this connection, implies a complete and final relinquishment, as because of weariness, discouragement, etc. [Do not *abandon* hope.] **Waive** suggests a voluntary relinquishing by refusing to insist on one's right or claim to something [to *waive* a jury trial]. **Forgo** implies the denial to oneself of something, as for reasons of expediency or altruism [I must *forgo* the pleasure of your company this evening.]

relinquish for antonyms see **keep.**

reluctant, disinclined, hesitant, loath, averse —**Reluctant** implies an unwillingness to do something, as because of distaste or irresolution [She was *reluctant* to marry.] **Disinclined** suggests a lack of desire for something, as because it fails to suit one's taste or because one disapproves of it [I feel *disinclined* to argue.] **Hesitant** implies a refraining from action, as because of fear or indecision [Don't be *hesitant* about asking this favor.] **Loath** suggests strong disinclination or a decided unwillingness [I am *loath* to depart.] **Averse** suggests a sustained, although not extreme, disinclination [She is *averse* to borrowing money.] —*Antonyms:* **inclined, disposed.** *For other antonyms see* **eager.**

rely, trust, depend, count, reckon, bank —To **rely** (*on* or *upon*) a person is to have confidence, usually on the basis of past experience, that the person will do what is expected [He can be *relied* on to keep the secret.] To **trust** is to have complete faith or assurance that one will not be let down by another [to *trust* in God]. To **depend** (*on* or *upon*) a person is to rely on him or her for support or aid [He can *depend* on his wife for sympathy.] To **count** (*on*) or, colloquially, to **reckon** (*on*) something is to consider it in one's calculations as certain [They *counted*, or *reckoned*, on my going.] To **bank** (*on*), a colloquial term, is to have confidence like that of one who is willing to risk money on something [Don't *bank* on his help.]

remain for synonyms see **stay.**

remainder, residue, residuum, remnant, balance —**Remainder** is the general word applied to what is left when a part is taken away [the *remainder* of a meal, the *remainder* of one's life]. **Residue** and **residuum** apply to what remains at the end of a process, as after the evaporation or combustion of matter or after the settlement of claims, etc. in a testator's estate. **Remnant** is applied to a fragment, trace, or any small part left after the greater part has been removed [*remnants* of cloth from the ends of bolts]. **Balance** may be used in place of **remainder**, but in strict use it implies the amount remaining on the credit or debit side.

remains for synonyms see **body**.

remark, observation, comment, commentary —**Remark** applies to a brief, more or less casual statement of opinion, etc., as in momentarily directing one's attention to something [a *remark* about her clothes]. An **observation** is an expression of opinion on something to which one has given some degree of special attention and thought [the warden's *observations* on prison reform]. A **comment** is a remark or observation made in explaining, criticizing, or interpreting something [*comments* on a novel]. **Commentary** is usually applied as a collective noun to a series of explanatory notes or annotations [a *commentary* on Aristotle's *Politics*].

remarkable for synonyms see **noticeable**.

remedy for synonyms see **cure**.

remember, recall, recollect, remind, reminisce —**Remember** implies a putting oneself in mind of something, often suggesting that the thing is kept alive in the memory so that it can be called to conscious thought without effort [He'll *remember* this day.] **Recall** and **recollect** both imply some effort of will to bring something back to mind, **recall**, in addition, often connoting an imparting of what is brought back [Let me *recall* what was said. It is fun to *recollect* the days of one's childhood.] **Remind** implies an agent as the cause of or stimulus for remembering [Your story *reminds* me of another.] **Reminisce** now usually implies the remembering and telling of past events or experiences in one's own life [They *reminisced* about school days.] —*Antonym:* **forget**.

remembrance for synonyms see **memory**.
remind for synonyms see **remember**.
reminisce for synonyms see **remember**.
reminiscence for synonyms see **memory**.
remiss, negligent, neglectful, derelict, lax, slack —**Remiss** implies the culpable omission or the careless or indifferent performance of a task or duty [*remiss* in one's obligations]. **Negligent** and **neglectful** both imply failure to attend to something sufficiently or properly, but **negligent** often stresses this as a habit or trait [*negligent* in dress] and **neglectful** carries an implication of intentional and culpable disregard [a mayor *neglectful* of his pledges to the voters]. **Derelict** implies flagrant neglect of a duty or obligation. **Lax** implies looseness in satisfying or enforcing requirements, observing standards or rules, etc. [*lax* discipline]. **Slack**, in this connection, implies lack of necessary diligence or efficiency, as because of laziness or indifference [*slack* service in a restaurant].

remnant for synonyms see **remainder**.
remonstrate for synonyms see **object**.
remorse for synonyms see **penitence**.
remote for synonyms see **far**.
remove for synonyms see **move**.
remove for antonyms see **introduce**.
removed for synonyms see **far**.
remunerate for synonyms see **pay**.
rend for synonyms see **tear**.

renew, renovate, restore, refresh, rejuvenate —**Renew** is the most direct but also the broadest term here, implying a making new again by replacing what is old, worn, exhausted, etc. [to *renew* a stock of goods]. To **renovate** is to clean up, replace or repair worn parts, etc. so as to bring back to good condition. To **restore** is to bring back to an original or unimpaired condition after exhaustion, illness, dilapidation, etc. [to *restore* an old castle]. **Refresh** implies a restoring of depleted strength, vigor, etc. by furnishing something needed [a *refreshing* sleep]. **Rejuvenate** implies a restoring of youthful appearance, vigor, etc. [She looked *rejuvenated* after the plastic surgery.]

renounce for synonyms see **abdicate**.

renovate for synonyms see **renew**.

renowned for synonyms see **famous**.

rent for synonyms see **hire**.

repair for synonyms see **mend**.

reparation, restitution, redress, indemnification —**Reparation** refers to the making of amends, specifically the paying of compensation, for some wrong or injury [war *reparations*]. **Restitution** implies return to the rightful owner of something that has been taken away, or of an equivalent [He made *restitution* for the libel.] **Redress** suggests retaliation or resort to the courts to right a wrong [to seek *redress* for an injury]. **Indemnification** refers to reimbursement, as by an insurance company, for loss, damage, etc.

repartee for synonyms see **wit**.

repay for synonyms see **pay**.

repeal for synonyms see **abolish**.

repeat, iterate, reiterate, recapitulate —**Repeat** is the common, general word meaning to say, do, make, or present over again [Will you *repeat* that question, please?] **Iterate** and **reiterate** both suggest a repeating, either once or several times, but **reiterate** strongly implies insistent repetition over and over again [He keeps *reiterating* his innocence.] **Recapitulate** suggests a repeating briefly of the main points in a discourse in summarizing [He will *recapitulate* his account of the ball game at 8:00 o'clock.]

repentance for synonyms see **penitence**.

replace, displace, supersede, supplant —**Replace** implies a taking the place of someone or something that is now lost, gone, destroyed, or worn out [We *replace* defective tubes.] **Displace** suggests the ousting or dislodgment of a person or thing by another that replaces it [He had been *displaced* in her affections by another man.] **Supersede** implies a replacing with something superior or more up-to-date [The steamship *superseded* the sailing ship.] **Supplant** suggests a displacing that involves force, fraud, or innovation [The prince had been *supplanted* by an impostor.]

replica for synonyms see **copy**.

reply for synonyms see **answer**.

report for synonyms see **tell**.

reprehend for synonyms see **criticize**.

reproduction for synonyms see **copy**.

repudiate for synonyms see **decline**.

repugnance for synonyms see **aversion**.

repugnant for synonyms see **hateful**.

require for synonyms see **demand**.

require for antonyms see **lack**.

requisite for synonyms see **essential** and **need**.

rescind for synonyms see **abolish**.

rescue, deliver, redeem, ransom, save —**Rescue** implies prompt action in freeing someone or something from imminent danger or destruction or in releasing someone from captivity [He *rescued* the drowning child.] **Deliver** implies a setting free from confinement or from some restricting situation [*Deliver* me from his interminable sermons.] **Redeem** suggests a freeing from bondage or from the consequences of sin, or a reclaiming, as from pawn, deterioration, etc. [How can I *redeem* my good name?] **Ransom** specifically implies the payment of what is demanded in order to free one held captive. **Save**, in this connection, is a general, comprehensive synonym for any of the preceding terms.

research for synonyms see **investigation**.
resemblance for synonyms see **likeness**.
resentment for synonyms see **offense**.
reserved for synonyms see **silent**.
residue for synonyms see **remainder**.
residuum for synonyms see **remainder**.
resign for synonyms see **abdicate, surrender**.
resilient for synonyms see **elastic**.
resist for synonyms see **oppose**.
resist for antonyms see **attack** and **yield**.
resolute for synonyms see **faithful**.
resolve for synonyms see **decide**.
resort for synonyms see **resource**.
resource, resort, expedient, makeshift, stopgap —Resource applies to any thing, person, or action to which one turns for aid in time of need or emergency [What *resource* is left us?] **Resort** is usually used of a final resource, qualified as by *last* [We'll take the train as a last *resort*.] **Expedient** refers to something used to effect a desired end, specifically to something used as a substitute for the usual means [The daybed was an excellent

expedient for unexpected guests.] **Makeshift** applies to a quick expedient and, as a somewhat derogatory term, connotes an inferior substitute, carelessness, etc. [She served sandwiches as a *makeshift* for dinner.] **Stopgap** refers to a temporary expedient, to be replaced when the usual means is again available [He's just a *stopgap* until a new manager is appointed.]

respect for synonyms see **regard**.

respect for antonyms see **disgrace**.

respond for synonyms see **answer**.

responsible, answerable, accountable —**Responsible** applies to one who has been delegated some duty or responsibility by one in authority and who is subject to penalty in case of default [He is *responsible* for making out the reports.] **Answerable** implies a legal or moral obligation for which one must answer to someone sitting in judgment [He is not *answerable* for the crimes of his parents.] **Accountable** implies liability for which one may be called to account [He will be held *accountable* for anything he may say.]

responsibility for synonyms see **duty**.

restful for synonyms see **comfortable**.

restitution for synonyms see **reparation**.

restive for synonyms see **contrary**.

restore for synonyms see **renew**.

restrain, curb, check, bridle, inhibit —**Restrain**, the term of broadest application in this list, suggests the use of strong force or authority either in preventing, or in suppressing and controlling, some action [Try to *restrain* your zeal.] **Curb, check,** and **bridle** derive their current implications from the various uses of a horse's harness. **curb** implying a sudden, sharp action to bring something under control [to *curb* one's tongue], **check** implying a slowing up of action or progress [to *check* inflationary trends], and **bridle** suggesting a holding in of emotion or feelings [to *bridle* one's envy]. **Inhibit**, as used in psychology, implies a suppressing or repressing of some action, thought, or emotion [Her natural verve had become *inhibited*.]

restrain for antonyms see **free, incite, indulge.**

restrict for synonyms see **limit.**

result for synonyms see **effect, follow.**

retain for synonyms see **keep.**

retain for antonyms see **relinquish.**

retard for synonyms see **delay.**

retard for antonyms see **advance.**

retarded for synonyms see **stupid.**

reticent for synonyms see **silent.**

retire for synonyms see **go.**

retort for synonyms see **answer.**

retreat for synonyms see **shelter.**

retrieve for synonyms see **recover.**

return, revert, recur —**Return** is the common word meaning to go or come back, as to a former place, person, or condition [Let us *return* home.] **Revert** implies a return to an earlier, usually more primitive, condition, or to the original owner, to a former topic of discussion, etc. [They have *reverted* to savagery.] **Recur** suggests the return of some action, occurrence, or experience, and often connotes its repeated return at intervals [Malaria is characterized by a *recurring* fever.]

reveal, disclose, divulge, tell, betray —**Reveal** implies a making known of something hidden or secret, as if by drawing back a veil [to *reveal* one's identity]. **Disclose** suggests a laying open, as to inspection, of what has previously been concealed [He refuses to *disclose* his intentions.] **Divulge** suggests that what has been disclosed should properly have been kept secret or private [Do not *divulge* the contents of this letter.] **Tell** may also imply a breach of confidence [kiss and *tell*] but more commonly suggests the making known of necessary or requested information [*Tell* me what to do.] **Betray** implies either faithlessness in divulging something [*betrayed* by an informer] or inadvertence in revealing something [Her blush *betrayed* embarrassment.]

reveal for antonyms see **hide**.

revenge for synonyms see **avenge**.

revengeful for synonyms see **vindictive**.

revere for synonyms see **venerate**.

reverence for synonyms see **awe, honor, venerate**.

reverse, invert, transpose —**Reverse**, the general term, implies a changing to a contrary position, direction, order, etc. [to *reverse* an automobile, to *reverse* a trend]. (*See also synonyms at* **opposite**.) **Invert**, in strictest application, implies a turning upside down or, less commonly, inside out [The image is *inverted* by the lens.] **Transpose** implies the reversing of the order of elements in a sequence [to *transpose* words in a sentence].

revert for synonyms see **return**.

revile for synonyms see **scold**.

revoke for synonyms see **abolish**.

revolt for synonyms see **rebellion**.

revolution for synonyms see **rebellion**.

revolve for synonyms see **turn**.

revulsion for synonyms see **aversion**.

reward, prize, award, premium —**Reward** usually refers to something given in recompense for a good deed, for merit, etc. [He received a *reward* for saving the child.] **Prize** applies to something won in competition or, often, in a lottery, game of chance, etc. [She won first *prize* in the golf tournament.] **Award** implies a decision by judges but does not connote overt competition [He received an *award* for the best news story of the year.] **Premium**, in this connection, applies to a reward offered as an inducement to greater effort, production, etc. [to pay a *premium* for advance delivery].

rhymer, rhymester for synonyms see **poet**.

ribald for synonyms see **coarse**.

rich, wealthy, affluent, opulent, well-to-do —Rich is the general word for one who has more money or income-producing property than is necessary to satisfy his or her normal needs. **Wealthy** adds to this connotations of grand living, influence in the community, a tradition of richness, etc. [a *wealthy* banker]. **Affluent** suggests a continuing increase of riches and a concomitant lavish spending [to live in *affluent* circumstances]. **Opulent** suggests the possession of great wealth as displayed in luxurious or ostentatious living [an *opulent* mansion]. **Well-to-do** implies sufficient prosperity for easy living.

rich for antonyms see **poor**.

ricochet for synonyms see **skip**.

riddle for synonyms see **mystery**.

ride for synonyms see **bait**.

ridicule, deride, mock, taunt —Ridicule implies a making fun of someone or something but does not necessarily connote malice or hostility [He *ridiculed* her new hairdo.] **Deride** suggests scorn or malicious contempt in ridiculing [to *deride* another's beliefs]. **Mock** implies a contemptuous ridiculing, especially by caricaturing another's peculiarities [It is cruel to *mock* his lisp.] **Taunt** implies insulting ridicule, especially by jeering and repeatedly calling attention to some humiliating fact

[They *taunted* him about his failure.]

ridiculous for synonyms see **absurd.**

rife for synonyms see **prevailing.**

righteous for synonyms see **moral.**

righteous for antonyms see **vicious.**

rigid for synonyms see **stiff, strict.**

rigid for antonyms see **elastic, pliable.**

rigor for synonyms see **difficulty.**

rigorous for synonyms see **strict.**

rim for synonyms see **border.**

rip for synonyms see **tear.**

ripe, mature, mellow, adult —Ripe, in its basic application, implies readiness to be harvested, eaten, or used [*ripe* apples, *ripe* cheese] and, in extended use, full readiness for action, etc. [*ripe* for change]. **Mature** implies full growth or development, as of living organisms, the mind, etc. [a *mature* tree, *mature* judgment]. **Mellow** suggests the qualities typical of ripe fruit, such as softness or sweetness, and therefore stresses the absence of sharpness or harshness [a *mellow* flavor, a *mellow* mood]. **Adult** is applied to a person who has reached complete physical or mental maturity, or legal majority, and to ideas and philosophies that show mature thinking. —*Antonyms:* unripe, immature.

ripple for synonyms see **wave.**

rise, arise, spring, originate, derive, flow, issue, emanate, stem —Rise and arise both imply a coming into being, action, notice, etc., but **rise** carries an added implication of ascent [Empires *rise* and fall.] and **arise** is often used to indicate a causal relationship [Accidents *arise* from carelessness.] **Spring** implies sudden emergence [Weeds *sprang* up in the garden.] **Originate** is used in indicating a definite source, beginning, or prime cause [Psychoanalysis *originated* with Freud.] **Derive** implies a proceeding or developing from something else that is the source [This word *derives* from the Latin.] **Flow** suggests a streaming from a source like water ["Praise God, from whom all blessings *flow.*"] **Issue** suggests emergence through an outlet [Not a word *issued* from his lips.] **Emanate** implies the flowing forth from a source of something that is nonmaterial or intangible [rays of lights *emanating* from the sun]. **Stem** implies outgrowth as from a root or a main stalk [Modern detective fiction *stems* from Poe.]

risk for synonyms see **danger**.

rite for synonyms see **ceremony**.

ritual for synonyms see **ceremony**.

rivalry for synonyms see **competition**.

roam, ramble, rove, range, stray, meander —Roam implies a traveling about without a fixed goal over a large area and carries suggestions of freedom and pleasure [to *roam* about the country]. **Ramble** implies an idle moving or walking about and connotes carelessness and aimlessness [We *rambled* through the woods.] **Rove** suggests extensive wandering, but it usually implies a special purpose or activity [a *roving* reporter]. **Range** stresses the extent of territory covered and sometimes suggests a search for something [buffalo *ranging* the plains]. **Stray** implies a wandering from a given place or fixed course [sheep *straying* from the fold]. **Meander** is used of streams, paths, etc., and, in extension, of people and animals, that follow a winding, seemingly aimless course.

robbery for synonyms see **theft**.

robust for synonyms see **healthy**.

robust for antonyms see **weak**.

roll for synonyms see **list**.

roller for synonyms see **wave**.
romantic for synonyms see **sentimental**.
romp for synonyms see **play**.
root for synonyms see **origin**.
rosy, rubicund, ruddy, florid —Rosy suggests the warm
pink or red characterizing a rose in bloom [*rosy* cheeks].
Rubicund implies a flushed, unnatural redness of the
face that results from intemperance in eating, drinking,
etc. [a *rubicund* nose]. **Ruddy** implies such healthy redness as results from an outdoor life [the *ruddy* face of the
ranger]. **Florid** implies the deep, often uneven facial redness of one suffering from hypertension or strong emotional agitation [His face grew *florid* as he shouted.]
rosy for antonyms see **pale**.
rot for synonyms see **decay**.
rotate for synonyms see **turn**.
rough, harsh, uneven, rugged, jagged —Rough applies
to any surface covered with projections, points, ridges,
bumps, etc. [*rough* skin, *rough* ground]. **Harsh** applies
to anything disagreeably rough to the touch [a *harsh* tex-
ture]. That is **uneven** which is not uniform in height,
breadth, etc. [an *uneven* floor, an *uneven* hem]. **Rugged**
implies a roughness of surface in which the sharp, irregular projections are obstacles to travel [*rugged* country] or
a roughness of countenance suggestive of strength [a
rugged jaw]. **Jagged** suggests uneven, sharp-pointed
projections or notches along an edge, as of broken glass
or ragged cloth. Most of these words have extended uses
suggested by their basic meanings [*rough* weather, *harsh*
sounds, an *uneven* performance, a *rugged* life]. —*Antonyms:* **smooth, soft**.
round, spherical, globular, circular, annular —Round,
the most inclusive of these words, applies to anything

shaped like a circle, sphere, or cylinder, or like a part of any of these. **Spherical** applies to a round body or mass having the surface equally distant from the center at all points. **Globular** is used of things that are ball-shaped but not necessarily perfect spheres. **Circular** is applied to round lines, or round flat surfaces, in the shape of a ring or disk, and it may or may not imply correspondence in form with a perfect circle. **Annular** applies to ringlike forms or structures, as the markings in a cross section of a tree.

rouse for synonyms see **stir**.

rout for synonyms see **conquer**.

rove for synonyms see **roam**.

rubicund for synonyms see **rosy**.

ruddy for synonyms see **rosy**.

ruddy for antonyms see **pale**.

rude, ill-mannered, boorish, impolite, discourteous, uncivil —Rude, in this comparison, implies a deliberate lack of consideration for others' feelings and connotes, especially, insolence or impudence [It was *rude* of you to ignore your uncle.] **Ill-mannered** connotes ignorance of the amenities of social behavior rather than deliberate rudeness [a well-meaning but *ill-mannered* fellow]. **Boorish** is applied to one who is rude or ill-mannered in a coarse, loud, or overbearing way. **Impolite** implies merely a failure to observe the forms of polite society [It would be *impolite* to leave so early.] **Discourteous** suggests a lack of dignified consideration for others [a *discourteous* reply]. **Uncivil** implies a disregarding of even the most elementary of good manners [her *uncivil* treatment of the waiter].

rude for antonyms see **civil**.

rugged for synonyms see **rough**.

ruin, destruction, havoc, dilapidation —**Ruin** implies a state of decay, disintegration, etc. especially through such natural processes as age and weather [The barn is in a state of *ruin*.] **Destruction** implies annihilation or demolition, as by fire, explosion, flood, etc. [the *destruction* of the village in an air raid]. **Havoc** suggests total destruction or devastation, as following an earthquake or hurricane. **Dilapidation** implies a state of ruin or shabbiness resulting from neglect [the *dilapidation* of a deserted house].

rule for synonyms see **govern, law**.

ruthless for synonyms see **cruel**.

ruminate for synonyms see **ponder**.

rural, rustic, pastoral, bucolic —**Rural** is the comprehensive, nonspecific word referring to life on the farm or in the country as distinguished from life in the city [*rural* schools]. **Rustic** stresses the contrast between the supposed crudeness and unsophistication of the country and the polish and refinement of the city [*rustic* humor]. **Pastoral** suggests the highly idealized primitive simplicity of rural life, originally among shepherds. **Bucolic**, in contrast, suggests a down-to-earth rustic simplicity or artlessness [her *bucolic* suitor]. —*Antonym:* **urban**.

ruse for synonyms see **trick**.

rustic for synonyms see **rural**.

S

sack for synonyms see **ravage**.

sacred for synonyms see **holy**.

sacrilege, profanation, desecration —**Sacrilege** implies a violation of something sacred, as by appropriating to oneself or to a secular use something that has been dedicated to a religious purpose. **Profanation** suggests a lack of reverence or a positive contempt for things regarded as sacred. **Desecration** implies a removal of the sacredness of some object or place, as by defiling or polluting it.

sad, sorrowful, melancholy, dejected, depressed, doleful —**Sad** is the simple, general term, ranging in implication from a mild, momentary unhappiness to a feeling of intense grief. **Sorrowful** implies a sadness caused by some specific loss, disappointment, etc. [Her death left him *sorrowful*.] **Melancholy** suggests a more or less chronic mournfulness or gloominess, or, often, merely a wistful pensiveness [*melancholy* thoughts about the future]. **Dejected** implies discouragement or a sinking of spirits, as because of frustration. **Depressed** suggests a mood of brooding despondency, as because of fatigue or a sense of futility [The novel left him feeling *depressed*.] **Doleful** implies a mournful, often lugubrious, sadness [the *doleful* look on a lost child's face].

sad for antonyms see **happy**.

sadness for synonyms see **sorrow**.

sadness for antonyms see **mirth**.

sagacious for synonyms see **shrewd**.

sage for synonyms see **wise**.

salary for synonyms see **wage.**

sally for synonyms see **joke.**

same, selfsame, very, identical, equal, equivalent
—**Same,** in one sense, agrees with **selfsame** and **very** in
implying that what is referred to is one thing and not
two or more distinct things [That is the *same,* or *selfsame*
or *very,* house we once lived in.] and, in another, implies
reference to things that are really distinct but without
any significant difference in kind, appearance, amount,
etc. [I eat the *same* food every day.] **Identical,** in one
sense, also expresses the first idea [This is the *identical*
bed where he slept.] and, in another, implies exact correspondence in all details, as of quality, appearance, etc.
[The signatures are *identical.*] **Equal** implies the absence
of any difference in quantity, size, value, degree, etc.
[*equal* weights, an *equal* advantage]. **Equivalent** implies
of things that they amount to the same thing in value,
force, meaning, etc. [$5 or its *equivalent* in merchandise].

same for antonyms see **different, opposite.**

sanctimonious for synonyms see **pious.**

sanction for synonyms see **approve.**

sanctuary for synonyms see **shelter.**

sang-froid for synonyms see **equanimity.**

sap for synonyms see **weaken.**

sapient for synonyms see **wise.**

sarcastic, satirical, ironical, sardonic, caustic —**Sarcastic** implies intent to hurt by taunting with mocking
ridicule, veiled sneers, etc. [a *sarcastic* reminder that
work begins at 9:00 A.M.] **Satirical** implies as its purpose the exposing or attacking of the vices, follies, and
stupidities of others and connotes the use of ridicule or
sarcasm [Swift's *satirical* comments]. **Ironical** applies to
a humorous or sarcastic form of expression in which the

intended meaning of what is said is directly opposite to
the usual sense ["My, you're early," was his *ironical*
taunt to the latecomer.] **Sardonic** implies sneering or
mocking bitterness in a person, or, more often, in his expression, remarks, etc. [a *sardonic* smile]. **Caustic** implies a cutting, biting, or stinging wit or sarcasm [a *caustic* tongue].

sardonic for synonyms see **sarcastic**.

sate for synonyms see **satiate**.

sated for antonyms see **hungry**.

satiate, sate, surfeit, cloy, glut —**Satiate** and **sate** in
their basic sense mean to satisfy to the full, but in current use **satiate** almost always implies, as **sate** often
does, a being filled or stuffed so full that all pleasure or
desire is lost [*satiated,* or *sated,* with food, success, etc.]
Surfeit implies a being filled or supplied to nauseating
or disgusting excess [*surfeited* with pleasure]. **Cloy**
stresses the distaste one feels for something too sweet,
rich, etc. that one has indulged in to excess [*cloying,* sentimental music]. **Glut** implies an overloading by filling
or supplying to excess [to *glut* the market].

satiated for antonyms see **hungry**.

satire for synonyms see **caricature, wit**.

satirical for synonyms see **sarcastic**.

satisfy, content —**Satisfy** implies complete fulfillment
of one's wishes, needs, and expectations. **Content** implies a filling of requirements to the degree that one is
not disturbed by a desire for something more or different
[Some persons are *satisfied* only by great wealth, others
are *contented* with a modest but secure income.]

saturate for synonyms see **soak**.

saucy for synonyms see **impertinent**.

savage for synonyms see **barbarian**.

save for synonyms see **rescue**.

savoir-faire for synonyms see **tact**.

saw for synonyms see **saying**.

saying, saw, maxim, adage, proverb, motto, aphorism, epigram —Saying is the simple, direct term for any pithy expression of wisdom or truth. A **saw** is an old, homely saying that is well worn by repetition [The preacher filled his sermon with wise *saws*.] A **maxim** is a general principle drawn from practical experience and serving as a rule of conduct (Example: "Keep thy shop and thy shop will keep thee.") An **adage** is a saying that has been popularly accepted over a long period of time (Example: "Where there's smoke, there's fire.") A **proverb** is a piece of practical wisdom expressed in homely, concrete terms (Example: "A penny saved is a penny earned.") A **motto** is a maxim accepted as a guiding principle or as an ideal of behavior (Example: "Honesty is the best policy.") An **aphorism** is a terse saying embodying a general, more or less profound truth or principle (Example: "He is a fool that cannot conceal his wisdom.") An **epigram** is a terse, witty, pointed statement that gains its effect by ingenious antithesis (Example: "The only way to get rid of a temptation is to yield to it.")

scan for synonyms see **scrutinize**.

scandal for synonyms see **disgrace**.

scant for synonyms see **meager**.

scant for antonyms see **plentiful, profuse**.

scanty for synonyms see **meager**.

scarce for synonyms see **rare**.

scarce for antonyms see **plentiful**.

scare for synonyms see **frighten**.

scared for synonyms see **afraid**.

scatter, disperse, dissipate, dispel —**Scatter** implies a strewing around loosely [to *scatter* seeds] or a forcible driving apart in different directions [The breeze *scattered* the papers.] (*See also synonyms at* **sprinkle.**) **Disperse** implies a scattering which completely breaks up an assemblage and spreads the individuals far and wide [a people *dispersed* throughout the world]. **Dissipate** implies complete dissolution, as by crumbling, wasting, etc. [to *dissipate* a fortune]. **Dispel** suggests a scattering that drives away something that obscures, confuses, troubles, etc. [to *dispel* fears].

scatter for antonyms see **gather.**

scene for synonyms see **view.**

scent, perfume, fragrance, bouquet, redolence —**Scent,** in this comparison, implies a relatively faint but pervasive smell, especially one characteristic of a particular thing [the *scent* of apple blossoms]. (*See also synonyms at* **smell.**) **Perfume** suggests a relatively strong, but usually pleasant, smell, either natural or manufactured [the rich *perfume* of gardenias]. **Fragrance** always implies an agreeable, sweet smell, especially of growing things [the *fragrance* of a freshly mowed field]. **Bouquet** is specifically applied to the fragrance of a wine or brandy. **Redolence** implies a rich, pleasant combination of smells [the *redolence* of a grocery]. —*Antonyms:* **stench, stink.**

scheme for synonyms see **plan.**

scholar for synonyms see **pupil.**

school for synonyms see **group** and **teach.**

scoff, sneer, jeer, gibe, flout —**Scoff** implies a showing of scorn or contempt as a manifestation of doubt, cynicism, irreverence, etc. [They *scoffed* at his diagnosis of the disease.] **Sneer** implies a display of contempt or disparagement, as by a derisive smile or scornful, insinuating tone of voice ["You call this a dinner?" he *sneered.*] **Jeer** suggests openly insulting, coarse remarks or mocking laughter [The crowd *jeered* at the speaker.] **Gibe** implies a taunting or mocking, either in amiable teasing or in sarcastic reproach [He kept *gibing* at me for my clumsiness.] **Flout** suggests a treating with contempt or disdain, especially by ignoring or rejecting [to *flout* the law].

scold, upbraid, berate, revile, vituperate —Scold is the common term meaning to find fault with or rebuke in angry, irritated, often nagging language [A mother *scolds* a naughty child.] **Upbraid** implies bitter reproach or censure and usually connotes justification for this [She *upbraided* me for my carelessness.] **Berate** suggests continuous, heated, even violent reproach, often connoting excessive abuse [The old shrew continued *berating* them.] **Revile** implies the use of highly abusive and contemptuous language and often connotes deliberate defamation or slander [He *reviled* his opponent unmercifully.] **Vituperate** suggests even greater violence in the attack [*vituperating* each other with foul epithets].

scope for synonyms see **range.**

scorch for synonyms see **burn.**

scorn for synonyms see **despise.**

scowl for synonyms see **frown.**

scrawny for synonyms see **lean.**

scream, shriek, screech —Scream is the general word for a loud, high, piercing cry, as in fear, pain, or anger. **Shriek** suggests a sharper, more sudden cry than **scream** and connotes either extreme terror or pain or loud, high-pitched, unrestrained laughter. **Screech** suggests an unpleasantly shrill or harsh cry painful to the hearer.

screech for synonyms see **scream.**

scruple for synonyms see **qualm.**

scrupulous for synonyms see **careful, upright.**

scrutinize, inspect, examine, scan —Scrutinize implies a looking over carefully and searchingly in order to observe the minutest details [He slowly *scrutinized* the bank note.] **Inspect** implies a close, critical observation, especially for detecting errors or flaws [to *inspect* a building for fire hazards]. **Examine** suggests a close observation or investigation to determine the condition, quality, or validity of something [*examined* thoroughly by a doctor]. **Scan,** in its earlier, stricter sense, implies a close scrutiny, but in current, popular usage, it more frequently connotes a quick, rather superficial survey [to *scan* the headlines].

sear for synonyms see **burn.**

seasonable for synonyms see **timely.**

seclusion for synonyms see **solitude.**

secret, covert, clandestine, stealthy, furtive, surreptitious, underhanded —Secret, the general term, implies a concealing or keeping from the knowledge of others, for whatever reason [my *secret* opinion of him]. **Covert** implies a concealing as by disguising or veiling [a *covert* threat]. **Clandestine** suggests that what is being kept secret is of an illicit, immoral, or proscribed nature [their *clandestine* meetings in the park]. **Stealthy** implies a slow, quiet secrecy of action in an attempt to elude notice and often connotes deceit [the *stealthy* advance of the panther]. **Furtive** adds to this connotations of slyness or watchfulness and suggests a reprehensible objective [the *furtive* movement of his hand toward my pocket]. **Surreptitious** connotes a feeling of guilt in the one who is acting in a furtive or stealthy manner [She stole a *surreptitious* glance at him.] **Underhanded** implies a stealthiness characterized by fraudulence or deceit [*underhanded* business dealings]. —*Antonyms:* **open, obvious.**

secrete for synonyms see **hide.**

secretive for synonyms see **silent.**

section for synonyms see **part.**

secure for synonyms see **get.**

sedate for synonyms see **serious.**

sedition, treason —**Sedition** applies to anything regarded by a government as stirring up resistance or rebellion against it and implies that the evidence is not overt or absolute. **Treason** implies an overt act in violation of the allegiance owed to one's state, specifically a levying war against it or giving aid or comfort to its enemies.

seduce for synonyms see **lure.**

sedulous for synonyms see **busy.**

see, behold, espy, descry, view —**See,** the most simple and direct of these terms, is the basic term for the use of the organs of sight. **Behold** implies a directing of the eyes on something and holding it in view, usually stressing the strong impression made [He never *beheld* a sight more beautiful.] **Espy** and **descry** both imply a catching sight of with some effort, etc. [He *espied* the snake crawling through the grass.] and **descry** the making out of something from a distance or through darkness, mist, etc. [She *descried* the distant steeple.] **View** implies a seeing or looking at what lies before one, as in inspection or examination [The jury *viewed* the evidence.]

seethe for synonyms see **boil.**

segment for synonyms see **part.**

seize for synonyms see **take.**

select for synonyms see **choose.**

selection for synonyms see **choice.**

self-confidence for synonyms see **confidence.**

self-esteem for synonyms see **pride.**

self-possession for synonyms see **confidence.**

selfsame for synonyms see **same.**

sell, barter, trade, auction, vend —**Sell** implies a transferring of the ownership of something to another for money [to *sell* books, to *sell* a house]. **Barter** implies an exchange of goods or services without using money [to *barter* food for clothes]. **Trade,** in transitive use, also implies the exchange of articles [Let's *trade* neckties.] and, intransitively, implies the carrying on of a business in which one buys and sells a specified commodity [to *trade* in wheat]. **Auction** implies the public sale of items one by one, each going to the highest of the competing bidders [to *auction* off unclaimed property]. **Vend** applies especially to the selling of small articles, as by peddling, coin-operated machine, etc. [*vending* machines]. —*Antonym:* **buy.**

semblance for synonyms see **appearance.**

sense for synonyms see **meaning.**

sensible for synonyms see **aware, material, perceptible, rational.**

sensible for antonyms see **absurd.**

sensual for synonyms see **carnal, sensuous.**

sensuous, sensual, voluptuous, luxurious, epicurean —**Sensuous** suggests the strong appeal of that which is pleasing to the eye, ear, touch, etc. and, of a person, implies susceptibility to the pleasures of sensation [soft, *sensuous* music]. **Sensual** refers to the gratification of the grosser bodily senses or appetite [*sensual* excesses]. **Voluptuous** implies a tending to excite, or giving oneself up to the gratification of, sensuous or sensual desires [her *voluptuous* charms]. **Luxurious** implies a reveling in that which lavishly provides a high degree of physical comfort or satisfaction [a *luxurious* feeling of drowsiness]. **Epicurean** implies delight in luxury and sensuous pleasure, especially that of eating and drinking.

sentiment for synonyms see **feeling, opinion.**

sentimental, romantic, mawkish, maudlin, gushy —**Sentimental** suggests emotion of a kind that is felt in a nostalgic or tender mood [*sentimental* music] or emotion that is exaggerated, affected, foolish, etc. [a trashy, *sentimental* novel]. **Romantic** suggests emotion aroused by that which appeals to the imagination as it is influenced by the idealization of life in literature, art, etc. [a *romantic* girl waiting for her Prince Charming]. That is **mawkish** which is sentimental in a disgustingly weak, insincere, or exaggerated way [a *mawkish* soap opera]. That is **maudlin** which is tearfully or weakly sentimental in a foolish way [an intoxicated, *maudlin* guest]. **Gushy,** an informal word, implies an effusive display of sentiment or enthusiasm [*gushy* congratulations].

separate, divide, part, sever, sunder —**Separate** implies the putting apart of things previously united, joined, or assembled [to *separate* machine parts, to *separate* a family]. **Divide** implies a separation into parts, pieces, groups, etc. by or as by cutting, splitting, or branching, often for purposes of apportionment [to *divide* the profits into equal shares]. **Part** is now usually applied to the separation of persons or things that have been closely connected or associated ["till death us do *part*"]. **Sever** implies a forcible and complete separation, as by cutting off a part from a whole [to *sever* a branch from a tree]. **Sunder,** now a literary term, implies a violent splitting, tearing, or wrenching apart.

separate for antonyms see **join, stick, tie.**

sequence for synonyms see **series.**

serene for synonyms see **calm.**

serenity for synonyms see **equanimity.**

series, sequence, succession, chain —**Series** applies to a number of similar, more or less related things following one another in time or place [a *series* of concerts]. **Sequence** emphasizes a closer relationship between the things, such as logical connection, numerical order, etc. [the *sequence* of events]. **Succession** merely implies a following of one thing after another, without any necessary connection between them [a *succession* of errors]. **Chain** refers to a series in which there is a definite relationship of cause and effect or some other logical connection [a *chain* of ideas].

serious, grave, solemn, sedate, earnest, sober —**Serious** implies absorption in deep thought or involvement in something really important as distinguished from something frivolous or merely amusing [He takes a *serious* interest in the theater.] **Grave** implies the dignified weightiness of heavy responsibilities or cares [a *grave* expression on his face]. **Solemn** suggests an impressive or awe-inspiring seriousness [a *solemn* ceremony]. **Sedate** implies a dignified, proper, sometimes even prim seriousness [a *sedate* clergyman]. **Earnest** suggests a seriousness of purpose marked by sincerity and enthusiasm [an *earnest* desire to help]. **Sober** implies a seriousness marked by temperance, self-control, and emotional balance [a *sober* criticism].

serious for antonyms see **witty.**

sermon for synonyms see **speech.**

servile, subservient, slavish, menial, obsequious —**Servile** suggests the cringing, submissive behavior characteristic of a slave [*servile* flattery]. **Subservient** applies to one who occupies an inferior or subordinate position that furthers another's ends, and may or may not connote servility [a faculty *subservient* to the board of trustees]. **Slavish** implies utter abjectness and submissiveness in obeying, depending on, or following another [*slavish* adherence to the rules]. **Menial** applies to work or a position of a kind regarded as low or degrading [restricted to the *menial* job of a porter]. **Obsequious** implies a servile, fawning attitude toward someone regarded as one's superior [an *obsequious* courtier]. —Antonyms: **domineering, imperious.**

servitude, slavery, bondage —**Servitude** refers to compulsory labor or service for another, often, specifically, such labor imposed as punishment for crime. **Slavery** implies absolute subjection to another person who owns and completely controls one. **Bondage** originally referred to the condition of a serf bound to his master's land, but now implies any condition of subjugation or captivity.

set for synonyms see **coterie.**

settle for synonyms see **decide.**

sever for synonyms see **separate.**

severe, stern, austere, ascetic —**Severe** applies to a person or thing that is strict and uncompromising and connotes a total absence of softness, laxity, frivolity, etc. [a *severe* critic, a *severe* hairdo]. **Stern** implies an unyielding firmness, especially as manifested in a grim or forbidding aspect or manner [a *stern* guardian]. **Austere** suggests harsh restraint, self-denial, stark simplicity [the *austere* diet of wartime], or an absence of warmth, passion, ornamentation, etc. [an *austere* bedroom]. **Ascetic** implies extreme self-denial and self-discipline or even,

sometimes, the deliberate self-infliction of pain and discomfort, as by religious fanatics [an *ascetic* hermit].
—*Antonyms:* **mild, lax, indulgent.**

shackle for synonyms see **hamper.**

shade for synonyms see **color.**

**shake, tremble, quake, quiver, shiver, shudder, wob-
ble** —**Shake** is the general word for a moving up and
down or back and forth with quick, short motions.
Tremble implies such an involuntary shaking of the
body as to suggest a loss of coordination or control, as
from fear or fatigue [She *trembled* at the lion's roar.]
Quake usually suggests a relatively violent trembling, as
in great agitation [to *quake* in one's boots with dread.]
Quiver suggests a slight, tremulous vibration, as of a taut
string that has been plucked [The leaves *quivered* in the
breeze.] **Shiver** implies a slight, momentary quivering of
the body, as from cold or in fearful apprehension [He
shivered at the thought of facing them.] **Shudder** implies
a sudden, convulsive quivering, as in horror of revulsion
[She *shuddered* at the grisly sight.] **Wobble** suggests a
shaking or tottering that connotes instability [The chair
wobbled on its unsteady legs.]

shallow for synonyms see **superficial.**

sham for synonyms see **false.**

sham for antonyms see **authentic.**

shame for synonyms see **disgrace.**

shape for synonyms see **form, make.**

sharp, keen, acute —**Sharp** and **keen** both apply to
that which is cutting, biting, incisive, or piercing, as because of a fine edge, but **sharp** more often implies a
harsh, cutting quality [a *sharp* pain, a *sharp* tongue, a
sharp flavor] and **keen**, a pleasantly biting or stimulating
quality [*keen* wit, *keen* delight]. **Acute** literally implies

sharp-pointedness and figuratively suggests a penetrating or poignant quality [*acute* hearing, *acute* distress].

sharp for antonyms see **dull**.

shatter for synonyms see **break**.

sheer for synonyms see **steep**.

shelter, refuge, retreat, asylum, sanctuary —**Shelter** implies the protection of something that covers, as a roof or other structure that shields one from the elements or danger [to find *shelter* from the rain]. **Refuge** suggests a place of safety that one flees to in escaping danger or difficulties [He sought political *refuge* in France.] **Retreat** implies retirement from that which threatens one's peace of mind or one's security, and withdrawal to a safe, quiet, or secluded place [a country *retreat*]. **Asylum** is applied to a refuge where one is immune from seizure or harm, as because it is beyond a particular legal jurisdiction [The convict sought *asylum* abroad.] A **sanctuary** is an asylum that has a sacred or inviolable character [the former right of *sanctuary* in churches].

shield for synonyms see **defend**.

shift for synonyms see **move**.

shimmer for synonyms see **flash**.

shine for synonyms see **polish**.

shining for synonyms see **bright**.

shiver for synonyms see **shake**.

shoal, bank, reef, bar —**Shoal** applies to any place in a sea, river, etc. where the water is shallow and difficult to navigate. **Bank**, in this connection, applies to a shallow place, formed by an elevated shelf of ground, that is deep enough to be safely navigated by lighter vessels. A **reef** is a ridge of rock, coral, etc. lying at or very close to the surface of the sea, just offshore. **Bar** applies to a ridge of sand, etc. silted up across the mouth of a river or harbor and hindering navigation.

shock, startle, paralyze, stun —**Shock** suggests the violent impact on the mind or emotions of an unexpected, overwhelming event that comes as a blow [*shocked* by her sudden death]. **Startle** implies a shock of surprise or fright of a kind that often causes one to literally jump or shrink [*startled* by the clap of thunder]. **Paralyze** implies such extreme shock as to make one temporarily unable to move, escape, etc. [*paralyzed* with fear]. To **stun** is to shock with such impact as to stupefy or daze [*stunned* by the disaster].

shore, coast, beach, strand, bank —**Shore** is the general word applied to an edge of land directly bordering on the sea, a lake, a river, etc. **Coast** applies only to land along the sea. **Beach** applies to a level stretch of sandy or pebbly seashore or lake shore, usually one that is washed by high water. **Strand** is a poetic word for **shore** or **beach**. **Bank** applies to the rising or steep land at the edge of a stream.

short for synonym see **brief**.

short for antonyms see **high**.

shorten, curtail, abridge, abbreviate —**Shorten** implies reduction in length, extent, or duration [to *shorten* a rope, to *shorten* a visit, to *shorten* one's life]. **Curtail** implies a making shorter than was originally intended, as because of necessity or expediency [expenditures *curtailed* because of a reduced income]. **Abridge** implies reduction in compass by condensing and omitting parts but usually connotes that what is essential is kept [to *abridge* a dictionary]. **Abbreviate** usually refers to the shortening of a word or phrase by contraction or by substitution of a symbol, but also has extended, sometimes jocular applications [an *abbreviated* costume].

shorten for antonyms see **extend**.

shove for synonyms see **push**.

shove for antonyms see **pull**.

show, display, exhibit, expose, flaunt —Show implies a putting or bringing something into view so that it can be seen or looked at [*Show* us the garden.] To **display** something is to spread it out before one so that it is shown to advantage [Much jewelry was *displayed* on the sales counter.] **Exhibit** implies prominent display, often for the purpose of attracting public attention or inspection [to *exhibit* products at an exposition]. **Expose** implies the laying open and displaying of something that has been covered or concealed [This bathing suit *exposes* her scar.] **Flaunt** implies an ostentatious, impudent, or defiant display [to *flaunt* one's riches, to *flaunt* vices].

showy for synonyms see **gaudy**.

shrewd, sagacious, perspicacious, astute —Shrewd implies keenness of mind, sharp insight, and a cleverness or sharpness in practical matters [a *shrewd* comment, a *shrewd* businessman]. (*See also* synonyms at **clever**.) **Sagacious** implies keenness of discernment and far-sightedness in judgment [a *sagacious* counselor]. **Perspicacious** suggests the penetrating mental vision or discernment that enables one clearly to see and understand what is obscure or hidden [a *perspicacious* judge of character]. **Astute** implies shrewdness combined with sagacity and sometimes connotes, in addition, artfulness or cunning [an *astute* politician].

shriek for synonyms see **scream**.

shrink for synonyms see **contract, recoil**.

shrivel for synonyms see **wither**.

shudder for synonyms see **shake**.

shy, bashful, diffident, modest, demure —Shy implies

a shrinking from the notice of others and a reticence in approaching them, either as an inherent trait or as resulting from inexperience. **Bashful** implies such shyness as is displayed in awkward behavior and embarrassed timidity. **Diffident** implies a self-distrust and lack of self-confidence that makes one reluctant to assert oneself. **Modest** implies an unassuming manner in one who, because of ability or achievements, might be expected to assert himself or herself strongly. **Demure**, in current usage, suggests a decorously modest manner, often one that is affectedly so. —*Antonyms:* **bold, confident.**

shyness for antonyms see **confidence.**

sick, ill, ailing, indisposed —**Sick** and **ill** both express the idea of being in bad health, affected with disease, etc., but **sick** is more commonly used than **ill**, which is somewhat formal [He's a *sick* person. He is *sick*, or *ill*, with the flu.] **Ailing** usually suggests prolonged or even chronic poor health [She has been *ailing* ever since her operation.] **Indisposed** suggests a slight, temporary illness or feeling of physical discomfort [*indisposed* with a headache.]

sick for antonyms see **healthy.**

sign, mark, token, symptom, indication —**Sign,** the broadest in scope of these terms, applies to an action, condition, quality, occurrence, or visible object that points to a fact or conveys a meaning [a *sign* of spring, a *sign* of decay, a *sign* of the zodiac]. **Mark** suggests that which is imprinted on, or is intrinsically characteristic of, something [Suffering left its *mark* on his face.] **Token** suggests something given or serving as a symbol or sign of some quality, feeling, or value [a *token* of good will]. A **symptom** is an outward, recognizable sign of the existence of a disease or disorder [Prejudice is a *symptom* of social maladjustment.]   **Indication** is interchangeable with any of the preceding words.

significance for synonyms see **importance, meaning.**

significant for antonyms see **petty.**

signification for synonyms see **meaning.**

silent, taciturn, reserved, reticent, secretive —**Silent** is the simple, direct word for one who is temporarily not speaking or one who seldom speaks. (*See also synonyms at* **still.**)   **Taciturn** applies to a person who is habitually uncommunicative.   **Reserved** implies a habitual disposition to be withdrawn in speech and self-restrained or aloof in manner.   **Reticent** implies a disinclination, sometimes temporary as from embarrassment, to express one's feelings or impart information.   **Secretive** suggests the furtive or evasive reticence of one who conceals things unnecessarily.

silent for antonyms see **talkative.**

silhouette for synonyms see **outline.**

silly, stupid, fatuous, asinine —**Silly** implies ridiculous or irrational behavior that seems to demonstrate a lack of common sense, good judgment, or sobriety [It was *silly* of you to dress so lightly.] (*See also synonyms at* **absurd.**)   **Stupid** implies a dullwittedness or lack of normal intelligence or understanding [He is *stupid* to believe that.]   **Fatuous** suggests stupidity, inanity, or obtuseness coupled with a smug complacency [a *fatuous* smile].   **Asinine** implies the extreme stupidity conventionally attributed to an ass [an *asinine* argument].

silly for antonyms see **intelligent, wise.**

silt for synonyms see **wash.**

similarity for synonyms see **likeness.**

simmer for synonyms see **boil.**

simper for synonyms see **smile.**

simple for synonyms see **easy**.

simple for antonyms see **complex, hard**.

simulate for synonyms see **assume**.

simultaneous for synonyms see **contemporary**.

sincere, unaffected, unfeigned, heartfelt, hearty
—**Sincere** implies an absence of deceit, pretense, or hypocrisy and an adherence to the simple, unembellished truth [a *sincere* desire to help]. **Unaffected** implies a natural, genuine simplicity and a freedom from artificial behavior [an *unaffected* prose style]. **Unfeigned** suggests behavior that is honestly spontaneous [She looked at him with *unfeigned* admiration.] **Heartfelt** stresses depth as well as sincerity of feeling, especially as expressed in warm words or acts [He extended his *heartfelt* sympathy.] **Hearty** adds to this connotations of exuberance and geniality [my *hearty* congratulations].

sincere for antonyms see **false**.

singe for synonyms see **burn**.

single, sole, unique, solitary, individual, particular
—**Single** simply refers to one that is not united with or accompanied by another [a *single* chair in the room, a *single* man]. **Sole** applies to the only one of its kind under consideration or in a particular situation [my *sole* dependent, his *sole* contribution]. **Unique** strictly applies to the only one of its kind in existence [a *unique* bronze statue], but in popular usage often implies mere rareness or unusualness [a *unique* experience]. **Solitary** adds to the sense of singleness connotations of isolation or separation [a *solitary* tree in the meadow]. **Individual** refers to every one of a group or class as distinguished from all the others [an *individual* listing of members]. **Particular** applies to a single, distinct instance, example, etc. of a group or class [Must you have this *particular*

seat?]

sinister, baleful, malign —Sinister, in this connection, applies to that which can be interpreted as presaging imminent danger or evil [a *sinister* smile]. **Baleful** refers to that which is inevitably deadly, destructive, pernicious, etc. [a *baleful* influence]. **Malign** is applied to that which is regarded as having an inherent tendency toward evil or destruction [a *malign* doctrine].

situation for synonyms see **position, state.**

skepticism for synonyms see **uncertainty.**

skepticism for antonyms see **conviction.**

skid for synonyms see **slide.**

skill for synonyms see **art.**

skin, hide, pelt, rind, peel, bark —Skin is the general term for the outer covering of the animal body and for the covering, especially if thin and tight, of certain fruits and vegetables [human *skin*, the *skin* of a peach]. **Hide** is used of the tough skins of certain large animals, as of a horse, cow, elephant, etc. **Pelt** refers to the skin, especially the untanned skin, of a fur-bearing animal, as of a mink, fox, sheep, etc. **Rind** applies to the thick, tough covering of certain fruits, as of a watermelon, or of cheeses, bacon, etc. **Peel** is used of the skin or rind of fruit that has been removed, as by stripping [potato *peel*, lemon *peel*]. **Bark** applies to the hard covering of trees and woody plants.

skinny for synonyms see **lean.**

skip, bound, hop, ricochet —Skip suggests a springing forward lightly and quickly, leaping on alternate feet, and, of inanimate things, deflection from a surface in a series of jumps. **Bound** implies longer, more vigorous leaps, as in running, or by an elastic object thrown along the ground. **Hop** suggests a single short jump, as on one leg, or a series of short, relatively jerky jumps. **Ricochet** is used of an inanimate object that has been thrown or shot and that bounds or skips in glancing deflection from a surface.

skirmish for synonyms see **battle.**

skulk for synonyms see **lurk.**

slack for synonyms see **remiss.**

slack for antonyms see **tight.**

slacken for synonyms see **delay.**

slap for synonyms see **strike.**

slaughter, massacre, butchery, carnage, pogrom —**Slaughter,** as applied to people, suggests extensive and brutal killing, as in battle or by deliberate acts of wanton cruelty. **Massacre** implies the indiscriminate and wholesale slaughter of those who are defenseless or helpless to resist. **Butchery** adds implications of extreme cruelty and of such coldblooded heartlessness as one might display in the slaughtering of animals. **Carnage** stresses the result of bloody slaughter and suggests the accumulation of the bodies of the slain. **Pogrom** refers to an organized, often officially inspired, massacre of a minority group, specifically of the Jews in czarist Russia.

slavery for synonyms see **servitude.**

slavish for synonyms see **servile.**

slay for synonyms see **kill.**

sleepy, drowsy, somnolent, slumberous —**Sleepy** applies to a person who is nearly overcome by a desire to sleep and, figuratively, suggests either the power to induce sleepiness or a resemblance to this state [a *sleepy* town, a *sleepy* song]. **Drowsy** stresses the sluggishness or lethargic heaviness accompanying sleepiness [The *drowsy* sentry fought off sleep through his watch.] **Somnolent**

is a formal equivalent of either of the preceding [the *somnolent* voice of the speaker]. **Slumberous**, a poetic equivalent, in addition sometimes suggests latent powers in repose [a *slumberous* city].

slender for synonyms see **thin**.

slide, slip, glide, skid —Slide implies easy movement, as over a smooth surface, and usually suggests continuous contact with it [to *slide* on ice, to *slide* back into old habits]. **Slip** more often implies that the surface is frictionless and the contact not continuous, therefore suggesting an involuntary movement or an accident [She *slipped* and fell on the ice. Her name *slipped* from his mind.] **Glide** suggests a flowing, smooth, easy, usually silent movement and continuous or intermittent contact with a surface [*gliding* dancers]. **Skid** means to slide or slip sideways and out of control, as a vehicle when not gripping an icy road.

slight for synonyms see **neglect** and **thin**.

slim for synonyms see **thin**.

slink for synonyms see **lurk**.

slip for synonyms see **error** and **slide**.

slipshod for synonyms see **slovenly**.

sloppy for synonyms see **slovenly**.

sloppy for antonyms see **neat**.

slothful for synonyms see **lazy**.

slovenly, slipshod, untidy, unkempt, sloppy —Slovenly implies a general carelessness or shiftlessness as characterized by a want of attention to cleanliness and orderliness [a *slovenly* housewife]. **Slipshod** suggests a carelessness about details and a resulting lack of precision, accuracy, thoroughness, etc. [*slipshod* work]. **Untidy** implies a lack of neatness in appearance or arrangement [an *untidy* room]. **Unkempt**, basically meaning uncombed, stresses untidiness as resulting from neglect [an *unkempt* ragamuffin, an *unkempt* lawn]. **Sloppy** suggests a careless spilling over of something loose and therefore implies messiness, lack of restraint, etc. [a *sloppy* eater, *sloppy* thinking]. —*Antonym:* **fastidious**. *For other antonyms see* **neat**.

slow for synonyms see **stupid**.

slow for antonyms see **fast, quick**.

slowness for antonyms see **haste**.

sluggish for antonyms see **agile**.

slumberous for synonyms see **sleepy**.

sly, cunning, crafty, tricky, foxy, wily —**Sly** implies a working to achieve one's ends by evasiveness, insinuation, furtiveness, duplicity, etc. [a *sly* bargain]. **Cunning** implies a cleverness or shrewd skillfulness at deception and circumvention [a *cunning* plot]. **Crafty** implies an artful cunning in contriving stratagems and subtle deceptions [a *crafty* diplomat]. **Tricky** suggests a shifty, unreliable quality rather than cleverness at deception [*tricky* subterfuges]. **Foxy** suggests slyness and craftiness that have been sharpened by experience [He was a *foxy* old trader.] **Wily** implies the deceiving or ensnarement of others by subtle stratagems and ruses [*wily* blandishments].

small, little, diminutive, minute, tiny, miniature, petite —**Small** and **little** are often used interchangeably, but **small** is preferred with reference to something concrete of less than the usual quantity, size, amount, value, importance, etc. [a *small* man, tax, audience, matter, etc.] and **little** more often applies to absolute concepts [he has his *little* faults], in expressing tenderness or indulgence [a cute *little* tyke], and in connoting insignificance, meanness, or pettiness [of *little* importance]. **Diminutive**

implies extreme, sometimes delicate, smallness or little-
ness [the *diminutive* Lilliputians]. **Minute** and the more
informal **tiny** suggest that is extremely diminutive,
often to the degree that it can be discerned only by close
scrutiny [a *minute,* or *tiny,* difference]. **Miniature** applies to a copy, model, representation, etc. on a very
small scale [*miniature* painting]. **Petite** has specific application to a girl or woman who is small and trim in figure.

small for antonyms see **large.**

smart for synonyms see **intelligent.**

smash for synonyms see **break.**

smell, scent, odor, aroma —**Smell** is the most general
word for any quality perceived through the olfactory
sense [foul and fresh *smells*]. **Scent** refers to the emanation from the thing smelled, often implying that it can be
discriminated only by a sensitive sense of smell [the *scent*
of a hunted animal]. **Odor** suggests a heavier emanation
and, therefore, one that is more generally perceptible
and more clearly recognizable [chemical *odors*]. **Aroma**
suggests a pervasive, pleasant, often spicy odor [the
aroma of fine tobacco]. *See also synonyms at* **scent.**

smile, grin, simper, smirk —**Smile** is the general term
for a facial expression somewhat resembling that in a
laugh but not accompanied by vocal sound. **Grin,** applied to a broad smile showing the teeth, implies mischievous amusement, unaffected cheerfulness, foolishness,
etc. [an impish *grin,* the *grin* of an idiot]. **Simper** is applied to a silly, affected, or coy smile [a coquette with a
simper on her face]. A **smirk** is a simpering smile that is
conceited, knowing, or annoyingly complacent [a self-
satisfied *smirk*].

smile for antonyms see **frown.**

smirk for synonyms see **smile**.

smite for synonyms see **strike**.

smog for synonyms see **mist**.

smooth for synonyms see **easy** and **level**.

smooth for antonyms see **rough**.

snare for synonyms see **catch, trap**.

snatch for synonyms see **take**.

sneak for synonyms see **lurk**.

sneer for synonyms see **scoff**.

snicker for synonyms see **laugh**.

snug for synonyms see **comfortable**.

soak, saturate, drench, steep, impregnate —**Soak** implies immersion in a liquid, etc. as for the purpose of absorption, thorough wetting, softening, etc. [to *soak* bread in milk]. **Saturate** implies absorption to a point where no more can be taken up [air *saturated* with moisture]. **Drench** implies a thorough wetting as by a downpour [a garden *drenched* by the rain]. **Steep** usually suggests soaking for the purpose of extracting the essence of something [to *steep* tea]. **Impregnate** implies the penetration and permeation of one thing by another [wood *impregnated* with creosote].

soar for synonyms see **fly**.

sob for synonyms see **cry**.

sober for synonyms see **serious**.

sober for antonyms see **drunk** and **witty**.

social for synonym see **friendly**.

social for antonyms see **unsocial**.

soft, bland, mild, gentle —**Soft**, in this connotation, implies an absence or reduction of all that is harsh, rough, or too intense, so as to be pleasing to the senses [*soft* colors, a *soft* voice]. **Bland** implies such an absence of irritation, stimulation, or pungency, as to be soothing, unexciting, and hence, sometimes, uninteresting [*bland* foods, a *bland* climate]. **Mild** applies to that which is not as rough, harsh, or irritating as it might be [a *mild* cigarette, *mild* criticism]. **Gentle**, often equivalent to *mild*, carries a more positive connotation of being pleasantly soothing or tranquil [a *gentle* breeze, a *gentle* voice].

soft for antonyms see **rough**.

soiled for synonyms see **dirty**.

solace for synonyms see **comfort**.

sole for synonyms see **single**.

solemn for synonyms see **serious**.

solemnize for synonyms see **celebrate**.

solicit for synonyms see **beg**.

solicitude for synonyms see **care**.

solid for synonyms see **firm**.

solidarity for synonyms see **unity**.

solitary for synonyms see **alone**, **single**.

solitude, isolation, seclusion —**Solitude** refers to the state of one who is completely alone, cut off from all human contact, and sometimes stresses the loneliness of such a condition [the *solitude* of a hermit]. **Isolation** suggests physical separation from others, often an involuntary detachment resulting from the force of circumstances [the *isolation* of a forest ranger]. **Seclusion** suggests retirement from intercourse with the outside world, as by confining oneself to one's home or a remote place.

somatic for synonyms see **bodily**.

somnolent for synonyms see **sleepy**.

sonance for synonyms see **sound**[1].

soothe for synonyms see **comfort**.

soothe for antonyms see **annoy**.

sorcery for synonyms see **magic**.

sordid for synonyms see **base**[2].

sorrow, grief, sadness, woe —**Sorrow** refers to the deep, often long-continued mental anguish caused by a sense of loss, disappointment, etc. [her secret, life-long *sorrow*]. **Grief** suggests a more painfully intense anguish, usually of relatively shorter duration, for some specific misfortune or disaster [his *grief* over the stricken child]. **Sadness** refers to a condition of low spirits or mournfulness, resulting either from a specific cause or from a general feeling of depression or hopelessness. **Woe** refers to intense unhappiness or sharp grief that cannot be consoled. —*Antonym:* **happiness.** *For other antonyms see* **pleasure.**

sorrowful for synonyms see **sad.**

sort for synonyms see **type.**

sound¹, noise, tone, sonance —**Sound** is the general term for anything that is or may be heard [the *sound* of footsteps]. **Noise** usually refers to a sound that is unpleasant or disagreeable because it is too loud, harsh, or discordant [the *noise* of a boiler factory]. **Tone** is generally applied to a sound regarded as pleasant or musical because it has regularity of vibration resulting in a constant pitch [the range of *tones* in a violin]. **Sonance,** in its general use, is an obsolete synonym for **sound,** but in its restricted use in phonetics, applies to the quality of a sound that is voiced [All vowels have *sonance.*] —*Antonym:* **silence.**

sound² for synonyms see **healthy** and **valid.**

sour, acid, acidulous, tart —**Sour** usually implies an unpleasant sharpness of taste and often connotes fermentation or rancidity [*sour* milk]. **Acid** suggests a sourness that is normal or natural [A lemon is an *acid* fruit.] **Acidulous** suggests a slightly sour or acid quality [*acidulous* spring water]. **Tart** suggests a slightly stinging

sharpness or sourness and usually connotes that this is
pleasant to the taste [a *tart* cherry pie]. —*Antonym:*
sweet.

source for synonyms see **origin.**

span for synonyms see **couple.**

spare for synonyms see **lean, meager.**

spare for antonyms see **profuse.**

sparing for synonyms see **thrifty.**

sparkle for synonyms see **flash.**

sparse for synonyms see **meager.**

spat for synonyms see **quarrel.**

speak, talk, converse, discourse —**Speak** and **talk** are
generally synonymous, but **speak** often connotes formal
address to an auditor or audience [Who will *speak* at the
dinner?] and **talk** often suggests informal colloquial conversation [We were *talking* at dinner.] **Converse** suggests a talking together by two or more people so as to
exchange ideas, information, etc. [They are *conversing* in
the parlor.] **Discourse** suggests a somewhat formal, detailed, extensive talking to another or others [He was *dis-
coursing* to us on Keats.]

special, especial, specific, particular —**Special** and
especial both imply that the thing so described has qualities, aspects, uses, etc. which differentiate it from others
of its class, and the choice of word generally depends on
euphony, but **especial** is usually preferred where pre-
eminence is implied [a matter of *especial* interest to you].
Specific and **particular** are both applied to something
that is singled out for attention, but *specific* suggests the
explicit statement of an example, illustration, etc. [He
cited *specific* cases.] and **particular** emphasizes the distinctness or individuality of the thing so described [in
this *particular* case]. —*Antonym:* **general.**

specific for synonyms see **special**.

specious for synonyms see **plausible**.

speculate for synonyms see **think**.

speech, address, oration, lecture, talk, sermon
—**Speech** is the general word for a discourse delivered
to an audience, whether prepared or impromptu. **Address** implies a formal, carefully prepared speech and
usually attributes importance to the speaker or the
speech [an *address* to a legislature]. **Oration** suggests an
eloquent, rhetorical, sometimes merely bombastic
speech, especially one delivered on some special occasion [political *orations* at the picnic]. A **lecture** is a carefully prepared speech intended to inform or instruct the
audience [a *lecture* to a college class]. **Talk** suggests informality and is applied either to an impromptu speech
or to an address or lecture in which the speaker deliberately uses a simple, conversational approach. A **sermon**
is a speech by a clergyman intended to give religious or
moral instruction and usually based on Scriptural text.

speechless for synonyms see **voiceless**.

speed for synonyms see **haste**.

speedy for synonyms see **fast**.

spherical for synonyms see **round**.

spicy for synonyms see **pungent**.

spicy for antonyms see **insipid**.

spin for synonyms see **turn**.

spite for synonyms see **malice**.

spiteful for synonyms see **vindictive**.

splendid, gorgeous, glorious, sublime, superb
—**Splendid** applies to that which literally or figuratively
dazzles or impresses with its brilliance, luster, etc. [a
splendid uniform, a *splendid* hero]. **Gorgeous** applies to
that which is striking for its brilliance and variety of

color [a *gorgeous* floral display]. **Glorious** refers to that
which is radiantly beautiful or distinctive [a *glorious* sun-
set]. **Sublime** implies such an exalted beauty or grandeur as to inspire awe or admiration [the *sublime* Grand
Canyon]. **Superb** is applied to that which exceeds all
others in grandeur, splendor, etc. [a *superb* performance
of an opera]. All of these words are now used hyperbolically, in informal speech, with weakened effect.

splenetic for synonyms see **irritable**.

splinter for synonyms see **break**.

split for synonyms see **break**.

spoil, spoils, pillage, plunder, booty, prize, loot
—Spoil (now, more commonly, **spoils**) refers to any
property or territory taken in war by the conqueror. (*See
also synonyms at* **decay, indulge, injure**.) **Pillage** suggests violence and destructiveness in the taking of spoils.
Plunder is equivalent to **pillage** but also applies to
property taken by bandits, highwaymen, etc. **Booty** suggests plunder taken by a band or gang, to be divided
among the members. **Prize** refers specifically to spoils
taken at sea, especially an enemy warship or its cargo.
Loot, a more derogatory equivalent for any of the
preceding, emphasizes the immorality or predatory nature of the act.

sponge or **sponger** for synonyms see **parasite**.

sponsor, patron, backer, angel —A **sponsor** is one who
assumes a certain degree of responsibility for another in
any of various ways [The *sponsors* of a television program assume the costs of production.] A **patron** is one
who assumes the role of protector or benefactor, now
usually in a financial capacity, as of an artist, an institution, etc. A **backer** is one who lends support, especially
financial support, to someone or something but does not

necessarily assume any responsibilities [The magazine failed when it lost its *backer.*] **Angel** is a colloquial term for the backer of a theatrical enterprise.

spontaneous, impulsive, instinctive, involuntary, automatic —**Spontaneous** applies to that which is done so naturally that it seems to come without prompting or premeditation [a *spontaneous* demonstration]. **Impulsive** applies to that which is prompted by some external incitement or sudden inner inclination rather than by conscious, rational volition [an *impulsive* retort]. **Instinctive** suggests an instantaneous, unwilled response to a stimulus, as if prompted by some natural, inborn tendency [He took an *instinctive* liking to her.] **Involuntary** refers to that which is done without thought or volition, as a reflex action [an *involuntary* flicker of the eyelid]. **Automatic** suggests an unvarying, machinelike reaction to a given stimulus or situation [an *automatic* response].

spontaneous for antonyms see **voluntary**.

sport for synonyms see **play**.

sprightly for synonyms see **agile, lively**.

spring for synonyms see **rise**.

sprinkle, scatter, strew —To **sprinkle** is to cause to fall in small drops or particles [to *sprinkle* water, to *sprinkle* sugar over berries]. To **scatter** is to disperse the units of a group in different directions, usually in an irregular distribution [The wind *scattered* the papers on the desk.] To **strew** is to scatter, either regularly or irregularly, especially so as to more or less cover a surface [to *strew* sawdust on a floor].

spry for synonyms see **agile**.

spur for synonyms see **motive**.

spurious for synonyms see **artificial**.

spurious for antonyms see **authentic**.

spurn for synonyms see **decline**.

squabble for synonyms see **quarrel**.

squeamish for synonyms see **dainty**.

squirt for synonyms see **flow**.

stack for synonyms see **pile**.

stagger, reel, totter —**Stagger** implies unsteady movement characterized by a loss of equilibrium and failure to maintain a fixed course [to *stagger* under a heavy load]. **Reel** suggests a swaying or lurching so as to appear on the verge of falling [The drunken man *reeled* down the hall.] **Totter** suggests the uncertain, faltering steps of a feeble old person or of an infant learning to walk.

stalwart for synonyms see **strong**.

stance for synonyms see **posture**.

stanch for synonyms see **faithful**.

stand for synonyms see **bear**.

standard, criterion, gauge, yardstick —**Standard** applies to some measure, principle, model, etc. with which things of the same class are compared in order to determine their quantity, value, or quality [*standards* of purity for drugs]. (*See also synonyms at* **model**.) **Criterion** applies to a test or rule for measuring the excellence, fitness, or correctness of something [Mere memory is no accurate *criterion* of intelligence.] **Gauge** literally applies to a standard of measurement [a wire *gauge*], but figuratively it is equivalent to **criterion** [Sales are an accurate *gauge* of a book's popularity.] **Yardstick** refers to a test or criterion for measuring genuineness or value [Time is the only true *yardstick* of a book's merit.]

stare for synonyms see **look**.

start for synonyms see **begin**.

start for antonyms see **close²**, **stop**.

startle for synonyms see **shock**.

starved for synonyms see **hungry**.

state, condition, situation, status —**State** and **condition** both refer to the set of circumstances surrounding or characterizing a person or thing at a given time [What is his mental *state*, or *condition?*] but **condition** more strongly implies some relationship to causes or circumstances [His *condition* will not permit him to travel.] **Situation** implies a significant interrelationship of the circumstances, and connection between these and the person involved [She is in a difficult *situation.*] **Status**, basically a legal term, refers to one's state as determined by such arbitrary factors as age, sex, training, mentality, service, etc. [His *status* as a veteran exempts him from certain taxes.]

stately for synonyms see **grand**.

stature for synonyms see **height**.

status for synonyms see **state**.

statute for synonyms see **law**.

staunch for synonyms see **faithful**.

stay, remain, wait, abide, tarry, linger —**Stay**, the general term, implies a continuing in a specified place [*Stay* there until you hear from me.] **Remain** specifically suggests a staying behind while others go [He alone *remained* at home.] **Wait** suggests a staying in anticipation of something [*Wait* for me at the library.] **Abide**, now somewhat archaic, implies a staying fixed or a relatively long period, as in settled residence [He came for a visit and has been *abiding* here since.] **Tarry** and **linger** imply a staying on after the required or expected time for departure, **linger** especially implying that this is deliberate, as from reluctance to leave [We *tarried* in town two days. He *lingered* at his sweetheart's door.]

stay for antonyms see **go.**

steady, even, uniform, regular, equable —**Steady** implies a fixed regularity or constancy, especially of movement, and an absence of deviation, fluctuation, or faltering [a *steady* breeze]. **Even,** often interchangeable with **steady,** emphasizes the absence of irregularity or inequality [an *even* heartbeat]. **Uniform** implies a sameness or likeness of things, parts, events, etc., usually as the result of conformity with a fixed standard [a *uniform* wage rate]. **Regular** emphasizes the orderliness or symmetry resulting from evenness or uniformity [*regular* features, *regular* attendance]. **Equable** implies that the quality of evenness or regularity is inherent [an *equable* temper]. —*Antonyms:* **changeable, jerky.**

steal, pilfer, filch, purloin, lift, swipe, pinch —**Steal** is the general term implying the taking of another's money, possessions, etc. dishonestly or in a secret or surreptitious manner [to *steal* jewelry, to *steal* a writer's idea]. **Pilfer** implies the stealing of small sums or petty objects [a *pilfering* house guest]. **Filch** also implies petty theft, but connotes that it is done by surreptitious snatching [to *filch* candy in a store]. **Purloin,** a literary word interchangeable with any of the preceding, stresses the removal of that which one means to appropriate for his or her own purposes [letters *purloined* by a blackmailer]. **Lift, swipe,** and **pinch** are slang terms meaning to steal, pilfer, or filch, **lift,** in addition, having specific colloquial application to plagiarism.

stealthy for synonyms see **secret.**

steep[1], abrupt, precipitous, sheer —**Steep** suggests such sharpness of rise or slope as to make ascent or descent very difficult [a *steep* hill]. **Abrupt** implies a sharper degree of inclination in a surface breaking off suddenly from the level [an *abrupt* bank at the river's edge]. **Precipitous** suggests the abrupt and headlong drop of a precipice [a *precipitous* height]. **Sheer** applies to that which is perpendicular, or almost so, and unbroken throughout its length [cliffs falling *sheer* to the sea].

steep² for synonyms see **soak**.

steer for synonyms see **guide**.

stem for synonyms see **rise**.

stereotyped for synonyms see **trite**.

sterile, infertile, barren, unfruitful, impotent —Sterile and **infertile** imply incapability of producing offspring or fruit, as because of some disorder of the reproductive system. **Barren** and **unfruitful** are specifically applied to a sterile woman or to plants, soil, etc. **Impotent** is specifically applied to a man who cannot engage in sexual intercourse because of an inability to have an erection. All of these words have figurative uses [*sterile* thinking, an *infertile* mind, a *barren* victory, *unfruitful* efforts, *impotent* rage].

sterile for antonyms see **fertile**.

stern for synonyms see **severe**.

stew for synonyms see **boil**.

stick, adhere, cohere, cling, cleave —Stick is the simple, general term here, implying attachment by gluing or fastening together in any way, by close association, etc. [to *stick* a stamp on a letter, to *stick* to a subject]. **Adhere** implies firm attachment and, of persons, denotes voluntary allegiance or devotion to an idea, cause, leader, etc. [to *adhere* to a policy]. **Cohere** implies such close sticking together of parts as to form a single mass [Glue made the particles of sawdust *cohere.*] **Cling** implies attachment by embracing, entwining, or grasping with the arms, tendrils, etc. [a vine *clinging* to the trellis].

Cleave is a poetic or lofty term implying a very close, firm attachment [His tongue *cleaved* to the roof of his mouth. Ruth *cleaved* to Naomi.] —*Antonym:* **detach.** For other antonyms see **separate.**

stiff, rigid, inflexible, inelastic —**Stiff** implies a firmness of texture which makes a substance resist a bending force to a greater or lesser degree and figuratively connotes formality or constraint [a *stiff* collar, a *stiff* manner]. (See also synonyms at **firm.**) **Rigid** implies such stiffness in a thing that it resists a bending force to the breaking point and figuratively connotes strictness or severity [a *rigid* framework, a *rigid* disciplinarian]. **Inflexible** is applied to that which cannot be bent or, figuratively, diverted [an *inflexible* rod, an *inflexible* will]. **Inelastic** implies a lack of resilience and, figuratively, of adaptability [the brittle, *inelastic* bones of the aged, *inelastic* regulations]. —*Antonyms:* **limp, pliant.** For other antonyms see **elastic.**

still, quiet, noiseless, hushed —**Still** implies the absence of sound and, usually, of movement [the *still* hours before dawn, a *still* pool]. **Quiet** also implies the absence of sound but usually stresses freedom from excitement, commotion, or agitation [a *quiet* town, a *quiet* motor]. **Noiseless** stresses the absence of noise or sound and often suggests movement unaccompanied by sound [a *noiseless* typewriter]. **Hushed** suggests the suppression of noise or sound [the *hushed* corridors of a hospital]. —*Antonyms:* **noisy, stirring.**

stimulate for synonyms see **animate, provoke.**

stingy, close, niggardly, parsimonious, penurious, miserly —**Stingy** implies a grudging, mean reluctance to part with anything belonging to one. **Close** suggests the keeping of a tight hold on what one has accumulated.

Niggardly implies such closefistedness that one grudgingly spends or gives the least amount possible. **Parsimonious** implies unreasonable economy or frugality, often to the point of niggardliness. **Penurious** implies such extreme parsimony and niggardliness as to make one seem poverty-stricken or destitute. **Miserly** implies the penuriousness of one who is meanly avaricious and hoarding. —*Antonyms:* **generous, bountiful.**

stink for antonyms see **scent.**

stinking, fetid, malodorous, noisome, putrid, rank, rancid, musty —**Stinking** and the more formal **fetid** both imply foulness of odor [a *stinking* cesspool, a *fetid* gum resin]. **Malodorous** is the broadest term here, ranging in application from an unpleasant smell to one that is strongly offensive [*malodorous* cheeses]. **Noisome** stresses the unwholesomeness or harmfulness of that which gives off a foul odor [the *noisome* stench of open sewers]. **Putrid** suggests the disgusting foul smell of decomposed or rotting organic matter [buzzards feeding on *putrid* corpses]. **Rank** implies a disagreeably strong odor that offends to a greater or lesser degree [the *rank* smell of a goat]. **Rancid** specifically suggests the bad smell or taste of stale fats or oils [*rancid* butter]. **Musty** suggests the stale, moldy smell of a long-closed room, food kept in a damp place, etc.

stint for synonyms see **task.**

stipend for synonyms see **wage.**

stir, arouse, rouse, awaken, waken, rally —**Stir** (in this sense, often **stir up**) implies a bringing into action or activity by exciting or provoking [The colonies were *stirred* to rebellion.] **Arouse** and **rouse** are often used interchangeably, but **arouse** usually implies merely a bringing into consciousness, as from a state of sleep [She was *aroused* by the bell.] and **rouse** suggests an additional incitement to vigorous action [The rifle shot *roused* the sleeping guard.] **Awaken** and **waken** literally mean to arouse from sleep, but figuratively they suggest the elicitation of latent faculties, emotions, etc. [It *awakened,* or *wakened,* her maternal feelings.] **Rally** implies a gathering of the component elements or individuals so as to stir to effective action [to *rally* troops, to *rally* one's energy].

stirring for antonyms see **still.**

stoic for synonyms see **impassive.**

stoicism for synonyms see **endurance.**

stolid for synonyms see **impassive.**

stoop, condescend, deign —**Stoop,** in this connection, implies a descending in dignity, as by committing some shameful or immoral act [to *stoop* to cheating]. **Condescend** implies a voluntary descent by one high in rank or power to act graciously or affably toward one regarded as inferior [The general *condescended* to talk with the private.] **Deign** is usually used in negative constructions or with such qualifications as *hardly* or *barely* and, hence, connotes unwilling or arrogant condescension [She scarcely *deigned* to answer me.]

stop, cease, quit, discontinue, desist —**Stop** implies a suspension or ending of some motion, action, or progress [My watch *stopped.*] **Cease** implies a suspension or ending of some state or condition or of an existence [The war had *ceased.*] **Quit** is equivalent to either **stop** or **cease** [To *quit* working means either to stop working, as for the day, or to cease working, that is, to retire.] **Discontinue** suggests the suspension of some action that is a habitual practice, an occupation, etc. [He has *discontinued* the practice of law.] **Desist** implies a ceasing of some action that is annoying, harmful, or futile [*Desist* from further bickering.]

stop for antonyms see **begin, continue.**

stopgap for synonyms see **resource.**

storm for synonyms see **attack.**

story, narrative, tale, anecdote —**Story,** the broadest in scope of these words, refers to a series of connected events, true or fictitious, that is written or told with the intention of entertaining or informing. **Narrative** is a more formal word, referring to the kind of prose that recounts happenings. **Tale,** a somewhat elevated or poetical term, usually suggests a simple, leisurely story, more or less loosely organized, especially a fictitious or legendary one. **Anecdote** applies to a short, entertaining account of a single incident, usually personal or biographical.

stout for synonyms see **fat, strong.**

stout for antonyms see **lean.**

strait or **straits** for synonyms see **emergency.**

strand for synonyms see **shore.**

strange, peculiar, odd, queer, quaint, outlandish —**Strange,** the term of broadest application here, refers to that which is unfamiliar, as because of being uncommon, unknown, or new [a *strange* voice, a *strange* idea, a *strange* device]. **Peculiar** applies either to that which puzzles or to that which has unique qualities [a *peculiar* smell, a *peculiar* pattern]. **Odd** suggests that which differs from the ordinary or conventional, sometimes to the point of being bizarre [*odd* behavior]. **Queer** emphasizes an element of eccentricity, abnormality, or suspicion [a *queer* facial expression]. **Quaint** suggests an oddness, especially an antique quality, that is pleasing or appealing [a *quaint* costume]. **Outlandish** suggests an oddness that is decidedly, often outrageously, fantastic or bizarre [*outlandish* customs]. —*Antonym:* **ordinary.** *For other antonyms see* **familiar.**

stranger for synonyms see **alien.**

stratagem for synonyms see **trick.**

stray for synonyms see **roam.**

strength, power, force, might, energy, potency —**Strength** refers to the inherent capacity to act upon or affect something, to endure, or to resist [the *strength* to lift something, tensile *strength*]. **Power,** somewhat more general, applies to the ability, latent or exerted, physical or mental, to do something [the *power* of the press, the *power* of a machine]. **Force** usually suggests the actual exertion of power, especially in producing motion or overcoming opposition [the *force* of gravity]. **Might** suggests great or overwhelming strength or power [with all one's *might*]. **Energy** specifically implies latent power for doing work or affecting something [the *energy* in an atom]. **Potency** refers to the inherent capacity or power to accomplish something [the *potency* of a drug]. —*Antonyms:* **weakness, impotence.**

strengthen for antonyms see **weaken.**

strenuous for synonyms see **active.**

strew for synonyms see **sprinkle.**

strict, rigid, rigorous, stringent —**Strict,** in this connection, implies exact, undeviating conformity to standards, rules, or conditions [the *strict* interpretation of a law]. **Rigid** implies an unyielding inflexibility, often connoting excessive firmness [*rigid* rules]. **Rigorous** implies such uncompromising strictness as to impose hardships or difficulties [*rigorous* discipline]. **Stringent** implies such strictness as to limit, bind, curb, or confine [a *stringent* censorship code]. —*Antonyms:* **lax, flexible.**

strident for synonyms see **vociferous.**

strife for synonyms see **discord**.

strike, hit, punch, slap, smite, knock —Strike and hit are more or less interchangeable in meaning to deliver a blow to or toward someone or something [He *struck*, or *hit*, the boy.] but each is more frequently used in certain connections than the other [Lightning *struck* the barn. She *hit* the bull's-eye.] **Punch** implies a hitting with or as with the closed fist [to *punch* one on the jaw]. **Slap** implies a hitting with or as with the palm of the hand [to *slap* one's face]. **Smite**, a literary or rhetorical word, emphasizes the force used in striking or hitting [He will *smite* you dead.] **Knock** implies either a hitting so as to displace [He *knocked* the vase from the table.] or a repeated striking [She *knocked* at the window.]

striking for synonyms see **noticeable**.

stringent for synonyms see **strict**.

strip, denude, divest, bare, dismantle —Strip implies the pulling or tearing off of clothing, outer covering, etc. and often connotes forcible or even violent action and total deprivation [to *strip* paper off a wall, *stripped* of sham]. **Denude** implies that the thing stripped is left exposed or naked [land *denuded* of vegetation]. **Divest** implies the taking away of something with which one has been clothed or invested [an official *divested* of authority]. **Bare** simply implies an uncovering or laying open to view [to *bare* one's head in reverence]. **Dismantle** implies the act of stripping a house, ship, etc. of all of its furniture or equipment [a *dismantled* factory].

strive for synonyms see **try**.

strong, stout, sturdy, tough, stalwart —Strong is the broadest in scope of these terms, implying power that can be exerted actively as well as power that resists destruction [a *strong* body, a *strong* fortress]. **Stout** implies

ability to stand strain, pressure, wear, etc. without breaking down or giving way [a *stout* rope, a *stout* heart].
Sturdy suggests the strength of that which is solidly developed or built and hence difficult to shake or weaken
[*sturdy* oaks, *sturdy* faith].   **Tough** suggests the strength
of that which is firm and resistant in consistency or
character [*tough* leather, *tough* opposition].   **Stalwart**
stresses staunchness or reliability [a *stalwart* support].

strong for antonyms see **weak.**

structure for synonyms see **building.**

struggle for synonyms see **conflict, try.**

stubborn, obstinate, dogged, pertinacious —**Stubborn** implies an innate fixedness of purpose, course, or
condition that is strongly resistant to change or manipulation [a *stubborn* child, a *stubborn* belief].   **Obstinate** applies to a person who adheres persistently, and often unreasonably, to his or her purpose, course, etc., against argument or persuasion [a panel hung by an *obstinate*
juror].   **Dogged** implies thoroughgoing determination or,
sometimes, sullen obstinacy [the *dogged* pursuit of a
goal].   **Pertinacious** implies a strong tenacity of purpose
that is regarded unfavorably by others [a *pertinacious*
critic]. —*Antonyms:* **compliant, tractable.**

student for synonyms see **pupil.**

study for synonyms see **consider.**

stun for synonyms see **shock.**

stupid, dull, dense, slow, retarded —**Stupid** implies
such lack of intelligence or incapacity for perceiving,
learning, etc. as might be shown by one in a mental stu-
por [a *stupid* idea].   (See also synonyms at **silly**.)   **Dull** implies a mental sluggishness that may be constitutional or
may result from overfatigue or disease [The fever left
him *dull* and listless.]   **Dense** suggests obtuseness, or an

irritating failure to understand quickly or to react intelligently [too *dense* to take a hint]. **Slow** suggests that the quickness to learn, but not necessarily the capacity for learning, is below average [a pupil *slow* in his studies]. **Retarded** is applied to those behind others of the same age or class because of mental deficiency [a *retarded* pupil]. —*Antonym:* **bright.** For other antonyms see **intelligent, wise.**

stupor for synonyms see **lethargy.**

sturdy for synonyms see **strong.**

sturdy for antonyms see **fragile, weak.**

style for synonyms see **fashion.**

suave, urbane, diplomatic, politic, bland —**Suave** suggests the smoothly gracious social manner of one who deals with people easily and tactfully [a *suave* sophisticate]. **Urbane** suggests the social poise of one who is highly cultivated and has had much worldly experience [an *urbane* cosmopolite]. **Diplomatic** implies adroitness and tactfulness in dealing with people and handling delicate situations, sometimes in such a way as to gain one's own ends [a *diplomatic* answer]. **Politic** also expresses this idea, often stressing the expediency or opportunism of a particular policy pursued [a *politic* move]. **Bland** is the least complex of these terms, simply implying a gentle or ingratiating pleasantness [a *bland* disposition].

suave for antonyms see **blunt.**

subdue for synonyms see **conquer.**

subject, theme, topic, text —**Subject** is the general word for whatever is dealt with in discussion, study, writing, art, etc. [the *subject* of a talk, the *subject* of a painting]. (*See also synonyms at* **citizen.**) A **theme** is a subject developed or elaborated upon in a literary or artistic work, or one that constitutes the underlying motif of the work [a novel with a social *theme*]. A **topic** is a subject of common interest selected for individual treatment, as in an essay, or for discussion by a group of persons [Baseball is their favorite *topic* of conversation.] **Text** is specifically applied to a Biblical passage chosen as the subject of a sermon.

subject for antonyms see **alien**.

subjugate for synonyms see **conquer**.

sublime for synonyms see **splendid**.

submit for synonyms see **surrender**.

submit for antonyms see **oppose**.

subservient for synonyms see **servile**.

subservient for antonyms see **chief**.

subside for synonyms see **wane**.

substantiate for synonyms see **confirm**.

subterfuge for synonyms see **deception**.

succeed, prosper, flourish, thrive —Succeed implies the favorable outcome of an undertaking or career or the attainment of a desired goal [to *succeed* as a businessman]. (*See also synonyms at* **follow**.) **Prosper** implies continued, often increasing, good fortune or success [The nation *prospered* under his administration.] **Flourish** more specifically suggests a figurative state of flowering, when a person or thing is at the peak of development, influence, etc. [Militarism *flourishes* in a fascist state.] **Thrive** implies vigorous growth or development, as because of favorable conditions [Industry *thrived* in the North.] —*Antonym:* **fail**.

succession for synonyms see **series**.

succinct for synonyms see **concise**.

succor for synonyms see **help**.

succumb for synonyms see **yield**.

succumb for antonyms see **oppose**.

sudden, precipitate, abrupt, impetuous —**Sudden** implies extreme quickness or hastiness and, usually, unexpectedness [a *sudden* outburst of temper]. **Precipitate** adds the implication of rashness or lack of due deliberation [a *precipitate* decision]. **Abrupt** implies a breaking in or off suddenly and, hence, suggests the lack of any warning or a curtness, lack of ceremony, etc. [an *abrupt* dismissal]. **Impetuous** implies vehement impulsiveness or extreme eagerness [an *impetuous* suitor]. —*Antonym:* **deliberate.**

sue for synonyms see **appeal.**

suffer for synonyms see **bear** and **let.**

suffering for synonyms see **distress.**

sufficient, enough, adequate —**Sufficient** and **enough** agree in describing that which satisfies a requirement exactly and is neither more nor less in amount than is needed [A word to the wise is *sufficient*. We have *enough* food for a week.] **Adequate** suggests the meeting of an acceptable (sometimes barely so) standard of fitness or suitability [The supporting players were *adequate*.] —*Antonyms:* **deficient, inadequate.**

suggest, imply, hint, intimate, insinuate —**Suggest** implies a putting of something into the mind either intentionally, as by way of a proposal [I *suggest* you leave now.] or unintentionally, as through association of ideas [The smell of ether *suggests* a hospital.] **Imply** stresses the putting into the mind of something involved, but not openly expressed, in a word, a remark, etc. and suggests the need for inference [Her answer *implied* a refusal.] **Hint** connotes faint or indirect suggestion that is, however, intended to be understood [He *hinted* that he would come.] **Intimate** suggests a making known obliquely by a very slight hint [He only dared to *intimate* his feelings.] **Insinuate** implies the subtle hinting of something disagreeable or of that which one lacks the courage to say outright [Are you *insinuating* that she is dishonest?]

suitable for synonyms see **fit**.

sulky for synonyms see **sullen**.

sullen, glum, morose, surly, sulky —**Sullen** suggests a gloomy, withdrawn silence, usually connoting anger, resentment, or bitterness [The *sullen* prisoners marched along.] **Glum** implies a dejected silence resulting from low spirits or a feeling of depression [He listened with a *glum* expression.] **Morose** suggests a sour, unsociable glumness [She took a *morose* view of the future.] **Surly** suggests a brusque, ill-tempered gruffness [a *surly* answer]. **Sulky** suggests a sullenness characterized by petulance and discontent [a *sulky* child].

sullen for antonyms see **amiable**.

sum, amount, aggregate, total —**Sum** refers to the number or amount obtained by adding individual units [The *sum* of 3 and 5 is 8.] **Amount** applies to the result obtained by combining all the sums, quantities, measures, etc. that are involved [He paid the full *amount* of the damages.] **Aggregate** refers to the whole group or mass of individual items gathered together [the *aggregate* of his experiences]. **Total** stresses the wholeness or inclusiveness of a sum or amount [The collection reached a *total* of $200.]

summary for synonyms see **abridgment**.

summit, peak, climax, acme, apex, pinnacle, zenith —**Summit** literally refers to the topmost point of a hill or similar elevation and, figuratively, to the highest attainable level, as of achievement. **Peak** refers to the highest of a number of high points, as in a mountain range or, figuratively, in a graph. **Climax** applies to the highest point, as in interest, force, or excitement, in a scale of ascending values. **Acme** refers to the highest possible point of perfection in the development or progress of something. **Apex** suggests the highest point (literally, of a geometric figure such as a cone; figuratively, of a career, process, etc.) where all ascending lines, courses, etc. ultimately meet. **Pinnacle**, in its figurative uses, is equivalent to **summit** or **peak**, but sometimes connotes a giddy or unsteady height. **Zenith** literally refers to the highest point in the heavens and hence figuratively suggests fame or success reached by a spectacular rise.

summon for synonyms see **call**.

sunder for synonyms see **separate**.

superb for synonyms see **splendid**.

supercilious for synonyms see **proud**.

superficial, shallow, cursory —**Superficial** implies concern with the obvious or surface aspects of a thing [*superficial* characteristics] and, in a derogatory sense, lack of thoroughness, profoundness, or significance [*superficial* judgments]. **Shallow**, in this connection always derogatory, implies a lack of depth of character, intellect, or meaning [*shallow* writing]. **Cursory**, which may or may not be derogatory, suggests a hasty consideration of something without pausing to note details [a *cursory* inspection]. —*Antonyms:* **deep, profound**.

supersede for synonyms see **replace**.

supine for synonyms see **prone**.

supplant for synonyms see **replace**.

supple for synonyms see **elastic**.

supplicate for synonyms see **appeal**.

support, uphold, sustain, maintain, advocate, back, back up —**Support**, the broadest of these terms, suggests a favoring of someone or something, either by giving active aid or merely by approving or sanctioning [to *support* a candidate for office]. **Uphold** suggests that what is being supported is under attack [to *uphold* civil rights for all]. **Sustain** implies full active support so as to strengthen or keep from failing [*sustained* by his hope for the future]. **Maintain** suggests a supporting so as to keep intact or unimpaired [to *maintain* the law, to *maintain* a family]. **Advocate** implies support in speech or writing and sometimes connotes persuasion or argument [to *advocate* a change in policy]. **Back** (often **back up**) suggests support, as financial aid or moral encouragement, given to prevent failure [I'll *back* you *up* in your demands.]

supporter for synonyms see **follower**.

sure, certain, confident, positive —**Sure**, the simple word, suggests merely an absence of doubt or hesitancy [I'm *sure* you don't mean it.] **Certain** usually suggests conviction based on specific grounds or evidence [This letter makes me *certain* of his innocence.] **Confident** stresses the firmness of one's certainty or sureness, especially in some expectation [She's *confident* she'll win.] **Positive** suggests unshakable confidence, especially in the correctness of one's opinions or conclusions, sometimes to the point of dogmatism [He's too *positive* in his beliefs.]

sure for antonyms see **doubtful**.

surfeit for synonyms see **satiate**.

surly for synonyms see **sullen**.

surly for antonyms see **amiable**.

surmise for synonyms see **guess**.

surpass for synonyms see **excel**.

surprise, astonish, amaze, astound, flabbergast

—**Surprise**, in this connection, implies an affecting with wonder because unexpected or unusual [I'm *surprised* at your concern.] **Astonish** implies a surprising with something that seems unbelievable [to *astonish* with sleight of hand]. **Amaze** suggests an astonishing that causes bewilderment or confusion [*amazed* at the sudden turn of events]. **Astound** suggests a shocking astonishment that leaves one helpless to act or think [I was *astounded* by his proposal.] **Flabbergast** is a colloquial term suggesting an astounding to the point of speechlessness.

surrender, relinquish, yield, submit, resign —**Surrender** commonly implies the giving up of something completely after striving to keep it [to *surrender* a fort, to *surrender* one's freedom]. **Relinquish** is the general word implying an abandoning, giving up, or letting go of something held [to *relinquish* one's grasp, to *relinquish* a claim]. To **yield** is to concede or give way under pressure [to *yield* one's consent]. To **submit** is to give in to authority or superior force [to *submit* to a conqueror]. **Resign** implies a voluntary, formal relinquishment and, used reflexively, connotes submission or passive acceptance [to *resign* an office, to *resign* oneself to failure].

surreptitious for synonyms see **secret**.
survive for synonyms see **outlive**.
suspend for synonyms see **adjourn, exclude**.
sustain for synonyms see **support**.
swagger for synonyms see **boast**.
swarm for synonyms see **crowd, group**.
swarthy for synonyms see **dusky**.
sway for synonyms see **affect, power, swing**.
swearing for synonyms see **blasphemy**.
swell for synonyms see **expand**.
swerve for synonyms see **deviate**.

swift for synonyms see **fast**.

swindle for synonyms see **cheat**.

swing, sway, oscillate, vibrate, fluctuate, undulate
—**Swing** suggests the to-and-fro motion of something
that is suspended, hinged, pivoted, etc. so that it is free
to turn or swivel at the point or points of attachment [a
swinging door]. **Sway** describes the swinging motion of
something flexible or self-balancing, whether attached or
unattached, in yielding to pressure, weight, etc. [branches
swaying in the wind]. To **oscillate** is to swing back and
forth, within certain limits, in the manner of a pendulum.
Vibrate suggests the rapid, regular, back-and-forth motion of a plucked, taut string and is applied in physics to
a similar movement of the particles of a fluid or elastic
medium [sound *vibrations*]. **Fluctuate** implies continual,
irregular alternating movements and is now most common in its extended sense [*fluctuating* prices]. **Undulate**
implies a gentle wavelike motion or form [*undulating*
land].

swipe for synonyms see **steal**.

sycophant for synonyms see **parasite**.

symmetry, proportion, harmony, balance —**Symmetry**, with reference to the interrelation of parts to
form an aesthetically pleasing whole, strictly implies correspondence in the form, size, and arrangement of parts
on either side of a median line or plane. **Proportion** implies a gracefulness that results from the measured fitness in size or arrangement of parts to each other or to
the whole. **Harmony** implies such agreement or proportionate arrangement of parts in size, color, form, etc. as
to make a pleasing impression. **Balance** suggests the
offsetting or contrasting of parts so as to produce an aesthetic equilibrium in the whole.

sympathetic for synonyms see **tender**.
sympathy for synonyms see **pity**.
symptom for synonyms see **sign**.
synchronous for synonyms see **contemporary**.
syndicate for synonyms see **monopoly**.
synopsis for synonyms see **abridgment**.
synthetic for synonyms see **artificial**.
system for synonyms see **method**.
system for antonyms see **confusion**.
systematic for synonyms see **orderly**.

T

taciturn for synonyms see **silent**.
tact, poise, diplomacy, savoir-faire —Tact implies the skill in dealing with persons or difficult situations of one who has a quick and delicate sense of what is fitting and thus avoids giving offense [It will require *tact* to keep him calm.] **Poise** implies composure in the face of disturbing or embarrassing situations [Despite the social blunder, she maintained her *poise*.] **Diplomacy** implies a smoothness and adroitness in dealing with others, sometimes in such a way as to gain one's own ends [His lack of *diplomacy* lost him the contract.] **Savoir-faire** implies a ready knowledge of the right thing to do or say in any situation.
tactful for antonyms see **blunt**.
taint for synonyms see **contaminate**.
take, seize, grasp, clutch, grab, snatch —Take is the general word meaning to get hold of by or as by the hands [to *take* a book, to *take* the opportunity]. (*See also synonyms at* **bring** *and* **receive**.) To **seize** is to take sud-

denly and forcibly [He *seized* the gun from the robber. The general planned to *seize* power.] **Grasp** implies a seizing and holding firmly [to *grasp* a rope, to *grasp* an idea.] **Clutch** implies a tight or convulsive grasping of that which one is eager to take or keep hold of [She *clutched* his hand in terror.] **Grab** implies a roughness or unscrupulousness in seizing [The child *grabbed* all the candy. The teacher wanted to *grab* credit.] **Snatch** stresses an abrupt quickness and, sometimes, a surreptitiousness in seizing [She *snatched* the letter from my hand.]

tale for synonyms see **story**.

talent, gift, aptitude, faculty, knack, genius —**Talent** implies an apparently native ability for a specific pursuit and connotes either that it is or can be cultivated by the one possessing it [a *talent* for drawing]. **Gift** suggests of a special ability that is bestowed upon one, as by nature, and not acquired through effort [a *gift* for making plants grow]. **Aptitude** implies a natural inclination for a particular work, specifically as pointing to special fitness for, or probable success in it [*aptitude* tests]. **Faculty** implies a special ability that is either inherent or acquired, as well as a ready ease in its exercise [the *faculty* of judgment]. **Knack** implies an acquired faculty for doing something cleverly and skillfully [the *knack* of rhyming]. **Genius** implies an inborn mental endowment, specifically of a creative or inventive kind in the arts or sciences, that is exceptional or phenomenal [the *genius* of Edison].

talk for synonyms see **speak** and **speech**.

talkative, loquacious, garrulous, voluble —**Talkative**, implying a fondness for talking frequently or at length, is perhaps the least derogatory of these words [a happy, *talkative* girl]. **Loquacious** usually implies a disposition to talk incessantly or to keep up a constant flow of chatter [a *loquacious* mood]. **Garrulous** implies a wearisome loquacity about trivial matters [a *garrulous* old man]. **Voluble** suggests a continuous flow of glib talk [a *voluble* oration].

talkative for antonyms see **silent**.

tall for synonyms see **high**.

tally for synonyms see **agree**.

tangent for synonyms see **adjacent**.

tangible for synonyms see **perceptible**.

tardy, late, overdue —**Tardy** applies to that which comes or occurs after the proper or appointed time, either from a lack of punctuality or because of inadvertent delay [Two of the pupils were *tardy* this morning.] **Late** applies to that which fails to occur at the usual or proper time, as because of slowness of movement, development, etc. [Summer came *late* that year.] **Overdue** is applied to something delayed, unpaid, etc. beyond the scheduled time, as because of someone's tardiness or procrastination [an *overdue* ship, *overdue* rent]. —*Antonym:* **prompt**.

tarry for synonyms see **stay**.

tart for synonyms see **sour**.

task, chore, stint, assignment, job —**Task** refers to a piece of work assigned to or demanded of someone, as by another person, by duty, etc., and usually implies that this is difficult or arduous work [He has the *task* of answering letters.] **Chore** applies to any of the routine domestic activities for which one is responsible [His *chore* is washing the dishes.] **Stint** refers to a task that is one's share of the work done by a group and usually connotes a minimum to be completed in the allotted time [We've all done our daily *stint*.] **Assignment** applies to a specific, prescribed task allotted by someone in authority [classroom *assignments*]. **Job**, in this connection, refers to a specific piece of work, as in one's trade or as voluntarily undertaken for pay [the *job* of painting our house].

taunt for synonyms see **ridicule**.

taut for synonyms see **tight**.

tawdry for synonyms see **gaudy**.

tawny for synonyms see **dusky**.

teach, instruct, educate, train, school —**Teach** is the basic, inclusive word for the imparting of knowledge or skills and usually connotes some individual attention to the learner [He *taught* her how to skate.] **Instruct** implies systematized teaching, usually in some particular subject [She *instructs* in chemistry.] **Educate** stresses the development of latent faculties and powers by formal, systematic teaching, especially in institutions of higher learning [He was *educated* in European universities.] **Train** implies the development of a particular faculty or skill, or instruction toward a particular occupation, as by methodical discipline, exercise, etc. [He was *trained* as a mechanic.] **School**, often equivalent to any of the preceding, sometimes specifically connotes a disciplining to endure something difficult [He had to *school* himself to obedience.]

tear, rip, rend —**Tear** implies a pulling apart by force, so as to lacerate or leave ragged edges [to *tear* paper wrapping]. **Rip** suggests a forcible tearing, especially along a seam or in a straight line [to *rip* a hem]. **Rend**, a somewhat literary term, implies a tearing with violence [The tree was *rent* by a bolt of lightning.]

tease for synonyms see **annoy**.

tell, relate, recount, narrate, report —**Tell**, in this connection, is the simple, general word meaning to convey the facts or details of some circumstance or occurrence [*Tell* me what happened.] (*See also synonyms at* reveal.) **Relate** suggests the orderly telling of something that one has personally experienced or witnessed [*Relate* your dream to us.] **Recount** implies the telling of events in consecutive order and in elaborate detail and, hence, often takes a plural object [to *recount* one's adventures]. **Narrate** suggests the use of the techniques of fiction, such as plot development, building up to a climax, etc. [to *narrate* the story of one's life]. **Report** suggests the recounting for others' information of something that one has investigated or witnessed [He will *report* the convention proceedings.]

tell for antonyms see **ask**.

telling for synonyms see **valid**.

temerity, audacity, effrontery, nerve, brass, cheek, gall —Temerity refers to a rashness or foolish boldness that results from underrating the dangers or failing to evaluate the consequences [He had the *temerity* to criticize his employer.] **Audacity** suggests either great presumption or defiance of social conventions, morals, etc. [shocked at the *audacity* of her proposal]. **Effrontery**, always derogatory in usage, connotes shamelessness or insolence in defying the rules of propriety, courtesy, etc. [We were shocked at his *effrontery* in addressing the teacher by her first name.] **Nerve, brass, cheek,** and **gall** are colloquial equivalents of **effrontery**, but **nerve, brass,** and **cheek** usually suggest mere impudence or sauciness and **gall**, unmitigated insolence.

temper for synonyms see **disposition, mood**.

temperament for synonyms see **disposition**.

temperate for synonym see **moderate**.

temporary, provisional, ad interim, acting —**Temporary** applies to a post held (or to the person holding such a post) for a limited time, subject to dismissal by those having the power of appointment [a *temporary* mail carrier]. **Provisional** is specifically applied to a government established for the time being in a new state until a permanent government can be formed. **Ad interim** refers to an appointment for an intervening period, as between the death of an official and the election of his or her successor. **Acting** is applied to one who temporarily takes over the powers of a regular official during the latter's absence [A vice-president often serves as *acting* president.]

temporary for antonyms see **continual, permanent.**

tempt for synonyms see **lure.**

tenacity for synonyms see **perseverance.**

tendency, trend, current, drift, tenor —**Tendency** refers to an inclination or disposition to move in a particular direction or act in a certain way, especially as a result of some inherent quality or habit [He has a *tendency* toward exaggeration.] **Trend** suggests a general direction, with neither a definite course nor goal, subject to change or fluctuation by some external force [a recent *trend* in literature]. **Current** differs from **trend** in connoting a clearly defined course, but one also subject to change [the *current* of one's life]. **Drift** refers either to the course along which something is being carried or driven [the *drift* toward absolute conformity] or to a course taken by something that has unstated implications [What is the *drift* of this argument?] **Tenor,** equivalent in this connection to **drift,** connotes more strongly the clarity or purport of the unstated purpose or objective [the general *tenor* of the Bill of Rights].

tender¹, compassionate, sympathetic, warm, warm-hearted —**Tender**, in this connection, implies a softness or gentleness in one's relations with others that is expressive of warm affection and concern [a *tender* caress]. **Compassionate** is applied to one who is easily affected by another's troubles or pains and is quick to show pity or mercy [a *compassionate* judge]. **Sympathetic** implies the ability or disposition to enter into another's mental state or emotions and thus to share his or her sorrows, joys, and desires [a *sympathetic* interest in a colleague's career]. **Warm** and **warmhearted** suggest a sympathetic interest or affection characterized by cordiality and generosity [*warm*, or *warmhearted*, hospitality].

tender² for synonyms see **offer**.

tenet for synonyms see **doctrine**.

tenor for synonyms see **tendency**.

tense for synonyms see **tight**.

tenuous for synonyms see **thin**.

terminal for synonyms see **last**.

terminate for synonyms see **close²**.

terrestrial for synonyms see **earthly**.

terrified for synonyms see **afraid**.

terrify for synonyms see **frighten**.

terror for synonyms see **fear**.

terrorize for synonyms see **frighten**.

terse for synonyms see **concise**.

terse for antonyms see **wordy**.

test for synonyms see **trial**.

testimony for synonyms see **proof**.

text for synonyms see **subject**.

thaw for synonyms see **melt**.

theft, larceny, robbery, burglary —**Theft** is the general term and **larceny** the legal term for the unlawful or felonious taking away of another's property without the person's consent and with the intention of depriving him or her of it. **Robbery** in its strict legal sense implies the felonious taking of another's property from his or her person or in the person's immediate presence by the use of violence or intimidation. **Burglary** in legal use implies a breaking into a house with intent to commit theft or other felony and is often restricted to such an act accomplished at night.

theme for synonyms see **subject**.

theory, hypothesis, law —Theory, as compared here, implies considerable evidence in support of a formulated general principle explaining the operation of certain phenomena [the *theory* of evolution]. **Hypothesis** implies an inadequacy of evidence in support of an explanation that is tentatively inferred, often as a basis for further experimentation [the nebular *hypothesis*]. **Law** implies an exact formulation of the principle operating in a sequence of events in nature, observed to occur with unvarying uniformity under the same conditions [the *law* of the conservation of energy].

thick for synonyms see **close¹**.

thick for antonyms see **thin**.

thin, slender, slim, lean, slight, tenuous —Thin implies relatively little extent from one surface or side of a thing to the opposite and connotes lack of fleshiness, fullness, substance, etc. **Slender** and **slim** suggest a physical spareness that is more or less pleasing in proportion, but in extended senses, the words carry connotations of meagerness or scantiness [a *slender* income, a *slim* possibility]. **Lean,** implying an absence of fat, figuratively connotes a lack of richness or productiveness [*lean* years]. **Slight** implies smallness and lightness or

fragility in form or build and, in extended senses, suggests inconsiderableness in amount, extent, or significance [a *slight* figure, a *slight* difference in weight]. **Tenuous** implies extreme physical thinness or fineness and, in extended senses, suggests insubstantiality, flimsiness, extreme subtlety, etc. [a *tenuous* film, a *tenuous* plot].
—*Antonyms:* **thick, substantial.**

think, reason, cogitate, reflect, speculate, deliberate —**Think** is the general word meaning to exercise the mental faculties so as to form ideas, arrive at conclusions, etc. [Learn to *think* clearly]. **Reason** implies a logical sequence of thought, starting with what is known or assumed and advancing to a definite conclusion through the inferences drawn [He *reasoned* that she would accept]. **Cogitate** is used, sometimes humorously, of a person who is, or appears to be, thinking hard [I was *cogitating,* not daydreaming.] **Reflect** implies a turning of one's thoughts on or back on a subject and connotes deep or quiet continued thought [He *reflected* on the day's events.] **Speculate** implies a reasoning on the basis of incomplete or uncertain evidence and therefore stresses the conjectural character of the opinions formed [to *speculate* on the possibility of life on Mars]. **Deliberate** implies careful and thorough consideration of a matter in order to arrive at a conclusion [The jury *deliberated* on the case.]

thought for synonyms see **idea.**

thoughtful, considerate, attentive —**Thoughtful,** as compared here, implies the showing of thought for the comfort or well-being of others, as by anticipating their needs or wishes [It was *thoughtful* of you to call.] **Considerate** implies a thoughtful or sympathetic regard for the feelings or circumstances of others, as in sparing them pain, distress, or discomfort [*considerate* enough to extend the time for payment]. **Attentive** implies a constant thoughtfulness as shown by repeated acts of consideration, courtesy, or devotion [an *attentive* suitor]. —*Antonym:* **thoughtless.**

thrash for synonyms see **beat.**

threaten, menace —**Threaten** implies a warning of impending punishment, danger, or evil by words, actions, events, conditions, signs, etc. [He *threatened* to retaliate. The clouds *threaten* rain.] **Menace** stresses the frightening or hostile character of that which threatens [She *menaced* me with a revolver.]

thrifty, frugal, sparing, economical, provident —**Thrifty** implies industry and clever management of one's money or resources, usually so as to result in some savings [The *thrifty* housewife watched for sales.] **Frugal** stresses the idea of saving and suggests spending which excludes any luxury or lavishness and provides only the simplest fare, dress, etc. [The Amish are a *frugal* people.] **Sparing** implies such restraint in spending as restricts itself to the bare minimum or involves deprivation [*sparing* to the point of niggardliness]. **Economical** implies prudent management of one's money or resources so as to avoid any waste in expenditure or use [It is often *economical* to buy in large quantities.] **Provident** implies management with the foresight to provide for future needs [Never *provident*, he quickly spent his inheritance.] —*Antonyms:* **lavish, prodigal, wasteful.**

thrive for synonyms see **succeed.**

throng for synonyms see **crowd.**

throw, cast, toss, hurl, fling, pitch —**Throw** is the general word meaning to cause to move through the air by a rapid propulsive motion of the arm. **Cast,** the preferred word in certain connections [to *cast* a fishing line], generally has a more archaic or lofty quality [They *cast* stones at him.] To **toss** is to throw lightly or carelessly and, usually, with an upward or sidewise motion [to *toss* a coin]. **Hurl** and **fling** both imply a throwing with force or violence, but **hurl** suggests that the object thrown moves swiftly for some distance [to *hurl* a javelin] and **fling**, that it is thrust sharply or vehemently so that it strikes a surface with considerable impact [She *flung* the plate to the floor.] **Pitch** implies a throwing with a definite aim or in a definite direction [to *pitch* a baseball].

thrust for synonyms see **push**.

thwart for synonyms see **frustrate**.

tidy for synonyms see **neat**.

tidy for antonyms see **slovenly**.

tie for synonyms see **bind**.

tie for antonyms see **separate**.

tight, taut, tense —**Tight**, in this connection, implies a constricting or binding encirclement [a *tight* collar] or such closeness or in a compactness of parts as to be impenetrable [*airtight*]. **Taut** (and, loosely, also **tight**) is applied to a rope, cord, cloth, etc. that is pulled or stretched to the point where there is no slackness [*taut* sails]. **Tense** suggests a tightness or tautness that results in great strain [*tense* muscles]. —*Antonyms:* **loose, slack, lax.**

timely, opportune, seasonable —**Timely** applies to that which happens or is done at an appropriate time, especially at such a time as to be of help or service [a *timely* interruption]. **Opportune** refers to that which is so timed, often as if by accident, as to meet exactly the needs of the occasion [the *opportune* arrival of a supply train]. **Seasonable** applies literally to that which is suited to the season of the year or, figuratively, to the moment or occasion [*seasonable* weather].

timid, timorous for synonyms see **afraid.**

tinge, tint for synonyms see **color.**

tiny for synonyms see **small.**

tired, weary, wearied, exhausted, fatigued, fagged
—Tired is applied to one who has been drained of much
of his or her strength and energy through exertion, boredom, impatience, etc. [*tired* by years of hard toil].
Weary (or **wearied**) suggests such depletion of energy or
interest as to make one unable or unwilling to continue
[*weary* of study]. **Exhausted** implies a total draining of
strength and energy, as after a long, hard climb. **Fatigued** refers to one who has lost so much energy
through prolonged exertion that rest and sleep are essential [*fatigued* at the end of the day]. **Fagged,** an informal
word, suggests great exhaustion or fatigue from hard, unremitting work or exertion [completely *fagged* after a set
of tennis].

titter for synonyms see **laugh.**

toady for synonyms see **parasite.**

toil for synonyms see **work.**

token for synonyms see **pledge, sign.**

tolerate for synonyms see **bear.**

tone for synonyms see **sound**[1].

tool for synonyms see **implement.**

tooth, tusk, fang —Tooth is the general, inclusive word
for any of the set of bonelike structures set in the jaws of
most vertebrates and used for biting, tearing, and chew-
ing. **Tusk** refers to a long, pointed, enlarged tooth
projecting outside the mouth in certain animals, as the
elephant, wild boar, and walrus, and used for digging or
as a weapon. **Fang** refers either to one of the long, sharp
teeth with which meat-eating animals tear their prey or

to the long, hollow tooth through which poisonous snakes inject their venom.

topic for synonyms see **subject**.

torment, torture, rack —Torment implies harassment or persecution by the continued or repeated infliction of suffering or annoyance [*tormented* by the mosquitoes]. (*See also* synonyms *at* **bait**.) **Torture** implies the infliction of acute physical or mental pain, such as to cause agony [*tortured* by his memories]. **Rack** suggests the excruciating pain suffered on the rack, an ancient instrument of torture on which the limbs were pulled out of place [*racked* by the pain of arthritis].

torment for antonyms see **comfort**.

torpor for synonyms see **lethargy**.

torture for synonyms see **torment**.

toss for synonyms see **throw**.

total for synonyms see **complete, sum**.

totter for synonyms see **stagger**.

touch for synonyms see **affect**.

touching for synonyms see **moving**.

touchy for synonyms see **irritable**.

tough for synonyms see **strong**.

tough for antonyms see **fragile**.

tow for synonyms see **pull**.

towering for synonyms see **high**.

toy for synonyms see **trifle**.

trace, vestige, track —Trace, literally applying to a mark, footprint, etc. left by the passage of an animal or vehicle, commonly refers to any mark showing that something has existed or occurred [a faint *trace* of egg on his vest]. **Vestige** applies to some slight remains of something that is no longer in actual existence [the *vestiges* of an ancient civilization]. **Track**, equivalent to

trace in its literal sense, suggests a continuous mark or series of marks that can be followed for some distance [automobile *tracks* in the sand].

track for synonyms see **trace**.

tractable for synonyms see **obedient**.

tractable for antonyms see **stubborn, unruly**.

trade for synonyms see **business** and **sell**.

train for synonyms see **teach**.

trait for synonyms see **quality**.

traitorous for synonyms see **faithless**.

tramp for synonyms see **vagrant**.

tranquil for synonyms see **calm**.

transcend for synonyms see **excel**.

transfer for synonyms see **move**.

transfigure for synonyms see **transform**.

transform, transmute, convert, metamorphose, transfigure —Transform, the broadest in scope of these terms, implies a change either in external form or in inner nature, in function, etc. [She was *transformed* into a happy girl.] (*See also synonyms at* **change**.) **Transmute**, from its earlier use in alchemy, suggests a change in basic nature that seems almost miraculous [*transmuted* from a shy youth into a lighthearted man about town]. **Convert** implies a change in details so as to be suitable for a new use [to *convert* an attic into an apartment]. **Metamorphose** suggests a startling change produced as if by magic [A tadpole is *metamorphosed* into a frog.] **Transfigure** implies a change in outward appearance which seems to exalt or glorify [his whole being *transfigured* by love].

transient, transitory, ephemeral, momentary, evanescent, fleeting —Transient applies to that which lasts or stays but a short time [a *transient* guest, a *transient* feeling]. **Transitory** refers to that which by its very nature must sooner or later pass or end [Life is *transitory*.] **Ephemeral** literally means existing only one day and, by extension, applies to that which is markedly short-lived [*ephemeral* glory]. **Momentary** implies duration for a moment or an extremely short time [a *momentary* lull in the conversation]. **Evanescent** applies to that which appears momentarily and fades quickly away [*evanescent* mental images]. **Fleeting** implies of a thing that it passes swiftly and cannot be held [a *fleeting* thought].

transient for antonyms see **continual, permanent.**

transitory for synonyms see **transient.**

translation, version, paraphrase, transliteration —**Translation** implies the rendering from one language into another of something written or spoken [a German *translation* of Shakespeare]. **Version** is applied to a particular translation of a given work, specifically of the Bible [the King James *Version*]. **Paraphrase**, in this connection, is applied to a free translation of a passage or work from another language. **Transliteration** implies the writing of words with characters of another alphabet that represent the same sound or sounds [In an English language dictionary, Greek words are *transliterated* with letters of the English alphabet].

transliteration for synonyms see **translation.**

translucent for synonyms see **clear.**

transmit for synonyms see **carry.**

transmute for synonyms see **transform.**

transparent for synonyms see **clear.**

transpire for synonyms see **happen.**

transport for synonyms see **banish, carry, ecstasy.**

transpose for synonyms see **reverse.**

trap, pitfall, snare —**Trap,** as applied to a device for capturing animals, specifically suggests a snapping device worked by a spring. (*See also synonyms at* **catch**.) **Pitfall** is applied to a concealed pit with a collapsible cover, and **snare** to a noose which jerks tight upon the release of a trigger. In extended senses, these words apply to any danger into which unsuspecting or unwary persons may fall, **trap** specifically suggesting a deliberate stratagem or ambush [a speed *trap*], **pitfall**, a concealed danger, source of error, etc. [the *pitfalls* of the law], and **snare**, enticement and entanglement [the *snares* of love].

travail for synonyms see **work**.

travesty for synonyms see **caricature**.

treacherous for synonyms see **faithless**.

treason for synonym see **sedition**.

treasure for synonyms see **appreciate**.

tremble for synonyms see **shake**.

tremendous for synonyms see **huge**.

trenchant for synonyms see **incisive**.

trend for synonyms see **tendency**.

trespass, encroach, infringe, intrude, invade —**Trespass** implies an unlawful or unwarranted entrance upon the property, rights, etc. of another [to *trespass* on a private beach]. To **encroach** is to make such inroads by stealth or gradual advances [squatters *encroaching* on his lands]. **Infringe** implies an encroachment that breaks a law or agreement or violates the rights of others [to *infringe* on a patent]. **Intrude** implies a thrusting oneself into company, situations, etc. without being asked or wanted [to *intrude* on one's privacy]. **Invade** implies a forcible or hostile entrance into the territory or rights of others [to *invade* a neighboring state].

trial, experiment, test —**Trial** implies the trying of a person or thing in order to establish worth in actual performance [hired on *trial*]. *(See also synonyms at* **afflic-tion.**) **Experiment** implies a showing by trial whether a thing will be effective [The honor system was instituted as an *experiment*.] and, in addition, is used of any action or process undertaken to discover something not yet known or to demonstrate something known [*experiments* in nuclear physics]. **Test** implies a putting of a thing to decisive proof by thorough examination or trial under controlled conditions and with fixed standards in mind [a *test* of a new jet plane].

tribulation for synonyms see **affliction.**

tribute, encomium, eulogy, panegyric —**Tribute,** the broadest in scope of these words, is used of praise manifested by any act or situation, as well as that expressed in speech or writing [Their success was a *tribute* to his leadership.] **Encomium** suggests an enthusiastic, sometimes high-flown expression of praise [*encomiums* lavished on party leaders at a convention]. **Eulogy** generally applies to a formal speech or writing in exalting praise, especially of a person who has just died. **Panegyric** suggests superlative or elaborate praise expressed in poetic or lofty language [Cicero's *panegyric* upon Cato].

trick, ruse, stratagem, maneuver, artifice, wile —**Trick** is the common word for an action or device in which ingenuity and cunning are used to outwit others and implies deception either for fraudulent purposes or as a prank, etc. *(See also synonyms at* **cheat.**) **Ruse** applies to that which is contrived as a blind for one's real intentions or for the truth [Her apparent illness was merely a *ruse*.] A **stratagem** is a more or less complicated ruse, by means of which one attempts to outwit or entrap an enemy or antagonist [military *stratagems*]. **Maneuver,** specifically applicable to military tactics, in general use suggests the shrewd manipulation of persons or situations to suit one's purposes [a political *maneuver*]. **Artifice** stresses inventiveness or ingenuity in the contrivance of an expedient, trick, etc. [*artifices* employed to circumvent the tax laws]. **Wile** implies the use of allurements or beguilement to ensnare [womanly *wiles*].

trickery for synonyms see **deception**.

tricky for synonyms see **sly**.

trifle, flirt, dally, coquet, toy —Trifle is the general term meaning to treat with earnestness, full attention, or definite purpose [to *trifle* with a person, to *trifle* with an idea]. **Flirt** implies a light, transient interest or attention that quickly moves on to another person or thing [She's always *flirting* with men.] **Dally** implies a playing with a subject or thing that one has little or no intention of taking seriously [to *dally* with painting]. **Coquet** suggests the behavior of a flirtatious woman who promiscuously seeks attention or admiration without serious intent. **Toy** implies a trifling or dallying with no purpose beyond that of amusement or idling away time [to *toy* with an idea].

trifling for synonyms see **petty**.

trim for synonyms see **neat**.

trip, journey, voyage, jaunt, expedition —Trip strictly implies a relatively short course of travel, although it is also commonly used as an equivalent for **journey** [a vacation *trip*]. **Journey**, a more formal word, generally implies travel of some length, usually over land, and does not necessarily suggest the idea of return [The *journey* was filled with hardships.] **Voyage**, in current use, implies a relatively long journey by water [a *voyage* across the Atlantic]. **Jaunt** is applied to a short, casual trip taken for pleasure or recreation [a *jaunt* to the city]. **Ex-**

pedition is applied to a journey, march, etc. taken by an organized group for some definite purpose [a military *expedition*, a zoological *expedition* to Africa].

trite, hackneyed, stereotyped, commonplace —Trite is applied to something, especially an expression or idea, which through repeated use or application has lost its original freshness and impressive force (Example: "like a bolt from the blue"). **Hackneyed** refers to such expressions which through constant use have become virtually meaningless (Example: "last but not least"). **Stereotyped** applies to those fixed expressions which seem invariably to be called up in certain situations (Example: "I point with pride" in a political oration). **Commonplace** is used of any obvious or conventional remark or idea (Example: "it isn't the heat, it's the humidity.") —*Antonyms:* **original, fresh.**

triumph for synonyms see **victory**.

trivial for synonyms see **petty**.

troop, troupe, company, band —Troop is applied to a group of people organized as a unit [a cavalry *troop*] or working or acting together in close cooperation [*troops* of sightseers]. **Troupe** is the preferred form with reference to a group of performers, as in the theater or a circus. **Company** is the general word for any group of people associated in any of various ways. **Band** suggests a relatively small group of people closely united for some common purpose [a *band* of thieves, a brass *band*].

true, actual, real —These three words are often used interchangeably to imply correspondence with fact. But in discriminating use, **true** implies conformity with a standard or model [a *true* democrat] or with what actually exists [a *true* story], **actual** stresses existence or occurrence and is, hence, strictly applied to concrete things [*actual* and hypothetical examples], and **real** implies conformity between what something is and what it seems or pretends to be [*real* rubber, *real* courage].

truism for synonyms see **platitude**.

trust for synonyms see **belief, monopoly, rely**.

trustworthy for synonyms see **dependable**.

trusty for synonyms see **dependable**.

truth, veracity, verity, verisimilitude —Truth suggests conformity with the facts or with reality, either as an idealized abstraction ["What is *truth*?" said jesting Pilate.] or in actual application to statements, ideas, acts, etc. [There is no *truth* in that rumor.] **Veracity**, as applied to persons or to their utterances, connotes habitual adherence to the truth [I cannot doubt his *veracity*.] **Verity**, as applied to things, connotes correspondence with fact or with reality [the *verity* of his thesis.] **Verisimilitude**, as applied to literary or artistic representations, connotes correspondence with actual, especially universal, truths [the *verisimilitude* of the characterizations in a novel]. —*Antonyms:* **falseness, falsity**.

try, attempt, endeavor, essay, strive, struggle —Try is commonly the simple direct word for putting forth effort to do something [*try* to come], but specifically it connotes experimentation in testing or proving something [I'll *try* your recipe.] **Attempt**, somewhat more formal, suggests a setting out to accomplish something but often connotes failure [He had *attempted* to take his life.] **Endeavor** suggests exertion and determined effort in the face of difficulties [We shall *endeavor* to recover your loss.] **Essay** connotes a tentative experimenting to test the feasibility of something difficult [She will not *essay* the high jump.] **Strive** suggests great, earnest exertion to accomplish something [*Strive* to win.] **Struggle** suggests a violent striving to overcome obstacles or to free oneself from an impediment [She *struggled* to reach the top.]

tug for synonyms see **pull**.

tune for synonyms see **melody**.

turbid for synonyms see **opaque**.

turbid for antonyms see **clear**.

turgid for synonyms see **bombastic**.

turn, rotate, revolve, gyrate, spin, whirl —Turn, the general word in this connection, implies motion around, or partly around, a center or axis [A wheel *turns*. He *turned* on his heel.] (*See also synonyms at* **curve**.) **Rotate** implies movement of a body around its own center or axis [The earth *rotates* on its axis.] **Revolve** is sometimes interchangeable with **rotate**, but in strict discrimination, it suggests movement in an orbit around a center [The earth *revolves* around the sun.] **Gyrate** implies movement in a circular or spiral course, as by a tornado. **Spin** and **whirl** suggest very fast and continuous rotation or revolution [A top *spins*. The leaves *whirled* about the yard.]

tusk for synonyms see **tooth**.

twist for synonyms see **curve**.

type, kind, sort, nature —Type is used of a group or category of persons or things whose distinguishing characteristics held in common clearly set it apart from related groups or categories [a new *type* of shock absorber]. **Kind** basically refers to a natural group or division [the rodent *kind*], but it is sometimes interchangeable with **sort** when used in vague reference to a less explicit group [all *sorts*, or *kinds*, of games]. **Nature**, in precise use, implies that the distinguishing characteristics are inherent or innate [earthquakes and other phenomena of that *nature*].

typical for synonyms see **normal**.
tyro for synonyms see **amateur**.

U

ubiquitous for synonym see **omnipresent**.
ultimate for synonyms see **last**.
umbrage for synonyms see **offense**.
umpire for synonyms see **judge**.
unaffected for synonyms see **sincere**.
unbecoming for synonyms see **improper**.
unbelief, disbelief, incredulity —Unbelief implies merely a lack of belief, as because of insufficient evidence, especially in matters of religion or faith. **Disbelief** suggests a positive refusal to believe an assertion, theory, etc. because one is convinced of its falseness or unreliability. **Incredulity** implies a general skepticism or disinclination to believe. —*Antonym:* **credulity.** *For other antonyms see* **belief**.
unbeliever for synonyms see **atheist**.
unbiased for synonyms see **fair**.
uncanny for synonyms see **weird**.
uncertainty, doubt, dubiety, dubiosity, skepticism —Uncertainty ranges in implication from a mere lack of absolute sureness [*uncertainty* about a date of birth] to such vagueness as to preclude anything more than guesswork [the *uncertainty* of the future]. **Doubt** implies such a lack of conviction, as through absence of sufficient evidence, that there can be no certain opinion or decision [There is *doubt* about his guilt.] **Dubiety** suggests uncertainty characterized by wavering between conclusions. **Dubiosity** connotes uncertainty characterized by vague-

ness or confusion. **Skepticism** implies an unwillingness to believe, often a habitual disposition to doubt, in the absence of absolute certainty or proof. —*Antonyms:* **conviction, assurance, certitude.**

uncivil for synonyms see **rude.**

uncommon for synonyms see **rare.**

unconcerned for synonyms see **indifferent.**

underhanded for synonyms see **secret.**

undermine for synonyms see **weaken.**

understand comprehend, appreciate —**Understand** and **comprehend** are used interchangeably to imply clear perception of the meaning of something, but, more precisely, **understand** stresses the full awareness or knowledge arrived at, and **comprehend,** the process of grasping something mentally [A foreigner may *comprehend* the words in an American idiom without *understanding* at all what is meant.] **Appreciate** implies sensitive, discriminating perception of the exact worth or value of something [to *appreciate* the difficulties of a situation.]

undulate for synonyms see **swing.**

unearth for synonyms see **learn.**

unearthly for synonyms see **weird.**

uneducated for synonyms see **ignorant.**

uneven for synonyms see **rough.**

unfeeling, unkind, ill-natured —**Unfeeling** indicates a lack of sensitivity or sympathy [The *unfeeling* driver never stopped when her car hit the dog.] **Unkind** refers to behavior that is meant to hurt others or make them unhappy [His *unkind* remarks made her cry.] **Ill-natured** suggests attitudes, comments, etc. of a person with a mean, disagreeable disposition [He is *ill-natured* toward children.]

unfeeling for antonyms see **kind**.

unfeigned for synonyms see **sincere**.

unfruitful for synonyms see **sterile**.

ungovernable for synonyms see **unruly**.

uniform for synonyms see **steady**.

union for synonyms see **alliance, unity**.

unique for synonyms see **single**.

unite for synonyms see **join**.

unite for antonyms see **separate**.

unity, union, solidarity —Unity implies the oneness, as in spirit, aims, interests, feelings, etc., of that which is made up of diverse elements or individuals [national *unity*]. **Union** implies the state of being united into a single organization for a common purpose [a labor *union*]. **Solidarity** implies such firm and complete unity in an organization, group, class, etc. as to make for the greatest possible strength as in influence or action.

universal, general, generic —Universal implies applicability to every case or individual, without exception, in the class, category, etc. concerned [a *universal* practice among primitive peoples]. **General** implies applicability to all, nearly all, or most of a group or class [a *general* election]. **Generic** implies applicability to every member of a class or, specifically in biology, of a genus [a *generic* name].

universe for synonyms see **earth**.

unkempt for synonyms see **slovenly**.

unkind for synonyms see **unfeeling**.

unkind for antonyms see **kind**.

unlawful for synonyms see **illegal**.

unlawful for antonyms see **legal**.

unlearned, unlettered for synonyms see **ignorant**.

unlikely, improbable —Unlikely and improbable both

mean not likely to happen or be true, but **unlikely** may also be used of something that is not promising or likely to succeed [an *unlikely* candidate for the office].

unlikely for antonyms see **likely, probable**.

unman for synonyms see **unnerve**.

unmanageable for synonyms see **unruly**.

unnatural for synonyms see **irregular**.

unnerve, enervate, unman —**Unnerve** implies a causing to lose courage or self-control as by shocking, dismaying, or frightening a person [The terrified screams of the children *unnerved* her.] **Enervate** implies a gradual loss of strength or vitality, as because of climate or indolence [We stayed in the air-conditioned apartment all day because of the *enervating* heat.] **Unman** implies a loss of manly courage, fortitude, or spirit [He was so *unmanned* by the news that he broke into tears.]

unreasonable for synonym see **irrational**.

unripe for synonym see **immature**.

unripe for antonyms see **ripe**.

unruffled for synonyms see **cool**.

unruly, unmanageable, ungovernable, intractable, refractory, recalcitrant —**Unruly** implies a lack of submissiveness or obedience to rule or restraint [an *unruly* child]. **Unmanageable** and **ungovernable** both imply incapability of being controlled or directed [a delirious, *unmanageable* patient, an *ungovernable* temper]. **Intractable** and **refractory** both imply stubborn resistance to or a balking at direction, control, manipulation, etc. [an *intractable*, or *refractory*, will]. **Recalcitrant** implies defiant resistance to authority or control [The guards have difficulty dealing with a *recalcitrant* prisoner.] —*Antonyms:* **tractable, manageable, docile**.

unseemly for synonyms see **improper**.

unsocial, asocial, antisocial, nonsocial —Unsocial implies an aversion for the society or company of others [an *unsocial* neighbor]. **Asocial** implies complete indifference to the interests or welfare of society and connotes abnormal or irresponsible self-centeredness [the *asocial* behavior of a sociopath]. **Antisocial** applies to that which is believed to be detrimental to or destructive of the social order or social institutions [*antisocial* racism]. **Nonsocial** expresses simple absence of social relationship [*nonsocial* fields of interest]. —*Antonym:* **social**.

unsophisticated for synonyms see **naive**.

unstable for synonyms see **inconstant**.

untidy for synonyms see **slovenly**.

untruthful for synonyms see **dishonest**.

untutored for synonyms see **ignorant**.

unusual for synonyms see **rare**.

unusual for antonyms see **common, normal, usual**.

upbraid for synonyms see **scold**.

uphold for synonyms see **support**.

upright, honest, just, honorable, scrupulous —Upright implies an unbending moral straightness and integrity. **Honest** implies complete fairness and openness in one's dealings with others and stresses freedom from deceit or fraud. **Just**, of things, stresses fairness or equitableness and, of persons, high moral rectitude. **Honorable** implies a keen sense of, and strict adherence to, what is considered morally or ethically right, especially in one's social class, profession, position, etc. **Scrupulous** implies meticulous conscientiousness with regard to the morality of one's actions, aims, etc. —*Antonym:* **unjust**. *For other antonyms see* **dishonest**.

uprising for synonyms see **rebellion**.

uproar for synonyms see **noise**.

upset, overturn, capsize —**Upset** is the ordinary word implying a toppling, disorganization, etc. as a result of a loss of balance or stability [to *upset* a glass, to *upset* one's plans, emotionally *upset*]. **Overturn** implies a turning of a thing upside down or flat on its side and, in extended use, connotes the destruction of something established [to *overturn* a chair, to *overturn* a government]. **Capsize** specifically implies the overturning or upsetting of a boat.

urbane for synonyms see **suave**.

urge, exhort, press, importune —**Urge** implies a strong effort to persuade one to do something, as by entreaty, argument, or forceful recommendation [He *urged* us to accept the offer.] **Exhort** implies an earnest urging or admonishing to action or conduct considered proper or right [The minister *exhorted* his flock to work for peace.] **Press** suggests a continuous, insistent urging that is difficult to resist [We *pressed* him to stay.] **Importune** implies persistent efforts to break down resistance against a demand or request, often to the point of being annoying or wearisome [not too proud to *importune* for help].

usage for synonyms see **habit**.

use, employ, utilize —**Use** implies the putting of a thing (or, usually in an opprobrious sense, a person regarded as a passive thing) to a given purpose so as to accomplish an end [to *use* a pencil, to *use* a suggestion, he *used* his brother to advance himself]. **Employ**, a somewhat more elevated term, implies the putting to useful work of something not in use at that moment [to *employ* a vacant lot as a playground] and, with reference to persons, suggests a providing of work and pay [He *employs* five mechanics.] **Utilize** implies the putting of something to a practical or profitable use [to *utilize* byproducts].

useless for synonyms see futile.

usual, customary, habitual, wonted, accustomed
—**Usual** applies to that which past experience has shown
to be the normal, common, hence expected thing [the
usual results, the *usual* price, the *usual* answer]. (*See also
synonyms at* **normal.**) **Customary** refers to that which
accords with the usual practices of some individual or
with the prevailing customs of some group [He had his
customary mid-morning coffee. It was *customary* to dress
for dinner.] **Habitual** implies a fixed practice as the result of habit [her *habitual* tardiness.] **Wonted** is a somewhat literary equivalent for **customary** or **habitual** [ac-
cording to their *wonted* manner]. **Accustomed** is
equivalent to **customary** but suggests less strongly a settled custom [He sat in his *accustomed* place.] —*Antonyms:* extraordinary, unusual.

utensil for synonyms see implement.

utilize for synonyms see use.

utter, express, voice, broach, enunciate —**Utter** implies the communication of an idea or feeling by means
of vocal sounds, such as words or exclamations [He *uttered* a sigh of relief.] **Express,** the broadest of these
terms, suggests a revealing of ideas, feelings, one's personality, etc. by means of speech, action, or creative
work [to *express* oneself in music]. **Voice** suggests expression through words, either spoken or written [*voicing*
one's opinions in letters to the editor]. **Broach** suggests
the utterance or mention of an idea to someone for the
first time [I'll *broach* the subject to him at dinner.]
Enunciate suggests the announcement or open attesta-
tion of some idea [to *enunciate* a theory, to *enunciate* a
doctrine].

V

vacant for synonyms see **empty**.

vacillate for synonyms see **hesitate**.

vacuous for synonyms see **empty**.

vagabond for synonyms see **vagrant**.

vagary for synonyms see **caprice**.

vagrant, vagabond, bum, tramp —**Vagrant** refers to a person without a fixed home who wanders about from place to place, begging for food and lodging rather than working, and in legal usage, implies such a person regarded as a public nuisance, subject to arrest. **Vagabond**, originally implying shiftlessness and rascality, now often connotes no more than a carefree, roaming existence. **Bum** and **tramp** are informal equivalents for the preceding, variously discriminated, but **bum** always connotes an idle, dissolute, often alcoholic person who never works, while **tramp** connotes a vagrant, whether living by begging or by doing odd jobs.

vain, idle, empty, hollow, otiose —**Vain**, in this connection, applies to that which has little or no real value, worth, or meaning [*vain* studies]. (*See also synonyms at* **futile**.) **Idle** refers to that which is baseless or worthless because it can never be realized or have a real effect [*idle* hopes, *idle* talk]. **Empty** and **hollow** are used of that which lacks real substance and only appears to be genuine, sincere, and worthwhile [*empty* threats, *hollow* pleasures]. **Otiose** applies to that which has no real purpose or function and is therefore useless or superfluous [*otiose* remarks].

vainglory for synonyms see **pride**.

valiant for synonyms see **brave**.

valid, sound, cogent, convincing, telling —**Valid** applies to that which cannot be objected to because it conforms to law, logic, the facts, etc. [a *valid* criticism]. **Sound** refers to that which is firmly grounded on facts, evidence, logic, etc. and is therefore free from error or superficiality [a *sound* method]. **Cogent** implies such a powerful appeal to the mind, as because of validity, as to appear conclusive [*cogent* reasoning]. **Convincing** implies such validity as to persuade or overcome doubts or opposition [a *convincing* argument]. **Telling** suggests the power to have the required effect by being forcible, striking, relevant, etc. [a *telling* rejoinder]. —*Antonym:* **fallacious.**

validate for synonyms see **confirm.**
valuable for synonyms see **costly.**
value for synonyms see **appreciate** and **worth.**
vanish, disappear, fade —**Vanish** implies a sudden, complete, often mysterious passing from sight or existence [The stain had *vanished* overnight.] **Disappear**, a more general term, implies either a sudden or gradual passing from sight or existence [customs that have long since *disappeared*]. **Fade** suggests a gradual, complete or partial disappearance, as by losing color or brilliance [The design on this fabric won't *fade*. His fame has *faded*.] —*Antonyms:* **appear, emerge.**
vanity for synonyms see **pride.**
vanquish for synonyms see **conquer.**
vapid for synonyms see **insipid.**
various for synonyms see **different.**
vary for synonyms see **change.**
vaunt for synonyms see **boast.**
veer for synonyms see **deviate.**
vend for synonyms see **sell.**

venerate, revere, reverence, worship, adore —**Venerate** implies a regarding as sacred or holy [to *venerate* saints, to *venerate* relics]. **Revere** implies a regarding with great respect, affection, honor, or deference [He is a poet *revered* by all.] **Reverence**, more or less equivalent to **revere**, is usually applied to a thing or abstract idea rather than to a person [They *reverence* the memory of their parents.] **Worship**, in strict usage, implies the use of ritual or verbal formulas in paying homage to a divine being, but broadly suggests intense love or admiration of any kind [He *worshiped* his wife.] **Adore**, in strict usage, implies a personal or individual worshiping of a deity, but in broad usage, it suggests a great love for someone and, colloquially, a great liking for something [I *adore* your hat.]

veneration for synonyms see **awe**.

vengeful for synonyms see **vindictive**.

veracity for synonyms see **honesty, truth**.

verbal for synonym see **oral**.

verbose for synonyms see **wordy**.

verify for synonyms see **confirm**.

verisimilitude for synonyms see **truth**.

veritable for synonyms see **authentic**.

verity for synonyms see **truth**.

vernacular for synonyms see **dialect**.

versifier for synonyms see **poet**.

version for synonyms see **translation**.

vertical, perpendicular, plumb —**Vertical** is specifically applied to that which rises in a straight line so as to form a right angle with the plane of the horizon [the *vertical* studs in a wall]. **Perpendicular**, the preferred term in geometry, refers to a straight line forming a right angle with any other line or plane [a line *perpendicular* to the hypotenuse of a triangle]. **Plumb** is a term used by carpenters, masons, etc. with reference to the perpendicularity or, especially, verticality of something, as determined by dropping a weight at the end of a line [This door is now *plumb.*] —*Antonym:* **horizontal.**

very for synonyms see **same.**

vestige for synonyms see **trace.**

vex for synonyms see **annoy.**

vibrate for synonyms see **swing.**

vice for synonyms see **fault.**

vicious, villainous, iniquitous, nefarious, infamous —**Vicious** suggests such reprehensible qualities as wickedness, depravity, or cruelty [a *vicious* bigot, a *vicious* remark]. **Villainous,** more or less synonymous with **vicious,** suggests the evil or criminality of a villain [a *villainous* attack]. **Iniquitous** implies the absence of all righteousness or justice and indifference to moral principles [the *iniquitous* practices of colonialism]. **Nefarious** implies unspeakable wickedness and total disregard of morality and ethics [a *nefarious* scheme for robbing the poor]. **Infamous** suggests scandalous or notorious wickedness [an *infamous* crime].

vicissitude for synonyms see **difficulty.**

victory, conquest, triumph —**Victory** implies the winning of a contest or struggle of any kind [a *victory* in battle, a *victory* in football]. **Conquest** implies a victory in which one subjugates others and brings them under complete control [the *conquests* of Napoleon]. **Triumph** implies a victory in which one exults because of its outstanding and decisive character [the *triumphs* of modern medicine]. —*Antonym:* **defeat.**

victuals for synonyms see **food.**

view, prospect, scene, vista —**View** is the general word for that which is exposed to the sight or lies within the range of vision [The *view* is cut off by the next building.] (*See also synonyms at* **opinion** *and* **see**.) **Prospect** suggests an extensive view as afforded by a position from which one can look out to a distance [a commanding *prospect* of the countryside]. **Scene** has aesthetic or dramatic connotations with reference to a view or a representation of a view [a rustic *scene*]. **Vista** suggests a view seen through a long narrow passage, as between rows of trees.

vigilant for synonyms see **watchful**.

vigorous for synonyms see **active**.

vile for synonyms see **base²**.

villainous for synonyms see **vicious**.

vindicate for synonyms see **absolve**.

vindictive, vengeful, revengeful, spiteful —**Vindictive** stresses the unforgiving nature of one who is animated by a desire to get even with another for a wrong, injury, etc. [*vindictive* feelings]. **Vengeful** and **revengeful** more directly stress the strong impulsion to action and the actual seeking of vengeance [a *vengeful*, or *revengeful*, foe]. **Spiteful** implies a mean or malicious vindictiveness [*spiteful* gossip].

virile for synonyms see **male**.

virtuoso for synonyms see **aesthete**.

virtuous for synonyms see **chaste, moral**.

virtuous for antonyms see **base²**, **vicious**.

visage for synonyms see **face**.

visionary for synonyms see **imaginary**.

visitor, visitant, guest, caller —**Visitor** is the general term for one who comes to see a person or spend some time in a place, whether for social, business, or professional reasons, or for sightseeing, etc. **Visitant** now generally suggests a supernatural rather than a human visitor and, in biology, is applied to a migratory bird in any of its temporary resting places. **Guest** applies to one who is hospitably entertained at the home of another, as at dinner, or, by extension, to one who pays for his or her lodgings, meals, etc. at a hotel. **Caller** applies to one who makes a brief, often formal visit, as for business or social reasons.

vista for synonyms see **view**.

vital for synonyms see **living**.

vitalize for synonyms see **animate**.

vituperate for synonyms see **scold**.

vivacious for synonyms see **lively**.

vivid for synonyms see **graphic**.

vociferous, clamorous, blatant, strident, boisterous, obstreperous —**Vociferous** suggests loud and unrestrained shouting or crying out [a *vociferous* crowd, *vociferous* cheers]. **Clamorous** suggests an urgent or insistent vociferousness, as in demand or complaint [*clamorous* protests]. **Blatant** implies a bellowing loudness and, hence, suggests vulgar or offensive noisiness, clamor, etc. [*blatant* heckling]. **Strident** suggests a harsh, grating loudness [a *strident* voice]. **Boisterous** implies roughness or turbulence and, hence, suggests unrestrained exuberance in noisemaking [*boisterous* revels]. **Obstreperous** implies an unruliness that is noisy or boisterous in resisting control [an *obstreperous* child].

vogue for synonyms see **fashion**.

voice for synonyms see **utter**.

voiceless, speechless, dumb, mute —**Voiceless** is applied to one who has no voice, either from birth or through deprivation [The throat operation left him *voiceless*.] **Speechless** usually implies temporary or momentary deprivation of the ability to speak [*speechless* with horror]. **Dumb** implies a lack of the power of speech and is now more often applied to brute animals and inanimate objects than to persons with impaired speech organs [a *dumb* beast]. **Mute** is applied to persons who are incapable of speech, specifically as because of congenital deafness and not through absence or impairment of the speech organs. —*Antonym* **articulate.**

void for synonyms see **empty** and **nullify.**

volition for synonym see **will.**

voluble for synonyms see **talkative.**

voluble for antonyms see **silent.**

volume for synonyms see **bulk.**

voluntary, intentional, deliberate, willful —**Voluntary** implies the exercise of one's own free choice or will in an action, whether or not external influences are at work [*voluntary* services]. **Intentional** applies to that which is done on purpose for a definite reason and is in no way accidental [an *intentional* slight]. **Deliberate** implies full realization of the significance of what one intends to do and of its effects [a *deliberate* lie]. **Willful** implies obstinate and perverse determination to follow one's own will despite influences, arguments, advice, etc. in opposition [a *willful* refusal].

voluntary for antonyms see **spontaneous.**

voluptuous for synonyms see **sensuous.**

voyage for synonyms see **trip.**

vulgar for synonyms see **coarse, common.**

W

wage, wages, salary, stipend, fee, pay, emolument
—**Wage** (also often **wages**) applies to money paid an employee at relatively short intervals, often daily or weekly, especially for manual or physical labor. **Salary** applies to fixed compensation usually paid at longer intervals, often monthly or semimonthly, especially to clerical or professional workers. **Stipend** is a somewhat lofty substitute for **salary**, or it is applied to a pension or similar fixed payment. **Fee** applies to the payment requested or given for professional services, as of a doctor, lawyer, artist, etc. **Pay** is a general term equivalent to any of the preceding, but it is specifically used of compensation to members of the armed forces. **Emolument** is an elevated, now somewhat jocular, substitute for **salary** or **wages**.

wail for synonyms see **cry**.

wait for synonyms see **stay**.

waive for synonyms see **relinquish**.

waken for synonyms see **stir**.

wan for synonyms see **pale**.

wane, abate, ebb, subside —**Wane** implies a fading or weakening of that which has reached a peak of force, excellence, etc. [His fame *waned* rapidly.] **Abate** suggests a progressive lessening in degree, intensity, etc. [The fever is *abating*.] **Ebb**, applied specifically to a fluctuating force, refers to one of the periods of recession or decline [their *ebbing* fortunes]. **Subside** suggests a quieting or slackening of violent activity or turbulence [Her temper had *subsided*.] —*Antonyms:* **wax, revive.** *For other antonyms see* **increase**.

want for synonyms see **desire, lack, poverty**.

want for antonyms see **have**.

wanton for synonyms see **immoral**.

wanton for antonyms see **chaste**.

warlike, martial, military —Warlike stresses the bellicose or aggressive nature or temperament that leads to war or results from preparations for war [a *warlike* nation]. **Martial** refers to anything connected with or characteristic of war or armies, connoting especially pomp and discipline [*martial* music, *martial* law]. **Military** applies to anything having to do with armies or soldiers [*military* uniforms, *military* police]. —*Antonyms:* **pacifist, peacelike**.

warm, warmhearted for synonyms see **tender**.

warn for synonyms see **advise**.

warp for synonyms see **deform**.

warrant for synonyms see **assert**.

wary for synonyms see **careful**.

wash, drift, alluvium, silt —Wash, the most general of these words, refers to any earthy material carried and deposited by running water. **Drift**, the more precise term as used in geology, is usually qualified by a word descriptive of the manner in which the material is transported [glacial or fluvial *drift*]. **Alluvium** usually refers to a deposit of relatively fine particles, such as soil, left by a flood, etc. **Silt** applies to material composed of very fine particles, such as that deposited on river beds or suspended in standing water.

waste, desert, badlands, wilderness —Waste, in this connection, is the general word for any stretch of uncultivable, hence uninhabitable, land. A **desert** is a barren, arid, usually sandy tract of land. **Badlands** is applied to a barren, hilly waste where rapid erosion has cut the soft

rocks into fantastic shapes. **Wilderness** refers to an un-
inhabited waste where a lack of paths or trails makes it
difficult to find one's way, specifically to such a region
thickly covered with trees and underbrush.

watchful, vigilant, alert, wide-awake —**Watchful** is
the general word implying a being observant and prepared, as to ward off danger or seize an opportunity [She
is under the *watchful* eye of her guardian.] **Vigilant** implies an active, keen watchfulness and connotes the immediate necessity for this [a *vigilant* sentry]. **Alert** implies a quick intelligence and a readiness to take prompt
action [*alert* to the danger that confronted them]. **Wide-
awake** more often implies an alertness to opportunities
than to dangers and connotes an awareness of all the
surrounding circumstances [a *wide-awake* young sales-
man].

wave, ripple, roller, breaker, billow —**Wave** is the general word for a curving ridge or swell in the surface of
the ocean or other body of water. **Ripple** is used of the
smallest kind of wave, such as that caused by a breeze
ruffling the surface of water. **Roller** is applied to any of
the large, heavy, swelling waves that roll in to the shore,
as during a storm. **Breaker** is applied to such a wave
when it breaks, or is about to break, into foam upon the
shore or upon rocks. **Billow** is a somewhat poetic or
rhetorical term for a great, heaving ocean wave.

waver for synonyms see **hestitate**.

way for synonyms see **method**.

weak, feeble, frail, infirm, decrepit —**Weak**, the
broadest in application of these words, basically implies
a lack or inferiority of physical, mental, or moral
strength [a *weak* muscle, mind, character, foundation, excuse, etc.] **Feeble** suggests a pitiable weakness or inef-

fectiveness [a *feeble* old man, a *feeble* joke]. **Frail** suggests an inherent or constitutional delicacy or weakness, so as to be easily broken or shattered [her *frail* body, a *frail* conscience]. **Infirm** suggests a loss of strength or soundness, as through illness or age [his *infirm* old grandfather]. **Decrepit** implies a being broken down, worn out, or decayed, as by old age or long use [a *decrepit* old pensioner, a *decrepit* sofa]. —*Antonym:* robust. *For other antonyms see* **strong.**

weaken, debilitate, enervate, undermine, sap —**Weaken,** the most general of these words, implies a lessening of strength, power, soundness, etc. [*weakened* by disease, to *weaken* an argument]. **Debilitate** suggests a partial or temporary weakening, as by disease or dissipation [*debilitated* by alcoholic excesses]. **Enervate** implies a lessening of force, vigor, or energy, as through indulgence in luxury [*enervated* by idleness]. **Undermine** and **sap** both suggest a weakening or impairing by subtle or stealthy means [His authority had been *undermined* by rumors. Her strength was *sapped* by disease.] —*Antonyms:* strengthen, energize.

weakness for synonyms see **fault.**
weakness for antonyms see **strength.**
wealthy for synonyms see **rich.**
wealthy for antonyms see **poor.**
wearied, weary for synonyms see **tired.**
wedding, wedlock for synonyms see **marriage.**
weep for synonyms see **cry.**
weigh for synonyms see **consider.**
weight for synonyms see **importance, influence.**
weighty for synonyms see **heavy.**
weird, eerie, uncanny, unearthly —**Weird** applies to that which is supernaturally mysterious or fantastically

strange [a *weird* experience]. **Eerie** applies to that which inspires a vague, superstitious uneasiness or dread [the *eerie* howling of a dog]. **Uncanny** applies to that which is unnaturally strange or remarkable [*uncanny* insight]. **Unearthly** applies to that which is so strange or extraordinary as to seem to belong to another world [an *unearthly* light].

well for synonyms see **healthy**.

well for antonyms see **sick**.

well-to-do for synonyms see **rich**.

wet, damp, dank, moist, humid —Wet is applied to something covered or soaked with water or other liquid [*wet* streets, *wet* clothes] or to something not yet dry [*wet* paint]. **Damp** implies slight, usually undesirable or unpleasant wetness [a *damp* room]. **Dank** suggests a disagreeable, chilling, unwholesome dampness [a *dank* fog]. **Moist** implies slight wetness but, unlike **damp**, often suggests that the absence of dryness is desirable [*moist* air]. **Humid** implies such permeation of the air with moisture as to make for discomfort [a hot, *humid* day].

wet for antonyms see **dry**.

wheedle for synonyms see **coax**.

whim for synonyms see **caprice**.

whimper for synonyms see **cry**.

whimsy for synonyms see **caprice**.

whip for synonyms see **beat**.

whirl for synonyms see **turn**.

whole for synonyms see **complete**.

whole for antonyms see **part**.

wicked for synonyms see **bad**.

wide for synonyms see **broad**.

wide-awake for synonyms see **watchful**.

wilderness for synonyms see **waste**.

wile for synonyms see **trick**.

will, volition —Will, the more inclusive term here, basically denotes the power of choice and deliberate action or the intention resulting from the exercise of this power [freedom of the *will*, the *will* to succeed]. **Volition** stresses the exercise of the will in making a choice or decision [He came of his own *volition*.]

willful for synonyms see **voluntary**.

wily for synonyms see **sly**.

wince for synonyms see **recoil**.

wind, breeze, gale, gust, blast, zephyr —Wind is the general term for any natural movement of air, whether of high or low velocity or great or little force. **Breeze** is popularly applied to a light, fresh wind and meteorologically, to a wind having a velocity of from 4 to 31 miles an hour. **Gale** is popularly applied to strong, somewhat violent wind and, meteorologically, to a wind having a velocity of from 32 to 63 miles an hour. **Gust** and **blast** apply to sudden, brief winds, **gust** suggesting a light puff, and **blast** a driving rush, of air. **Zephyr** is a poetic term for a soft, gentle breeze.

wink, blink —Wink usually implies a deliberate movement in the quick closing and opening of one or both eyelids one or more times [He *winked* at her knowingly.] **Blink** implies a rapid series of such movements, usually performed involuntarily and with the eyes half-shut [to *blink* in the harsh sunlight].

wisdom for synonyms see **information**.

wise, sage, sapient, judicious, prudent —Wise implies the ability to judge and deal with persons, situations, etc. rightly, based on a broad range of knowledge, experience, and understanding [a *wise* parent]. **Sage** suggests the venerable wisdom of age, experience, and philosophical reflection [*sage* counsel]. **Sapient,** a literary term now sometimes used ironically, implies sageness or learnedness [a *sapient* assembly]. **Judicious** implies the ability to make wise decisions, based on the possession and use of sound judgment [a *judicious* approach to a problem]. **Prudent,** as compared here, suggests the wisdom of one who is able to discern the most suitable or politic course of action in practical matters [a *prudent* policy]. —*Antonym:* **foolish.** *For other antonyms see* **silly, stupid.**

wisecrack for synonyms see **joke.**

wish for synonyms see **desire.**

wit, humor, irony, satire, repartee —**Wit** refers to the ability to perceive the incongruous and to express it in quick, sharp, spontaneous, often sarcastic remarks that delight or entertain. **Humor** is applied to the ability to perceive and express that which is comical, ludicrous, or ridiculous, but connotes kindliness, geniality, sometimes even pathos, in the expression and a reaction of sympathetic amusement from the audience. **Irony** refers to the humor implicit in the contradiction between literal expression and intended meaning or in the discrepancy between appearance and reality in life. **Satire** applies to the use, especially in literature, of ridicule, sarcasm, irony, etc. in exposing and attacking vices or follies. **Repartee** refers to the ability to reply or retort with quick, skillful wit or humor.

witchcraft for synonyms see **magic.**

withdraw for synonyms see **go.**

withdraw for antonyms see **introduce.**

wither, shrivel, wizen —**Wither** implies a drying up, decaying, wilting, fading, etc., as from a loss of natural juices [apples *withering* on the bough]. **Shrivel** implies a shrinking, wrinkling, or curling, as from exposure to intense heat [blossoms *shriveling* in the hot sun]. **Wizen,** now usually in the past participle, implies a shrinking and wrinkling, as from advanced age, malnourishment, etc. [the *wizened* face of the old beggar].

withhold for synonyms see **keep.**

withstand for synonyms see **oppose.**

witticism for synonyms see **joke.**

witty, humorous, facetious, jocular, jocose —**Witty** implies sharp cleverness and spontaneity in perceiving and expressing, sometimes sarcastically, the incongruous, especially as evidenced in quick repartee. **Humorous** connotes more geniality, gentleness, or whimsicality in saying or doing something that is deliberately comical or amusing. **Facetious** is now usually derogatory in suggesting an attempt to be witty or humorous that is unsuccessful because it is inappropriate or in bad taste. **Jocular** implies a happy or playful disposition characterized by the desire to amuse others. **Jocose** suggests a mildly mischievous quality in joking or jesting, sometimes to the point of facetiousness.

witty for antonyms see **serious.**

wizardry for synonyms see **magic.**

wizen for synonyms see **wither.**

wobble for synonyms see **shake.**

woe for synonyms see **sorrow.**

woman, female, lady —**Woman** is the standard general term for the adult human being of the sex distinguished from *man.* **Female,** referring specifically to sex, is applied to plants and animals, but is now regarded as a contemptuous equivalent for **woman** [That strong-minded *female* is here again.] except in scientific, technical, or statistical use, as in population tables. **Lady,** once restricted to a woman of the upper classes or high social position, is now used in polite or genteel reference to any woman [there's a *lady* to see you, the *ladies'* room] or, in the plural, in addressing a group of women [*ladies* and gentlemen].

womanish, womanly for synonyms see **female**.

wont for synonyms see **habit**.

wonted for synonyms see **usual**.

wordy, verbose, prolix, diffuse, redundant —Wordy is the general word implying the use of more words in speaking or writing than are necessary for communication [a *wordy* document]. **Verbose** suggests a wordiness that results in obscurity, tediousness, bombast, etc. [a *verbose* acceptance speech]. **Prolix** implies such a tiresome elaboration of trivial details as to be boring or dull [his *prolix* sermons]. **Diffuse** suggests such verbosity and loose construction as to lose all force and sharpness [a rambling, *diffuse* harangue]. **Redundant**, in this connection, implies the use of unnecessary or repetitious words or phrases [a *redundant* literary style].

wordy for antonyms see **concise**.

work, labor, travail, toil, grind —Work, in this connection, is the general word for effort put forth in doing or making something, whether physical or mental, easy or difficult, pleasant or unpleasant, etc. **Labor** more often implies strenuous physical work [sentenced to three years at hard *labor*]. **Travail**, now a somewhat literary word, suggests painful exertion or oppressive labor [wearied by long *travail*]. **Toil** implies long, exhausting work, whether physical or mental [the irksome *toil* of cataloging]. **Grind** suggests prolonged, tedious, uninspiring work [the *grind* of routine tasks]. —Antonym: **rest**. For other antonyms see **play**.

world for synonyms see **earth**.

worldly for synonyms see **earthly**.

worry for synonyms see **care**.

worship for synonyms see **venerate**.

worth, value —These two words are used interchangeably when applied to the desirability of something material as measured by its equivalence in money, goods, etc. [the *worth* or *value* of a used car]. But, in discrimination, **worth** implies an intrinsic excellence resulting as from superior moral, cultural, or spiritual qualities, and **value** suggests the excellence attributed to something with reference to its usability, importance, etc. [The true *worth* of Shakespeare's plays cannot be measured by their *value* to the commercial theater.]

wrangle for synonyms see **quarrel**.

wrath for synonyms see **anger**.

wrong, oppress, persecute, aggrieve, abuse —Wrong implies the inflicting of unmerited injury or harm upon another [He was *wronged* by false charges.] (*See also synonyms at* **injustice**.) **Oppress** implies a burdening with harsh, rigorous impositions or the cruel or unjust use of power [*oppressed* by heavy taxation]. **Persecute** suggests constant harassment or the relentless infliction of cruelty and suffering [the *persecuted* minorities of Nazi Germany]. **Aggrieve** suggests the inflicting of such wrongs or injuries as seem a just cause for complaint or resentment [*aggrieved* by her ill-treatment of him]. **Abuse** suggests improper or hurtful treatment, as by the use of insulting or coarse language [her much *abused* husband].

wrong for antonyms see **correct**.

Y

yardstick for synonyms see **standard**.

yield, capitulate, succumb, relent, defer —Yield implies a giving way under the pressure or compulsion of force, entreaty, persuasion, etc. [to *yield* to demands]. (*See also relent* at **surrender**.) **Capitulate** implies surrender to a force that one has neither the strength nor will to resist further [to *capitulate* to the will of the majority]. **Succumb** stresses the weakness of the one who gives way or the power and irresistibility of that which makes one yield [She *succumbed* to his charms.] **Relent** suggests the yielding or softening of one in a dominant position who has been harsh, stern, or stubborn [He *relented* at the sight of her grief.] **Defer** implies a yielding to another because of respect for his or her dignity, authority, knowledge, etc. [to *defer* to another's judgment]. —*Antonym:* **resist**.

yielding for antonyms see **inflexible**.

yoke for synonyms see **couple**.

young, youthful, juvenile, puerile, adolescent —Young is the general word for one in an early period of life and variously connotes the vigor, strength, immaturity, etc. of this period [a *young* child, a *young* man, *young* blood]. **Youthful** applies to one who is, or appears to be, in the period between childhood and maturity or to that which is appropriate to such a person [a *youthful* executive, *youthful* hopes]. **Juvenile** applies to that which relates to, is suited to, or is intended for young persons [*juvenile* delinquency, *juvenile* behavior, *juvenile* books]. **Puerile** implies reference to adults who unbecomingly display the immature qualities of a child [*puer-*

ile petulance]. **Adolescent** applies to one in the period between puberty and maturity and especially suggests the awkwardness, emotional instability, etc. of this period [*adolescent* yearnings]. —*Antonym:* **mature.** *For other antonyms see* **old.**

youthful for synonyms see **young.**

Z

zeal for synonyms see **passion.**

zealot, fanatic, enthusiast, bigot —**Zealot** implies extreme or excessive devotion to a cause and vehement activity in its support [*zealots* of reform]. **Fanatic** suggests the unreasonable overzealousness of one who goes to any length to maintain or carry out his or her beliefs [a temperance *fanatic*]. An **enthusiast** is one who is animated by an intense and eager interest in an activity, cause, etc. [a sports *enthusiast*]. **Bigot** implies blind and intolerant devotion to a creed, opinion, etc. [a religious *bigot*].

zenith for synonyms see **summit.**

zephyr for synonyms see **wind.**